The World of the Paris Café

THE JOHNS HOPKINS UNIVERSITY STUDIES
IN HISTORICAL AND POLITICAL SCIENCE

114th Series (1996)

1.
Antwerp in the Age of Reformation:
Underground Protestantism in a Commercial Metropolis, 1550–1577
by Guido Marnef

2.
The World of the Paris Café:
Sociability among the French Working Class, 1789–1914
by W. Scott Haine

3.
A Provincial Elite in Early Modern Tuscany:
Family and Power in the Creation of the State
by Giovanna Benadusi

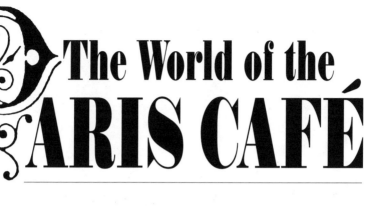

The World of the Paris CAFÉ

Sociability among the French Working Class, 1789-1914

W. SCOTT HAINE

THE JOHNS HOPKINS UNIVERSITY PRESS

Baltimore and London

This book has been brought to publication with the generous
assistance of the National Endowment for the Humanities.

Johns Hopkins Paperbacks edition, 1999
9 8 7 6 5 4 3 2 1

THE JOHNS HOPKINS UNIVERSITY PRESS
2715 North Charles Street
Baltimore, Maryland 21218-4363
www.press.jhu.edu

Library of Congress Cataloging-in-Publication Data will be found at
the end of this book.
A catalog record for this book is available from the British Library.

ISBN 0-8018-6070-9 (pbk.)

To the memory of
EDWARD T. GARGAN,
Professor, Mentor, and Friend

Contents

Preface

Proletarian cafés in nineteenth-century Paris met a wide set of needs. In some ways, café life was very modern, flourishing amid rapid urban transformation; in others, it was very traditional, facilitating face-to-face social interactions of the sort found in village life. To the extent that it contained elements of both the "modern" and the "traditional," the café suited the needs of a proletariat negotiating the transition from life in small cities, towns, and villages to the experience of a large modern city. The daily and weekly rituals surrounding the café reveal that social perception and purpose may be generated as much through the collective experience of public assembly as through the intentions of private individuals.[1] As a result, Paris workers transformed an otherwise anonymous piece of urban space into their own place.[2] Over the past thirty years, historians such as George Rudé, Eric Hobsbawm, E. P. Thompson, and Natalie Z. Davis have rescued collective forms of protest such as the food riot and the charivari from the condescending view that they were mindless pathological disorders.[3] Ordinary forms of collective gathering such as cafégoing need to be saved from similar misinterpretations. The café provided Paris workers with an accessible, public, and open forum for social life.

A study of the working-class café in Paris must address innumerable facets of working-class history. One of these is the controversy that has arisen in the study of the working class over the relation between the "organized" elements of the labor movement and left-wing political parties (that is, unions and the socialists) and the "spontaneous" elements within the working class (for example, wildcat strikes, demonstrations, or seditious sociability in the streets and in cafés). To what degree do these factors complement or contradict each other? The study of the café, by encompassing the interface between the formal and informal aspects of working-class life, as well as the relation between public and private life, provides a more rounded picture of working-class identity and incorporates gender issues as well. Studies of the working class that focus on work or strikes, Gerhard Haupt has noted, are dangerously teleological, because they suppose workers have only one identity when, instead, they have many.[4] Café sociability provides a privileged space within which to view these myriad identities, to see workers in the café interact as customers, friends, lovers, relatives, strangers, and enemies.

The following chapters show how workers transformed these spaces into places. In Chapter 1, I trace perceptions of the café, delineate its laws and regulations, and then explore the policing of this social space. Condemned de jure but tolerated de facto by the officials on the street, the café confronted virtually all regimes with moral and political ambiguities. Chapter 2 places the café in the context of housing and family life and shows that the rise of the café did not represent the decline of private or family life. Rather, the large number of adults—fathers, mothers, and spouses—charged with infractions relating to cafés reveal that they used it as a complement, rather than an antidote, to their family life. Chapter 3 reveals the relations between work and the café. Here again, café sociability transcends the dire stereotypes of nineteenth-century moralists. Rather than distracting people from work, café sociability helped preserve the preindustrial connection between work and community life and provided a valuable space in times of strikes. Chapter 4 then tackles café drinking. The rise of mass alcoholic consumption altered but did not abolish the communal and symbolic rituals structuring the activity. Chapter 5 explores the role of the café owner and traces the evolution of this petty entrepreneur from simple shopkeeper to social entrepreneur, at the center of neighborhood and community life.[5] Chapter 6 finds that the social life over which these entrepreneurs presided was not the commonly supposed promiscuous anarchy. Instead, an etiquette of café sociability emerged. Chapter 7 explores the role of women and the question of gender politics. Although usually a minority among café clienteles, women played a distinctive role there, which transcended narrow nineteenth-century characterizations of harlots and housewives. Finally, Chapter 8 integrates café sociability into Parisian politics, from the storming of the Bastille to the Syndicalist offensive before the Great War.

To clarify the working of the French court system, a vital element of this book, please keep in mind the following points. Following the 1789 Revolution, petty offenses (*contraventions*) were heard by the *tribunal de simple police* (police court); misdemeanors (*délits*), by the *tribunal de prèmiere instance, police correctionnelle* (correctional tribunal); and felonies (*crimes*), by the *cour d'assises* (assize court). This tripartite court system was in place, without important modifications, until the twentieth century. Thus it did not change during the era covered by this book. The punishments meted out by the police courts usually consisted of fines of a few francs and jail terms of a few days. The correctional tribunal handed down substantially harsher punishments. In the cases I deal with, the defendants, if found guilty, might spend anywhere from a few weeks to a few years in jail and pay fines of from five francs to several hundred. The assize courts, of course, handed down much more severe sentences, including death, but aside from the case of the Décoré, this seldom included people involved in café incidents, other than murder. Appeals were heard by the *cour d'appel* (appeals court).

This book was born in the fall of 1976. I had come into the graduate program at the University of Wisconsin committed to the study of traditional intellectual history. From the first day of Edward T. Gargan's seminar, however, the innovative nature of the projects of the other new graduate students, especially that of Joe Lunn, opened my eyes to new territory in the rapidly expanding domain of social history.

Professor Gargan was there to guide me, and within a few class sessions, he was suggesting dozens of superb topics. One in particular caught my fancy: the cafés. I had already been attuned to the importance of the café from taking Lynn Hunt's "Old Regime and Revolution" course at the University of California, Berkeley. I then went to the library and read some dazzling descriptions of French café life in the age of Jean Jaurès and Emile Zola and was caught up in a passion to recover the words, gestures, and deeds of café life.

Along the way, I have collected a lifetime's worth of intellectual debts. Heading the list is Edward T. Gargan, whose insatiable curiosity about all things French was a constant source of inspiration and support. I thus dedicate this book to his memory. I am also most thankful to other professors in the superb Wisconsin History Department: George L. Mosse has been unstinting in his help; Ron Aminzade, then at the Wisconsin Sociology Department, guided me expertly through my minor in sociology and provided invaluable assistance based upon his own deep historical knowledge of the French working class; and Domenico Sella, Harvey Goldberg, and Michael McDonald were also inspirational in their teaching and vital in their assistance. My fellow graduate students at Wisconsin—Tyler Stovall, Robert Frost, Mark Miller, Fred (Bud) Burkhard, Kathy Alaimo, Whitney Walton, Alice Brock, Joe Lunn, Steven Kale, and David Wright—were models of comradely collegiality and have continued to be so. Robert A. Nye, another Wisconsin alumnus, has also provided continuous encouragement, help, and letters over the years. Also a special word of thanks to Judy Cochrane in the office of the Wisconsin History Department.

In the archives and at professional meetings, I have also incurred obligations almost beyond enumeration. Ruth Harris, who did her research in the Archives de la Seine at the same time as I did, provided constant help with the judicial records and has been of great assistance ever since. Joëlle Guillais and Nicholas Papayanis were also most helpful in the archives. For the past decade, too, I have drawn on the expertise of Donna Evleth, whom I also met in the archives. At the Archives départementales de la Seine et de la Ville de Paris, Brigitte Lainé, Philippe Grand, and Alain Grassie have been unstinting in their assistance over the years. Maurice Agulhon and Michelle Perrot showed great generosity in letting me attend their classes and seminars and in providing critiques of my early drafts. Jacqueline Lalouette has been steadfast and endless in her kindness throughout my many Paris sojourns. At historical conferences, I have had the good fortune to have many eminent scholars comment on my work, some of whom later played an essential part in getting this book into print. David Harvey kindly agreed to read my dissertation and then magnanimously sent it to the Johns Hopkins University Press. Michael Hanagan's enthusiastic evaluation was also much appreciated, as were the responses of William H. Sewell, Elinor Accampo, George Sheridan, Jr., Rachel G. Fuchs, Susan P. Conner, Philip G. Nord, and Eugen Weber. I thank all my former colleagues at the University of South Alabama and the American University, especially Leonard Macaluso, Terry Murphy, Charles McLaughlin, Peter Kuznick, Ira Klein, Pam Nadell, Michael Kazin, Brett Williams, and Vivian Shayne for her expert help with the computer. Membership in the Alcohol and Temperance History Group and the editorship now of its *Social History of Alcohol Review* have great-ly enhanced my work. David Gutzke, David Kyvig, David Fahey, Thomas Brennan, Patricia Prestwich, Jack Blocker, Geoffrey Giles, and other members of the group have all expanded my horizons. I have also been lucky to have three sharp proofreaders, Cathy Kreche, Polly Tooker, and David Paoli. Finally, my thanks to former students Pat Simmonds and Joellyn Wallen, who helped with the research, and to Tina Hummel, who prepared the index.

At the Johns Hopkins University Press, Henry Tom displayed a masterly combination of patience and encouragement throughout the gestation of this book. I wish to thank especially Lenard R. Berlanstein for a deft and incisive reading of the manuscript. Peter Dreyer has been a superb copy editor and has made this a stronger and leaner book. Barbara Lamb, Douglas Armato, and Robert J. Anthony have also been of great assistance.

In addition, I wish to thank the editors of *Historie sociale / Social History, Contemporary Drug Problems, Contemporary French Civiliza-tion,* the *Proceedings of the Consortium on Revolutionary Europe,* the *Proceedings of the Western Society for French History,* the *Journal of Family History,* and the *Journal of Contemporary History* for permission to use copyrighted material that appeared in those publications.

Finally, I salute my family. My parents kindled my love of history and a passionate concern about social problems from an early age. My uncle Bud Scott provided my first archival experience with an assign-ment to do research in the Bancroft Library at the University of California, Berkeley, for his books on the history of Lake Tahoe. My wife, Gano, and my two children, Emily and Bert, have ensured that I have not only studied but also lived social history. I cannot thank them all enough. I wish I could gather everyone who has assisted in the produc-tion of this book in one big café banquet room. Naturally, any faults in this work are part of my tab, not theirs.

The World of the Paris Café

N° 1076. — Dix centimes.

JOURNAL POUR TOUS

MAGASIN LITTÉRAIRE ILLUSTRÉ.

PUBLICATION DE CH. LAHURE, IMPRIMEUR A PARIS.

22 Janvier 1868. On s'abonne à Paris : au Bureau du Journal, rue de Fleurus, 9 ; chez MM. L. Hachette et Cie, boulevard St-Germain, et chez tous les Libraires. **Tome vingt-unième.**

Les abonnements se prennent du 1er de chaque mois. Paris, six mois, 5 fr. ; un an, 9 fr. Départements, six mois, 5 fr. 50 c. ; un an, 10 fr. — Les manuscrits déposés ne sont pas rendus.

« Ne l'aguiche point, il nous surveillerait. » (Page 258, col. 3.)

PÉRINE ROSIER.

XIII. — A la Girafe.

Le café-restaurant de *la Girafe*, lieu de rendez-vous fixé par Tromb-Alcazar et Passé-la-Jambe à Gontran de Strény d'une part, et, de l'autre, à Georges de la Brière et Lionel Morton, jouissait, dans le quartier de la place Maubert, d'une estime qui n'était point usurpée.

Il occupait tout le rez-de-chaussée d'une vielle maison décrépite, et se composait d'une vaste salle très-basse d'étage, dont le plafond noirci et gercé aurait certainement menacé ruine s'il n'avait été soutenu, de distance en distance, par des piliers de bois vermoulu.

A droite et à gauche de cette salle, on avait ménagé trois ou quatre cabinets particuliers pour les consommateurs en partie fine.

Ces cabinets étaient clos par des vitrages à petits carreaux que recouvraient, à l'intérieur, des rideaux de calicot rouge trop étroits.

Au fond de la salle, une porte, également vitrée, donnait accès dans un jardin muni de *tonnelles*, c'est-à-dire de berceaux en treillage recouverts d'une maigre verdure.

L'ameublement de chaque tonnelle se composait d'une table de bois inamovible, fichée en terre par ses quatre pieds, et de deux bancs sans dossiers.

De chaque côté du jardin, le long des murs, les amateurs de plaisirs innocents trouvaient, d'un côté un jeu de tonneau, de l'autre un jeu de boules.

Au-dessus de la grande salle, au premier étage, le maître de l'établissement avait installé un vieux billard d'occasion, dont le tapis était reprisé en cent endroits.

Les murailles du rez-de-chaussée (dans toute

Small group socializing in a typical café (*Journal pour tous*, no. 1076 [22 January 1868]). The *Journal pour tous* catered to a broad audience, including the working class.

Working class women not only went to cafés but were willing to assert themselves when necessary (*Journal pour tous*, no. 1077 [25 January 1868]).

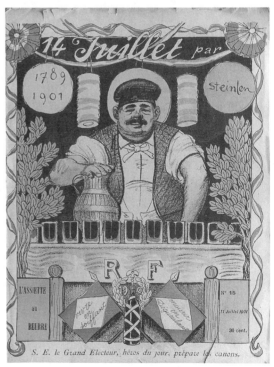

Café owner on Bastille Day (*L'Assiette au beurre*, no. 120 [18 July 1903]: 2026). The caption reads "His eminence, the Great Elector, hero for a day, prepares his canons." (The term *"les canons"* means guns, but also is slang for "glasses of liquor"; the "Great Elector" refers to the power of café owners to influence male voters during elections.)

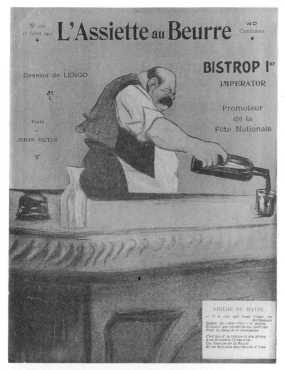

Café owner behind the bar, serving a glass of his staple product, red wine. (*L'Assiette au beurre*, no. 120 [18 July 1903]).

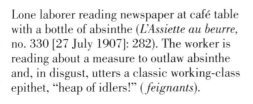

Lone laborer reading newspaper at café table with a bottle of absinthe (*L'Assiette au beurre*, no. 330 [27 July 1907]: 282). The worker is reading about a measure to outlaw absinthe and, in disgust, utters a classic working-class epithet, "heap of idlers!" (*feignants*).

Worker at café table with wife and children (*L'Assiette au beurre*, no. 330 [27 July 1907]: 286). The caption reads "My kids? They should be like me, they should work!" Beyond its satire and social commentary, the image conveys the permeability of public and private space in the working-class café.

Female café owner (*Journal amusant*, no. 346 [16 August 1862]: 3).

Above right:
Café owner behind the bar pronouncing a couple's wedding vows (*Journal amusant*, no. 334 [24 May 1892]: 3). Between the 1860s and 1880s, almost one-fourth of the couples who got married in a civil ceremony in Paris had a café owner witness their wedding contract (and likely preside over the wedding party as well).

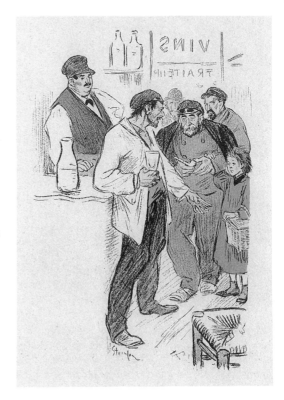

Café politics being discussed in the late nineteenth century (Alexandre Théophile Steinlen, *Dans la vie* [Paris: Sevin & Rex, 1901]). The worker is saying "If it was up to me, if I was in the government . . ."

Terrace of an upper-class café at aperitif time (between 5 and 7 P.M.) in 1906
(© Collection Viollet). Police typically kept cafés under close surveillance,
especially in working-class districts. During the café waiters' strike in 1906,
which affected mainly upper-class cafés, police were stationed on café terraces.

Soireé du peuple around 1840 (Pigal; © Collection Viollet). The drawing shows the connection between café sociability and musical entertainment in working-class districts.

A Corner of the Moulin de la Galette (Henri de Toulouse-Lautrec, 1892; © 1995 Board of Trustees, National Gallery of Art, Washington; Chester Dale Collection). The painting captures the anonymity and ambiguity of café life. The standing woman looking at the man might be a prostitute; the woman sitting next to him might be his lover, friend, or just another customer.

CHAPTER ONE

Regulation and Constraint

The nineteenth-century cafés of Paris were much more than places to get drink and food. Explaining why Paris had become the social center of the world, Ralph Waldo Emerson wrote that its "supreme merit is that it is the city of conversation and cafés."[1] Visiting Paris in the early 1840s, the young Karl Marx attended meetings of artisans and noted that "smoking, eating, and drinking are no longer simply means of bringing people together. Society, association, entertainment which also has society as its aim, is sufficient for them; the brotherhood of man is no empty phrase but a reality, and the nobility of man shines forth upon us from their toil-worn bodies."[2] Indeed, Marx's historic first meeting with Friedrich Engels took place in a Paris café, the famous café de la Régence.[3]

Parisians had similar sentiments about this informal institution in their city. At the café Procope, Jules Janin, the preeminent literary critic of the 1830s and 1840s, believed, "French *causerie* [small talk] has exhibited its most lively impatience, its most dangerous zeal; all its briefs, all its paradoxes, all its scandals, all its resistance, all its opposition."[4] Victor Hugo depicted working-class café sociability in a remarkably similar fashion in *Les Misérables*: "The wine-shops of the Faubourg [Saint-] Antoine have a notoriety which is historic. In times of trouble their words are more intoxicating than their wine. A sort of prophetic spirit and an odor of the future circulates in them, swelling hearts and enlarging souls."[5] The Paris café, in short, was one of the cauldrons of conversation and thought in this "capital of the nineteenth century."[6]

1

Study of its cafés discloses how Paris was able, in the course of the long nineteenth century, to be both a center of revolutions and a birthplace of modern leisure. In 1789, standing on a marble-topped table in the café de Foy in the Palais-Royal, Camille Desmoulins exhorted the people of Paris to take the Bastille. In 1895, the Lumière brothers showed the first commercial film in the basement of the café de Paris on the boulevard des Capucines. In the years between these two events, café conversations and rituals helped shape modern republicanism, socialism, bohemianism, anarchism, and syndicalism. The crossroads of nineteenth-century Paris were not its streets but rather its cafés. And cafés were a primary circuit for Parisian social networks.

The above quotations hint at the breadth of Parisian café life. This book seeks to show that working-class cafés in nineteenth-century Paris produced a distinctive subculture. More than any other group, proletarians made the café their home, and they formed the chorus from which the distinctive voices of café culture emerged. The great writers gained as much as they gave by going to cafés. When the journalist Henri Leyret decided in the early 1890s to discover the "real" Paris worker, he set up a café in the working-class stronghold of Belleville. In his book about these experiences, he concluded: "There is no better place than the small *marchand de vin* of the suburb in which to observe the worker. There he is at home."[7] Café sociability refutes simple notions of economic or political determination and, paradoxically, reveals the idea of class consciousness to be more than merely a Marxist abstraction.

Most of these establishments catered to the overwhelming majority (over 80%) of the population of Paris who either belonged to the working class or were on its periphery (e.g., white-collar clerks, small shopkeepers, and petty entrepreneurs). Whereas in upper-class cafés, the clientele had contact primarily with waiters or waitresses, customers in working-class cafés focused upon the owner(s), usually a husband and wife, behind the counter. The servers in these modest shops were usually the children and relatives of the proprietors. Café owners who catered to the working class realized, often from personal experience, that working-class customers came as often for space and sociability as for drink or food. As the most immediate, open, and neutral space available to them, the café was a protean place for proletarians. "The specialty is not listed anywhere— indeed has never been pinned down. . . . Perhaps it had to do with the people somehow, with pedestrian mortality, restless crisscrossing of needs or desperations in one fateful piece of street," the American novelist Thomas

Pynchon muses about a café patronized by intellectuals, but his speculation is perhaps even truer of the cafés frequented by Paris workers in the nineteenth century.[8] Parisian proletarian cafés were at the interface between the worlds of work and leisure, the public and the private, male and female, order and disorder, government regulation and community life, the collective and the individual, political engagement and apathy. All these relations were mediated, naturally, by the consumption of drink and food. In such an atmosphere, alcoholic beverages and food were of symbolic as well as instrumental importance. Although the history of café sociability cannot be divorced from the history of drink, neither should they be considered one and the same.

The multifunctional nature of the Paris café is attested to by the myriad analogies made between the café and other social spaces. Cafés were likened to homes, salons, theaters, churches, sewers, streets, stock exchanges, parliaments, and festivals—figuratively every space imaginable between heaven and hell (and in fact, two cafés opened in Paris in the 1880s whose exterior and interior decorations had eschatological motifs). The allusion to churches is especially apt, because the rise of the café after 1789 coincided not only with the decline in religious belief among the Parisian lower orders but also with a dramatic decline in the number of places of worship in the city. Of the 290 churches in Paris before the Revolution, more than 200 were later either sold as national properties or demolished. By the 1860s, churches had fallen on such hard times in the eastern working-class sections of Paris that some of them did not have enough seats for the women and children who were virtually their only clientele.[9]

Cafés could serve so many functions and resemble so many spaces in nineteenth-century Paris precisely because there were so many of them. In the matter of cafés, as in so many other areas, the French capital led and the provinces followed. Thus in a century in which the number of French drinking establishments soared from approximately 100,000 at the time of the taking of the Bastille to 500,000 by the guns of August 1914, Paris witnessed an explosion in the number of its drink shops: there were approximately 3,000 in 1789, 4,500 by the late 1840s, and then, following the Haussmannization of Paris, 22,000 in 1870. Even this sevenfold increase did not satisfy demand. By 1885, five years after the Second Empire restrictions on café commerce had been lifted, 20,000 additional publicans had opened their doors. At some point in the mid 1880s, Paris may have had as many as 42,000 cafés. By the late 1880s, when an official census was conducted, the figure stood at 30,000 cafés. During the fin de siècle and Belle Epoque, the number of drink shops remained within the range of 30,000 to 33,000. While the nation as a whole saw a fivefold increase in the number of cafés across the 1789–1914 period, Paris cafés increased by a factor of ten to twelve.

Paris also had the highest number, and greatest density, of cafés of any major city in the world. In 1909, 30,000 drink shops sparkled each night in this city of light. London and New York evenings were much dimmer, with the lights of only 5,860 and 10,821 drinking establishments respectively. Even more impressive is the number per thousand inhabitants: 1 in London, 3.15 in New York, and a staggering 11.25 in Paris. The influential weekly *L'Illustration* lamented that Paris was much worse off than even "notorious" San Francisco, which had 8.81 per thousand.[10]

During the nineteenth century, these modest establishments were known by an ever-growing variety of terms. Along with names more familiar today, such as *bistro, café, cabaret,* and *brasserie,* the terms *bibine, boc, boite, cabremont, caboulot, cargot, abreuvoir, assommoir, bastringue, bouchon, bouffardière, bousin,* and *cabermon* were all widely used,[11] but as a knowledgeable contemporary American observer, Theodore Child, noted, the traditional *marchand de vin* (wine merchant) remained the usual term for premises with zinc counters, whose owners "varied in worthiness from respectable tradesmen and prominent elector[s] down to the keeper of a *tapis franc* (thieves den)."[12] *Cabaret* was originally used to describe drinking and eating establishments rather than music halls or nightclubs, a meaning that became current only at the end of the century.

To avoid overburdening my narrative with appellations, I chiefly employ the term *café,* which is not only convenient but expresses an important historical development in working-class drinking establishments, which assimilated many of the characteristics of the upper-class café after the Revolution of 1789. Coffee and, later, beer and absinthe became staples in working-class taverns, which in the eighteenth century had primarily served wine. In addition, the newspaper, which before the Revolution had largely been restricted to upper-class cafés, became commonplace in working-class establishments after 1789. Finally, after the Revolution, many café owners in working-class districts began imitating the interior decoration of fashionable eighteenth-century cafés, using mirrors, bas-reliefs, and other garish ornamentation.

The nineteenth-century working-class cafés of Paris were thus a synthesis of the eighteenth-century wine shop and the upper-class café.

American visitors provide excellent descriptions of these hybrids. One traveler described a workers' café as "simply a parlor, an elegant lounging place, where friends may meet, intrigues be commenced and carried on, and the latest and most popular journals be read for nothing."[13] Alvan Sanborn, a scholar of the American proletariat, also discusses the mixed nature of these drinking establishments:

> The furnishings are not in the best of taste; they are chiefly glitter and gaud. Nevertheless, the room is a beautiful sight; it is so full of the brighter aspects of humanity. Here are bloused and frocked laborers, with their whitecapped wives and their black-aproned children; petty tradesmen and trades-women, and one or two uniformed soldiers. On the tables are glasses of dark-brown coffee, light brown beer, red wine and pearly absinthe, beside cards, dice, dominoes, checker and back-gammon boards, tally slates and newspapers. Here are also tobacco smoke and good humor, and emulation and curiosity and labyrinthine chatter, but no drunkenness or rudeness or tobacco juice or saturated sawdust.[14]

A complex web of perception as well as of laws, regulations, and police practices surrounded and constrained this "labyrinthine chatter" of Parisian café life. Seldom in history has so large a gap existed between the literary and administrative image of a social institution and the police practice monitoring the reality. This gap developed because the police on the street had to deal with a café life that did not fit society's preconceived administrative and literary image. The perceived "laxity" of the police was one important result of this chasm. The police force of this capital of revolution and entertainment, usually including the prefect, realized that keeping order in these public places was a gargantuan task. During the early decades of the nineteenth century, the Paris police were extremely innovative in both the theory and the practice of café regulation. By the century's end, however, the regulation of cafés seemed, to a wide spectrum of opinion, anything but enlightened. As we shall see, this seeming police capitulation to café life may very well have reflected a grudging recognition of the café's centrality to working-class life.

Consequently, the perception and regulation of the café's complex social space abounded in paradoxes, contradictions, and ambiguities. Although each political set, from the far left to the far right, had their own favored cafés, there were no "schools of thought" on the café question. Almost all authors believed that social and economic progress would make the café obsolete. As a result, most social analyses saw the café as a symbol, specter, or symptom. Only a few peripheral writers gave this vital social institution the sustained attention it deserved. Here we confront a primary paradox: while observers admitted that the café had a profound social influence—and in fact frequented cafés often themselves—few tried to understand how this institution functioned. The only real difference between bourgeois and proletarian or the left and the right was that some republicans and socialists saw cafés as a means by which people could exercise their civil and political rights of assembly and association. However, virtually no thinker or observer viewed cafés as positive institutions in and of themselves; rather than as an issue for debate, they were seen as a problem to be solved.

The universal inability of political parties to comprehend the café led to the enactment of laws that were often contradictory and ambiguous, alternating between draconian severity and liberal leniency. Paradoxically, the actual policing of cafés was the area of regulation that showed the most consistency and least contradiction across the nineteenth century. This was because the police on the street had to find practical means of dealing with an institution intricately imbricated with daily life. Their basic response was to develop a set of informal measures to handle it, which were often not explicitly codified. Actual police surveillance and regulation changed surprisingly little even after the emergence of the much larger and more intensive system of police patrolling set in motion in 1854 by the Second Empire. Napoléon III's expanded and more sophisticated police force still had to deal with an institution embedded in social life. Monitoring the café meant in large part adapting to the rhythms of its life. The police did not have the luxury of acting in the bold, clear-cut fashion advocated by armchair theorists in parliaments, salons, academies, or even their own cafés.

Judged from the vantage point of their ideals, the nineteenth-century reformers who crusaded against the café seem to have fought a losing battle. In 1914, in Paris as in the rest of France, the café was an even more flourishing institution than it had been in 1789.

Perceptions

In France, as in most countries, the moral imagination traditionally triumphed over the sociological in perceptions of the café. Since biblical times, the public drinking establishment has been considered by many to be a place of perdition.[15] From at least the fifth century on, the French clergy had preached against the debauchery and blasphemy that occurred in taverns.[16] And it was in the reign of one of the first great French monarchs, Saint Louis (1226–70), that the crown developed a systematic set of tavern regulations reflecting the same attitude. One decree, for example, lumped tavern owners together with blasphemers, sorcerers, Jews, prostitutes, and the operators of gambling houses. Such attitudes became codified in Nicolas Delamare's pioneering *Traité de la police* (1694). In his study of eighteenth-century Parisian taverns, Thomas Brennan finds that even at the end of the Old Regime, the authorities still had a "profound ambivalence toward public places" and in particular about the tavern.[17]

During the 1680s, the advent of the coffeehouse, a public place of elegance and luxury, which drew the elite from their town houses and palaces, did nothing to dispel the crown's or its police's fear of public drinking establishments. The anxiety centered not on the consumption of drink but on the discussion of politics, especially among the Parisian elite. Almost immediately after the creation of the first Paris café, Louis XIV requested that his prefect of police monitor political discussions there closely. A police report near the end of his reign neatly summed up the difference between the popular tavern and the upper-class café: "In cabarets they sing of love and war, while in cafés politics is discussed by malcontents who speak wrongly of affairs of state."[18]

Across the eighteenth century, the café's social status declined, although its political significance increased. "It is no longer decent to stay in a café, because it announces a dearth of acquaintances and an absolute void of good society," the socially astute, if not always historically accurate, Louis-Sébastien Mercier wrote in the late 1780s.[19] Yet during the same years in which "good society" frowned on the café, Robert Darnton has traced the emergence of a French "Grub Street"—a network of marginal writers—frequenting and often working in cafés, where such struggling young writers and thinkers as Camille Desmoulins and Jean-Paul Marat rubbed shoulders with the kind of working people who would soon be called sansculottes.[20] The fusion of popular tavern and upper-class café had momentous consequences.

From the taking of the Bastille to Gracchus Babeuf's conspiracy of equals, many of the great events of the Revolution were planned or occurred in cafés, but few commentators reflected upon the café's contribution. Nor did any politician single out the café for particular or sustained praise or blame. No thinker or politician such as Robespierre, Danton, Sieyès, or Mirabeau commented, in print or in parliament, on the café as a major virtue or vice. No particular laws were proposed or passed dealing with café life or the consumption of alcohol, coffee, or other drinks.

The paradoxes of modern perceptions of the café thus begin with the Revolution: although a vital revolutionary venue, the café never received any detailed reflection. All parties attacked specific café politics, but not the principle of the café itself. Silence on the café seems, moreover, to have been equally maintained during the political turmoil of 1792–94 and during the successively more tranquil times of the Thermidorians, the Directory, and Napoléon.

A discourse specifically on the café did emerge under the Restoration and July Monarchy. The issue that brought the café into public discussion in a sustained and lasting fashion was not politics but rather the family. This concern for family was prompted by the first stirrings of the Industrial Revolution in northern and eastern France and the dramatic increase in the population of Paris, not the specter of another revolution. On a deeper level, the revolutionary concept of civil equality had politicized the issue of family morality, because such equality destroyed the Old Regime notion that several different types of family morality could coexist in the same society. As a result, immorality might become the basis not only for debauchery but also, potentially, for revolution. In the aftermath of the revolutionary era, even among conservative thinkers wedded to the traditional notions of order and hierarchy that had tolerated differing moralities, the family became the great key to social order. In particular, reformulated royalist ideology feared that the urban working-class family was disintegrating under the pressures of industrial expansion and demographic increase. Investigators of working-class family life paid close attention to proletarian work habits, social contacts, and leisure pursuits. Napoléon's prefect of the Seine, G. J. G. Chabrol de Volvic, who remained in office from 1812 until 1830, laid the foundations for the social analysis of Parisian life by creating a municipal statistical office, and in 1816 he ordered a comprehensive census of the city. By the early 1830s, investigators studying the social effects of the 1832 cholera epidemic, which took the lives of more than ten thousand Parisians, noted the high correlation between mortality and poverty. The impoverished districts containing the filthy, the hungry, and the intemperate poor were the most susceptible to the ravages of disease.[21] These findings simply reinforced the growing links being made between hygiene, morality, and public order.

This innovative new socio-medico-political vision quickly found a culprit for society's problems: the café. Count Alban de Villeneuve-Bargemont's *Economie politique chrétienne* (1834), one of the first systematic analyses of the emerging French industrial system, set the tone for more than a century of social investigation of the worker, who "without foresight of the morrow, . . . consumes his modest earnings in cabarets or places of debauchery."[22] Social Catholic philanthropists and investigators such as the count often disagreed with the moral economists, who were also developing a means of investigating and ameliorating the new urban industrial society. The difference, however, was more one of tactics than of strategy. Both schools of thought believed that a single standard of morality and family structure could produce prosperity, health, and order, and that cafés could play no role in a good society. Louis René Villermé, the count's counterpart among the moral economists, also took a dim view of the café. According to his biographer, William Coleman, "the cabaret" was "an institution whose mere mention usually left Villermé in a state of shocked breathlessness."[23] Yet his extensive statistical studies of the poor of Paris, especially of the cholera epidemic, have little to say about the café's role. H. A. Frégier, the moral economist who established the classic image of the popular Paris café as a haunt where the "dangerous" and "laboring" classes were indistinguishable, was quite innovative in his attempt, however futile, to interview café owners themselves. Although he felt Parisian workers were demoralized and intemperate, Frégier did not think the problem in Paris was as dire as that in France's industrial cities.[24]

Although representatives of the nascent socialist and working-class movements that emerged during these same decades (the 1820s through the 1840s) often met in cafés, their spokesmen did not defend the café as a site of working-class or radical republican culture. Few thinkers or leaders praised the potential of the café as a place in which to practice the virtues of communal sharing, camaraderie, or cooperation that were at the basis of socialist theories. Rather, most were defensive about working-class café sociability. In response to a hostile article in the *Courier français* on proletarian cafés, Jules Vinçard, director of the working-class journal *La Ruche populaire*, retorted: "That is a flat lie; it applies only to a very small minority. . . . Anyway, if the toilers do go to the barrières [i.e., go outside the Paris tollgates] on Sundays and holidays, is there so much harm in it? Where else do you suppose they can forget the neglect and misery to which they are abandoned?"[25] The agitator and writer Flora Tristan called the café the "workers' temple," but for her, too, its function was largely negative: cafés were the only places available to workers who did not believe in church or understand the theater; that was the reason they were always full. One of the first to articulate the later theory that bad housing "pushed" workers into the café, Tristan threw down a gauntlet to the bourgeoisie: when three-quarters of the workers lived in wretched, cramped, barracklike housing, where else did you expect them to go? Late-nineteenth-century reformers rallied to this cry.[26]

A rare exception to this radical myopia on the café, as we have seen, was the young Karl Marx. This appreciation of the sociable habits of the workers was very much a part of his youthful optimism of the 1840s. Among contemporary writers of the period, Marx's favorite novelist, Honoré de Balzac, was one of the few to achieve a nuanced portrait of the popular café. Indeed, Balzac coined a term that would become famous, calling the café "the parliament of the people." This insight does not appear in his Parisian novels, however, but as a chapter in his novel on rural life, *The Peasants*.

The mobilization of the 1848 revolution temporarily swept aside the image of the café as the wrecker of families and substituted that of destabilizer of governments. In short, Balzac's image of the "parliament of the people" shunted aside Tristan's notion of the "workers' temple." Indeed, Alexis de Tocqueville dreaded that the "parliament of the people" might literally take over the National Assembly. In March 1851, fearing that the Democ-Socs might make good on their predictions of winning the 1852 elections, conservative deputies proposed a law to bring cafés under strict governmental control. The brief but heated debate provided a forum for these warring views of the café. The "party of order" tried to avoid the question of politics by emphasizing that the law would curb the debauchery and immorality of the café. The left faction in the assembly viewed the law as a smoke screen to give local mayors power to close any café whose clientele leaned to the left.

The left mounted an eloquent, perceptive, even profound defense of the café. The Fourierist journalist Victor Hennequin, a provincial lawyer from the department of Saône et Loire, spoke first, calling the proposal an attempt to install the police in every meeting place, striking a blow at freedom of assembly and the inviolability of domicile. Anticipating Michel Foucault's theories in *Discipline and Punish*, Hennequin argued further that the ultimate goal of the bourgeoisie was to impose the cellular system of surveillance found in prisons on the entire nation. He defended the café as a place where news spread, political opinions circulated, and peasants shared newspapers. Drunkenness in such places was minimal, he declared, adding that the only difference between these meetings and ministerial gatherings was in the price of the wine. A political agenda was being foisted upon the nation under the guise of morality, Hennequin concluded.

Then the Limousin mason Martin Nadaud, whose politics had been formed in Paris cafés, rose "to defend the café against the salons." Nadaud charged that if workers were demoralized it was because of oppression by the upper classes and not cafés, where nomadic workers found food, refreshment, lodging, and often advances on their salaries. During these speeches, the right accused the left of turning the National Assembly into a café. Over the objections of Victor Hugo, among others, the right persuaded the Legislative Assembly to consider the proposition.[27]

Louis-Napoléon Bonaparte used much the same rhetoric to justify his draconian decree against cafés, imposed in December 1851, the month of his coup d'état. The preamble blamed the café for causing disorder and demoralization and also frankly admitted that the café caused the development of secret societies that threatened France with the despotism of red republicanism. (Ironically, this nephew of the great Napoléon had himself strongly sympathized with such a secret society, the Carbonari, in his youth.) Because the measure was an emergency decree issued at a time when the Assembly had been suspended and the press severely curtailed, no national debate on the measure ever occurred. During the 1850s, the French legislature, renamed the Corps législatif, remained essentially Napoléon III's puppet. During the 1860s, however, the Corps législatif gained greater autonomy and investigated a new problem connected with the café. For the first time in the nineteenth century, prefects and judges increasingly petitioned parliament for a law to punish drunkenness. The French medical community proved not to be as perspicacious. They ignored warnings, first voiced in 1853 by the Swedish doctor Magnus Huss, that chronic heavy consumption of alcohol produced the disease he called alcoholism. The problem, they felt, affected only cold northern populations who imbibed spirits, not their southern Latin counterparts who drank wine. The Paris Commune would shake the doctors out of their complacency.

The Second Empire's literary and scholarly worlds did not greatly enhance the debate on the café. Nevertheless, three authors from diverse milieus developed new and subsequently influential perspectives. The detective novels of the first, Emile Gaboriau, include hundreds of descriptions of café life that transcend the emphasis on exotic criminality in Eugène Sue's novels and the romantic radicalism of Hugo's work. Gaboriau's detectives, as they track criminals through various locales, reveal the strategies that govern café life in matters of friendship, politics, crime, and sexuality. The café emerges from these novels as a hub of Parisian society.

The second author, Denis Poulot, an entrepreneur in the Parisian metal trades, provides an even more sociological, but also more moralistic, treatment of working-class café life in *Le Sublime* (1870). The book's subtitle—*The Worker as He Is and as He Can Be*—encapsulates this combination of sociology and morality. Poulot's typology of working-class drinking and café sociability, especially as related to the quality of workers' labor, the level of their class consciousness, and the degree of their moral debauchery, is depicted as a product as much of time in the café as on the job. The novelist Emile Zola and the historian Georges Duveau relied on Poulot's portrait.

The third author, Jules Simon, a young republican politician and moral economist, would prove to be the most immediately influential. His book on women workers, *L'Ouvrière* (1860), is a ground-breaking analysis with rich policy implications. Simon offers a new wrinkle in the strategy for moral suasion: working-class wives could be a potential ally for the moralists in the struggle against the café. If the state passed laws limiting their work at home and in workshops, Simon felt, proletarian housewives could create a warm home environment that would keep men out of the café. Much subsequent social legislation concerning women and children, as well as the teaching of "home economics," drew on Simon's logic.

The Paris Commune and the subsequent eight years of conservative "moral order" government again focused attention on café politics. But this is not to say that social and moral issues disappeared. In fact, the cataclysmic end of the Commune melded the moral and political fears of the French upper classes into a composite nightmare: the alcoholic, communist café habitué. This specter ensured the continuing application of the December 1851 imperial decree as well as the passage of the first modern French law against public drunkenness in 1873. Needless to say, the Commune figured prominently in the debates.

By the mid 1870s, the resurgent republican movement adopted the café and its owner as yet further victims of imperial, royalist, and rightist despotism. The rehabilitation of the café, which embodied not only the virtues of free enterprise but also the freedoms of speech and assembly, figured nicely in their overall program. During the crisis of 16 May 1877 and the subsequent electoral campaign, when a circular from the minister of the interior resulted in the closing of almost three thousand provincial cafés, the republicans had no trouble linking the "moral order" with the discredited Second Empire. The following year, flush from republican electoral victory, the eloquent Léon Gambetta gave a speech to the Paris wine merchants' association in which he embraced café owners as part of his ascending "new social strata." He particularly praised them as the merchants most responsible for the flourishing of the rights of assembly and freedom of speech in the budding Third Republic.[28] Indeed, shortly after the republicans gained full control of the government, they abolished oppressive imperial decree on cafés (1880), along with restrictions on the press (1881), on the right of assembly (1881), and on labor unions (1884).

The final triumph of parliamentary government opened rather than closed the debate on the "parliament of the people." Between 1880 and 1914, more words were uttered or written on the café than during any comparable era. The impetus for this new wave of criticism was the ever-climbing rate of French (especially Parisian) alcohol consumption. Doctors and social hygienists connected with the public health movement, as well as journalists and the first generation of academically trained sociologists, joined the ranks of a new generation of Social Catholics and moral economists in denouncing the café. For the most part, the mountain of publications they produced recapitulated the arguments of the previous fifty years. The café became bonded as never before with virtually all aspects of the "social question."[29] The question of politics receded. The French left proved either unable or unwilling to offer an alternative perspective on the café.

Sadly, all this energy seldom added appreciably to an understanding of the café as an informal social institution. Epithet, analogy, and anecdote substituted for sustained analysis. Only the stray journalist, such as Leyret and Sanborn, and a few remarks at French socialist and labor conferences moved beyond these clichés. At the 1912 Conference of the French Socialists (SFIO), an empathic but as yet embryonic defense of the café emerged, prompted by the question of whether the Assembly should limit the number of cafés. The socialist leader Jean Jaurès remained silent, and Jules Guesde and Marcel Cachin carried the day with arguments similar to those of the German social democratic theoretician Karl Kautsky. There were socialist café owners who did not promote alcoholism so much as socialism and syndicalism, they asserted, Guesde taking examples from his stronghold in the Nord department and Cachin from the Seine. The café provided a refuge for the working class, Guesde and Cachin argued. If the number of cafés were limited, the café would become a tool of the rich and the police.[30] Unfortunately, these insights never developed into an official socialist policy.

The central question that this brief survey has raised is why no author developed a more nuanced image of the café. The lack of a strong tradition of grassroots community action—often used to explain why France has had fewer voluntary associations than the Anglo-American world—may be the main reason why this informal community center never received detailed analyses. How did perceptions of the café as an institution that was simultaneously ephemeral and egregious inspire such ambivalent legislative attitudes across the century?

Regulations

Much like the Old Regime monarchy, the various nineteenth-century French states pursued contradictory courses on café legislation, periodically shifting from lenience to severity. This is not surprising given the ambiguity of the café's status as at once private property and a public place; a commercial establishment and a community center. To make matters more complex, café behavior hovered unpredictably between sociability and sedition, entertainment and debauchery.[31] Logically, then, policies on cafés lurched back and forth between tolerance and harshness during the years 1789–1914. For the first eighty years of that period, Parisian café laws set the pattern for the nation, but after 1880 the capital ceased to be innovative.

This ambivalent pattern of café regulation developed first under the Old Regime. In 1256, to discourage immorality, the pious Saint Louis banned the inhabitants of (but not travelers in) Paris and his other cities from drinking "on tavern premises," although they could buy drinks and consume them off-premises. Political events of the religious wars in the sixteenth century prompted an ill-fated successor, the unpopular Henri III, to annul this law in 1585 with respect to Paris, although it remained in effect until 1789 for the rest of France. His leniency did Henri little good, but subsequent monarchs, especially Louis XIV, found it advantageous. The increased business at taverns and "cabarets" (the later term) from consumption of wine and food on the premises augmented the amount of indirect taxes collected. The Sun King raised this tax rate within Paris, precipitating the growth of a string of suburban taverns just outside the city limits.[32]

Louis XIV's reign was also significant for the drinking public in that he created a modern police force. The first lieutenant of police, Gabriel Nicolas La Reynie, instituted numerous procedures that persisted through the nineteenth century.[33] He placed a special contingent of police (called "exempts") in each district to maintain order in public places.[34] Their duty was to pay frequent visits to taverns, prevent the singing of "dissolute and slanderous songs," the "drawing of bows" and other weapons, gambling, and prostitution. Taverners who also took in lodgers had to keep a register of all guests.[35] Moreover, tavern owners had to warn the police immediately about any violence in their shops, respect closing hours—8 P.M. in winter and 10 P.M. in summer—and not allow "low smoking rooms," which were regarded as particularly immoral. La Reynie's improvements in street lighting and more systematic use of police spies additionally facilitated cabaret regulation.[36] These innovations allowed the lieutenant of police to send the Sun King detailed reports of activities in public places, which Louis read carefully.[37] Later Old Regime lieutenants of police merely augmented these basic regulations.

For the café, the Revolution was, perhaps, more important for the laws it abolished than for those it created. Between 1789 and 1799, the religious, political, and fiscal assumptions surrounding the café were overturned. The guilds of wine merchants and café sellers were abolished, and these merchants ceased to be considered as having immoral occupations. In the laws concerning municipal and correctional police (16–24 August 1790), which invested local mayors with the right to pass ordinances on police matters, the Constituent Assembly assimilated the café into the category of public places in which tranquility had to be maintained. Cafés were not singled out as particularly evil or dangerous places, and no attempt was made to continue Saint Louis's prohibition on their patronage by local inhabitants. The law simply said that the local authorities had to punish rows and disputes, disperse crowds, and silence late-night noise. The only specific requirement concerning cafés was that any concerts and dances therein had to have prior mayoral permission.[38] Café owners must have been even happier when in January 1791 the Constituent Assembly abolished all municipal entry taxes on wine (*octrois*). In the laws enacting freedom of commerce (2–17 March 1791), the café became just another unrestricted commercial establishment. These laws permitted the owner of a drinking establishment to sell whatever drinks he chose and thus ended the once-rigid distinction between a wine shop and a café. Only one of the Constituent Assembly's laws had the potential for inhibiting café sociability. The Le Chapelier law of 14 June 1791 could potentially be used to suppress café gatherings if the authorities judged them to be illegal associations attempting to restrict freedom of commerce by organizing a strike or a labor union. However, no member of the assembly recognized the possibility of suppression, not even Isaac Le Chapelier himself, although he had been one of the architects of the laws on freedom of commerce and had led the fight to abolish municipal entry taxes on wine.[39] Whereas the Old Regime had viewed cafés as places of disorder outside the corporate structure of society, the Revolution perceived these spaces as commercial establishments and granted them the freedom and dignity due any enterprise.

Despite his authoritarianism and mania for regulation, Napoléon subjected cafés to few restrictions until the end of his reign. The Napoleonic penal code of 1810 merely reconfirmed, in article 484, the existing police laws governing cafés. Some other penal code articles mentioned cafés, such as article 386 on theft and article 410 on gambling. But the articles most important for café regulation—215, 222, and 330 on physical or verbal abuse of public authorities and 291–94 on associations—did not mention cafés at all. Although some of Napoléon's prefects took individual initiative against cafés in their departments for religious, moral, or political reasons, the emperor demanded no uniform system of café regulation from his prefects. The only major effect of his governmental centralization was the emergence of a sustained scrutiny from the supreme court of appeals, the *cour de cassation*, which monitored café regulations closely after 1800. Its decisions, a vital element in café regulation, had a great impact on police procedure throughout the century. By the time of the Third Republic, indeed, the police prefecture had handbooks of the cour de cassation's decisions distributed to the officers on patrol.[40]

After 1808, growing political discussion and agitation in Paris, coupled with political and military setbacks, prompted the prefect of police to watch cafés more closely. In 1810, believing that the existing laws were insufficient, he ordered the retail sale of drink brought under much closer supervision, with a system of surveillance entailing corporate and police control of the retail drink trade. On 4 August 1810, the police established a corporation of wholesale and retail wine merchants. Merchants of each district chose delegates to sit on the corporation board charged with monitoring the trade.[41] On the same day, the prefect of police also decreed that all café owners must register with the police, prove that their business license (*patente*) was in good order, and show proof that they were members of the retail wine merchants' corporation. Finally, aspirants wishing to open a café or established merchants desiring to alter their trade in any fashion first had to receive the prefect's approval. The prefect could shut any shop that violated the law. Infractions entailed a substantial fine of 500 francs.[42]

Four regimes—Napoléon's Hundred Days, the renewed Restoration, the July Monarchy, and the Second Republic—each brought an initial waning and subsequent waxing of regulatory vigilance over the café. This pattern was especially clear in the matter of drink taxes, which were abolished after each upheaval, then reinstated with the return of order.[43]

However, the 1848 revolutionaries initially surpassed previous liberalizations and returned to the spirit of 1789 when they encouraged freedom of assembly and association. In April 1848, they announced that "the clubs are a necessity for the republic and a right for the citizens." Naturally, such pronouncements fostered café sociability. The former revolutionary Marc Caussidière, now prefect of police, also praised free discussion. But in an ominous and portentous note, he counseled the "citizens" that they must distinguish between discussion and anarchy.[44]

In extending his uncle's Paris system to the entire nation shortly after his coup d'état in December 1851, Louis-Napoléon Bonaparte instituted a national revolution in café regulation. Louis-Napoléon's decree of 29 December 1851 was, however, more detailed and specific in its instructions than the law of Napoléon I had been: all questions concerning the opening, running, and closing of an establishment that sold drink were to be supervised by the prefects of police. Moreover, unlike his uncle, Louis-Napoléon coordinated and synchronized the repression of cafés with that of the press. In February 1852, two months after this draconian café decree, the imperial authorities subjected French journalism to its harshest system of regulation since the First Empire. Both decrees contained similar graduated systems of warnings, fines, and other penalties.[45] Ironically, the decree had little effect on the place of its first implementation, Paris.

The imperial laws and regulations that had the greatest impact on Parisian café life were those of Baron Georges Eugène Haussmann, prefect of the Seine from 1853 to 1870, whose wholesale urban renovation transformed not only the capital's landscape but also its café geography. Haussmann's demolitions in the congested central city wiped out a large number of cafés, especially the thieves' dens on the Ile de la Cité immortalized by Eugène Sue. For example, Paul Niquet's establishment at 36 rue aux Fers disappeared in 1853, and the Lapin Blanc on the rue aux Fèves was demolished around 1860.[46] In addition, many of the other cafés that had helped hatch the 1789, 1830, and 1848 revolutions fell under the wrecker's hammer. Haussmann's 1860 annexation of the inner suburbs to the city also transformed suburban taverns and popular drinking habits, as these shops lost their allure of cheap wine and a rural holiday setting. Lightly settled suburban land became filled with housing as workers looked for replacements for their demolished inner-city domiciles. The weekly pattern of heavy suburban drinking on Sundays and Mondays, as compared to fairly frugal local drinking in the city on the other days, started to even out and increase.

Another parallel between the regulatory systems of uncle and nephew was manifest in the close attention the cour de cassation again paid cafés. The enormous number of decisions dwarfed that of preceding regimes. Nevertheless, the court's decisions, like the laws, often followed a contradictory course. Thus the court reversed itself by declaring in 1859 that owners were required to notify the police even in the case of minor incidents. And in 1855 the court revised earlier rulings and legal thinking by making café owners rather than parents responsible for alcohol consumption by minors. Only once did the court lighten rather than increase the café owner's burdens, when an 1866 decision lowered the fines for Parisian café owners who tolerated prostitution in their shops and removed such cases from the jurisdiction of the court of petty sessions, or correctional tribunal (*tribunal de police correctionnelle*), to that of an ordinary police court (*tribunal de simple police*). The cour de cassation consistently upheld police ordinances on closing hours and extended the application of article 475, number 5, of the penal code (prohibiting not only clandestine gambling houses but also gambling in public places) more fully to cafés. The court naturally upheld the 1851 decree and the prefect's prerogatives, but it did exempt restaurants and hotels from the need for prior prefectorial authorization.

During the Second Empire, the high court also started to hand down numerous decisions regarding café owners and public drunkenness. In 1860 the court maintained that owners were legally responsible if they neglected to turn away drunk customers, and, in an 1862 decision, it judged that the mere presence of an intoxicated individual in his café sufficed to convict the owner.[47] By the demise of the Second Empire, the cour de cassation had largely codified police procedure regarding café regulation for the rest of the century.

The so-called liberal period of the Second Empire and even the Paris Commune did not mitigate the 1851 decree. Although the empire tolerated strikes after 1864 and granted additional rights of assembly in 1868, legal restrictions on cafés remained in force. Notwithstanding that it was denounced by its opponents as government by café, the Commune generally endorsed the empire's strict policies. Many of the Commune's clubs and committees demanded that measures be taken against women of suspect morality, against drunkards "who have forgotten self-respect," and against cafés that stayed open past the traditional closing hour of 11 P.M. Measures such as these were taken by the Vigilance Committees of the 1st, 2nd, 15th, and 18th arrondissements, as well as by the women's club in the Latin Quarter and the municipal council of the 11th arrondissement.[48] Edouard Moreau, a civil commissioner in the War Department, demanded the closure of every drinking establishment that discharged a drunken man.[49] Militant women strove to punish alcoholic husbands who beat their wives.[50] Communard newspapers such as *La République* and *L'Affranchi* also stigmatized bourgeois café habitués. Pascal Grousset, editor of *L'Affranchi*, called for a military sortie against aristocratic and bohemian cafés and the "dandies and little fops who scheme, politic, and talk nonsense concerning the day's events."[51]

The return of Louis Adolphe Thiers and his Versailles troops brought seven days of savage repression in Paris, known appropriately as the bloody week (*semaine sanglante*), but no new laws against the café. Yet once again following the restoration of conservative government, the taxes on wine increased. In the fall of 1871, the royalist-dominated National Assembly raised entry and retail taxes on wine to help pay off the German war indemnity and to mount an attack on alcoholism, which many saw as the real cause of the Commune and its café politics.[52] The following year, a deputy and future Parisian prefect of police, Felix Voisin, had the National Assembly modify the 1851 decree to give judges and juries greater latitude in both the conviction and sentencing of offenders. The National Assembly also enacted a law specifically punishing public drunkenness, the first of its kind since Charlemagne. Passed in February 1873, this law, as Susanna Barrows has shown, with its complex gradation of fines for each new infraction, potentially gave the police a means of minutely monitoring working-class café behavior.[53] Despite the anti-café hysteria of the moment, the National Assembly also passed a law in 1873 that was seemingly friendly to the café owner. Hitherto there had been no specific statute to punish a café or restaurant customer who ordered and consumed, but could not pay for, food or drink. Voisin, who formulated this law, did so not because he was the café owner's friend but because he saw this type of swindle—commonly committed by vagabonds, beggars, and con men—

as a threat to the social order.[54] As we shall see in Chapter 5, café owners had traditionally relied on their physical and moral presence and had not needed such legal redress against customers who did not pay.

Moved no doubt by the zeal of the royalist and reactionary "moral order" government, the cour de cassation quickly made some important decisions concerning the 1873 public drunkenness law. Within a year of its passage, the court ruled that a café owner must request intoxicated customers to leave and must notify the police immediately. If the owner failed to comply, he or she could be fined. However, the court limited the café owner's liability by decreeing that the owner was liable only if the inebriate was found on the premises. If an individual became drunk in an establishment but was found drunk outside it, the owner was not culpable. One of the most important decisions of the court for the Paris police was an 1876 ruling that article 365 of the penal code, prohibiting the accumulation of penalties, did not apply to the 1873 law. This decision permitted the Paris police and the correctional tribunal to prosecute not only for drunkenness but also for other offenses, most especially the insulting of a police officer (outrage-aux-agents).[55]

The complete triumph of republican forces after 1879 brought a swift abrogation of the 1851 decree. In July 1880, the National Assembly enacted a much more liberal law, which removed the power of authorization from the prefects and required only a simple declaration to the prefect of police fifteen days before the opening of a drink shop.[56] After this date, the Paris prefect of police had no power to prevent an increase in the number of establishments and did not even know how many cafés existed in Paris.[57] This liberal law did, however, contain one potentially repressive article. If they wished, mayors (or in Paris the prefect of police) could prohibit cafés within a certain radius of their choosing around schools, churches, cemeteries, and hospitals.[58] In theory, if a mayor selected a large radius, this article could have greatly diminished, if not abolished, the café in cities and villages. However, no French mayor ever pursued this restrictive strategy. In Paris, in fact, despite mounting requests after 1890, no prefect of police ever promulgated such a decree.[59] The mayor of Lyon issued one in April 1901 and enforced it strictly, thereby significantly diminishing the number of cafés in his city, but his example did not persuade Paris prefects between 1901 and 1914 to take similar action.[60] In the Paris region, only a few municipalities, those with elected socialist mayors and city councils after 1900, enacted and enforced radial measures.

As in the case of the 1880 law, Paris police prefects generally took a liberal view of café regulation. The most visible sign of this freedom was a revision of closing-hour laws. The liberalization began during the 1878 Exposition, when the prefect granted an exemption to all cafés within pre-1861 boundaries and allowed those on the interior boulevards of Paris to stay open until two o'clock in the morning.[61] The next prefect, Louis Andrieux, generalized this exception in 1880 and 1881 to include the whole city. He moved the official closing hours of all cafés from twelve midnight to two A.M.[62] The one exception to this trend of lessening control over the café—especially in the eyes of the owners themselves—was the creation in 1880, the same year as the repeal of the 1851 decree, of a municipal laboratory.[63] The prefect of police appointed twenty-eight inspectors to gather samples of food and drink from Paris cafés and restaurants to test for adulteration.[64] Notwithstanding the assertions of café owners, this law was not a political measure intended to suppress their trade.

Despite the anti-café rhetoric of the decades after the early 1880s, French parliaments and Paris prefects of police passed no laws or decrees inhibiting the café trade. The only vigorous measures came in the areas of education and social welfare. The head of primary education in the department of the Seine developed an anti-alcoholism program for the schools shortly after the turn of the century.[65] In the same years, the office of public assistance printed and hung posters denouncing not only the usual villain, spirits, but also wine, commonly termed the "hygienic drink."[66] The sole strong measure taken by the prefect was a 31 May 1907 ordinance prohibiting vagrants and unaccompanied women from entering lodging houses and cafés.[67] This decree had a short life, however, because the Conseil d'état, the French administrative court, promptly annulled it as an excessive use of power.[68]

In summary, nineteenth-century legislation on the café, as in previous centuries, alternated between tolerance and repression. The Revolution ushered in a liberal period, which lasted until the Second Empire, when a repressive era commenced that persisted until 1880. Finally, with the consolidation of the Third Republic, liberalism returned, albeit with an uneasy conscience, which periodically chipped away at, but never extinguished, the freedom of the cafés. The city of Paris followed this theme, with a slight variation in terms of the length of these cycles but not in their nature. The liberal phase in Paris lasted only until 1810, and was followed by seven decades of authoritarianism. Thereafter, between 1880 and 1914, Paris had a more liberal regulatory system than many other large cities and even its own suburbs.

Policing

If perceptions of the café operated according to a set of dichotomies, and its regulation moved in cycles, then its actual policing can be seen in terms of an ever-expanding number of strategies piled one on top of another like geological strata. These levels include the formal police agenda elaborated by police manuals of procedure, prefectorial ordinances, and the tactics used by officers and detectives in the field, with the repertoire of police strategies growing more diverse with time. In Paris, paradoxically, prefects of police remained extremely rigid in their attitudes and instructions, while the police became increasingly more discerning and sophisticated in their actual work. Despite all the nuances and subtlety that the police gained across the century, their moral vision of the ideal citizen—that is, one who was not considered suspicious—exhibited the same sobriety and disdain of the café as the moral reformers already analyzed.

Police guides, dictionaries, manuals of procedure, and collections of laws and ordinances were often quite short and perfunctory on the subject of the café. They listed the rules concerning closing hours, dances and other entertainments, disorder and gambling. But they seldom went beyond this. Even the remaining sparse documentation, for Paris at least, on the enforcement of the 1851 decree and 1873 law does little to illuminate contemporary police practice. Judging from the copious number of blank forms in the archives of the Prefecture of Police, district commissioners devoted little or no time to a detailed enumeration of café regulations. This was not simply a question of shirking responsibility but rather a realization that it would be too time-consuming to collate the leads, tips, and anecdotes that formed the basis of café surveillance. This information, based on an oral culture, did not look impressive on government stationery.[69]

Much of the actual regulation of cafés, like their sociability, was therefore never recorded. It is not surprising that an informal institution elicited informal means of regulation. An examination of police reports, court cases, and novels reveals a much richer repertoire than could possibly be conjectured from the formal laws and regulations. These richer sources reveal that as the nineteenth century unfolded, the café became ever more important for police work. The installation of the modern serving counter early in the nineteenth century, explored in detail in Chapter 5, brought the café owner into much more intimate contact with his or her clientele. Consequently a complex interaction developed between the publican and the policeman. As Emile Gaboriau noted in one of his detective novels, every magistrate had his own system.[70]

The nineteenth-century police inherited many techniques from their predecessors of the Old Regime. Police patrols, night watches, and spies had all been staples in the arsenal of the eighteenth-century lieutenant general of police, and they remained integral to nineteenth-century police practice as well. The great innovation of the nineteenth century was the establishment in 1854 of the English model of "beat" policing and the resulting dramatic enlargement of the police force. This reform marked the emergence of a recognizably modern police force and finally ended the traditional reliance of the Paris police upon the army. The modern French policeman on his beat and the modern café owner behind his or her counter thus evolved within a generation of each other.

Patrols were the oldest and most basic weapon in the police arsenal. The night watch was already centuries old when La Reynie reorganized and expanded it as part of his new prefecture in 1667. Surveillance of cafés and taverns was naturally an important part of any patrol's job. Unlike many of their provincial counterparts, the Paris police focused on gaining information rather than on exacting repression, and they did not believe it necessary to have a special brigade for cafés. This may be found surprising in view of the fact that they used such brigades for the surveillance of lodging houses, card sharpers, gaming houses, prostitution, criminals, labor conflicts, and, during the 1880s and 1890s, anarchists,[71] but since these beats obviously covered cafés too, adding a special detachment for cafés alone may have seemed redundant.

The police raid complemented the patrol. Systematic sweeps of "dangerous" places—that is, those sustaining crime, debauchery or opposition politics—often specifically targeted cafés. The first step in a police raid was to put officers unfamiliar in the area on a watch to reconnoiter the terrain and clientele.[72] Then a sizable contingent descended on the establishment in question to ensure that no one escaped. Shortly after the Commune, for instance, the police staged a raid when a radical quarryman entered a café at 141 rue de Chemin Vert with ten other suspects.[73] Raids could not be successful unless all entrances were guarded, and in many shops the back entrance almost seemed reserved for getaways.[74] In Gaboriau's novels, the police make periodic raids upon fictional tables d'hôtes where the customers play baccarat after dinner on wine-stained tablecloths and on thieves' dens such as Widow Charpin's place and the Rainbow on the outskirts of Paris.[75]

The Paris police had used spies and agents provocateurs for gathering information and sowing intimidation at least since Richelieu's time, and nineteenth-century prefects continued to rely heavily on these agents. Consider the boast of the Old Regime police prefect Gabriel de Sartine to the king in 1759: "Sire, when three people are chatting in the street, one of them is surely my man." The general reading public found the same boast echoed in the memoirs of Louis Andrieux, one of Sartine's late-nineteenth-century successors.[76] Writers ranging from Mercier in the eighteenth century to Emile Gaboriau and various American observers in the late nineteenth noted that a café customer stood a good chance of running into a police spy or agent provocateur.[77] Indeed, police detectives from Vidocq to Rossignol bragged in their memoirs of disguising themselves and blending into the café life of conspirators and criminals in places such as the thieves' dens around the place Maubert.[78] The exact number of such spies can never be known precisely, but reasonable estimates in the mid nineteenth century put it at two thousand.[79] The actual number always fluctuated, because spies often recruited workers to help entrap their comrades.

Along with eavesdropping on conversations, spies were also notorious for provoking customers to utter seditious opinions. For example, when the police wished to remove foreign radicals from the city during the 1840s, one agent tried to entrap a group of German workers. Spies could also arrange to have customers followed from the café and arrested at home.[80] Undercover police work avoided the public protest that often ensued from overt, official repression. It also heightened suspicions and exacerbated divisions among a regime's opponents, who often felt that their meetings were never free of spies or agent. From the time of the early-nineteenth-century Carbonari to the communists in the twentieth, arguments frequently erupted over whether police had infiltrated the organization and whether spies were in their midst.[81]

After the 1789 Revolution, police patrols and spies developed a special vocabulary to describe various types of cafés and café behavior. In the prefect's reports to the minister of the interior and in the reports of police spies, the term "café scenes" occurs frequently.[82] This term was especially prevalent during the first half of the century and referred to brawls between soldiers or men fighting over women at suburban tavern dances, such as those at the barrière des Martyrs.[83] One "tumult without political significance" at a café doorstep in the Arcis district in November 1830 involved a scuffle between Vidocq, a famous former criminal turned police detective, and an amnestied prisoner, one M. Henault.[84] Another rubric in police reports, usually called either *police des cafés* or *cafés lieu de réunion*, concerned political discussion. By the time of the empire, police in general, and secret agents in particular, routinely referred to "political cafés" and "café politicians and agitators."[85] Their reports represent a primitive form of public opinion polling.[86] For example, the prefect of police happily reported to the king and the minister of the interior in 1820 that the disorder he had feared in the highly political Palais-Royal cafés (such as the Lemblin and the Valois) in response to the tumult in the Chamber of Deputies had not materialized.[87] After the upheavals of the revolutionary era, the police and the government were well aware that conversation can be far-reaching, and that what was said in the National Assembly resonated in the parliaments of the people.

The ineffectiveness of police patrols and spies under the Restoration and July Monarchy was a problem more of tactics than of strategy. There were simply not enough policemen or spies to monitor all the cafés of the city and suburbs adequately, so the police used the army or the national guard to patrol the streets late at night.[88] The prefect distributed his patrolmen and spies according to the fluctuations of daily life and the movements of suspected orators and organizers. Ordinarily, café life was characterized in terms of location, time, and social class. Middle-class and student cafés in central Paris warranted constant surveillance, whereas working-class cafés received varying attention according to the spatial and temporal rhythms of proletarian life.

Paris cafés frequented by the working class in small numbers between Tuesday and Friday received much less attention than those just beyond the toll-bars, which catered to massive crowds on Sunday and Monday. The weekly working-class trek to the country basically governed the pulse of public order. In Paris during the middle of the week, public drunkenness and the attendant brawling and carousing were rare.[89] The high cost of the wine limited the crowds in Paris cafés, making surveillance relatively easy.[90] In addition to being quieter, until the time of the July Monarchy, working-class Paris cafés are portrayed as having generally been politically inactive. On Sunday and Monday of each week, however, the prefect of police made a concerted effort to contain the disruptive revelry at the suburban taverns and to ensure serenity in the city.

As the prefects continually repeated to their superiors, suburban cafés at, for example, the Ivry or Monceau barrières had to be watched with extreme care on Sundays and Mondays; that is, a *surveillance de pré-*

caution was necessary to prevent the brawls (*rixes*) that seemed to be constantly erupting. The worst scenes occurred when the supply of wine was abundant and it was moderately priced. To contain this disorder, the prefect constantly demanded both of his officers and of suburban mayors (usually in vain) that the closing-hour regulations be punctually observed. Punctual closing occurred so infrequently as to merit special mention in reports to the king and minister of the interior. Only when the weather turned bad, and the workers consequently stayed in the interior cafés, could the prefect be assured of tranquil Sundays and Mondays.[91]

Restoration prefects paid particularly close attention to working-class singing societies that met in cafés. These were known as *goguettes* and had emerged under Napoléon. During the 1820s, the prefect of police alerted his force to the political threat the goguettes posed. In a 25 March 1820 decree, he emphasized that the goguettes were increasingly clandestine political clubs. His officers, he insisted, must ensure that the laws against illegal associations were not being violated and that the songs and poetry did not attack the "government and morality." A 5 January 1822 decree warned that goguettes were sprouting in rural areas around Paris. A month later, the prefect requested his agents to gather information about the vending of seditious and irreligious songbooks in cafés, and about customers singing these songs. On 2 September of that same year, citing a large increase in the number of street singers around cafés, he reminded district police officials that all musicians in public places needed police authorization.[92] Only under the Second Empire did the police succeed in substantially curtailing this café-singing culture.

The great change in the regulation of Paris cafés under the Second Empire was not the 1851 decree, which had for practical purposes been in force since 1810, but the establishment in 1854 of a system of beat policing. Based upon the recently instituted English system, the Paris police were augmented and segmented in such a manner that for the first time they could watch the city constantly and systematically without the immediate presence of the army.[93] By the 1870s, some café owners noted that police patrols passed their cafés every half hour.[94] Uniform and pervasive surveillance formed an ideal complement to Haussmann's transformation, which opened up and regularized Parisian urban space. Simultaneously with the decline of the taverns at the barrières and in the suburbs (because they were now within the city limits and their wine was no longer cheaper), the police force expanded sufficiently to be able to monitor all the districts of Paris. Both police surveillance and working-class café life thus ceased to exhibit dramatic geographic and temporal variations. While many scholars have noted the military advantages of the broad, straight new boulevards, virtually no one has indicated how they served to facilitate police regulation as well.[95] These broad boulevards and the increasing shift in commerce from the street to the shop permitted the police to scan café life more easily and efficiently. Only on the side streets did the old-fashioned sort of dense sociability persist, but these were now peripheral to the new Paris.

The prefects of police used beat policing to develop a strategy of omnipresent monitoring of cafés. This tactic was concerned with watching (or harassing) political discussion in cafés rather than with closing dangerous establishments. The police realized that in a city filled with cafés, if agitators were denied access to one drink shop, they would quickly find another. In any case, the growing social segregation of the city brought about by Haussmann's transformation permitted the police more easily to distinguish potentially dangerous working-class cafés as opposed to benign upper-class cafés. The Paris beat police used different tactics depending upon the social class of a particular café. On the great boulevards catering to the bourgeoisie, the police established "a system of liberty for circulation of strollers [*flâneurs*]" from the café de Madrid to the Gymnase and the Opéra-Comique. This opulent section was watched closely by police to ensure that nothing upset the enjoyment of the boulevardiers.[96] In working-class districts and on the side streets where proletarian life persisted, the police took just the opposite tack. Rather than ensuring the free play of sociability, they constantly intervened to inhibit and contest working-class expression. Cafés in the new suburban areas received little attention, however; throughout the entire period 1850–1914, the suburban prefectures under the command of the prefect of police closed only a few cafés and made café-related arrests at a significantly lower per capita rate than did their counterparts in Paris. The police seem to have lacked interest in rigorously policing a working class now far from the seat of power.

A vital part of the policeman's job was to try to establish a good relationship with the café owners on his beat. This relationship became both possible and necessary after the 1820s, with the rise of the modern counter as a site of sociability, an innovation that made the nineteenth-century café owner a much more integral part of the neighborhood than his or her eighteenth-century predecessor. The famous zinc tops of these counters became, as Leyret noted, the confessional of the working class. Consequently, the café owner also became an ideal source of information for the police. By the late nineteenth century, the surveillance of the quarter police was complemented by the investigations of police detectives (the Sûreté).[97] The greater informality of the detective was well suited to the informality of the café owner.

Along with literary sources, especially the detective novels of Emile Gaboriau, testimony in Paris court cases provides vivid insight into both police techniques and the types of information they acquired at the café counter. In Gaboriau's *Monsieur Lecoq*, the detective elaborates on how to make the café owner more communicative: go in, buy a drink, and treat the *patron* to one as well. In another of his novels, *Other People's Money*, we see the detective's strategy working: a few polite little glasses of cognac (*petits verres*) loosen the tongue of the café owner.[98] In this case, the café is the longest-established business on the street. In Gaboriau's previous novel, too, the young detective chooses a particular café owner because he has been in the neighborhood for ten years and enjoys "a certain amount of confidence" among habitués who are the servants of aristocratic families. During the 1860s, the Vieux Chien dance hall and bar, on the narrowest part of rue Mouffetard, was perhaps the "most notorious of entertainments of ill repute in Paris" and one of first places a policeman visited to get information on suspects.[99] Frequently, in court cases between 1870 and 1914, café owners such as Madame Vistat, at 115 rue de la Santé, Victor Saladin, at 9 rue Sauval, and Jean-Joseph Ganvin, at 70 rue Julien Lacroix, gave the police access to the intricacies of the neighborhood's social networks.[100]

These improved techniques of police surveillance explain why the 1851 decree had so much less of an impact on Paris than on the rest of the country. During the first three years following the coup d'état, when the number of cafés in the rest of the country fell from 340,000 to 290,00, the number of cafés in the capital remained stable. The disparity in the enforcement of the 1851 decree, especially between Paris and rural France, continued as long as the Second Empire lasted. The provincial prefects kept the number of cafés below 300,000 throughout the 1850s; only after 1860, with the advent of the "liberal empire," did the number shoot up to 310,000 by 1865, and then to just over 370,000 in 1870. In Paris no such fluctuations occurred. Instead, the number of cafés skyrocketed in a fivefold increase: from 4,500 in the late 1840s to over 22,000 in 1870. Why would the imperial prefect permit such a drastic multiplication of a "dangerous" space? The answer is no doubt linked to the general growth in commercial activity that the urban renovation and expansion facilitated. The emperor and his prefect of the Seine, Hauss-mann, clearly believed that cafés would contribute more to the animation of a great capital city than to the mobilization of malcontents, especially when the city was spatially more coherent and policed more efficiently. Another factor that may explain Paris' separate path is the fact that the Paris prefect of police gained a large measure of autonomy from the minister of the interior during the empire.[101] A final factor may simply be the dynamic of imperial urban renewal and development, which occurred in other cities beside Paris, for the number of cafés increased in all French agglomerations with populations above 50,000.

In the aftermath of the Commune, the Paris prefects exercised greater discrimination vis-à-vis these spaces that had helped to hatch the insurrection. To the repeated calls by the minister of the interior in August 1871, June 1873, and October 1877 the Paris prefects responded with a vigorous application of the 1851 decree, not so much by closing premises as by limiting the growth of new ones.[102] Whereas in the rest of the country, the number of cafés declined by over 4,000 annually from 1870 to 1875, only thirty-seven cafés were closed in Paris between 2 November 1872 and 31 December 1875,[103] and the Paris prefect allowed thirteen of these to reopen.[104] The most dramatic example of tolerant attitude of the Paris prefecture is that no cafés were closed between 16 May to 10 November 1877 during the Seize Mai crisis, when the monarchist government tried to repress the republicans by stifling political expression before the November elections.[105] In the provinces during this same period, 2,218 cafés closed.[106]

Even if the Paris prefects were not actually repressive, however, they were surely restrictive. The full extent of this restrictive regime became apparent only after the abrogation of the 1851 decree. An avalanche of café openings occurred after July 1880; between the summers of 1880 and 1884, the numbers reached over twenty thousand. The prefects could not determine which of these remained in operation and which replaced already-existing premises, since the July law required new owners to register only when they opened, not when they closed. This liberal system revealed the insatiable need of Parisian workers for sociability. At some point during the mid to late 1880s, there were probably over 40,000 cafés in Paris—in other words, almost double the number in existence under the Second Empire. Market forces would cause the number to drop to between 27,000 and 30,000 in the succeeding decades. Despite the decrease in numbers, notifications of new openings continued to stream in.

Between 1880 and 1910, the police received a total of over 150,000 notifications of café openings.[107]

A similar shift from rigor to laxity after 1880 also characterized the evolution of the prefect's enforcement of the 1873 law on public drunkenness. Under the "moral order" governments, the number of arrests for public drunkenness increased steadily from 11,825 in 1873 to 17,632 in 1877. After this, the year of the Seize Mai crisis, the number of arrests steadily declined to 7,370 in 1880. The 1880s and 1890s brought a further decline in the number of infractions, which reached a low of 1,084 in 1896 before rising to the 5,000 mark in 1900. Paris and the department of the Seine, with comparable numbers, faithfully reflected national trends. These low arrest figures illustrate the basic problem: the law was unpopular with the people, the police, and the courts. It simply demanded too much paper work and too much interference in the worker's daily life. Moreover, the police never applied the law to café owners who served intoxicated customers. As a result, the police sabotaged the intent of the law, to focus on café owners who encouraged working-class drinking as much as on the drinkers themselves. In general, the enforcement of the law unfortunately revealed the tremendous class bias of the police. Few members of the bourgeoisie or even of the petit bourgeoisie ever appeared in court to face charges of public drunkenness. They were usually escorted home or at worst (as had been the case prior to the law) were put in jail to sleep off their inebriation and then released in the morning.[108]

The Paris police nevertheless found the 1873 law advantageous in one vital aspect. After the Commune, the incidence of workers verbally insulting or physically attacking the police jumped dramatically.[109] These incidents rose from around one thousand in the late 1860s to over twice that number during the early 1870s. "Questioned by the judge of the ninth chamber, the accused blamed his drunken state for the insults he had liberally heaped upon the police. He probably would not have had recourse to this excuse if the law on public drunkenness had been passed," the *Gazette des tribunaux* said of a typical case in September 1871, probably expressing the sentiments of the ordinary police officer.[110] Once the law went into effect, in March 1873, the police could charge an aggressive worker not only with insult or physical abuse but also now with public drunkenness. The additional fine of five francs imposed on those found guilty of this may seem petty, but for most of the era's workers, it represented more than a day's wages.[111] From the inception of the law, the Paris police were much more likely than their counterparts elsewhere in urban or rural France to apply it in cases where they were insulted. In general, from 1873 to 1914, over 55 percent of the people arrested annually in Paris for insulting police officers were also charged with public drunkenness. The police used the 1873 law to maintain public order rather than, as its framers had hoped, to improve public health.

By the mid 1890s, however, the Parisian police started to relax their harassment of café life. The steady rise in infractions against public authority finally leveled off at 4,986 cases in 1893, and then, by 1904, began to fall below 2,000 cases annually.[112] After 1890, moreover, the offense of public drunkenness was much less frequently added to these infractions. Paris prefects, republicans ever since their party's triumph in Seize Mai 1877, finally succeeded in getting their officers to ease up on the surveillance of the workers.[113] The police shifted much of their concern about café life from politics to prostitution and gambling. An English observer returning to Paris in 1900 after a thirty-year absence noted that the police were no longer a semi-military force and claimed that they received more blows than they gave.[114]

Police perceptions of café owners and customers grew more discriminating over the course of the century. By 1914, it was no longer the case, as Richard Cobb has so brilliantly illuminated, that the police tarred most suspects with the same "drunken and disorderly brush" they had used during the revolutionary era. By the Third Republic, the reports of spies, detectives, ordinary policemen, and district commissioners made subtle distinctions among different types of behavior involving drink, café-going, politics, and crime. The dossiers of cases dropped because of lack of evidence reveal that police agents viewed suspects who did not frequent cafés in an especially favorable light. An investigation during the late 1870s of a group of clerks charged with swindling provides an especially good example. Many of them never went out except to shop and to go to work. A well-paid 27-year-old clerk at the post office lived in his own comfortable apartment with his wife, a seamstress. The couple were childless, extremely quiet, and morally upright. They received no one at home, and he seldom went out except on commonplace errands. Another suspect, a 33-year-old white-collar worker, also living in his own apartment, was so sickly, secretive, and reclusive that the detectives could not even determine whether he was married. Nevertheless, they described his conduct as "leaving nothing to be desired": his expenses were modest, he invited nobody over to his home—indeed, ate his meals at home and went out solely to go to work. The report concluded that his behavior was that of an honest man. These two reports typify what the police perceived as a completely unsuspicious individual. The other dossiers in the series of cases dropped for lack of evidence show that for the police, as for social reformers and moralists, a sort of secular celibacy was the only condition truly above reproach.[115]

The police were the one institution of social control flexible enough to be able to understand the dynamics of café life. Their regulation of the café was always firmly rooted in tradition, although open to innovation. Yet, they, too, subscribed to the abstract dichotomies of virtue and vice, home and the café, that underlay perceptions of cafés and the legal system surrounding them. Much of the meaning of café life unfortunately eluded even the police.

CHAPTER TWO

Privacy in Public

A s we have seen, one of the main sources of the nineteenth-century moralistic concern over the café involved the question of housing and home life. The underlying assumption of most writers, whether Flora Tristan on the left, Jules Siegfried in the center, or Catholic thinkers on the right, was that workers went to cafés because their housing was so poor.[1] The pillars of café sociability, the argument went, were young bachelors who lived in furnished rooms.[2] Lacking kitchens and stable family or social lives, these youths took their meals and found their friendships and sexual affairs in cafés, where the only women were either active or potential prostitutes. The café seemed central to the process by which poverty in large cities produced immorality and family breakdown.[3] Public and private life seemed totally incommensurable in such a setting. A flourishing café life therefore seemed to herald the end of family life among the workers.

Evolution of Private Life in Paris

The widely held belief among both nineteenth-century middle-class moralists and twentieth-century sociologists and historians of the "modernization" school that bad housing "pushes" people onto the street or into the café, which we might call the "push-pull" thesis, assumes that people *prefer* to stay at home and will go to places like cafés only if they cannot find similar amenities of space and comfort at home. There is good reason, however, to think that this idea is a culturally specific value rather than

33

an inherent human trait. Philippe Ariès and others have shown that the elites of early modern Europe, both noble and bourgeois, did not privilege domestic space or the nuclear family in their social lives. Sociability, amid larger family groups and in the immediate social terrain, whether château or neighborhood, was one of the dominant traits of this society. In his splendid study of eighteenth-century Parisian neighborhoods and communities, David Garrioch chronicles the growing space that the bourgeoisie put between itself and the street and neighborhood sociability it had earlier embraced. The eighteenth-century Parisian bourgeoisie did not effect this separation because they were suddenly able to afford much larger houses, but because their cultural values began to shift. Indiscriminate mixing with the general public in streets and taverns, as Thomas Brennan also observes, was increasingly viewed as indiscreet and coarse. Instead, the bourgeoisie adopted the ideal of a selective sociability centered on entertaining a carefully chosen number of guests at home. These changes were part of the growing privatization of French upper-class society that Ariès has been so innovative in tracing. We can now see the continued working-class reliance on street sociability in the eighteenth century, described most graphically by Arlette Farge in *Vivre dans la rue*, not merely as a question of necessity, as she argues, but also as an instance of cultural continuity.[4]

Along with the notion of different standards of morality for different classes, the fact that this cultural ideal was emerging in their own age explains why contemporary observers of tavern life did not develop this push-pull theory of tavern or café frequentation. This is also the reason for the lack of concern about the housing of the lower classes in eighteenth-century Paris.[5] The notion of a housing problem could emerge only when the ideal of the domestic unit encased within its own domestic space had become a widespread and pervasive cultural ideal. If a wealthy bourgeoisie did not formulate and accept this domestic ideal until the mid eighteenth century, then surely the impoverished, immigrant, and recently rural proletarian population of nineteenth-century Paris could not be expected to entertain it. The lack of a modern domestic ideal among nineteenth-century workers may therefore be attributed to cultural continuity or lag or preference, but certainly not to immorality or perversity. It was scarcely fitting for contemporaries, much less for historians, to chastise a group for failing to act according to an ethic that had only recently been formulated and only ambiguously developed in nineteenth-century Paris.

Inasmuch as the domestic ideal continued to advance only haltingly, this theory of housing deprivation did not become dominant even among bourgeois observers until late in the nineteenth century. Certainly, the middle-class residents who avoided the increasingly congested central city by building elegant residences on Paris's northwest side followed the domestic trend of their eighteenth-century forebears. But Baron Haussmann's urban renewal during the Second Empire completely altered this evolution. The relations among the café, the street, the neighborhood, and inevitably the bourgeois home were dramatically altered. As Jeanne Gaillard has noted, the city ceased to be a closed medieval city and became an open modern city.[6] As we have seen, cafés quickly multiplied on the broad new boulevards that now traversed Paris. The growth in the number of establishments and the ease with which the new street system permitted people to get to them suddenly gave both the bourgeoisie on the central boulevards and the workers on the old small side streets and in the crowded periphery an ever-expanding choice of cafés to frequent.

Ironically, the "modernization" of Paris under Haussmann, with the creation of a dazzling new boulevard culture filled with theaters, shops, cafés, and music halls, may have led to a decrease in bourgeois domesticity. Unlike their counterparts across the channel in London, the bourgeoisie of Paris fondly and fervently embraced dense urban living in apartments and public sociability in cafés. A graphic indication of the difference in the two orientations is that in 1901, the city on the Thames had well over six times more buildings and houses than the city on the Seine did (611,837 compared with 80,319) even though its population was not quite twice as large (4,536,500 as opposed to 2,714,00).[7] Moreover, in 1909, 30,000 cafés sparkled each night in the City of Light, compared to only 5,860 in foggy London. Even more impressive is the ratio of drink shops to inhabitants: 1 to 1,000 in London compared with 11.25 to 1,000 in Paris.[8]

Given these divergent statistics, it is not surprising that the French appeared to observers to be much more at home on the street than the English.[9] Anglo-Saxons also found it difficult to grasp that a Parisian bourgeois family were much more likely to invite a guest to their favorite café rather than to their home, and that this informal institution was the common ground where everyone went for both business and pleasure.[10] Cafés became steadily more important, until, as Léon Daudet observed shortly after the turn of the century, they had displaced the salons as the center of Parisian intellectual life.

Many critics feared that these effects of Haussmannization had destroyed private life among the Paris bourgeoisie. In an 1860 entry to their journal, the Goncourts drew this conclusion: "The home is dying. Life is threatening to become public. The club for the upper classes, the café for the lower."[11] A few years later, Octave Feuillet echoed the same sentiments.[12] In a more lyrical vein, the American Theodore Child felt that the café had taken the place of home life and satisfied the taste for low life.[13] David W. Bartlet noted that the cafés were so crowded between 5 and 8 P.M. that one might conclude Parisians lived entirely in public.[14] In the novel *La Curée*, an exposé of haute bourgeois life under the empire, Zola portrayed a family that did little more than camp in their spacious town house and used the private rooms (*cabinets noirs*) of the café Riche as bedrooms.[15] In August 1884, "Perdican," a writer on local color for the influential weekly *L'Illustration*, commented on the unsavory aspects of the boulevard: "if one means by the boulevard the café, the flânerie, the brasserie, the laziness, one has reason to fulminate against the infamous boulevard."[16] Bourgeois boulevard cafés were one of the few aspects of middle-class drinking that temperance and social reformers consistently attacked. The political economist Leroy Beaulieu condemned the "rows of cafés on our boulevards overflowing with idlers and absinthe drinkers" because workers were thus provided with corrupt examples of upper-class life that they might wish to imitate.[17] In Zola's *L'Assommoir* we find a fictional example of this imitation when Gervaise's pretentious profligate former lover Lantier returns to the working-class rue de la Goutte d'Or, and "might well have changed for the better; he always wore a frock-coat nowadays and had picked up a bit of polish in cafés and political meetings."[18]

If this new urban leisure culture tempted the middle class from their opulent hearths, why would it not have had an even greater appeal for the working class, whose domestic amenities were, to say the least, less commodious? This is more than a rhetorical question, because the frequenting of cafés by Parisian workers was not simply a response to miserable conditions but also an aspiration to achieve the new urban luxuries that increasingly abounded all around them.

The Housing Problem and the Café

Can the number of cafés provide an index to a worsening or improvement in working-class housing? It certainly does not do so for eighteenth-century Paris, when the number of drinking establishments seems not to have grown even though the population of the city probably increased from

500,000 to 650,000.[19] The answer for the nineteenth century is fluid and more complex.

If the push-pull theory were correct, one would expect the period 1789–1851, during which the population of Paris increased from approximately 600,000 to over a million, to have witnessed a great expansion in the number of cafés. By 1820, the start of the great nineteenth-century immigration into the city, the populace began to complain that rents had doubled since 1789. By this date, too, Claude Lachaise had shown the direct correlation between mortality rates and housing. These links became unmistakable for researchers in the following decades as they charted the grim toll of the 1832 cholera epidemic in Paris.[20] By the 1830s, immigrant influx was overwhelming the existing housing stock. For example, under the Restoration, the population jumped by 25 percent, but housing increased by only 10 percent. The figures for the July Monarchy reveal almost as stark a disproportion, the population increasing by 34 percent and housing by only 22 percent.[21]

Contemporary observers, often on the left, detected a crisis in working-class home life. The working-class journalist Anthime Corbon felt that workers did not so much live as "camp" in their apartments.[22] Flora Tristan, one of the first writers to connect deteriorating housing to café life, asserted that three-quarters of the working class either slept in "furnished barracks," if they were single, or lived in attics, if they were married.[23] However, she did not query whether the number of cafés was increasing in pace with the city's population. Naturally, police regulation had a great deal to do with the failure of the number of cafés to grow. Nevertheless, if the push-pull theory is correct, Restoration and July Monarchy cafés should have been filled with unprecedented crowds fleeing their cramped quarters.[24] The resulting trade should have made café ownership extremely lucrative. In fact, no contemporary noted a dramatic increase in cafés' clientele, and there was no extraordinary increase in the fortunes or assets of café owners. Indeed, they remained extremely prone to bankruptcy.

For the Haussmann era and the years immediately following (1854–85), when the processes of immigration and housing deterioration were well established, the number of cafés can at least be consistently correlated with the housing crisis. The inexorable increase in the number of cafés over these decades—from 4,000 in 1851 to 42,000 in 1885—sustains the argument of historians who believe that Haussmann's renovation resulted in an even more severe housing crisis for the working class than the Restoration and the July Monarchy did.[25] The demolition of the old working-class inner-city tenements was not offset by the construction of new affordable housing in the outlying districts to receive the displaced workers. During these decades, immigration, too, continued at a high rate. Consequently, the price of affordable housing for workers more than doubled during the sixteen years of Haussmann's tenure.[26] Increasingly, landlords subdivided apartments to accommodate the ever-growing demand for cheap housing. The proletarian apartment often seemed altogether less like a home and more like an extension of the street. Fathers, mothers, daughters, and sons lived together in "pell-mell" fashion, with the result that "their souls atrophy and their habits become corrupted."[27] Most observers used the term "promiscuity" to describe all working-class housing. Both furnished rooms and apartments promoted a "terrible" and "deplorable" promiscuity.[28] Logically, then, sons and daughters moved out of the family quarters as soon as they were able. By the 1870s, single-person households totaled approximately 33 percent of the population, and over 70 percent of such households lived in only one room. Moralists believed that single individuals were the most assiduous café habitués.

The fifteen years following the fall of the Second Empire brought no noteworthy improvements in Parisian working-class housing; however, after 1880, the number of cafés showed a dramatic surge. Proletarian housing deteriorated even further as the pace of immigration accelerated and the Third Republic failed to construct adequate or affordable working-class housing. Rents continued to soar, pushing ever more workers into the densely crowded apartment buildings and shanty towns on the periphery of Paris.[29] In addition, the ever-increasing rents forced much of the population to move frequently.[30] Evidence from the judicial archives is particularly revealing. In a sample of approximately one hundred cases from the correctional tribunal and assize courts, slightly fewer than half of the defendants had lived at one place for less than one year, twenty had lived in one place for between one and two years, and only eight had remained in the same domicile for more than three years. Jean Palat, a coachman, is representative: between 1870, the year he arrived in Paris, and 1876, he lived at 2 rue de la Grange-Batelière, 31 rue de Trévise, 39 rue Boissy-d'Anglas, 22 rue Caumartin, 8 rue Ménessier, and 4 rue Coustou.[31] This type of peripatetic life, observers felt, drove people into the cafés. During the decade of the 1880s, continued deterioration of working-class housing meshed exactly with the virtual doubling of the number of cafés. This correlation unquestionably provides support for theorists who link housing to cafégoing.

Despite the overall correlation between a worsening housing market and an accelerating café trade, however, the push-pull thesis often fails at the individual level. Many workers, from a diverse sample of occupations, simply did not frequent cafés. And surely not all working-class Parisians saw cafégoing as a social obligation. Dossiers of the Paris courts, as well as case studies of the Le Play school published in the series *Les Ouvriers des deux mondes*, provide abundant examples of abstention. The court records detail not only straitlaced white-collar clerks but also anarchists refraining from café life, despite the latter's reputation for conspiracy. In one case, for example, a 42-year-old official of long standing in the opticians' union who was allegedly a committed anarchist never frequented cafés or attended public meetings and invited only a few close friends home. In another case, from shortly after the 1871 Commune, a 39-year-old metalworker at the city bus company, who had lived at the rue des Poissonniers for over twelve years, was described as caring only about his job, going straight home after work, and seeing no one, even on Sundays.[32] Similarly, a suburban railroad worker profiled in *Les Ouvriers des deux mondes* always ate at home and never patronized theaters or cafés; promenading on the exterior boulevards was his family's sole diversion.[33] Even when workers were café habitués and lived in cramped apartments, most of them often invited close friends home for dinner. Joséphine de Ardaillon, a clothes ironer, and her lover, Eugène Tellier, a stonemason, improvised by using a chest for a dining table when they had a few guests for dinner.[34] In general, these dossiers and case studies suggest that working-class behavior was determined by social and economic factors, with no singular socioeconomic profile for people who did not go to cafés.

After 1895, even the one overt link between the housing crisis and the café becomes tenuous. By this date, the number of cafés had stabilized at a figure (between 27,000 and 30,000) that would remain steady until 1914. But the housing situation, most scholars believe, continued to deteriorate.[35] Indeed, some historians argue that the prewar decade was the nadir of the nineteenth-century housing crisis.[36] How can we explain this anomaly? Perhaps these historians are in error, and the period after 1890 did see an attenuation of the working-class housing crisis. Or it very well may be that meager working-class budgets simply could not sustain any more cafés. Although attractive, this explanation works no better for the late nineteenth century than for the earlier years. Indeed, the average assets of café owners seem to have declined dramatically during this period, even though the number of potential customers continued to rise. In any case, we must conclude that there is very little correlation between the number of cafés and the housing crisis in nineteenth-century Paris.

We have so far compared the evolution of café life and the housing question in a very broad manner and found no necessary connection between the two. Perhaps a more specific analysis, based not on aggregate figures of housing stock or cafés but on the details of housing and café-going, would reveal a more direct connection. Social observers pinpointed furnished rooms catering to the working class—and usually rented by the hour, day, week, or month—as one of the worst aspects of the housing crisis. Moreover, because these rooms were usually little more than cramped bedrooms for either young Parisians or immigrant provincial bachelors, these observers felt that the renters were literally forced to become assiduous cafégoers.[37] Observers found that some renters, unable to accumulate enough money to marry, had spent the rest of their lives in these furnished rooms.[38] The *maisons de la nuit* (night houses) that sheltered the intemperate, the immoral, and the destitute fell into Class 5, the lowest category of working-class accommodation.[39] Some of these places were more like barracks than apartment houses, with renters sleeping four or five to a room. For example, in 1876, a survey found that 1,131 such rooms contained 5,558 beds.[40] Given such sardinelike conditions, it is not surprising that the Paris judge Adolphe Guillot called these chambers "vipers' nests of vice."[41]

Lodging-house (*garni*) owners were often charged with aiding and abetting a spendthrift, rootless, and alcoholic existence by running cafés in their lobbies. The liberal reformer Georges Picot charged that nine out of ten garnis had bars, which usually sold hard liquor.[42] The socialist investigators of proletarian life Léon and Maurice Bonneff also link the garni and the café.[43] Indeed, many lodging-house owners gave their tenants no moral guidance whatever and rented to anyone able to pay. Testifying at a trial in 1868, the widow Patat, a lodger and street vendor, laughed at the judge when he recounted the criminal behavior of one of her tenants, saying that it was not her problem if they hocked the mattress, drapes, and covers to pay the rent.[44] A writer in the weekly magazine *L'Illustration* in 1886 believed that endless purchase of drink in working-class lodgings produced "desperate pleasures," "forgetfulness," and "promiscuity of the most depraved sort."[45]

How accurate was this portrayal of the café-garni connection? To answer this question, we can draw upon two sets of statistics: first, the evolution of the number of cafés compared with the number of lodgings and their renter population, and, second, the percentage of defendants charged with public drunkenness who lived in garnis. For the first part of the answer, we have available data that—despite the inherent imprecision in enumerating a floating population—span the entire century. For the second, we have precise figures, although they cover only the period after 1873, for those arrested under the law on public drunkenness.

For most of the first half of the century, there was no dramatic expansion in either the number of cafés or the garni population (which nonetheless correlates more closely than the population as a whole with the growth rate for cafés). In 1832, between 32,000 and 35,000 people lived in lodgings,[46] and this had risen to over 50,000 by 1846.[47] During the same period, the number of cafés remained essentially unchanged. Under the Second Empire, however, both the garni population and the number of cafés grew astronomically. In 1864, Paris garnis held approximately 200,000 renters, an increase corresponding closely to the fivefold increase in the number of cafés during the 1850s and 1860s (from approximately 4,000 to 22,000).[48] Haussmannization did not immediately alter the geography of the garnis, which continued to be located in the city center, particularly in the 4th arrondissement (Hôtel de ville), which also had a dense concentration of cafés.[49]

After the fall of the Second Empire, the correlation shifts. The number of renters increased substantially between 1876 and 1882—from 142,671 to 243,564.[50] The garni population thus experienced a big jump in the years prior to the reintroduction of freedom of commerce for the café. By 1890, after the number of cafés doubled and then leveled off at a figure that was a third more than during the 1870s, the number of garni residents had declined to 168,000. The garni population subsequently fluctuated between 160,000 and 200,000 between 1891 and 1910.[51] Although the garni population had a trajectory that was partially and fitfully similar to the growth rate in the number of cafés, the one-to-one relationship that most scholars have hypothesized is not apparent.

That cafés were not simply the antechambers of garnis is persuasively documented in the records of the Paris police courts. A tabulation of over four thousand public drunkenness cases between 1873 and 1901, indicating whether the defendant lived in a garni, an apartment, or a house, shows that only 17 percent of those charged with public drunkenness were garni residents. This is merely seven percentage points higher than the proportion of lodgers in the working-class population of Paris overall. In a sample of 600 proletarian families, for example, Louis Abanal found 66 of them living in garnis and 484 in apartments.[52] One would logically expect a higher proportion of lodgers among those arrested for public drunkenness, because, in theory, they spent more time in cafés and presumably thus consumed more alcohol than customers with better housing. If only 17 percent of the problem drinkers of Paris, at least as defined by the police, were garni residents, then we may speculate that their actual ratio among café habitués may have been lower.

These same court cases permit us to test a related assumption concerning café habitués: that they were primarily under the age of twenty-five. Here we can draw upon an extremely large sample, over ten thousand cases from both the Paris police courts and the correctional tribunal between 1873 and 1901. Data from both reveal that those between the teenage years and twenty-five were very much a minority among cafégoers throughout the entire period. "Youth" in this definition made up only 16 percent of those brought before the correctional tribunal during the 1870s, 23 percent during the 1880s, and 22.5 percent in subsequent decades. In the police courts, the figure is even lower, fluctuating between 10 and 14 percent over the same period.[53]

These figures are remarkably low, given that youthful inebriates were much more likely to contest police authority than were their elders. During this era, the percentage of defendants insulting the police declines in neat progression with the rise in their age: 87 percent of the defendants between the ages of 15 and 19 insulted the police; 80 percent of those between 20 and 29; 77 percent of those between 30 and 39; 74 percent of those in their forties; 69 percent of those in their fifties; and 66 percent of those above the age of sixty.[54] In short, a very straight correlation may be made between age, public drunkenness, and a propensity to insult or physically attack the police. After 1900, this propensity became embodied in the image of "Apache" bands of ferocious proletarian youths terrorizing the outer districts of Paris. Yet, as these statistics distinctly show, this type of youthful assertive drinking was a minority comportment in the profile of Parisian drunkenness.

Clearly, the café was not the center of a youth subculture. If anything, teenagers were probably overrepresented among the correctional tribunal defendants. The records for the one infraction in which teenagers constituted a large percentage of the offenders—namely, *filouterie*, or the ordering of food and drink by customers who knew they could not pay—tend to support, not undermine, this point by showing that working-class youths were marginal to café life.[55] Approximately 40 percent of the people arrested in cafés for filouterie during the 1870s through the 1890s were teenagers. But the number of swindling cases in the correctional tribunal was only about one-fifth the number of public drunkenness cases. Adding to the marginal nature of the defendants charged with filouterie is the fact that more of them (35%) were unemployed and homeless than those (10%) charged with public drunkenness.[56] Defendants in filouterie cases were thus far less representative of the café's clientele than were defendants in public drunkenness cases. Teenage cafégoers were, for the most part, on the margins not only of café life but of Parisian society as a whole.[57] Youth did not penetrate generally into the center of a café sociability premised upon being able to buy rounds for friends and fellow customers.

The café was thus an overwhelmingly adult institution. The largest single group of café customers (28.9%) were in their thirties, with habitués in their forties representing only a slightly lower figure (21.2%). The café continued to attract customers in their fifties and sixties (10.1%). In fact, a higher percentage of people were arrested for public drunkenness above the age of fifty (13.1%) than below the age of twenty-one (10.6%). Clearly, working-class Parisians did not stop frequenting cafés as they grew older. Judging from the age structure of the body of defendants brought before the correctional tribunal, cafés served the needs of people throughout their lives. These statistics match the profile of alcoholics that doctors developed based on the ages of people hospitalized for excessive drunkenness. One of the most careful studies of 2,493 Parisians hospitalized for excessive drinking found few twenty- to twenty-nine-year-olds being treated, a dramatic jump in the numbers of people between thirty and thirty-four, and further increases between thirty-five and thirty-nine and between forty and forty-four, after which there was a sharp decline.[58] (Interestingly, this decline does not show up in the judicial statistics.) Once again, cafégoing escapes easy generalizations based on notions of pathology.

If the café was not the center of a youth subculture, then was it, perhaps, a meeting place for a bachelor subculture?[59] Along with its reputation as a gathering place for lodgers, the café was also generally viewed as the preserve of bachelors. Judicial statistics once again undermine this logical assumption. Almost 27 percent of the men and women brought before the correctional tribunal on charges of public drunkenness were married, which is close to the overall proportion (33%) of married Parisian workers in this era.[60] The difference between the figures may be explained in several ways. First, a married person with a family to support might well be reluctant to get involved in disputes with the police or an employer. Second, the marital status of a defendant was frequently omitted by court recorders and, in the absence of evidence to the contrary, I tallied such individuals as unmarried, an arbitrary decision that may have resulted in an undercount. In addition, these statistics do not take account of couples living together without a marriage contract, a percentage the statistician Jacques Bertillon estimated in 1880 to be as high as one out of every ten couples.[61] In the dossiers of the correctional tribunal, the ratio of common-law unions to legal marriages among café habitués is two out of ten, double Bertillon's estimate. No official data are available, as the police and court clerks understandably took no note of common-law marriages in the court registers.

The detailed information of the assize court and correctional tribunal dossiers shows that even unmarried café habitués were not necessarily rootless. Of the more than five hundred defendants involved in café life found in the dossiers, 34.4 percent were either married or living with a lover; another 14 percent lived with parents or relatives; and a further 11 percent lived with friends or an employer, or had separated recently from wife or lover. Thus 60 percent of the café customers in the correctional tribunal's dossiers lived with some close connection. Only about 7 percent were without domicile. Most of the cafés' customers thus did not frequent them because they lacked other means of meeting people in Paris. These figures provide one more indication that cafés did not attract a disproportionate share of the city's rootless and transient population.

This perception of café habitués as connected to their city is also borne out by the fact that native Parisians comprised the same or a greater percentage of the café population as they did of the city's population as a whole. Social observers assumed that the typical café at the end of the century catered heavily to provincial and rural migrants, especially Bretons and Auvergnats.[62] Once again the underlying assumption was that café customers lacked connections in the community. Yet the correctional tribunal and police court statistics between 1873 and 1901 show that native Parisians were a consistently higher percentage (between 36 and 40%) among those prosecuted for public drunkenness than among the general population in this era (between 33 and 36%).[63] Once again, in another statistical index, the café proves to have been a space for natives as much as for immigrants.

The Café in Relation to Proletarian Family Life

Given the persuasive power of the moralist discourse, it may seem strange that married life and café life should complement each other. Nevertheless, a global and a particular set of statistics reveal a direct connection between the two spheres of ordinary life. Across the nineteenth century in Paris, an increase was noted in the number of weddings (in 1748 there were 8 weddings for every 1,000 people; in 1872 the rate was 11.5 weddings per 1,000) as well as in the number of cafés.[64] Thus the repugnance that Louis-Sébastien Mercier found for marriage decreased during the same century in which the café became a ubiquitous institution.[65]

The best evidence to support the thesis of the complementarity of family and café life is the fact that a complete enumeration of Paris marriage contracts for 1860, 1880, and 1900 reveals that café owners were chosen as witnesses more than any other group, except for relatives and friends. The signatures of café owners appear on 23 percent of the marriage contracts for 1860 and 1880, and on 16 percent of those for 1900. Couples requesting the presence of a café owner at the registry office were almost exclusively working-class. The percentages range from 85 percent in 1860 to over 90 percent in 1900.

An occupational comparison between people who chose café owners to witness their marriage contracts and those arrested for public drunkenness provides a privileged insight into the contrasting public and private, as well as respectable and disreputable, sides of café sociability. The working class dominated both groups, representing over 95 percent of those charged with public drunkenness and 85–90 percent, as just noted, of the marrying couples. Concerning the men, the two populations differ primarily in the percentages of clerks and day laborers.

As one might expect, white-collar clerks composed a small percentage of defendants charged with public drunkenness but a substantial number of the grooms who chose café owners to witness their weddings. Straddling the margins between bourgeois and working-class life, this growing sector of the Paris workforce (increasing from 16.5% in 1866 to 21.4% in 1911) was underrepresented among the correctional tribunal cases (constituting between 4.3% in the 1870s and 5.3% in the 1880s and 1890s) but virtually representative in the registry office (12.3% in 1860, 17.3% in 1880, and 16.8% in 1900).

Conversely, day laborers, at the bottom of the occupational hierarchy, but one of the three major groups within the working class, constituted a substantial portion of the defendants charged with public drunkenness (15.0% in 1873 and 18.9% in 1880) and only a small fraction of the grooms (6.4% in 1860 and 6.2% in 1880).

These percentages are virtually mirror images. They probably reflect the quiet, respectable demeanor of clerks, white-collar office workers with regular salaries, as opposed to the loud and raucous comportment of day laborers, men who engaged in a series of temporary jobs involving manual labor.[66] The statistical difference echoes their different status and work conditions.

Other occupational groups that had more grooms than public drunkenness defendants, aside from the bourgeois and petit bourgeois, were domestics, butchers, and bakers. However, their percentages were extremely small, altogether totaling only a scant 3.9 to 4.3 percent of the defendants to merely 6 and 7 percent of the grooms. What is remarkable is that café life could encompass such a wide diversity of behavior.

Within the Parisian male working class, major occupational groups occur in roughly the same proportion in both sets of statistics, revealing the extremely small gaps between public and private and between respectability and disrepute. Carriage builders, harness makers, printers, and artisans in Paris's famous luxury trades—jewelers, bronze workers, and engravers—were groups with virtually identical percentages: 8.3 percent among the defendants during the 1870s and 6.9 percent in later decades, and between 8.3 and 8.9 percent among the grooms. Metalworkers and workers in small service industries (cabbies, street vendors, etc.) were also close. Among the public drunkenness defendants, metalworkers held steady at 8.3 percent; among the grooms, the figure ranged from 5.9 to 7.4 percent across these decades. Percentages of service workers declined among the defendants from 16.4 to 15.6 percent, but increased among the grooms from 13.2 to 15.0 percent. Construction laborers and men in trades undergoing mechanization (as in the clothing, shoe, and furniture sectors) showed a greater tendency to appear with café owners as defendants in court than as grooms at the city hall. Construction workers formed roughly 14.4 to 18.3 percent of the defendants and between 12.2 and 10.3 percent of the grooms; and workers in the evolving trades showed a similar divergence in their two populations, between 14.6 and 12.2 percent of the defendants and only 8.4 and 8.5 percent among the grooms. However, while the gap between the two populations was widening among the construction workers, it was narrowing among the trades in transition.

The variations among women's occupations in the two populations is much more dramatic than the comparable variations among the men. Female oppression accounts for much of the difference. Prostitutes, a category absent among the brides, made up 15.1 percent of those charged with public drunkenness, accounting for a good part of the difference between the two populations. Women day laborers, too, represent a big disparity in the two sets of data: 15.6 percent of the defendants (the second highest percentage), but only 6.3 percent of the brides. Clearly, women on the bottom rungs of Parisian society were not often chosen by male café habitués to be their wives, but were likely to have confrontations with the police involving drink. Garment and textile workers, one of the two dominant female trades in Paris, and women with no listed occupation, another substantial part of the population, represented sizable proportions of each group. While women in the "needle trades" totaled 27.6 percent among the brides and 19.2 percent among the defendants, those without an occupation constituted 18.2 percent of the brides and 11.5 percent of the defendants. The biggest surprise in these data sets is the small percentage of domestics, the other paramount women's occupation in Paris. They account for only 9.3 percent of the brides and 8.1 percent of the defendants, well under their percentages in the general population. Among the less populous occupations, the cooks stand out. Although only a minuscule 3.8 percent of the defendants, they made up a substantial 11.8 percent of the brides. Finally, laundresses and street vendors, two notoriously argumentative and bibulous female professions, meet the stereotype by constituting only 5.1 and 1 percent (respectively) of the newlyweds but 8.7 and 5.5 percent (respectively) of the defendants. These percentages of women, much more than in the case of men, reflect nineteenth-century notions of respectability. The issue of women in cafés is discussed further in Chapter 7.

There were many reasons why workers chose a café owner as witness to a wedding. First, the role of the shopowner in working-class social and festive life was certainly central. Cafés played a vital role in working-class courtship. The link between café sociability and courtship was epitomized in the popular expression "to do a wedding" (*faire la noce*), which became a synonym for going on a spree.[67] Second, the slightly elevated social standing of the café owner—manager of a business and perhaps a property owner—may have given the occupation a certain cachet. Couples usually chose marriage witnesses who were older and slightly more elevated in status than themselves.[68] The dynamics of the special relationship between café owners and their customers will be explored at greater length in Chapter 5. Suffice it to say here that the café owner represented sociability, stability, and a certain sense of respectability in the chaotic world of working-class Paris in the mid to late nineteenth century. A third possible reason for the high percentage of café owners witnessing weddings may have been the rootlessness of the particular couples involved. Further research might determine whether or not these brides and grooms were well connected with kinship, neighborhood, or immigrant networks. The high percentage of café owners serving as witnesses during the 1860s and through the 1880s may well reflect the unsettled nature of the newly annexed working-class districts. By 1900, these areas may have achieved sufficient solidarity to permit more reliance on neighbors as witnesses and less on café owners. Even after 1900, however, café owners remained the preferred choice of a sizable percentage of the Paris working class.

After the marriage contract had been signed, working-class wedding parties frequently took place in cafés. Perhaps in return for the honor of being chosen to witness the wedding, the café owner gave a discount on the food and rent of the room for the party. In any case, a long-standing feature of Paris cafés, dating at least from the eighteenth century, as Garrioch shows, was a ballroom for dancing and weddings.[69] During the Revolution, Parisian couples staged and celebrated "revolutionary marriages" in cafés. In late January 1794, a police report noted a series of weddings of revolutionary sansculottes at the Père Duchesne café (undoubtedly named after Hébert's popular paper) near the Bicêtre hospice. Thirty to forty neighbors around this café in the faubourg Saint-Marceau gathered to celebrate the marriages of a "worker," a clerk, and a street sweeper. The festivities included drinking, patriotic songs, toasts to the Convention, and children shouting "Death to the tyrants! Long live Liberty and Equality!" The police observer commented approvingly that "in their wine they spoke with a religious respect for the Convention."[70] Such respect for working-class café weddings was seldom found among the police after the 1789 Revolution.

The closing-hour circulars of the Paris prefects of police during the nineteenth century attest to the prevalence of café wedding parties and to the distrust with which the police generally viewed them. These circulars specifically cite wedding celebrations in cafés as a frequent cause of after-hours violations. The prefects also complain that café owners wanting to extend the closing hour for a wedding or banquet almost always put in their requests just before the actual event, preventing the police from following the proper procedures.[71] The prefects did have cause for concern, because sometimes these celebrations, such as one at the barrière des Martyrs in January 1829, might last until 2 A.M. or even 4 A.M.[72]

The geography of working-class café weddings changed during the course of the century in response to urban renovation and expansion. During the first half of the century, proletarian wedding parties frequently chose the suburban taverns (*guinguettes*) of Belleville and Ménilmontant in the northeast and the Martyrs barrière in the southwest, all beyond the then limits of Paris. The more sedate workers probably chose the guinguettes of Ménilmontant because they were reputed to be less rowdy and noisy than those of Belleville.[73] Even after Haussmannization brought these areas into the city, their cafés still played an integral role in weddings. For example, in Ménilmontant there was only one church, and an adjacent café sometimes served as a convenient place to catch the overflow of large wedding parties.[74] By the end of the century, the working-class wedding had become more standardized and less tied to the local neighborhood. The connection to the café, however, remained strong. Working-class marriages usually occurred on Saturday, or to a lesser degree on Sunday, and the custom developed of starting at 11 A.M. Three other customs had also become "absolutely indispensable": the wedding party would go to the town hall, then to church, and then to the Bois de Boulogne, a fashionable park on the west side of Paris. Here the wedding party would tour the artificial lakes and finally proceed either to café de la Cascade or to one of the cheaper cafés across the river in Suresnes. Other cafés across the city also began to specialize in weddings.[75]

Couples continued their association with the café after their wedding parties. They also used the owners extensively to witness, again at the city hall, the happy event of a baptism or the tragic event of a death in the family.[76] Café owners witnessed only half as many births and deaths as they did weddings. The lower figure (10%) in this case may have been a consequence of the law requiring only two witnesses for baptisms and deaths rather than the four needed for weddings. The paucity of other types of shopkeeper recorded as witnesses reveals that café owners purveyed much more than food and drink to their customers. Their relationships frequently broke through the boundaries separating public and private life and the usual interaction between patron and customer.

There is mounting evidence that simultaneously with the expansion of café owners' influence in the decades from 1860 to 1900, working-class families became more affectionate toward their children and concerned about their welfare. Two of the leading historians of the Parisian family, Rachel Fuchs and Lenard Berlanstein, have found that bonds of affection within working-class families increased steadily after 1860.[77] By 1900, the rate of illegitimacy had perceptibly decreased, along with a declining proletarian birthrate. As Berlanstein notes, most authorities believe a declining birthrate reveals a growing attention to each individual child. Greater attention to children may explain why by 1900, begging among youth seemed to contemporaries to be diminishing, too.[78] Moreover, the percentage of teenagers arrested in Paris was appreciably lower than it had been forty years earlier: 20–26 percent in 1900 compared to 33 percent in 1860.

The fact that familial affection and cafégoing could be related is revealed in a wide range of evidence indicating that working-class parents frequently took their children to cafés. The tradition in artisanal Paris had been for the male worker to spend Sunday walking with his family in the country or on the boulevards and Monday drinking with his comrades.[79] Yet during the July Monarchy (1830–48), bronze founders, members of one of the main luxury trades, often took their children with them to the barrière cafés on Mondays.[80] Indeed, in some cases, workers brought their families to Belleville two to three times a week.[81] The setting for this tradition shifted to the boulevards after Haussmann's renovations and annexations. In his 1876 novel *Jack*, Alphonse Daudet depicts whole families at the tables of small cafés on Sundays, reading illustrated papers and drinking beer.[82] In 1884, the leftist paper *Le Cri du peuple* observed that workers now took their children to the café for New Year's Day dinner rather than celebrating with a family feast at home as had once been the custom.[83] On a different date, the editor of the paper, the former Communard Jules Vallès, published his fears that the accessibility of prepared food in cafés and delicatessens was producing a decline in home cooking in particular and, consequently, of proletarian home life in general.[84] While this may have been the case with some families, the detailed case studies in the series *Les Ouvriers des deux mondes* show that cafégoing on holidays and special occasions did not necessarily lead to the families' becoming regular customers.[85] Abundant evidence suggests that white-collar workers also took their families to cafés. Thus the pattern of choosing café owners to witness weddings and baptisms continued as the children grew up and joined family outings.

Children's behavior in cafés, generally speaking, seems to have been monitored closely by their parents. The empathic and empirical American observer Alvan Sanborn noted that the typical café contained "bloused and frocked laborers, with their whitecapped wives and their black-aproned children." He believed, as we saw earlier, that Paris working-class cafés were a much more conducive space for children than American saloons.[86] A similarly vivid image of working-class café life, in this case among the upwardly mobile clerks, is found in an 1911 *L'Illustration* article. The chronicler of local Paris color relates how once a week, especially at the end of winter between five and seven in the afternoon, the face of the boulevard changed; the crowd ceased to be a mixture of international cosmopolitan tourists, and it became a boulevard of Parisians and their families. After a long walk in the still largely open spaces of the Champs-Elysées, the Champs-de-Mars, and the Invalides, the families went back to the central and peripheral boulevards and sat at the brightly lighted sidewalks. The clerks concentrated on keeping their hats on straight and the grandmothers held the children tightly by the hand so they would not stray.[87] There are few accounts in the judicial archives, in the newspapers, or in the periodical press of unattended children roaming through cafés. Even the *gamins*, the street-smart urchins, seem to have kept their distance from this adult institution by scavenging for cigar butts on the sidewalks next to cafés rather than inside.[88]

In the case of Paris, little evidence exists of heavy or widespread alcoholic drinking among children. Across the century, social observers documented the heavy childhood drinking that they found in the textile towns of the northeast, such as Rouen, Nancy, Amiens, Besançon, and Douai, but significantly not in Paris.[89] A youth's first drink and initial overindulgence were not as important a rite of passage into adulthood among Parisian youth as they were in Brittany or Picardy.[90] Adolescent Parisian proletarian culture was focused much more around the dance floor than the bar.[91] The family surveys in *Les Ouvriers des deux mondes* and working-class autobiographies sometimes reveal sons to be more sober than their fathers. Unfortunately, these studies did not explore whether or not this was in reaction to or rebellion against the father.[92]

Families, with or without their children, may have socialized in cafés, but did they feel at "home" there? Nineteenth-century moralists worried that workers might very well feel this way. For the moralists, such domesticity in the public domain represented one of the ultimate degradations of modern urban life, because it meant that public life had obliterated private life. Except for Henri Leyret and Alvan Sanborn, few nineteenth-century observers considered that café sociability might represent precisely the opposite historical trend—that is, a means for private life to expand into a previously public sphere. A comparison with eighteenth-century taverngoing and street life lends support to the idea that private life slowly encroached on public life between 1700 and 1900.

Arlette Farge and Thomas Brennan, in particular, provide a standard by which to compare the evolution of the expression of private sentiments in public places. Farge has demonstrated that family quarrels on the street or in cafés usually prompted the intervention of neighbors or strangers.[93] Brennan, finding similar behavior, notes how families in taverns coped with this possibility of public intervention in their private affairs: "The public character of the cabaret evidently had the opposite effect on family conflict. The family seemed to close ranks in the public space of the tavern. There are enough cases of husbands' defending their wives' honor, of brothers defending each other, of the family generally exhibiting its solidarity to suggest that domestic conflict was possible only in the relative isolation of the home."[94] Farge, however, shows that workers may have felt more at home in the street than in the tavern, for she provides numerous examples of families fighting in public thoroughfares.[95] That the laborers' tavern of the time was clearly not a place where private feelings could be expressed is also indicated in the autobiography of an eighteenth-century Paris glassmaker, Jacques-Louis Ménétra. We find him courting, seducing, and frolicking with women in taverns, but never taking his wife there to discuss family relationships or business.[96]

Over the course of the nineteenth century, cafés became places where customers discussed and argued intimate family matters with ever-increasing freedom. This slowly emerging right to privacy in public was a product both of changing architecture and changing mores. The emergence of the counter, and, in some cafés, of different rooms for various clienteles and functions, engendered an increased sense of privacy. Some suburban taverns provided separate rooms for conversation and for merrymaking. At Rochechouart, the vast suburban tavern (*guinguette*) named the Petit Ramponeau exemplified how tavern space had become more specialized. Besides the main room, there were two smaller ones, each containing a dozen tables. One room, named the Chamber of Peers, was specifically for tranquil habitués, retirees from the fast-paced life, and enemies of noise and dance who wanted only a simple basic tavern for food and drink. The other room, dubbed the Chamber of Deputies, was reserved for loud, young argumentative types.[97] In other cases, both literary and archival, café habitués simply appropriated a particular space in a café as their own. In Zola's novel *Le Ventre de Paris*, the radical Gavard virtually lives in the paneled side room of a café in the market district. He leaves overcoats, books, and papers there. Lebigre, the proprietor, accommodates such nesting by removing one of the room's tables to provide an upholstered settle that Gavard uses for a bed.[98] Zola's fictional character had a real-life alter ego in Joseph Fabre, a supervisor who fought for the Commune. At his trial, Fabre compared the way in which he lived in and moved out of a particular person's home with the way he did so at a café.[99]

A touching scene from the life of that son of the working class Jean Renoir provides a telling indication of this sense of café domesticity. In the early days of the impressionist school, Renoir and some of his friends often visited a small café at the intersection of rue des Saints-Pères and rue de l'Université. This café was exclusively frequented by habitués, who always sat at the same tables. One night, an elderly couple entered and found that Renoir's group had taken their customary table. Their vexation did not last long, because the artists moved on. Delighted, the couple immediately sat down to play their usual game of dominoes.[100] No eighteenth-century historian has offered comparable evidence of a sense of place in eighteenth-century wine shops.

This growing sense of being at home there explains why family fights and lovers' quarrels in cafés became common during the nineteenth century. Unlike their eighteenth-century forebears, couples aired family or personal problems with little fear of intervention from bystanders. Couples, brothers, or cousins did not feel inhibited in arguing with or even physically attacking each other.[101] From at least the 1830s on, the Paris courts and newspapers were filled with dramatic stories of family conflict in cafés. For example, a prostitute and a hauler at the grain depot lived as husband and wife for three years. One day, at a wine shop near the Palais-Royal, she reproached him for infidelities, and he responded by hitting her twice.[102] The fact that the woman was a prostitute does not detract from the fact that she was with her lover, not a client, that she chose a public venue to express her anger over a personal matter, and that no one intervened to stop the fight.

The number of couples who fought in public grew steadily across the century; accounts of such fights are especially numerous in judicial archives and newspaper reports from the 1870s through 1914. On 29 May 1874, Honoré-Marie de Lisle, an unemployed clerk, had a violent argument with his legally separated wife over the custody of his children. When the fight erupted on the terrace of the café de la Rotonde at 50 boulevard Courcelles, in the Ternes neighborhood of the 17th arrondissement, the owners and the few customers inside ran out at the sound of the woman's screams. The ex-husband's assertion that it was a family quarrel immediately persuaded them to go back inside.[103] Two years later, Sébastien Billoir, a retired army sergeant who was soon to be notorious for murdering and dismembering his lover, Jeanne Bellengé, shocked the habitués of a series of Montmartre cafés by his tyrannical treatment of her. There is not the faintest indication, however, that anyone ever tried to intervene in their quarrels, perhaps because he did not at that point resort to the brutal physical attacks that he would later commit. A much more banal case involved a worker named Henri Houdremont, who, after one of his all-night revels on 13 April 1885, encountered his estranged wife Marie in Madame Lefebvre's café at 39 rue des Amandiers, Belleville, where they immediately began to argue about Houdremont's lack of support or concern for their children.[104]

These cases reveal that nineteenth-century working-class Parisians felt sufficiently at home in their cafés not only to discuss their private affairs there but also to argue and fight over them. The reason people felt they could express such private emotions in public is that they could count on other customers not to meddle the way their eighteenth-century predecessors had done.[105] I have found no evidence in the nineteenth-century judicial archives of outside intervention in a nonviolent domestic quarrel. In the instances where couples or families were insulted in cafés, neighborhood feuds were involved, and it was by definition a public, not a private, matter. A similar trend toward greater public discretion in the expression of private matters in community settings also seems to have occurred in England. However, the explanation given for this change—that is, the general increase in the size of English homes—does not apply to Paris.[106] Henry Steele, an English mechanic who worked in Paris for a year at the turn of the century and wrote a book on his experiences, shows how pervasive this right to privacy in public had become among the workers by this time. "The families come and go away together, and though social intercourse with utter strangers is free in the course of the day's enjoyment, no one presumes on that freedom to the extent of entering into more intimate acquaintance with any family."[107]

This growing tolerance and distancing of others in the café relations of the nineteenth-century Paris working-class should not be mistaken for the callous indifference to neighbors that is often thought to be the effect of large modern cities on the human psyche. Nor can their tolerance be ascribed to the rapid growth of the city and deteriorating housing conditions, which might in some fashion make the population increasingly indifferent, callous, or passively anonymous. Café owners and their customers did enter the fray if they felt the argument was becoming violent (the etiquette that governed café life is examined in depth in Chapter 6).

This proletarian sense of privacy was not purely personal and individual in the middle-class sense. Instead, it had a communal and class basis. Workers had a keen sense that if they wanted more living space than they had in their crowded apartments and furnished rooms, they would have to create it in the café. Thus they were especially resentful of the constant surveillance of the police, because this intrusiveness appeared to be an attempt to deprive them of one of the few locations at which they could attain a measure of control over their environment.[108]

By insulting or even physically attacking the police, workers tried to ensure that the police would stay clear and let them have an autonomous space. Throughout the nineteenth century, there were many cafés that the police were frightened to enter, resorting, instead, to police raids.[109] Although sometimes physically violent, this hostility more often took the form of verbal abuse. The dossiers and judgments of the Correctional Tribunal record numerous instances when this assertion of privacy had a political edge, especially in the aftermath of the Commune and its bloody repression. In an incident just a few months after the Commune's fall in August 1871, Jean van der Speck, a commercial traveler of Dutch extraction, voiced such sentiments, shouting at the police, "These affairs do not concern you and I will give my story to Victor Hugo." A year after the bloody week, on 29 April 1872, the house painter Louis Houbert shouted at the police, "Idlers, good-for-nothings, cowards, you should not mix in things that do not concern you. If I had been at Montmartre, I would have taken your measure."

The privacy motif continued to be found in the epithets hurled at the police during the 1880s. For example, in February 1885, a café waiter, Louis Bugnard, stigmatized a policeman in the following terms: "You are only good for breaking open doors, you bunch of murderers." Two months later, in separate incidents, police officers arrested Pierre Jeandin, a coachman, and Achille Barbier, a mason, for remonstrating, "This is not your affair."[110] Although the location of such disputes is seldom given in the registers, the remaining insult cases in the dossiers indicate that they usually did take place in or around cafés.

Numerous newspaper accounts and contemporary observers also provide examples of this quest for privacy in the café. The radical republican paper *La Lanterne* reported in June 1880 that a patron of a café in the suburb of Lavallois-Perret joined the owners and their waiter in an attack on some tax collectors. "They jumped on me, yelling, 'Screw you! Police spy, scum [*canaille*]; we are in our house,'" one official noted.[111] Working-class Parisians reacted to police penetration of their cafés the way any homeowner would react to an intrusion into his home. Lacking houses, workers made the café their castle. The left-wing political parties of the 1880s and 1890s tried to connect resistance to police harassment to the worker's rights of freedom of speech and assembly. In the halls of the Parisian and suburban municipal councils, as well as in the Chamber of Deputies, socialist militants such as Edouard Vaillant and Jules Joffrin vigorously protested police intimidation and harassment in working-class neighborhoods.[112]

After 1870, much like the sansculottes before them, emerging socialist and anarchist groups and the labor movement annexed the culture of proletarian café privacy to their movements. In the 1870s, in a bid to end the Church's control of the rites of passage, socialists in Parisian suburbs such as Saint-Denis and Boulogne-sur-Seine created the socialist baptism. Such baptisms were held, naturally, in cafés, restaurants, and dance halls.[113] A hostile article in *Le Pays* (19 September 1876) queried: "A civil baptism, what can that be?" The answer given by the article was that the ceremony would have to take place at the counter of a café, and that in place of baptismal water, there would undoubtedly be some mixture of cassis, but that the entire proceedings would only be a pretext for demagogic talk and toasts. A more sympathetic description of a socialist baptism presents a very different picture. On 15 October 1876, a baptism "with great cordiality" happened in Saint-Denis at a restaurant on the place des Armes, which was attended by a municipal counselor by the name of Grossetette and 150 other people. The ceremony was accompanied by songs, toasts to the republican virtue of fraternity and to the cause of de-Christianization, and a collection for the families of political prisoners. In 1892, the socialist municipal council of Saint-Denis approved the practice of socialist baptisms.[114] Clearly, the city's socialist leaders hoped by connecting the celebration of baptisms in cafés to some variant of socialism, the workers would not only be weaned from Catholicism but would also come to see their café sociability as part of a wider class solidarity.

This leftist strategy was both possible and effective because the Parisian working-class café was at the intersection between public and private life. Unlike the bourgeois, the working class did not hold a dichotomous view of café and the home. Despite the flowering of a seductive and opulent boulevard café culture, the Parisian bourgeoisie did not, for instance, use café owners to witness their weddings. In fact, although bourgeois café culture reached its zenith during the same decades (1860–1900), the paltry number of middle-class couples who did choose a café owner to witness their marriages fell from 6.4 percent (1860) to 3.8 percent (1880) to less than 2 percent (1900). The percentage of bourgeois using a café owner to witness baptisms was even lower. Thus even though both classes may have been assiduous cafégoers, the working class relied on the café for support in their private lives much more than did those above them in the social hierarchy.

Working-class domestic space extended into the café. Middle-class reformers seldom realized this. Their strategy of enlisting the working-class wife to get her husband out of the café in the name of domestic virtue was thus bound to fail, because this strategy did not adapt to the manner in which the workers, including women, defined domesticity and privacy. Workers patently did not define public and private life in the simple dichotomies used by the middle class.[115] Moreover, the movement to make workers better parents did not recognize the fact that the sense of domesticity created in the café by the workers may have actually helped to strengthen working-class families.[116]

Working-class café sociability was not part of the housing problem; rather, it was a grassroots attempt to solve it. The Paris working class coped with a severe housing crisis by appropriating the café. Workers as individuals and families lacked the money necessary to own private property and enjoy the accompanying prerogatives of privacy, but they did have the strength of numbers and myriad available milieus in the cafés for a collective appropriation of space. By continually frequenting a neighborhood, a group, or even a couple, could make a café into their own space. Such frequentation could lead to sense of belonging, a sense of being "at home," as shown by the much greater ease with which nineteenth-century Parisians let private emotions and family matters become part of café life, and also by the café owner's position as a pillar of the community with respect to such benchmarks in a person's and family's life as marriage, birth, and death.

Instead of seeing this type of privacy in public as moral degeneration, as contemporary moralists believed it to be, we should see it as part of a larger social and spatial evolution that has been occurring for the past three centuries. From this perspective, the age of the café lies halfway between the communal public street life of the eighteenth century and the private familial home life of the contemporary "new towns" of France. The café, in short, was a transitional space between the public life of eighteenth-century laboring people and the privacy of the late-twentieth-century working class. In this sense, the café served as an apprenticeship in behavior in small enclosed places, comportment to which rural peasants and denizens of the early-modern city had not been accustomed. This explains how both the family and the café could develop at the same time. The intimacy that developed among workers in the ambience of the café made it more of a home than the wretched apartments they were forced to live in. The satisfactions of café sociability explain, in part, why Paris workers spent more time on questions of political and economic rights and improvements and so little time on the housing question.[117] The sense of dwelling in the café, of creating a space through habitual behavior, laid the social foundations for the labor movement and working-class politics.

CHAPTER THREE

Work and the Café

Strategies of Sociability

T he café served not only as a living room for the working class but also as an annex to the workshop and factory. A study of the relationship between the workplace and the café reveals that leisure could pattern work almost as much as work patterned leisure. Moreover, such a study uncovers the complexity of the work/leisure dynamic: much working-class café behavior fits the standard definition of neither work nor leisure. This behavior pattern midway between work and leisure is best termed "indiscipline," because it encompasses various tactics designed to elude or undermine the authority of bosses or overseers.[1] Indiscipline became all the more prevalent after 1830 as the division of labor, an increased pace of production, and mechanization commenced in the Paris area. Café life thus provides a unique vantage point from which to observe the culture of work and its discontents.[2]

Although tradesmen owned them, and employers often hired or paid laborers there, workers usually out of necessity made their cafés their own. After 1789, with their traditional organizations illegal, their artisanal skills and customs eroding under the impact of new work techniques and organizations, the distance between home and work growing, and discipline increasing, the Paris proletariat developed a series of rituals connecting the café and the workplace. They wanted to maintain a degree of control over the pace of work, to perpetuate the interconnection between sociability and labor, strong in artisanal production, and to have a site of organization and mobilization, especially during strikes.[3] Its ability to adapt to the changing needs of its customers made the café a valuable institution. Cafés proved flexible enough to encompass the rituals of the *compagnonnage*, or trade guild, the confidentiality of secret societies, and the public show of organization and solidarity of the strike. Whether in back rooms or at the counter, workers transmitted traditions from generation to generation. Cafés, in short, provided a space for the "informal collective practices" that Alain Cottereau sees as one of the hallmarks of French working-class life, helping compensate for the perpetual lack of a strong formal working-class movement like those of England and Germany.[4]

The Paris Environment

The most important factor in the relationship between the Paris café and the labor process was the city itself. As Georges Duveau astutely observed, the Paris milieu determined the consciousness of the workers as much as their labor.[5] Paris had long been a center of the production and consumption of luxury goods, especially since the age of Louis XIV. The artisans who made the fine furniture, jewelry, tapestries, and mirrors had a wider set of options for combining work, sociability, and leisure than almost any other continental urban working population. The capital of French culture contained a diverse array of drinking establishments, offering a wide variety of food, drink, and entertainments geared to the working class. A characteristic workers' café has been described as a "shelter for workers who want to eat a snack [*casser une croûte*] and to wash it down with a glass of wine; the table always ready for someone who wants to eat a cutlet or cheese; the room is open to all comers."[6] There at mealtimes one found "masons, stonecutters, and day laborers soaking up bread in soup for four sous."[7] Parisian bosses found it almost impossible to isolate workers from the "vices" of urban life as their provincial counterparts, especially in the textile towns of the northeast, had done with the creation of company towns, company canteens, and company restaurants. Paris was clearly the antithesis of the company town.[8]

The rhythm and pattern of proletarian labor and leisure in Paris in the eighteenth and early nineteenth centuries had been defined by the practice of working in the city from Tuesday through Saturday and then going to the suburban taverns beyond the barrières on Sunday and Monday.[9] Even though bosses usually paid workers on Saturday, the merriment did not start until the following day. Workers preferred the barrière taverns not only for eating and drinking but also for the dances and outdoor entertainments there. Each barrière had five or six dance halls—each with a capacity for 200 to 300 revelers—located amid spacious gardens, salons, courtyards, and shops.

Most observers—from Honoré de Balzac to the prefects of police to modern historians—have felt that these festivities beyond the barrières prevented clashes in Paris itself. In the mid 1830s, the author of the *Comédie humaine* asserted in his inimitable fashion:

> First of all look at the class which has no possessions. The artisan, the proletarian. . . . When Monday comes—as rich as lords, they fling their wages away in the taverns which surround the city as with a girdle of foulness. . . . This population amounts to three hundred thousand souls. Would not the government be overturned every Tuesday were it not for the taverns? Fortunately, by Tuesday, these sons of toil are in a state of torpor, sleeping off their excesses and penniless; they go back to their work and dry bread.[10]

Working-class revelry, in short, was an opiate of the masses. It was commonly assumed that "a revolution coming from the people without hidden leaders is never to be feared as long as you do not close the barrières."[11] In an article on strikes under the July Monarchy, Peter Stearns has echoed this nineteenth-century conclusion, suggesting that these strikes had no true organization but were rather the product of spontaneous discontent. Often conceived in a tavern the evening before or on the same morning as the action, such rebellions lacked any real leadership or strategy. While many strikes may have been born or ended in a bar, Stearns argues, far more were drowned there.[12] This view overlooks the fact that such sociable gatherings could produce more than dissipation and diversion and could provide a catalyst for thought, organization, and action.

The revolutions of 1830 and 1848 disprove this perception of cafés as an opiate of the masses. By abolishing the guilds, prohibiting workers' associations, and destroying numerous Paris churches, the French Revolution had forced the workers to use cafés as organizational centers. The imbrication of leisure time and labor issues increased after 1789 not because the workers had become more perverted but because they were strictly policed. The enforcement of the Le Chapelier law politicized working-class tavern life in an unprecedented fashion. Until the repeal of the law in the 1880s, compagnonnages and journeymen's confraternities, which had been a vital part of eighteenth-century laboring life, remained illegal associations. Café life ensured that this law did not succeed in suppressing these organizations. The autobiography of the artisan turner Jacques-Etienne Bédé elaborates in detail how the early Restoration working class synthesized the old compagnonnage rituals with café sociability.[13] Michael Sibalis has recently shown that by 1800, barrière cafés had become the chief meeting places of carpenters and food sellers.[14] House painters serve as another good example of the way the café permitted a particular trade to adapt to the changed environment. Before the Revolution, the most active members of the association met every Sunday afternoon in various wine shops at the corner of rue des Arcis and the quai near Notre Dame cathedral. Despite the Le Chapelier law, these café meetings continued and indeed grew, and the group became known as the "chapel." Such gatherings provided a venue for exchanging trade information and for getting a job, further evidence that the early workers' associations still did not clearly distinguish between workers and bosses. Because most painters lived in the adjoining 4th and 5th arrondissements, these cafés were extremely convenient, but this practice ceased in 1850 with the disappearance of rue des Arcis.[15]

Usually these clandestine coalitions met at the barrières. Napoléon's police often raided the various compagnons' "mother" taverns and seized their papers and money, thus pushing workers' groups out of the city.[16] In 1810, the prefect of police asserted that he had eradicated the carpenters' compagnonnages in Paris and exiled them to the suburban cabaret de l'Etoile in the suburb of Pantin. Throughout the following decades, the carpenters' headquarters, among others, remained outside of Paris.[17] This was not as much of a defeat as the prefect hoped, because the compagnonnages had traditionally done much business (such as settling disputes) outside the city limits.[18] The police usually tolerated barrière meetings—for example, the typographers' trimesterly Sunday banquets for from three to five hundred members—as long as their talk and their toasts did not concern labor conditions.[19]

The police became much more concerned about these barrière meetings after the 1830 revolution, when workers were found to have used their Sunday and Monday festivities for labor organization. From the summer of 1830 through 1851, the prefects watched the barrière taverns carefully for any sign of labor agitation. In November 1833, the prefect noted nineteen meetings at barrière cafés each Sunday or Monday. Only with the creation of the Bourse du travail, or labor exchange, in 1885 did workers gain the right to organize legally within the city, thus ending both juridical and spatial marginality at the same time for Parisian workers.[20]

After 1850, under Haussmann, the relationship between the café and the labor process changed dramatically. The destruction of the barrières and the annexation of the surrounding suburbs resulting from his urban renovation produced a veritable revolution in both work and leisure. These transformations were as decisive as those already achieved by the changes in the labor process and the labor market. The end of the barrières, Belleville's in particular, brought an end to the climate of continual fête that had been one of the most important characteristics of the work/leisure dialectic.[21] The fairs, and later amusements parks, on the new outskirts of Paris simply did not combine, in Yves Marie-Berce's terminology, fête and revolt as the barrières had. As new and more distant leisure spots developed after the 1870s, such as the beach at Neuilly's Grande Jatte island and the taverns and dance halls of the towns of Bougival, Argenteuil, and Charenton, the connection between work and leisure grew even less direct.[22] These new entertainments could often be reached easily only by railroad. The greater physical distance was accentuated by the greater psychological and social distance engendered by train travel. Workers simply could not go as a group to a riverside tavern in the same way they had done to a barrière tavern. They had to arrange the trip based upon the train schedule and synchronize their plans. All these factors helped make working-class leisure more "mechanical," less spontaneous, and tied more to the rhythm of transportation than to the rituals of work.[23] By 1900, workers had won the right to organize but had largely lost the opportunity to integrate work and leisure.

Complementing this transformation in the landscape of leisure was the reordering of relations at the workplace. After 1830, as the Industrial Revolution penetrated France, Paris-area employers increasingly resorted to the division of labor and the introduction of machinery to cut production costs and raise productivity. As artisanal skills became subdivided, the individual was no longer assured of control over his or her labor. As a result, the semi-skilled increasingly became the norm. Such laborers, because their talents and training were circumscribed, could more easily be retrained or replaced than the old-fashioned artisan. Bosses and foremen could more easily control this new type of worker, and it thus became easier to impose greater discipline and introduce more machinery. This process occurred at an extremely uneven rate within the region because of the great diversity of Paris industry. The first sectors affected were the garment, textile, woodworking, and leather industries.[24] The introduction of the sewing machine facilitated the growth of large workshops for seamstresses. Analogous machinery transformed jobs in hat-making, textiles, and wool-cutting.[25] In textile workshops and factories, employers often imposed stiff fines on any worker who left the factory before closing time.[26]

Shoemakers—increasingly located in the large factories of Helbronner, Godillot, Lecerf, and Sarda in Paris—lost their traditional right to drink at work.[27] In the woodworking sector, too, the cabinet and furniture makers' traditions of high skill and craftsmanship eroded in the wake of the growth of a furniture industry oriented toward cheap reproductions for a mass market and dedicated to the priorities of speed and efficiency.[28] By the 1870s and 1880s, socialist journals furnished a running account of the struggle between employers and their workers over customary and traditional liberties to take a break, eat, drink, joke, or even swear on the job.[29]

One of management's goals in the transformation of the labor process was to break the interconnection between work and sociability. The café, naturally, was a prime target. Bosses and overseers tried to effect change through their own example. Increasingly, after 1850, they stopped drinking with their workers. Although isolated instances of the custom continued—for example, at the slaughterhouses of Vilette—reports of bosses or foremen clinking glasses or getting tipsy with their workers become rare after 1870.[30] Absence of such notations in public drunkenness cases in either the correctional tribunal or the police courts is especially telling. In his *Le Sublime*, a work aimed at promoting social mobility among workers in much the same fashion as the efforts of Samuel Smiles in England or Benjamin Franklin in America, Denis Poulot skillfully registers this transformation in the consciousness of Parisian bosses.

Before 1914, bosses had great difficulty in breaking the work/sociability link and instilling more formal discipline. Even though Haussmann got rid of the barrières, his renovation of Paris, as we have seen, dramatically increased the number of cafés, which were often right next door to workshops and factories. Although workers lost the concentrated carnival atmosphere of the barrière taverns, they now had closer and more convenient temptations, which ensured numerous temporary breaks during the day. The ubiquitous café frustrated management's attempt to impose greater discipline through the creation of company canteens, dormitories, and restaurants.[31] The great irony of the Second Empire's transformation of Paris may well be that while it destroyed the barrières and encouraged the rationalization of space (with the new street system) and the modernization of industry, the resulting increase in the number of cafés may well have undermined the hoped-for augmentation in social order.

In truth, during the three prewar decades, the workers gained evergreater powers to organize and form unions, and the café remained a vital venue in their work culture. Despite the hopes of leaders such as Fernand

and Maurice Pelloutier, the rise of labor exchanges and the cooperative movement after the mid 1880s did not displace cafés. Even the long-running and ever-bitter struggle against the many café owners who ran employment agencies in their shops did not dent the workers' use of this informal institution. The 1848 demand for the abolition of these agencies did not gather sufficient force until the 1890s. Butchers and housepainters were two of the most prominent occupations to resist this continued overlap between the publican and the patron. Butchers engaged in continuous litigation with the offending café owners, and in August 1898, housepainters switched from seeking work in cafés to the labor exchange.[32] Proletarian opposition to job placement bureaus led to their formal abolition by the Chamber of Deputies in March 1904, but a police ordinance three months later provided a loophole allowing such bureaus to operate in cafés if someone other than the owner ran them.[33] Critics, especially the socialist investigators Maurice and Léon Bonneff, charged that over nine hundred such shops exploited workers mercilessly. The laborer had to "work like a machine and drink like a sponge" to keep in the good graces of the boss and the café owner. The struggle culminated in a strike against placement bureaus in September 1909.[34] Hostility to café owners never, however, became general. Paradoxically, by decreasing the role of the boss or the owner, these legal actions helped make cafés even more of a workers' space.

The Relationship between Occupation and Cafégoing

Which occupations relied most heavily on the café? Nineteenth-century observers examining the relation between work and the café were less concerned about the occupation profile of cafégoers than about their moral attributes. Indeed, few commentators provide any detailed occupational data, because in their minds, the moral issues transcended occupational categories. The most lively debate for them was over whether the most able or the most debased workers were the more assiduous cafégoers. In short, two schools developed: one emphasizing workers' "indiscipline," the other their "immorality." Occupational data from judicial and civil archives cited below are not sufficiently qualitative on individual morality for us to determine fully which nineteenth-century view was correct. Nevertheless, important trends do emerge, which show that skilled and well-paid artisans generally predominated in cafégoing over outcasts and the poverty-stricken.

Eighteenth-century observers did not formulate a systematic view of the relationship between labor and the café. As described in Louis-Sébastien Mercier's *Tableau de Paris* in the 1780s, contemporary elite thought confirmed the traditional police perception that workers who frequented taverns were either lazy or unemployed. Significantly, the eighteenth century did not produce a French version of Ben Franklin—the upwardly mobile artisan who consciously reflected upon and analyzed the impact of café rituals on the labor process. Instead, Paris produced a glassmaker, Jacques-Louis Ménétra, and a typographer, Nicolas Contat, *dit* Lebrun, whose autobiographical writings not only reveal but also positively revel in the link between the tavern and the workshop. Recent historical work by Thomas Brennan, David Garrioch, and Daniel Roche has convincingly confirmed these memoirs and refuted Mercier's stereotypes.

The idea that the most energetic and skilled workers rather than the most lazy and unskilled were the most likely to frequent cafés developed only slowly across the nineteenth century. Napoleonic police spies compiled the first systematic typology of Paris occupations according to their work and leisure habits in 1811. They concluded that indiscipline and immorality were not identical: while the former could produce disputes, the latter often led to resignation. Sadly, the best evidence linking the café, work, and disputation, the autobiography of Jacques-Etienne Bédé, written during the Restoration, did not appear in print until the 1980s. By 1840, the great social observer Louis René Villermé had come to the conclusion that the best-paid workers were the most prone to alcoholism, but he never elaborated upon this point.[35] An attentive reading of the judicial newspaper the *Gazette des tribunaux* does, however, furnish this evidence. Although usually episodic and anecdotal, court accounts from the late 1820s provide examples of highly paid, diligent, sober, and skilled workers engaging in disputes in cafés, especially against the police.

These disparate pieces of evidence and analysis finally found an appropriate synthesis in Denis Poulot's *Le Sublime, ou le travailleur comme il est en 1870, et ce qu'il peut être* (The Sublime, or the Worker as He Is in 1870, and as He Might Be [1870]). With this work, the upwardly mobile Parisian artisan had finally found his Ben Franklin. The tardy emergence of this type of "Protestant work ethic" in Paris testifies to the intimate and long-standing imbrication of café sociability with Parisian work culture. Poulot's analysis may have come after Franklin's, but Poulot was much more thorough. In his "thick description," workers are divided into seven categories in regard to their work habits and café frequentation:

1. "True workers" displayed "exemplary sobriety" and were "conscientious" but not as skilled as "sublimes."

2. "Workers" labored hard but had only an acceptable level of skill and were not as exemplary in their sobriety, having a few drinks at home on Sunday and sometimes drinking with their mates.

3. "Mixed workers" were followers and easily led by the stronger personalities in the shop. They tended to drink more frequently than "true workers" and "workers" and got drunk on payday (Saturday), Monday mornings, and at workshop celebrations.

4. "Simple sublimes," despite being skillful workers, felt that undermining the boss was a duty and heavy drinking a necessity, at least every two weeks on Saturday and Monday.

5. "True sublimes" were top workers, exceptionally skillful and indispensable, but they were also "cynical" and frequently defied or teased the boss. "He does more work at the bar than in the workshop," Poulot averred.

6. "Sons of God" were the "soul of the workshop" and had great influence over other workers; they organized resistance to the bosses. Rarely getting drunk on alcohol, but almost always on politics, they drank with their mates in order to participate in collective discussions.

7. The "sublime of sublimes" either worked in the metal industry or subcontracted in other fields. They were the "prophets of resistance" but used the "sons of God" as their instruments rather than confronting management directly. Curiously, Poulot has little to say about the drinking habits of the "sublime of sublimes": they tended to be like "true workers" in their drinking, but their exact opposite in politics.[36]

Poulot's work had an extremely wide influence, but, in general, received no systematic test. The Le Play school's studies of individual workers, *Ouvriers des deux mondes*, many of which profiled Paris-region workers, substantiated all of Poulot's categories except the "sublime of sublimes." Instead, his insight concerning the best or highest-paid workers having tendencies to indiscipline was simply recapitulated by most authors, among them the student of alcoholism Dr. Joseph Lefort, the eminent late-nineteenth-century observer of working-class life Emile Levasseur, the sociologist G. L. Duprat, and such twentieth-century historians as Georges Duveau and Lenard Berlanstein.[37] In his classic novel *L'Assommoir* (The Dramshop; 1877), Zola relied heavily upon Poulot's work. However, as Alain Cottereau has shown, Zola dropped the nuances of Poulot's typology and created hardworking, sober characters, such as the metal forger Gougot; drinkers with a hereditary disposition to alcoholism, as in Gervaise and her husband Coupeau; and idlers, such as Gervaise's early lover Lantier. Emile Levasseur was also prone to reduction-ism, as when he asserted that "sublimes" formed half of the Paris working population. By contrast, in the later 1889 edition of his book, Poulot averred that café-inspired indiscipline had declined.[38]

The quantitative and qualitative data of the Parisian judicial archives between 1873 and 1901 permit systematic testing of Poulot's thesis. The preponderance of artisans in both police court and correctional tribunal infractions shows a strong correlation with public drunkenness. In the police courts, artisans made up 54.1 percent of the defendants, while the unskilled constituted 36.3 percent. The proportion of the unskilled among those brought before the correctional tribunal was slightly higher, 48.2 percent to 42.5 percent. However, when we distinguish between the various types of crime handled by the correctional tribunal and separate the public drunkenness cases involving disputes with the police (that is, when a worker physically or verbally assaulted a policeman) from public drunkenness cases connected with "ordinary crime" (that is, theft, assault and battery, begging, or loitering), we find a statistically significant difference between artisans and unskilled workers (see table 3.1). Workers in the construction, metal, clothing, furniture, and printing trades were all more likely to insult the police than were day laborers, the largest group among the unskilled.[39]

This finding points to a fundamental difference in the daily comportment of skilled and semi-skilled workers in contrast to unskilled and marginal day laborers. The contrast in the behavior of skilled and unskilled workers is consistent with the much greater organization and militancy found among the skilled workers than among the unskilled and also tallies with Michelle Perrot's discovery that at the national level, grassroots labor organizers were frequently convicted for insulting policemen.[40] A review of the rich collection of judicial dossiers from the 1880s confirms that working-class and socialist militants in the Paris region acted in the same fashion.[41] Skilled workers thus expressed their militancy not only during strikes but also in everyday life.[42]

Perhaps the best evidence that those who got drunk and then insulted the police were indeed examples of Poulot's "sublime" workers is found in the two hundred remaining correctional tribunal dossiers concerning public drunkenness. Sixty percent of the workers were considered by their employers, landlords, and neighbors to be hardworking, sober, and steady. In contrast, two-thirds of the defendants brought before the court for public drunkenness and "ordinary" crime were judged by their employers or landlords to be irregular, dissipated, and lazy. Thus many "good" workers

Table 3.1

CLASS AND OCCUPATIONAL DISTRIBUTION OF PUBLIC DRUNKENNESS INFRACTIONS, 1873–1902 (*percentages in parentheses*)

Sector	Police Courts		Correctional Tribunal	
Bourgeois	170	(2.9)	193	(2.4)
Petit-bourgeois	175	(2.7)	197	(3.0)
White-collar	215	(3.8)	322	(4.1)
Artisan	3,168	(54.2)	3,230	(42.4)
Unskilled	2,126	(36.4)	3,663	(48.1)
Total	5,854	(100)	7,605	(100)

Sources: Figures for the police courts are based on a complete enumeration from 18 November 1873 to 3 January 1874 (series D22U1, no. 79); 2 June to 24 July 1874 (D22U1, no. 81); 18 August to 10 November 1876 (D22U1, no. 87); 17 January to 26 September 1901 and 3 January to 27 June 1902 (D22U1, nos. 88–92). Figures for the correctional tribunals are based on the registers of judgments for March–December 1873 (D1U6, nos. 28–37); all of 1880 (D1U6, nos. 111–28); February–June 1885 (D1U6, nos. 225–34); May 1890 (D1U6, nos. 354–56); and January, February, and May 1899 (D1U6, nos. 666–71 and 678–80).

Note: The sheer size of the judicial archives prevented a complete enumeration of all the public drunkenness cases. To ensure that my collection procedures were not biased, a random statistical sample was taken of all the data to determine the continuity in occupational distribution. This was confirmed on the SAS program.

Although data for the 1873 time period (from the implementation of the 1873 law) and for the 1880 time period approximate population data, for the later years between 1885 and 1889, the data were extrapolated for monthly intervals (selected at random). In order to determine if there were any statistical differences as a function of time, a series of chi-square analyses were conducted using the SAS system running on IBM model 9121. The chi-square analysis was chosen because it is an especially appropriate analysis for categorical data (i.e., gender, occupation, etc.). Indeed, it is probably the most popular nonparametric test used. Essentially, this statistic is used to test for statistically significant differences between the frequency of occurrence between different categories.

First, the data were divided into three time periods: March–December 1873 (N = 2,057); January–December 1880 (N = 3,398); and the months listed above for the years 1885 through 1889 (N = 1,450). In addition, occupation was categorized into about eighty-five categories and was reorganized into five categories: bourgeois, petit-bourgeois, white-collar, skilled, and unskilled. When a chi-square test was conducted on this "sample," chi-square was found to be statistically significant across collapsed occupational categories (x = 19.6, p = .012) as well as the original detailed occupational categories (x = 341.29, p = 0.000). Of course, the detailed categorization is especially problematic given the paucity of data within most of the cells. Moreover, the results obtained for both analyses appear to be an artifact of the large N. Indeed, the other measures of association, *lambda*, were uniformly small: less than .026. When the size of the sample for each time period or stratum was reduced to 330 (a rather large sample size), the results obtained were no longer statistically significant. Because the size of the original "sample" approximated (or was equivalent—except for missing data—to the population), it is appropriate to generate a random sample across the three time periods across the three time strata (N = 330 or less for each stratum) and circumvent the excessive power problem. Technically, hypothesis testing should not be conducted on population data. Unfortunately, few guidelines for choosing appropriate sample sizes for multinomial data of this kind exist. However, use of a total sample size of 990—equivalent to almost 12 percent of the original sample/population—should

Table 3.1 (continued)

constitute an acceptable sample size for a population like this. It seems reasonable to conclude that time did not have a significant impact on occupational distribution.

Of course, the sampling frame used was incomplete to the extent that data were often absent or incomplete. It is probable that the cause of absence was not random, and the estimate of "population" is thus likely to be somewhat biased.

did indeed drink and contest the authority of the police and most probably also of their bosses. But their skills were valuable enough that their employers wanted to keep them and therefore gave them favorable references.

The "indiscipline" interpretation receives further support when we examine the frequency of specific occupations in the judicial data. The stereotype of the drunken and disorderly ragpicker receives no confirmation. Indeed, ragpickers are virtually absent from the ranks of public drunkenness defendants. Even though Paris had roughly 40,000 ragpickers, 5,937 of whom were certified "medalists" by the police, only about 30 were charged in the two court systems over the entire period between 1871 and 1901.[43] In stark contrast, coachmen, another group with a widespread reputation for public drunkenness, are extremely well represented. In fact, they form one of the largest groups within the service sector. Significantly, the coachmen, unlike the ragpickers, had a notorious reputation not only for drinking but also for challenging authority, causing the police to regulate them and their customers closely.[44] Another group prominently represented in the courts, street vendors, had a similar reputation and received similar scrutiny.

In general, the service sector—which included street vendors, coachmen, teamsters, coachmen, café/restaurant waiters, laundresses, and other laborers in commercial establishments as well as ragpickers and other scavengers—totaled about 15 percent of Paris's population and 16 percent of defendants before the police courts and correctional tribunal. In one fashion or another, all of these occupations combined work with café sociability. While shopkeepers' assistants, such as laundresses, bakers, and barbers often received part of their wages or tips in the form of a drink, coachmen, street vendors, and waiters performed their work around cafés all day.[45] While waiting for passengers, for example, a coachman customarily had a drink at the counter.[46] Street vendors often did much of their hawking among the concentrated clienteles of cafés.[47] Teamsters, in the course of their hauling, also took frequent café breaks. Workers in these occupations had no bosses looking over their shoulders. Rather, as they did their jobs on the streets, their main nemesis was the police. It is not surprising, then, that street vendors, coachmen, and teamsters figure prominently among those arrested for public drunkenness.[48]

If being under the eyes of the public and the police explains the predominance of these service-sector occupations in prosecutions, the factors of gender and discipline account for the textile, garment, and clothing industries' showing the greatest disparity vis-à-vis both the working population of Paris as a whole and the imbibers who came to the courts' attention. The textile, garment, and clothing sectors jointly made up the largest occupational group in Paris—roughly 20 percent of the population—but represented only 8.2 percent of the defendants in the police courts and an even smaller 6.8 percent before the correctional tribunals. The predominance of women working in this sector and the underrepresentation of women among public drunkenness defendants doubtless explains this disparity. Women constituted merely 12 and 5 percent respectively of such defendants in the correctional tribunal and police courts. However, gender was not the only factor operating here. A similar underrepresentation is also found in occupations in which men were either in the majority (such as shoemakers) or a high percentage (such as tailors). During the first half of the nineteenth century, both trades had distinguished records of labor militancy and political action.[49] Tailors in particular had been notorious for their drinking, but after 1870, neither they nor shoemakers were frequently charged with being publicly drunk and insulting a police officer.[50] Their absence from the public records provides compelling evidence that employers in the garment and leather trades had succeeded in imposing greater discipline at the workplace. Shoemakers and tailors seem no longer to have had either the time or the opportunity to drink on the job or in cafés during working hours.

The three occupations that produced the largest percentages of public drunkenness defendants, especially in comparison with their numbers in the city's population as a whole, were those that had not been subjected to growing work discipline and had a reputation for elaborate drinking rituals in connection with their labor. Two of these occupations—metal and construction workers—were in the artisanal sector, and unskilled day laborers were the third. Metalworkers constituted under 4 percent of the city's population but some 11 percent of the defendants in the police courts and 10 percent in the correctional tribunal. Construction workers composed 7 percent of the Parisian population but over 15 percent of the defendants in the police courts and approximately 16 percent in the correctional tribunal. The fact that metal and construction workers engaged so frequently in this type of daily struggle against the police is consistent with their leading position in the labor unrest of the 1899–1908 decade. These data persuasively demonstrate that metal and construction workers more often challenged the police and enjoyed a much greater level of workplace autonomy than other Paris artisans.

In contrast, these judicial statistics indicate that other artisanal trades had lost much of their ability to combine work and sociability. For example, wood and leather workers respectively constituted approximately 8.5 percent and 6 percent of the Paris population but only about 6 percent and less than 3 percent in the courts. An analogous ratio is found in the Paris luxury industries among bronze workers and jewelry makers. Finally, printers and bookbinders were also underrepresented. The evidence of the differential distribution of public drunkenness among these various artisanal groups suggests that by the 1870s and 1880s, employers in the tailoring, woodworking, shoemaking, leather, and luxury trades had succeeded in breaking the link between workplace and café. An intriguing conclusion to be drawn from this evidence is that the discipline workers were subjected to on the job seems to have carried over into their leisure time. The wood, clothing, and leather workers seem to have indulged neither in drinking on the job nor in wild binges after work to any appreciable degree. Thus, the intensification of the labor process did not necessarily lead to an intensification of pleasure-seeking in workers' leisure time. This finding refutes the commonly held belief that intense work and recreation complemented each other.[51]

The last two categories of workers to be considered, both unskilled, again reveal the importance of gender and accessibility to public space. The cases of day laborers and domestics represent a dramatic study in the contrast between unskilled men and women. Male day laborers represented about 8 percent of the urban population, but 11 percent in the police courts and approximately 17 percent in the correctional tribunal. Domestic servants, a largely female population, are conspicuous by their absence from these courts. They composed close to 12 percent of the Paris population but less than 1 percent in the police courts and less than 2 percent in the correctional tribunal. Much of this difference can be explained in terms of the amount of freedom of movement the two groups could exercise. Day laborers, like metal and construction workers, enjoyed greater freedom during the workday than did most other occupations.[52] However, their lack of restraint was directly related to the fact that they had no steady jobs rather than to work rituals and sociable customs as was the case with artisans. This probably explains why day laborers, when drinking, were much more likely to be involved in stealing, brawling, or begging than in contesting police authority like the artisans. Conversely, domestics had little workplace autonomy and often had to work and live almost the entire week in the homes of their masters, so that the amount of time they could spend in cafés was minimal. These statistics on domestics and day laborers indicate that depending on the specific occupation, being an unskilled worker could either inhibit or facilitate caféoing. In either case, such behavior did not have the ritual tradition or the political edge it did among the artisans.

Rituals of Camaraderie and Resistance

Workers fit these rituals within the context of the workday, the workweek, and the demands of the labor process. Elite perception was at its most myopic on this latter issue, for it seemed inconceivable to the establishment that a place reserved for recreation and refreshment could serve any useful function. The prefect of police usually typified this sentiment. On 8 March 1825, in his daily report to King Charles X and the interior minister, the prefect noted that instead of satisfying their real needs, the laborers of the outlying districts had as usual been filling the suburban taverns and engaging in orgies for several days running. Despite his disgust, he confidently asserted that none of this had anything to do with politics.[53] Typically, the prefect could not conceive that the workers might be reinforcing their bonds of solidarity.

The early social investigator H. A. Frégier, an observer of the July Monarchy of the "citizen king" Louis Philippe, sketched a portrait of workers using cafés to enhance their power in the workshop. When a worker met a long-lost comrade, he noted, the first thing that came into his mind was to take him to a café for a drink. While drinking wine and shaking hands, the proletarians criticized their work and their bosses. Frégier's description then turns disparaging: he asserts that workers spent hours drinking and completely forgot about their work. Laborers timid about frequenting cafés were subject to verbal attacks.[54] Stripped of its moralizing gloss, this description does, however, capture the essence of café culture and work culture.

The first ritual connecting café and work, as we have seen in the case of the employment bureaus, involved finding a job. Then, upon completing his first day's work, the novice frequently had to treat his new workmates to rounds of drinks at a nearby café. Workers generally dubbed this long-standing ritual, dating from at least the eighteenth century, the "welcome" (*bienvenue*) or the "when is it?" (*quand est-ce?*).[55] The workers in the most highly skilled Parisian trades—engravers, jewelers, and enamelers—especially in the Marais district, practiced the ritual in a most elaborate fashion. The initiate often spent between ten and fifteen francs "to give drinks for the comrades" who had accepted him in their shop. Such an amount at that time represented a day's salary even for the highest-paid workers and at least three or four days' salary for those less fortunate. And although less affluent trades such as the quarrymen, nail makers, and tailors also imposed this workplace rite of passage, it does not seem to have been practiced by unskilled workers such as day laborers.[56] In their studies of the Paris area's working class during the second half of the nineteenth century, Alain Cottereau and Lenard Berlanstein suggest that these rituals had great staying power among artisans.[57]

The bienvenue and the quand est-ce? show how a café celebration could lay the foundation for a close relationship at work. The ritual had similarities to the charivari documented by such early-modern French historians as Natalie Z. Davis. In both cases, the lucky individual—who had gained a wife in the case of the charivari or a job in the case of the bienvenue—either shared his good fortune with the community or risked being ridiculed by "rough music." In the case of the nail makers, when a novice entered the workshop, the workers sang in chorus:

> As soon as a comrade
> Comes to work here,
> He must pay for many rounds of drinks
> To his new friends.
> To this ancient custom
> We all conform.
> We hope that he will act wisely.

Next, everybody shouted, "When is the time?" meaning, when would the new worker pay for his welcome? If the worker ignored the refrain, his fellows repeated it at ever-increasing pitch and volume until the newcomer agreed to follow tradition. At this point the entire workshop made their way in a procession to the café, singing:

Lead the victim to the counter,
Lead the victim!

If the newcomer proved stingy and balked at paying for the rounds, a noisy and raucous yell erupted:

O rat! O rat! O ratiapia!

Yet when enough rounds had been consumed to satisfy his new comrades, all was well. Then the initiate became truly one of them and was called "old friend."[58] Café sociability thus eased the functioning of the labor process.

The ordinary workday was also punctuated by ritually sanctioned café stops. The entry and exit from work were especially filled with the recurring, patterned activity that highlights the ritual process. Work for most laborers—Maxime du Camp claims for at least 999 out of 1,000—could not begin until they had "killed a glass" (*tuer le verre*) of white wine at a café counter.[59] At the barrières during the 1840s, "every morning at 6 A.M. there is a crowd drinking white wine . . . always composed of the same workers. . . . If several habitués come at the same time, then a round of shots [*tournée de cannons*] must be consumed. No one wants to avoid or omit this obligatory courtesy [*politesse*], even if eight or ten people are around. . . . That means some drink two bottles before lunch."[60]

Thirty years later, Zola described early morning at the central markets and noted a similar scenario: "morning customers trying to wake up with white wine and brandy [*eau de vie*] . . . bowls of punch and warm wine, . . . milk, . . . rolls steaming hot."[61] By the end of the century, the dictionaries of Parisian slang were recording the addition of brandy to this morning ritual, and doctors noted the ill effects of drinks consumed on an empty stomach.[62]

Once at work, laborers intermittently interrupted their tasks to take breaks in the café. In typographer's slang *tric*, probably derived from the verb *tricher* (to cheat), meant the hand signal or gesture used by comrades when they wanted to escape the workshop and go to a café. This centuries-old expression sanctified the worker's sense of play and the employer's exasperation.[63] The daily pattern of breaks varied widely across the century and between diverse trades. The commonest pause, of course, was for lunch. For some workers, this meal was a simple slice of bread, piece of meat, and glass of wine; for others, it was much more elaborate. Around midcentury, butchers around the various barrières, such as Grenelle,

Villejuif, Roule, Ménilmontant, and Montmartre, would bring pieces of beef to cafés and have the café owners make a special bouillon, which they would wash down with a quarter of a liter of wine (demi-setier).[64] Another break that achieved almost universal status was the afternoon snack break (casser la croûte).[65] Quitting time was another peak time, but this daily rite of passage did not produce any particular ritual or slang. Much more colorful was the last celebration of the day. Workers thought of their last drink as the "consolation" (la consolation) or "charming the fleas" (charmer les puces). Cooks, for example, usually had this drink at around 9 P.M.[66]

Workers in the building and metal trades had the best-developed set of drinking rituals during the workday, a conclusion consistent with the occupational statistics noted earlier. Both groups enjoyed a large degree of control over the pace and timing of their work and were notorious for the number of breaks they took during the day, as well as for an elaborate set of drinking procedures.[67] The ritual quality of these occasions is clearly apparent in the names given to the drinks. Between 7 and 8 A.M., these trades took their first break with a petite verre or a demi-setier of wine. Then, at 11 A.M., another break was taken. For bricklayers and metalworkers, this was an apéritif of absinthe; for the other building trades, especially masons, it was a liter of wine. At 3 P.M., both metal and building workers took a break for a raccord, a quarter-liter of white wine. At 6 P.M., before quitting for the day, workers had another apéritif, again absinthe. With minor variations, this pattern of ritual drinking occurred throughout the construction and metal trades.[68] The breaks of the metal founders, workers in one of the most difficult and exhausting occupations within metallurgy, were most directly correlated with their labor process: "They have the habit of taking a glass after each cooling, and, as there are on average seven or eight coolings a day," they went to the café almost on the hour.[69]

An examination of the hours throughout the day when café incidents occurred confirms the café/work connection. The hourly pattern of these cases demonstrates just how frequently workers punctuated their long workday—on average between nine and ten hours—with trips to the café. Seventy percent of the café incidents in Parisian court records happened during the workday, between 8 A.M. and 10 P.M. The Paris workday did indeed differ from that in strictly industrial cities, like Lille in the north or Saint-Etienne in the southeast, because there was no standard "quitting time." In Paris, metal and construction workers usually ceased work at

6:30 P.M., and consequently could have their own version of the bourgeois "apéritif hour," but workers in the clothing, textile, and furniture sectors more often ended their labors at 8 or 9 P.M.[70] The city's workforce clearly did not all move to the same rhythm.

The hour at which the highest number of café incidents happened, 8 P.M., probably reflects the diversity of Parisian labor patterns. Undoubtedly, some workers were just coming off work, others just finishing their dinner and settling into the period of evening recreation. This was also the hour when most entertainment and public meetings occurred. After 10 P.M., the number of incidents fell dramatically and steadily with each succeeding hour. In marked contrast, in bourgeois cafés, there were two peaks of attendance, one in the late afternoon between 5 and 7 P.M. and another in the late evening after 9 P.M. and on into the early morning hours.[71]

A comparison with the hours of tavern incidents during the eighteenth century reveals a remarkable consistency in working-class life. Brennan found that the busiest hours were between 8 and 10 P.M., and that activity fell off sharply after that.[72] Despite the growth of an ever-more-dazzling night life, nineteenth-century Parisians did not go to bed much later, at least during most of the week, than had their eighteenth-century forebears.

The weekly pattern is also fully apparent across the days of the week, a pattern more "traditional" during the nineteenth century than in the preceding one.[73] Confirming an earlier insight of Michelle Perrot's, Brennan found that the ritual of *saint-lundi*, or "Holy Monday," was not prevalent during the eighteenth century, as had at first been assumed. In his tabulation of tavern incidents by day, Brennan discovered that attendance dropped unevenly from a high on Sunday to a low on Saturday; thus "'Saint Monday' was no 'holier' than any other day."[74] Approximately one quarter of all the customers, he found, drank on either Sundays or holidays; Monday accounted for 17 percent, and the following days gradually declined to a low of 9 percent on Saturday.[75] The lack of judicial data from the first half of the nineteenth century prevents a determination of exactly when "Holy Monday" began, but it can be said with certainty that by the 1870s, the custom had become a café ritual. The daily percentages of arrests for public drunkenness for the police courts (6,500 cases) and the correctional tribunal (7,000 cases), shown in table 3.2, support this point. The data for the two courts show virtually no variation from 1873 to 1902.

Table 3.2

	Sunday	Monday	Tuesday	Wednesday	Thursday	Friday	Saturday
Police Court	23	22.6	13.7	10.9	9.4	.8	10.6
Correctional Tribunal	122.5	22.2	14.0	11.0	9.7	10.0	10.7

Sources: As for table 3.1.

Another surprising and significant finding here is that Saturday—payday for upwards of 85 percent of the Paris workforce, as well as the preferred night, by the 1870s, to go the theater, the dance hall, or the music hall (*café-concert*)—had so few incidents.[76] This finding flies in the face of much contemporary thinking. Restoration police prefects reported that disputes erupted around principal workshops on Saturday.[77] During the Second Empire, according to Maxime du Camp, the week following Saturday paydays was "in large part lost for work, as a lot of workers prolong Monday till the following Thursday or Friday."[78] In Alphonse Daudet's 1870s novel *Jack*, a mason is dead drunk four times a month, on payday. In his short story "Arthur," the worker spends his week's pay on drink.[79] Some observers even said Saturday was the only day cafés were overwhelmed with customers.[80] This discrepancy between the statistics and contemporary testimony may be owing to the decisions of the police, who perhaps permitted carousing on Saturdays but suppressed it on Mondays, when they felt the drinkers should be at work. In any case, thousands of workers took this day as their own in the cafés.

Holy Monday persisted until at least 1914,[81] but there are increasing signs of its decline after 1900. Berlanstein has noted that in the Parisian suburbs of Saint-Denis and Puteaux, the number of requests by café owners to hold entertainments in their shops on Monday had declined markedly by this date. He also notes that the new suburban automobile and bicycle factories, with rigorous production schedules and tight discipline, also discouraged a Monday celebration.[82] Nevertheless, Holy Monday remained an important point of dispute for labor arbitration councils in the early twentieth century.[83] Moreover, the statistics generated by the 9 April 1889 law governing work-related accidents reveal that, especially in the construction industry, for example, by far the worst day for accidents in 1906 was Monday.[84] Thus the new commercialized and mechanized culture of leisure, embodied in such institutions as amusement parks, cinemas, and sporting contests, had not yet begun to corrode a café culture based on participant interaction.[85] Workers still joined in joyous camaraderie, glass in hand, singing J. B. Clément's "Heap of Rogues" ("Tas de coquins") and Jules Jouy's "The Wall" ("Le Mur"), whose lines were reminiscent of the resistance expressed during the Commune.[86]

Was cafégoing tied as closely to the work experience as these rituals imply? An examination of the insults directed at the police by workers indeed indicates an intimate connection. Yearly and monthly samples of the correctional tribunal judgments reveal that throughout the 1870–1900 era, one of the major themes of workers' invective was that the police performed no useful labor in society. One of the most common epithets was "idler" (*fainéant*). Moreover, workers used terms drawn directly from their jobs. In May 1872, Philippe Clermontet, a copper founder, called two policemen "idlers" and "cowards," and added that he would get them in a corner one day and "thread them" (*tarauder*: to tap screws or nuts). In the same month, Antoine Deliard and Henri Noël, two marble sculptors, threw their tools at the head of a policeman, yelling, "I defecate on you" and calling him a "nothing." Laborers also commonly threatened the police by shaking their fists. Given the Paris workers' opinion of the police, such a gesture surely symbolized the power of the workers, the people who worked with their hands, as opposed to the impotent idleness of the police.[87] These epithets indicate the close connection between work and leisure, labor and personal identity, among Parisian workers even in the Belle Epoque. Their picturesque verbal abuse also underscores the conviction of Lazar Sainéan, one of the era's scholars of Parisian argot, who called the café a veritable crucible of Parisian working-class slang.[88]

Rituals and Their Relation to Strikes

How did Paris workers integrate these café rituals into labor agitation? Exploring this question shows how café life helped mediate relations between the informal and formal parts of the labor movement, especially from 1871 to 1914.[89] Even though the Parisian labor movement and its strikes became more "modern," less "festive," and better organized with the advent of the labor exchange, the café retained its vital role. During strikes, for example, police repression or perhaps the sheer intensity of the goings-on often made the cafés around the Paris Bourse du travail complementary or substitute labor exchanges. "Sublimes," too, still had a role to play in inspiring or intimidating any wavering or recalcitrant workers during these disputes.[90] These details are found in the copious records of court cases involving "restraints to the liberty of work," an infraction instituted during the Second Empire but used heavily by republican governments after 1890.[91] These cases and other sources amply demonstrate that cafés served both labor leaders and strikers as spaces for solidarity, sabotage, intimidation, and boycott.[92]

The ritual of Holy Monday provides one of the clearest links between the labor process and the labor movement. A daily report of the Paris prefect of police to the minister of the interior in December 1871, within six months of the Commune, makes this point clear. The prefect observed that a political demonstration could very easily grow out of the working-class custom of strolling on Monday: "I have been told by diverse sources that they have planned some demonstrations for tomorrow, Monday. The return of the Assembly will be their pretext. These indications must not be overlooked, because the workers' enjoyment on Saturday makes Monday a day of rest, relaxation, and excursions. The difference between a promenade and a demonstration is not great. I have therefore had the principal districts of Paris put under close surveillance. I have been told of no particular agitation, no secret meetings in the café. Therefore, for the moment all is totally calm."[93]

Ever since the early nineteenth century, strikes had usually started on Mondays. From the labor actions of carpenters in early nineteenth century to those of white-collar employees in the 1820s and of post office workers in the 1900s, Monday café sociability facilitated strike activity.[94] During the 1871–1914 period, workers in the construction and metal trades, two of the groups most likely to celebrate Holy Monday, were also the two groups that struck most frequently.[95]

Workers often prepared their strikes in the cafés surrounding workshops or factories. This happened, for example, when coachmen struck during the 1867 Universal Exposition, and in the case of the October 1869 strike by commercial employees.[96] Even after the legalization of labor unions in 1884 and the establishment of the Bourse du travail two years later, unions still used cafés as their headquarters when they declared strikes. A leader of the leather dressers' union admitted as much in an August 1894 court case: "The union's headquarters are on rue Saint-Hippolyte, but during a strike we meet at private places and especially at cafés."[97] The auto mechanics at a suburban Billancourt auto factory during a dispute in 1906 kept their union's register at one Rappenne's café on the route de Versailles at the intersection of rue Billancourt.[98] During the same years, while a branch of the butchers' union met at a café de la Fontaine at 49–51 rue d'Auteuil, a section of the metalworkers' union met at the taverne Voltaire. The Federation of Unions in Boulogne-Billancourt had their rendezvous at the café des Amateurs on the boulevard de Strasbourg. Master printers used the café de Commerce at 62 boulevard de Magenta. Some cafés had rooms for sizable meetings: the café de la Rotonde, for example, served as the venue for a hair cutter's union meeting that drew over four hundred attendees.[99] Even from this small sample, we can understand why a painting entitled *Before the Strike* shown at the Paris Salon of 1895 pictured a leader addressing a meeting in a café.[100]

During strikes, cafés served as sites for both surveillance and negotiation. The café's ubiquity in the Paris region made it a convenient observation post. During the strike at a wallpaper factory at 208 boulevard Voltaire in February 1883, workers guarded the site from their "posts" at the neighborhood cafés and were thus able to observe all who entered and left the factory.[101] Strikers often tried to persuade working comrades to join the conflict by offering to go to the café for a glass of wine. For example, in May 1885, a strike of longshoremen occurred on the docks of Paris. Charles Aubertin, nicknamed "the battern," and two other strikers tried to persuade their comrades to join the strike. One of the longshoremen still working, Jean Conu, explained how they ended up at a riverside café: "You came to the place where we were working, and in the interests of peace you gave us a glass of wine."[102] During a saddlers' strike in 1906 in the suburb of Levallois, 20-year-old Eugene Perchet approached the still-laboring Henri Martin and upbraided him for not joining the strike. But then, in Martin's words, "I followed him into a café and made peace."[103] Striking workers used this same tactic when employers brought in strike-breakers. Over a glass of wine, the strikers would exhort the newly arrived workers not to break the strike.[104] As these instances show, a glass of wine at the counter became a central ritual during strikes.

When drink and discussion failed, the strikers often resorted to verbal threats and physical force. In his daily report of 8 July 1876 to the minister of the interior, the prefect of police noted: "This morning a certain number of striking joiners went to the cafés near the Luxembourg with the intention of preventing their fellows from continuing work on the Senate. By threats and even by some physical assaults, they succeeded in scaring about twenty workers."[105] The judicial dossiers amply demonstrate the pervasiveness of this behavior, especially among carpenters, mechanics, and machinists.[106] When Jean Bonnet tried to go back to work during the 1883 strike of wallpaper makers, his fellow worker and union president Jean Hubé pulled him into a café and threatened: "This person is not going to keep his cap on his head for long; if the head falls with the cap, what a shame!"[107] Fortunately, Bonnet was never actually attacked. During an 1884 strike of machinists at the Châtelet theater, however, a operator who refused to join was bloodied after an encounter with a dozen strikers at one Detain's café, 25 avenue Victoria.[108] The very ambiguity and fluidity of café encounters prevented the police and the courts from prosecuting anyone for assault and battery or for obstruction of the liberty of work. A confusing situation resulting in acquittals occurred during a printers' strike in suburban Issy in May 1886, when a crowd of typographers and compositors were moving between a café at 12 Grand rue and an establishment on the rue de Vaugirard.[109] Similar ambiguities were found in approximately one-third of the cases involving restraint of the freedom to work.

Café intimidation was particularly prevalent during the 1906–10 strike wave, the apogee of post-Commune labor agitation.[110] More often than during earlier strikes, bosses were the target of intimidation or violence. For example, in 1910 as M. Chatelit, a wholesale wood dealer, passed a café on the quai de la Gare, some of the striking cabinetmakers from his factory, who were sitting at tables on the terrace, yelled, "Throw him into the water! Into the water!"[111] As the level of violence rose, café owners became frightened. The newspaper of the café owners' association noted that it was impossible to prevent strikers from breaking glasses and dishes if they found nonstriking workers eating and drinking in the café. If the owner protested this constraint of his or her own liberty, the café was boycotted by the union. Without customers, a café owner then had only two options: either to close the shop or sell it for a pittance.[112]

Many of the workers involved in these confrontations fit Poulot's profile of the sublime. Police reports of the 1880s and later detailing these individuals are a good example of the fine sense of nuance and distinction of the police of that time. Their reports show no clear and easy distinction between sober and peaceable as opposed to drunk and belligerent workers on the side of either the opponents or the proponents of strikes. Frequently, both the leaders and the supporters of a strike who made these threats had been previously convicted of the standard infraction of public drunkenness and insulting public authorities. This was true, for instance, of the day laborer Jacques Kolten, involved in a strike at Pantin in 1888; of the grocery clerk René Delahay during an 1898 strike in Paris; of a machinist in the 1884 strike mentioned above; and of the painter Joseph Morin during a strike in Paris in the 1890s.[113] M. Bertin, boss of a leather shop at 121 rue de la Glacière described "J," one of the supposed leaders, as "one of my best workers. Unfortunately, he often gets drunk after working regularly for a week or two. He goes three or four days without showing up."[114]

The most effective weapon during strikes was probably neither the threats nor the violence of labor militants but public opinion in the cafés, which usually heavily favored the strikers. Those who returned to work while their comrades were still on strike were often intimidated and threatened. Ferdinand Bossu, a tinsmith, was one of the early proponents of a strike in 1884 at the shop of Nicolas and Chamon in Paris, but returned to work before most of his comrades. As he explained to the prosecuting attorney, he avoided retribution by staying away from cafés: "Besides this letter, I have not been subjected to any threat from either the former workers at the shop or from outside workers. The former workers no longer talk to me, and I no longer talk to them and, as I do not habitually frequent cafés, I avoid all discussion."[115] Other workers who bucked their comrades' sentiments during strikes or on other occasions were not so fortunate. One such incident occurred in the suburb of Charenton at Joslain's café, 8 rue des Carrières, in May 1884. After the Compagnie générale des omnibus fired Louis Breton and his father, the two nursed a grudge against another coachman, Joseph Hackenspiel, because they felt the company had given him an unfair advantage by giving him the best horses. This jealousy was widespread at the company and had earned Hackenspiel the epithets of "potato eater" and "Prussian." One night Louis Breton paid some other disgruntled coachmen to insult and attack Hackenspiel at the café.[116] These incidents reveal the price workers paid when they ignored the opinions of their café comrades.

Cafés were also used as part of another weapon the workers wielded: the demonstration. The celebration of May Day in 1889 ushered in an era of great working-class demonstrations. Not surprisingly, the day most often selected for these active statements of collective solidarity was Monday.[117] During the period 1889 to 1907, Paris workers marched on Mondays to demand the enactment of laws guaranteeing them an eight-hour workday and an official day of rest each week. Some hoped these demonstrations would help launch their ultimate goal, a general strike.[118]

The events of 20 January 1907 are a good example of these demonstrations and their relationship to the café. The Confédération general du travail (CGT) and the Union des syndicats hoped for a mammoth demonstration in support of the day of rest, including a cortege to the place de la République. At the last moment, Prime Minister Georges Clémenceau banned the meeting, mobilized foot and horse brigades, and temporarily closed the Bourse du travail. These measures, and similar ones used earlier and later, touched off a spate of café incidents. At the angle of rue de Bondy and boulevard Saint-Martin, serious tussles broke out on the terrace of the café Balthazar and at a café at the intersection of boulevard Magenta and the rue du Château-d'eau. In both spots, tables, chairs, carafes, and saucers were transformed into projectiles, hitting the police and many bourgeois lounging on the terrace. Around the Bourse du travail, at Chatel's bar, a similar disturbance erupted. Crying, "Long Live the Day of Rest!" workers tore the sliding metal screens off these cafés to use as weapons. In response, the police tried to evacuate each of the cafés.[119] Naturally, at these demonstrations the police arrested many for both physically and verbally insulting public authority. At a demonstration at the place Wagram on 6 February 1906, for instance, the police detained forty-two offenders on such charges.[120]

The final link between the café and the strike involves the question of indiscipline. The daily rituals of recreation, sociability, and drink were often a source of subtle but never-ending tensions between employers and workers, which frequently flared into the open and provoked a strike. In May 1874, for example, the foreman at Nicolas and Chamon, makers of gas meters, dismissed Victor Ramange and some other tinsmiths for the rest of the day because they had returned tardily from their traditional 3 P.M. break. This incident, as Ramange noted, precipitated a strike: "One day at the start of last May my comrades and myself returned to the shop two or five minutes late (each day we take ten minutes to go take a glass of wine from three o'clock till ten past three). The foreman said to us that we were too late and that we must pick up our work the next morning. It is from this day that we agreed to demand an increase in salary."[121] This case was not an isolated incident in the metal trades and illustrates how questions of salary and questions of work discipline were often closely intertwined.[122] In other cases, a boss's attempt to impose stricter discipline by prohibiting or shortening breaks at the café, forbidding socializing on the job, or refusing to allow drink on the shop floor, could also prompt a walkout. The English mechanic Henry Steele, who worked in the Paris metal trade in the 1890s, noted that any attempt to limit a metalworker's freedom was resented as deeply as was an attack on wages or hours of work.[123] Berlanstein has recently argued that artisans in the luxury trades—jewelers and bronze makers, for example—had a great deal of autonomy at work. Any encroachment on their privileges would send them to the "nearest wineshop."[124]

As the nineteenth century progressed, bosses increasingly viewed this interpretation of work and sociability as grossly inefficient and a severe impediment to their profits. As in so many other areas of the labor process, the Second Empire marks an important threshold in management's growing intolerance of workplace sociability. An 1860 investigation into Parisian industry by the Paris Chamber of Commerce was optimistic regarding the workers' moral habits (for example, the inquiry noted improvement in workers' morality and in particular a decline in the observance of Holy Monday) but nevertheless paid more attention to the questions of drink and cafégoing than in the earlier investigation in 1848.[125] The onset of a severe economic crisis in the 1880s precipitated a long litany of complaints against indiscipline linked with cafégoing. In response to a questionnaire from the minister of commerce in 1883 regarding the laws regulating women's and children's work, the Association of Brushmakers lamented: "Experience shows that the majority of workers really work only forty-five hours a week, and then, as in the case of Holy Monday, at their own whim."[126] At the 1884 parliamentary investigation into the crisis in Paris industry, M. Dietz-Monnin, a senator and member of the Chamber of Commerce of Paris, complained about the numerous "frivolous workers" who tried to get the biggest possible salary for the least possible work. Another witness, an entrepreneur dealing in plumbing and gas fixtures, M. Lalanne, was much more blunt. The worker, he felt, was the enemy of the employer: "We pay the workers for eight- or nine-hour days, but I say, and I dare anyone to refute me, that the worker works in a real and effective fashion for only five hours out of eight.[127] The indiscipline of Paris workers, along with their high salaries and foreign competition, persuaded many Paris employers to relocate their workshops or factories in the provinces.

Only during the Belle Epoque prosperity of 1896–1914 did Paris employers push for a much more rapid and thorough mechanization of production and disciplining of labor. This new strategy was a crucial contributing factor in the great strike wave during the same era. Michelle Perrot views this period as the "crisis" of Parisian factory discipline, when the nineteenth-century artisanal work organization fought its last great battle against the forces of modern industrial development.[128] As a consequence, strikes shifted from the previous emphasis on salary increases to an abiding concern about the organization of work and the authority of management. Employers and workers fought fiercely over café breaks and the question of bringing wine onto the shop floor. As in the past, metalworkers (in this case, copper-plate engravers) and auto workers were at the forefront of the protest.[129] Like their colleagues throughout the country, employers in Paris wanted both to impose a more intense rhythm of work and to preserve the long workday of ten or eleven hours. As Gary Cross shows in his study of labor's conquest of the eight-hour day, French management did not accept the argument of either "scientists" of work or socialists that an increase in the pace of work accompanied by the implementation of the eight-hour day would result in more efficient, sober, and family-oriented workers.[130]

During and after World War I, the café-workshop nexus eroded. Cross argues compellingly that despite employers' recalcitrance and the 1930s depression, enactment of the eight-hour day after the war did decrease the old type of workplace sociability. Robert Garric, who was involved in social work and education in Belleville, the heart of proletarian Paris, found that by the 1930s, Poulot's "sublime" category no longer existed. Few workers squandered their pay in cafés, became disorderly, and had to be thrown out, as they had prior to 1914.[131]

Across the nineteenth century, workers in many occupations varied greatly in their attempts and ability to sustain the link between sociability and labor that had been one of the hallmarks of eighteenth-century Paris. By the 1870s, tailors and shoemakers in particular, and workers in the garment, textile, and woodworking sectors in general, had to surrender much of their work-related sociability. In contrast, metal and construction workers and day laborers maintained a lively work-oriented café sociability. This helps explain why the first two groups were at the forefront of working-class militance between 1870 and 1914. Work remained the principal socializing experience for Paris proletarians, and workplace factors directly explain working-class political actions.[132] The strategy of using the café to prolong the link between work and sociability evolved as a means of prolonging the traditions of the artisanal world, and it thus ran directly counter to the most powerful economic forces of the era: rationalization and mechanization. This strategy stemmed more from a desire on the part of Paris proletarians to preserve a sense of space and place than from narrow economic motives. Nevertheless, these maneuvers had a great impact upon industrial organization and efficiency, as well as on the evolution of the Paris labor movement and working-class life.

Although there may indeed have been a "commanding stability" in the economic and social structure of the Parisian working class during the late nineteenth century, as Berlanstein contends, there was a growing heterogeneity in work cultures, with some groups able to maintain much better control than others. But one of Berlanstein's most insightful hunches—that the work cultures and leisure lives of people in workshops differed substantially from those of factory workers—is supported by the evidence. The virtual absence of factory workers from the culture of the café, or at least from activities that the police found suspicious, supports his idea that these workers preferred more commercialized and passive forms of leisure, such as the music halls, amusement parks, and cinemas. It is noteworthy, too, that unlike the music hall crowds analyzed by Timothy J. Clark who wished to lose their class identity, workers in cafés insistently demanded to be defined by their class.[133]

CHAPTER FOUR

The Social Construction of the Drinking Experience

lcoholic drink, the primary item sold in cafés, should be viewed from three perspectives: as a commodity, as a symbol, and as an agent of activity—that is, in its effects on behavior. The study of drink in nineteenth-century Paris reveals that insights on all three perspectives can be fruitfully applied. As in the case of the labor process, the Paris milieu played a vital role in shaping the drinking experience. The upper classes of this capital of fashion, luxury, and politics had traditionally viewed drink as one of the great expressions of their opulent lifestyles. The assimilation and diffusion of aristocratic eating and drinking habits brought by the Revolution, which forced the cooks of the great noble houses to open restaurants after their patrons had emigrated or been killed, made the conspicuous consumption of drink and food ever more public.[1] It should not be surprising that lower social classes would wish to imitate such aristocratic behavior. In no other French and in few foreign cities did drink become the consummate art form throughout the class hierarchy that it did in Paris. Thus the history of drinking in Paris is as much about social aspirations as it is about social degradation and misery.

This tripartite approach combines, where appropriate, the various interpretive theories that have so far informed the history of French drinking. This nascent historiography has three basic schools of thought. The first stems from the nineteenth-century doctors and temperance advocates who argued that alcohol consumption was a symptom alternately of economic misery or moral degradation brought on by poverty. Few bothered to explain, if this were so, why the French upper classes probably consumed more alcohol per capita than any other European or American ruling class during the late nineteenth century. A more balanced assessment had to await Roger Dion's magisterial *Histoire de la vigne et du vin en France* (1959), which covered the Old Regime and demonstrated the aristocratic origins of wine-drinking and its steady assimilation by the lower orders.[2]

Dion's cultural perspective remained largely undeveloped until the 1980s. In the meantime, in a pioneering 1974 essay on social drinking during the Belle Epoque, Michael Maurras developed another interpretation. Viewing drink through the lens of modernization theory, then still in vogue, Maurras argued that the heavy alcohol consumption in the decades before World War I represented, not the decline of the social structure, but rather the rise of modern consumer society.[3] Once consumer goods began to increase rapidly in number and decline in cost, workers diversified their purchases, visited cafés less often, and drank less alcohol (a constant theme in my interviews with café owners and habitués in the Paris region in 1989, 1990, and 1994). The 1980s and 1990s have, however, seen Dion's cultural and historical interpretation attain dominance, and French historians of the past decade have studied drink, not as a pathology or commodity, but as a form of cultural expression.[4]

Drink as a Commodity

The story of the evolution of working-class consumption of alcoholic beverages in Paris between 1789 and 1914 is that of successive waves of different alcoholic drinks (first wine, then brandy, then beer, then absinthe) becoming cheap and plentiful in turn, although wine was never displaced as the central drink in the proletarian diet. Overall, working-class drink consumption paralleled the increase in food consumption. The century divides fairly neatly into an impoverished and stagnant first half (1789–1851) and a second half of rising but uneven abundance (1851–1914). Only during this second period did drunkenness and alcoholism become major problems. Alcoholism in Paris thus emerged at a time when the city was undergoing a rapid but disparate modernization: the amount and variety of alcoholic drinks rose faster than the food supply. Alcoholic drinks were all the more alluring because they were inexpensive compared to food. In addition, the increasingly chaotic and constricted housing conditions and the growing distance between home and work resulted in a decline of home cooking. These social forces made the increasing panoply of alcoholic drinks seem a cheap and quick way to gain either energy for work or happiness for sociability. Each of the alcoholic drinks—wine, brandy, beer, and absinthe—arrived in a specific historical context and produced a distinctive pattern of consumption and intoxication.

To understand the importance of drink in working-class life, we must first place it in the context of the working-class diet. Students of this class have found that its diet was one of its most distinctive traits. This finding provides added evidence for the conclusion in Chapter 3 that café life, set in one of the main spaces where workers ate, was a decisive and formative factor shaping working-class identity. Until the 1930s, food was the principal expense of the French working class; about half of the average worker's budget was spent on food.[5] This percentage of food expenditure was higher than that of clerks and lower civil servants, to say nothing of the upper classes.[6] Moreover, dietary habits differed even among proletarians between the bottom and the top of the class. The occupational dietary variations were often evident in the same café. An article in *L'Illustration* (October 1886) concerning the café Munier on the rue des Amandiers, 20th arrondissement, noted that in the first room "absinthe flows . . . at the six white wooden tables arranged in order before the zinc counter." Here during this time of economic crisis, employed workers ate "copious dinners" of rabbit complemented with liters of *piccolo* (light or new) wine. In the adjoining room, "the habitués are more miserable. Rarely do plates of meat and vegetables appear," and those that do are "devoured along with a portion of beef that they wash down with a glass of wine."[7]

In general, highly paid artisans were much more likely to exhibit care and discrimination in their diets than unskilled workers. Ragpickers especially, in some cases, lacked regular mealtimes and simply ate or drank when they felt hungry or thirsty.[8] Nevertheless, this distinction should not be overdrawn, because differences in pay among the various working-class strata were not as wide as they were in England, for example, and noticeable differences in diet were thus not constant.[9] Workers seldom planned their food consumption in advance, but rather purchased what they needed to eat each day. The lack of kitchens or proper storage space in most working-class apartments, to say nothing of furnished rooms, which usually lacked any kitchen amenities, explains the impracticability of forethought. Workers found it made more sense to buy even wine in small quantities in a café, because they lacked the space to store large quantities at home.[10]

Across the entire century, bread, meat, and wine remained the three staples of the Paris working-class diet.[11] Wine was considered a necessity rather than a luxury. The great turn-of-the-century labor historian François Siminad found that workers resented any reduction in wages because that would mean giving up wine.[12] This concern was expressed, for example, at a workers' congress at Le Havre in 1880, where Louis Hébrard, a delegate from the Lot department, plaintively asked, "Do you not see that the worker can no longer drink wine?"[13] In general, Paris workers between 1789 and 1914 constantly spent the same percentage of their budgets on alcoholic drinks, primarily wine.[14] At the time of the French Revolution, Parisians allotted about 15 percent of their budgets to wine. Most families in the period 1870–1914 expended virtually the same percentage—between 12 and 18 percent—of their budgets on drink.[15]

Although wine had been a staple of the Parisian working-class diet for centuries, it became a ubiquitous and daily beverage only during the second half of the nineteenth century. During the first half of the century, wine consumption, both gross and per capita, actually declined. In 1809–18, for example, official consumption declined almost by half. From the reign of Napoléon I to the ascent of his nephew's Second Empire, population growth far outpaced the growth in wine consumption: between 1811 and 1851, the population nearly doubled, from 622,636 to 1,053,261, while wine consumption increased by only one-third.[16]

Consumption beyond the barrières of Paris on Sundays and Mondays was nonetheless heavy, accounting for an estimated one-fifth to one-third of the wine drunk in the city, but this pattern was a carryover from the Old Regime.[17] During the period 1814–40, the average adult Parisian male is thought to have drunk between 100 and 175 liters of wine per year, an amount substantially under the estimates for the late eighteenth century.[18] Even though the price of wine rose more slowly than the rate of inflation, workers could not afford to drink more. The growing immiseration of the Paris working class that historians have noted for this period thus finds powerful confirmation in the matter of wine consumption.

The Second Empire brought a great revolution in wine drinking. The gross figures went from 1,272,000 hectoliters in 1852 to 3,694,100 in 1869. This nearly fourfold increase easily outstripped the doubling of the population and the expansion of the city limits. By 1865, the figure for per capita yearly consumption of wine had more than doubled to 225 liters, along with 80 liters of beer and 12 of various spirits.[19] Much of this increased wine supply came not from the traditional Paris-area vineyards but from the great wine-growing regions of the south, made accessible by the establishment of a national railroad network by 1860. This new national market in wine ensured that for the first time, the average Parisian could consume wine on a regular basis throughout the day, week, month, and year.

Most historians believe that working-class consumers participated fully in this increased drinking.[20] Drawing wine from the national market also ensured that the periodic problems with the Paris-area wine harvest did not hamper consumption in the capital. Thus the ravages of the fungal disease oidium in wine-growing regions during the period 1853 to 1857 increased the price but did not greatly diminish the supply of wine in Paris.[21] Only the unprecedented catastrophe wrought by the phylloxera aphid, which devastated French vineyards from the 1870s through the 1890s, seriously hampered the Paris wine trade. But even during the worst of this crisis, the resourceful French found "wine" of one variety or another.

The Second Empire also saw a dramatic increase in the consumption of other alcoholic drinks. Although brandy and then beer became regular components of the working-class diet in this era, consumption patterns followed different historical trajectories. From the end of the First Empire, brandy achieved a remarkable rate of increase; its consumption tripled between 1811 and 1851. By 1840, the average adult male Parisian drank between 9 and 10 liters of spirits annually. Under the regime of Louis-Napoléon, consumption of brandy continued to climb: in 1852, 63,000 hectoliters had entered the old Paris city limits; by 1869, the figure had risen to 132,419 hectoliters.[22] By this latter date, Armand Husson, one of the leading contemporary authorities on Paris consumption, believed that brandy had replaced wine as the main drink in the working-class diet.[23] Although patently an exaggeration, this suggestion nonetheless contains an important truth: by the 1870s, Parisian workers were almost as likely to drink brandy as wine, often consuming a glass of brandy with, or in, their coffee after their wine. In the early 1870s, brandy consumption stabilized at an annual figure of approximately 135,000 hectoliters per year, and it remained at that level for the next few decades.

In contrast to brandy, beer consumption remained low until the 1850s, at which point it became a Paris craze and beerhalls (*brasseries*) mushroomed throughout the city. Consumption rose steadily during the subsequent decades. In 1855, 140,000 hectoliters of beer were drunk in the city, but the figure had ballooned to over 6,000,000 hectoliters by 1880.[24] The fad was so formidable that even the classic café de la Rotonde in the Palais-Royal started selling beer in 1866.[25] The fashion also overcame the post-1871 revulsion at things German.[26] By the mid 1880s, the writer on Paris mores for *L'Illustration* claimed that 150,000 glasses of beer (*bocks*) were imbibed each evening on the *grands boulevards* between 9 P.M. and 1 A.M.[27] These same decades witnessed a decline in the consumption of alcoholic drinks made from apples and pears, which had customarily complemented wine consumption, and these drinks ceased to be an integral part of working-class drinking.[28]

The increase in wine, brandy, and beer consumption occurred in the general context of an improved working-class diet during the Second Empire, concurrently with similar increases in the consumption of meat and bread, the other two staples. These increases reflect the fact that even the working class received some of the benefits of the new Paris, which was becoming more than ever before the capital of luxury and leisure in both cuisine and entertainment. During the Second Empire, Parisian workers acquired a reputation, in the eyes of provincial workers, for being both gourmets and gourmands, and their improved diet endeared the Empire to the Paris proletariat up until the late 1860s.[29]

The best evidence for this sea change in working-class diet comes from the 1884 investigation into the economic crisis in Paris, at which senior industry and labor movement officials emphasized that workers in the 1880s had far more money to spend on food and drink than workers had had forty years earlier. "Before . . . we spent 25 sous [approximately 1 franc] at the maximum for our morning meal; today the workers spend 3 francs or 3 francs 50, and then there is the wine at noon. . . . Bread is a better buy today, and [where] we used to drink a *demi-setier* [quarter liter,] now they drink a liter, have a cup of coffee, and smoke a cigar," the carpenters' President Bertrand noted.[30]

What these former workers, now bosses, did not mention is that Haussmannization also had many negative effects on the working-class diet. The growing separation between home and work meant that it was much more difficult for workers to go home for lunch. Previously workers who had worked at a shop close to their homes had returned home for their noon meal.[31] Increasingly, after 1850, they had to lunch at cafés, which added greatly to their expenses, as café meals generally cost twice what the same meals would have cost at home.[32] Another witness at the 1884 investigation, a delegate representing various woodworkers' and joiners' organizations, also provided illustrative testimony: "When his work is far from home, the worker cannot take his noonday meal at his domicile, and this happens almost always now. He must eat out, and this usually costs about 1 franc 25. Take away 1 franc 25 from his salary, taking account of his rent and the money necessary for clothing and feeding his family, and judge for yourself if he can save."[33] Moreover, the number of cheap eating establishments catering to the working class was on the decline, forcing workers to pay even more for their lunches and breaks.[34] At the Paris Municipal Council hearings on the economic crisis of the 1880s, a witness noted: "Previously in Paris there were a number of establishments where the worker could have an *ordinaire* at 35 centimes, and with 35 centimes of bread, he ate lunch. Today they say they must spend 1 franc 50 for their lunch. There are no longer any old-style restaurants."[35] The growing expense of lunch reinforced the tendency among some workers just to grab a few things to eat from a delicatessen near their work rather than have a formal meal. Such workers were also considered those most likely to get drunk on Sundays and Mondays, and their employers regarded them as "sublimes."[36]

The growing abundance and cheapness of alcoholic drinks, the rising cost of prepared meals, and the increasing distance between home and workplace produced the noxious new custom of consuming alcohol on an empty stomach, especially in the early morning.[37] Maxime du Camp reported in 1870 that a small glass (*petite verre*) of brandy had replaced breakfast (*premier déjeuner*), which Louis Girard confirms in his book *La Deuxième République et le Second Empire, 1848–1870* (1981).[38] By the 1890s, the practice had entered working-class slang: the phrase "to kill a glass of white wine or brandy" was intimately associated with morning drinking on an empty stomach.[39] Doctors provide the main source of documentation on this practice, which they felt was one of the workers' most unhealthy habits. In the era's most authoritative studies on the diet of working-class Parisians, Dr. L. Landouzy estimated that 58 percent of the male and 42 percent of the female Paris-area workers started their workday without any food.[40]

The economic crisis of the 1880s and early 1890s exacerbated the emerging proletarian tendency to privilege drink over food. The most dramatic increase in living expenses occurred in the area of housing, but food costs also increased significantly.[41] Between 1866 and 1890, the cost of food increased between 23 and 29 percent.[42] Fernand and Maurice Pelloutier estimated in 1900 that the consumption of food had declined by 21 percent and the consumption of wine had increased by 29 percent over the previous twenty years. They felt that wine and spirits were the only items in the budget of the working-class family that did not increase in price.[43] Inflation may thus have encouraged intoxication.

This economic crisis produced another revolution in working-class drinking habits. During this era of economic retrenchment, meat consumption fell and wine consumption faltered.[44] Phylloxera was devastating the French vineyards, and the Paris wine depot at Bercy was periodically flooded.[45] Café owners resorted to every possible stratagem to hold down the cost of wine. Paris workers had come to expect this, for it had risen more slowly than the cost of living since 1788.[46] In desperation, café owners kept prices down by selling cheap Italian and Spanish wines, diluting wine with water (an age-old practice), and adulterating it with spirits or chemicals.[47] During the 1880s, for example, to satisfy the workers' preference, café owners turned much of their white wine into red.[48] As noted, police laboratories to test the quality of food and drink also opened in this decade. In consequence, the adulteration and falsification of drink became a major dispute between the police and the publicans (see also Chapter 5).[49] Despite their best efforts, café owners could not prevent the price of wine from climbing during the 1880s.[50] The effects of phylloxera began to lift after 1890, and imports of foreign wine declined.[51]

During this decade of diminished wine production, however, absinthe, a green, wormwood-flavored liqueur, became popular among Paris workers.[52] Although introduced to Paris during the 1830s by soldiers returning from the Algerian campaign, absinthe became a standard bar offering only in the 1860s, and fashionable bourgeois and artists were its main consumers until the late 1870s.[53] Workers seldom drank it. In Alphonse Daudet's working-class novel *Jack*, for example, absinthe is still associated with poets rather than with proletarians.[54] Writing in 1877, one of the leading Paris medical authorities, Dr. Legrand de Saulle, was confident that the "enormous" Paris consumption of absinthe would never spread to the working class.[55] The 1880s would belie this optimistic assumption. In 1881, the realist writer Octave Mirbeau described the Renaissance bar and dance hall at 7, rue d'Allemagne, a Paris working-class street, as having a main barroom filled with customers and "smelling of absinthe and white wine."[56] A late 1880s *Ouvriers des deux mondes* study of a shoemaker in the town of Malakoff noted absinthe-drinking among suburban workers.[57]

By the 1890s, evidence of the detrimental effects of absinthe among the working class had become pervasive.[58] Jules Simon, one the leading bourgeois politicians and reformers, noted the harm done to family life by working-class absinthe-drinking, and documentation of its ravages was provided by the doctor in charge of the Paris police infirmary, Paul Garnier, in his treatise *La Folie à Paris*.[59] Temperance journals also focused on this issue. In 1895, the *Bulletin de la société française de tempérance*, journal of the Ligue national contre l'alcoolisme, alerted its readers to the "legion" of workers who drank absinthe. On any given day, it asserted, both on the grands boulevards, frequented by the bourgeois, and on the exterior boulevards and the place Maubert, populated by the working class, one could witness the celebration of "absinthe hour," generally between 5 and 7 P.M. Another journal, *La Tempérance*, described working-class suburban cafés on Sundays as "smoky rooms" stinking of "stale wine, absinthe, and *'eau de mort'*"—a term it found more applicable than *eau de vie*.[60] Observers on the left, such as the Pelloutier and Bonneff brothers and the novelist Gustave Geoffroy also lamented the rise of working-class "absinthism."[61] Almost all observers agreed that absinthe consumption had drawn women into the drink culture in an unprecedented fashion and had thus exposed children to the threat.[62] Working-class "absinthism" is also attested to by its incorporation into popular slang. Absinthe became known as "the serpent with green eyes," or simply as "the green" (*la verte*) or "the blue" (*la bleue*).[63] This latter term represents a continuity in working-class drink terminology, because the same nickname had been used for pre-1860s barrière wine. When working-class families went absinthe-drinking on the exterior boulevards and the fortifications, they were "strangling a parrot."[64]

Absinthe deserved all this attention. Between 1885 and 1895, its consumption rocketed from 57,732 to 165,000 hectoliters.[65] Absinthe was the most prominent and popular of the era's new *alcools d'industrie* to flood the French market. Suddenly absinthe had displaced brandy and beer to become the second most consumed alcoholic drink in Paris. New processes ensured that alcohol distilled from beets, potatoes, or cereals soared in quantity while plummeting in cost.[66] The great advantage of these beverages was that their production was much less susceptible than wine to fluctuations in the weather, and impervious to diseases of the vine.

Absinthe rivaled wine in the working-class diet because it was both cheap and fashionable. In an era of economic crisis, it had a decisive price advantage over wine. In workers' bars a glass of absinthe, rum, kirsch, or vermouth varied in cost from 10 centimes in the outlying Paris suburbs such as Clichy to 30 centimes in the city.[67] In contrast, a glass of wine usually cost between 20 and 25 centimes.[68] By drinking absinthe, moreover, workers could imitate the stylish bourgeois boulevardiers. By the mid 1880s, Paris workers had wholeheartedly adopted the bourgeois ritual of the aperitif and the habit of drinking absinthe or bitters (*amers*).[69]

French temperance journals perceptively analyzed the working-class absinthe cult. Articles in both *Les Annales antialcooliques* and *La Tempérance* noted that in Paris drinking had become an art, with an elaborated symbolism unrivaled in any other city. Working-class drinking, in particular, had "attained a degree of intellectuality not found elsewhere." If paydays and Mondays were times of vulgar excess, the rest of the week showed that workers felt a need to express "their well-developed sociality" on the terraces of the exterior boulevards after the fashion of the middle class. Proximity to a "rich and hedonistic" bourgeoisie had generated "an unconscious desire to enjoy café life in the same manner." Yet—and here social analysis becomes class snobbery—the result was not a refinement of mores but an alcoholism "more frightening than in the bourgeoisie because it did not know any measure or decorum and was in defiance of good sense." Despite this class bias, the author saw more clearly than most contemporaries that much working-class drinking during the Belle Epoque was the product, not of moral degradation, but of social aspiration.[70]

Absinthe's green tide steadily mounted between 1880 and 1914 despite governmental efforts, via taxation, to counteract it. Throughout the era, the French parliament believed that the best way to fight alcoholism was to encourage the drinking of wine, dubbed the "hygienic drink," instead of spirits. The tax measures of 1880 and 1901, which respectively lowered and abolished wine duties, followed this logic but achieved only mixed results. Wine merchants nullified the impact of the 1880 measure because they refused to pass along the savings to their customers.[71] In testimony at the 1884 investigation, both employers and workers provided evidence on this point.[72] In addition, of course, the production cutback caused by the phylloxera crisis also undermined the legislators' intentions. By 1901, with absinthe consumption continuing to rise, the French parliament took even more drastic action. On January 2, it abolished the Paris entry tax (*octroi*) on wine, with the result that the cost of a glass of wine fell to 10 centimes, exactly the cost of an absinthe.[73] This substantive action, along with the end of the phylloxera ravages and the consequent increase in wine production, did result in a dramatic increase in wine consumption and a compensating decrease in absinthe consumption.[74] Now suburban workers were often drinking 317 liters of wine per year.[75] Although the temperance journals congratulated themselves that the strategy of substituting wine for absinthe had worked, absinthe consumption in Paris was on the upswing again by 1910. Observers in these same journals began to realize that the increased wine consumption was also producing alcoholics, especially among women.[76]

The onset of a revolution in the Parisian working-class diet at the turn of the century also failed to halt the growing intake of wine and absinthe. The increased availability and diversity of vegetables, fruit, and milk in the 1890s resulted in a decline in the consumption of meat but not of alcoholic drinks.[77] When Landouzy and his students analyzed the Paris working-class diet in the 1900–1910 period, they still found it unbalanced. Landouzy characterized it as "irrational, insufficient, sometimes unhealthy and unclean, and always too costly." He especially deplored the imbalance between drink and solid food: the average male worker spent 2 francs 38 centimes on food and 1 franc 24 centimes on drinks each day; the figures for women were, respectively, 1 franc 22 centimes and 92 centimes, with only 24 centimes for hard liquor.[78] Doctors also found that workers still tended, despite the improved economic circumstances after 1895, to drink to compensate for a diet deficient in solid food.[79] Workers in the pre–World War I decade simply did not have enough time to adjust to the wider range of foods that finally began to be available.

How did the successive increases in consumption of these various alcoholic drinks affect occupational, ethnic, and gender-based drinking patterns? Judicial archives, newspapers, and novels provide copious data on the particular drinks individuals consumed. But an analysis of these data by occupation fails to reveal any clear-cut patterns. The primary impression is that café customers consumed a wide variety of drinks according to personal whim rather than any set pattern of preference. For example, one morning in August 1871, the accountant Octave Pruvost struck up a fast friendship with a café owner after discovering he was from Pruvost's native Alsace. The two men spent the whole day drinking. They had three glasses of absinthe in the morning; then the café owner made a *politesse* by opening a complementary bottle of Mâcon wine at lunch; and then they had more unspecified drinks after dinner. On the day after Easter 1875, the master joiner Charles Akerman had a glass of wine at a table, then a glass of absinthe and another glass of wine, both at the counter. Mathurin Bourre, an attendant who watched patients at Paris's Beaujon hospital, and his co-worker Alphonse Doublet usually had a coffee and a small glass of kirsch at noon at the café next to the hospital where they worked, then went to another café for a glass of wine. On New

Year's night 1886, Bourre and four co-workers went to a café for diner; they drank four liters of wine among them, then each had a coffee with cognac and a small glass of kirsch. Because one of them was celebrating a birthday, the café owner gave them all a second glass of kirsch. In January 1872, the *Gazette des tribunaux* recorded a prodigious drinking bout between two longtime friends, during which they consumed "liqueurs, beer, punch, wine, cider, sugared water, syrups, tea, and all the liquors Paris can provide."[80] Workers undoubtedly felt that one of the great luxuries of living in Paris was its diversity of drinks, and they certainly took full advantage of it.

Café owners added to the complexity of the workers' drinking pattern by concocting a wide variety of mixed drinks. The adulteration of wine was one of the most obvious ways in which café owners altered the nature of their drinks, and only one of many strategies to increase their sales and profits. During the first half of the century, the wine and brandy workers drank was often made stronger and more flavorful by blending different wines or adding spices. One of the wines of the period was called "blue wine" from its color. According to observers these "horribly thick bluish nauseous mixtures in vogue at the barrières" were "an execrable medicine whose virtue is the power of intoxication." Around the barrières, workers sipped a drink known as "French wine"—a mixture of water, wine, and sugar—from bowls.[81] Other drinks, all with a brandy or spirit base, were called "yellow fire water," the "stomach breaker," and the "perfect lover." The "stomach breaker," low-grade brandy laced with Cayenne pepper, reputed to be the "staple drink of at least twenty shops of lowest order," must have been an especially lethal concoction.[82] A variation on the stomach breaker added water, caramel, and sugared molasses to the spirits; this blend was considered "dear to drunks and [one] whose abuse produces delirium tremens."[83] These mixtures continued to be popular even after the destruction of the barrières and the arrival of absinthe.

Although fully aware of the dangers of adulteration, the legal and medical authorities failed to understand the menace of alcohol addiction. Thus Joseph Lefort's recommendation in the 1870s that coffee should replace brandy overlooked the practice, common in working-class cafés, of mixing the two.[84] The combination was well known, for instance, as a *mazagran*, or a *gloria*.[85] Temperance advocates were sometimes more astute in this matter. Jules Bergeron considered the "mixture" (*mêlé*)— a drink with blackcurrant, anisette, or mint liqueur added to a strong dose of brandy—a "pernicious drink," and "almost as bad as absinthe" in its tendency to produce chronic alcoholics.[86] No observer, however, has ever tried to explore the effects of all these mixtures on the working-class mind and body.

An enumeration of the drinks mentioned in judicial dossiers between 1871 and 1914 reveals the workers' continued preference for wine over all other drinks. In 63 percent of the surviving cases, the defendants consumed wine; in 30 percent of the cases, absinthe is mentioned, and in 11 percent of the cases, beer is noted. (The percentages add up to over 100 percent, because often the defendants, as we have seen, consumed more than one type of drink.) This finding confirms Henri Leyret's perception that "the Parisian worker drinks wine almost exclusively, which maintains and sustains him," as well as studies of working-class Paris budgets that reveal the predominance of wine over spirit consumption.[87] In his 1984 study of Belleville, Gérard Jacquemet found that the proletariat "remained faithful to wine."[88]

Few observers from any field or ideological camp understood the hazards of wine consumption. Landouzy, the expert on the Paris working-class diet, was a rare exception. He stressed that when workers consumed more than three liters of wine per day, it ceased to be "hygienic."[89]

Alcohol as Symbol and Representation

"Alcohol is the literature of the people," the historian and literary critic Hippolyte Taine once remarked.[90] A study of the vocabulary surrounding the drinking experience reveals that it was indeed a liquid text by which workers commented upon their emotional life. Drink, like literature, generated multiple meanings and interpretations. The number of popular terms and expressions connected to drink was almost infinite. Compilations of Paris slang and argot such as Alfred Delveau's *Dictionnaire de la langue verte* contain thousands of references to drink, drunkenness, and café life.[91] Even so, the Paris judicial archives and newspaper press contain dozens of additional expressions.

Was there a logic to the popular perceptions of sobriety and intoxication? What were the social meanings associated with drinking? The destruction of the nineteenth-century court records during the fall of the Commune in 1871 prevents an analysis of these questions for the period 1789–1870. Nevertheless, Thomas Brennan's book on the Paris working-class tavern between 1690 and 1770 does permit a *longue durée* comparison between this period and the 1870–1914 years. The tremendous amount of reflection that workers obviously devoted to describe the drinking experience is at odds with the traditional notion that the intoxicated state diminishes, distorts, and eventually destroys the brain's ability to reason. This folklore on drink also reveals that the biological state of inebriation is conditioned by economic and cultural changes, as in the rise of new beverages, and cultural and political constraints, as in the growing legal and medical concern about "alcoholism."[92]

Drink held such a powerful grip on the worker's mentality because it was intimately tied to values at the very heart of working-class life: strength, equality, and sociability. Traditionally, for artisans, drink was not seen merely as a diversion from work but rather as a preparation for and a sustaining factor in labor. In popular imagination, alcohol provided the energy necessary for work.[93] During the 1830s, according to H. A. Frégier, workers considered wine a "first necessity." They believed it restored their strength after a hard day's labor and that it "enlivened their spirits and charmed" their sufferings.[94] Eugène Sue's novel *Les Mystères de Paris* (1843), which was hugely popular among the workers themselves, expressed the same sentiments: wine, for example, "refreshed and strengthened" an exhausted worker.[95] Ideas like these lasted until at least 1914. Consider the Bonneff brothers, who found in the early twentieth century that workers in both workshops and factories believed that the more one drank, the better one worked.[96] A cartoon in the journal *Les Annales antialcooliques* attacked the same sentiment. It portrayed a withered, half-dead alcoholic with a glass of absinthe on the rostrum of a public meeting saying, "At the hospital, do you know what they said, comrades? If you continue to drink absinthe, you will become a *phtisique*. Liar! Liars! They want to deprive us of the drink that gives us strength and health."[97]

The connection between drink and equality was embodied in the working-class ritual of the round (*tournée*) of drinks consumed with one's working comrades. Often an integral part of the *tournée* was the ritual clinking of glasses (called *trinquer*). Much of the café drinking among the working-class occurred within the ritualized context of the round, common among workmates, friends, lovers, and even draftees heading off for induction. *L'Illustration* reported in 1872 on the rounds for outgoing reservists paid for by their "joyous" fellow workers, concluding that at Paris, "it is necessary to drink to everything."[98] Rounds consumed by a husband and wife often consisted in the couple's passing a "loving cup" back and forth.[99] A round usually involved a group of friends, occasionally a group of strangers sitting together, and could as easily occur at the counter as at a table.[100] Paying for a round in one's turn was considered a point of honor as well as an obligation that an imbiber did not ignore lightly, for fear of ostracism.[101] Although there are pictures of employers clinking glasses with their workers in the twentieth century, by the 1870s, the ritual had become essentially a badge of working-class distinction.[102] Although most writers on alcoholism believed that the round was one of the primary causes of excessive alcohol consumption, the ritual seems likely, rather, to have been able to constrain disorderly behavior as well as excessive consumption by forcing drinkers to imbibe in an orderly fashion.[103]

After the round had been offered, the *politesses* given, and the glasses clinked, the drink was supposed to work its magic effects of making people congenial. Unlike many bourgeois, workers believed that wine enlivened the spirit and stimulated the passion for sociability. Novels by and about workers—from Sue's *Mysteries of Paris* to Gustave Geoffroy's *The Apprentice* in the early 1900s—portray the wine drinker as voluble and communicative.[104] In contrast, Geoffroy depicts the absinthe drinker as silent.[105] Rank-and-file workers expressed the same opinion. For example, a day laborer in the 1870s boasted, "I am loquacious when I drink."[106]

Yet workers also realized that drink had an ambivalent impact on sociability. Courtroom testimony shows the ease with which conviviality could slide into irascibility, and fraternity into fratricide. Arguments were also intimately associated with drink. "He gets drunk often, and when he is under the influence, he insults everyone," a laundress noted of her cousin, a stableman. "When he is drunk, he is, as they say, hot-headed," a landlady said of one of her tenants, a housepainter. Drunkenness could also transform sociability into meddling. "The accused was drunk, we saw very clearly that he looked for stories and that he had become involved in something that did not concern him," complained a policeman who had arrested one of *Le Cri du peuple*'s reporters. Café owners often remarked of a habitué: "He drinks often, and when he is drunk he tries to argue with everyone. When this happens I have to throw him out." The connection between drink and argumentation was so strong in people's minds that if an individual was not argumentative, he was not considered truly a drunkard. A café owner and a concierge both expressed this sentiment about a glassmaker: "He has sometimes been seen drunk [*pris de boisson*], but he is never noisy nor does he get into fights."[107]

Workers also realized that drunkenness sometimes produced the exact opposite of sociability: stupor and solitude. On this point, literary and popular expression were in complete agreement. An expression from the

Restoration asserted that drunkenness, like all other great passions, was solitary.[108] In his memoirs, Dr. L. Véron noted that when workers and soldiers became drunk, they lost their reason as well as their ability to speak or walk.[109] Working-class witnesses in court cases spoke of the same condition: "The person was so drunk that he could not have pronounced the least word."[110] One of the minor characters in an Emile Gaboriau novel was a "father absinthe," who, when he had a moment's leisure and a little money, invariably got drunk and never rose above a condition of semi-lucidity.[111] In his working-class novel *Jack*, Alphonse Daudet remarked that café owners sometimes named their shops "consolation," as though drunkenness and oblivion were the worker's only refuge.[112]

Nineteenth-century working-class Parisians not only elaborated on the connections between sociability and drink but also elucidated the various shadings of intoxication in unprecedented fashion. Unlike their Old Regime forebears, chronicled by Brennan, workers after 1789 progressively constructed a vocabulary to distinguish the various gradations between simple drunkenness and acute alcoholism and adopted a term for sobriety. During the eighteenth century, popular perception did not make a clear distinction between degrees of drunkenness and had no terms for sobriety. Moreover when people spoke of inebriation they used the euphemisms "to be taken by, or full of, the wine" (*pris* or *plein de boisson*) instead of the straightforward word "drunkenness" (*ivresse*). Half the references Brennan found refer to *pris* or *plein de boisson*, with *pris* used most often. Only in one-third of the cases did laborers use terms Brennan feels were more damning: *saoul, yvre*, or *mort yvre*.[113] Slowly but surely between 1830 and 1870, as the *Gazette des tribunaux* reveals, *saoul* and *ivre* displaced *pris de boisson* as the favored popular terms for drunkenness. Parallel to a more clearly defined sense of the state of intoxication, there also developed a sense that drunkenness occurred in a series of graduated steps. Dr. Véron, for example, distinguished between two types of drunkards, the *ivrogne* and the *soulard*. The former, found especially among the wealthy youth, pushed drunkenness to the point of brutishness and muscular paralysis. Véron felt that such behavior represented an illness rather than a vice, thus anticipating Magnus Huss, the doctor who developed the disease concept of alcoholism.[114]

By 1870, when the judicial archives recommence, the euphemisms and softer expressions had given way to a much richer set of terms. The spectrum was much wider and now included gradations of sobriety as well as of drunkenness. Sobriety might be considered *sang-froid, sobre, jeun,* and *état normal*. Although the term *sang-froid* may seem more "traditional," with possible connections to humoral medicine, it was not found by Brennan in the eighteenth-century archives, and thus was no more archaic than these other expressions. Both in the courtroom and on the stage, these terms were used in conscious juxtaposition to drunkenness (*ivresse*). For example, we find this differentiation in Tristan Bernard's classic play *The Small Café*, as well as in a case involving a café owner and his son. In this latter case, the son's girlfriend described the father as drinking as much as the son but as being able to keep his sangfroid despite insulting his son.[115] In a real-life case, defendants described themselves as halfway between sobriety and drunkenness. "I was neither drunk [*ivresse*] nor sober [*jeun*] but had drunk [*bu*] in different cafés."[116] The new set of terms to describe drunkenness had also become more specific and more emphatic. On the one hand, the simple word for drunkenness (*ivresse*) was now three times more likely to be used than during the eighteenth century. On the other hand, we note a decrease in the eighteenth-century preference for softer language: *pris de boisson*, for instance, was now used in a fifth rather than a half of the cases.

By the 1870s, the Paris working class had developed a sophisticated drinking vocabulary, including a whole range of terms coined for the intermediate stages between full drunkenness and stone-cold sobriety. Dr. Ernest Monin and other leading experts found much merit in these popular distinctions. The popular expression "he is moved" (*il est ému*) very accurately described the "first period of drunkenness," Monin thought.[117] Café owners and workers did, indeed, frequently use this phrase to indicate the onset of inebriation. For example, "The accused was not drunk [*gris*], but probably a little moved by the drink."[118] In a variation on this expression, defendants might simply say that they were just "a little bit drunk" (*un peu bu*). These phrases were used in 28 percent of the court cases. By the 1870s, the term *pris de boisson* had been added to describe this first stage. In one case, during the summer of 1871, the waiter at the Montmartre brasserie Graff used this wording: "These two individuals were not drunk; maybe they were *pris de boisson*." In general, the popular mentality associated this early stage of drunkenness with beer drinking. Thus a *limonadier* noted "no one seemed drunk; they had consumed beer."[119]

The intermediate stage of drunkenness encompassed a wide variety of popular expressions. These included "not bad" (*pas mal*), "gay" (*gai*), "dazed" (*étourdi*), and having "dined well" (*bien diné*).[120] The true meaning of these terms emerges only in their social context and is enhanced by the vocal inflection and facial expression of the speaker. The term *bien diné* was often considered the closest to sobriety. The *Gazette des tribunaux* described it as "an agreeable state of carelessness that dining well produces."[121] Such positive connotations were usually uppermost in the courtroom use of the term. Thus Emmanuel Pelurson, a merchant, thought "although I may have dined well, I retained all my sangfroid." Naturally, such subtle distinctions have never received definitive codification, and the terms were often used interchangeably. A café owner describing the state of two of his customers, for example, used *gai* and *bien diné* as equivalents: "Having evidently dined very well, they were what one might call gay [*gai*]." The term "not bad" referred to a slightly more inebriated state." Defendants often used it to indicate that they had not been the only ones drinking. A coachman explained the difference between his state and that of the butcher he killed: "I was not drunk [*ivre*], but he was not bad [*pas ma (sic)*]."[122] "Gay" signified a more definite state of intoxication, although one that was still viewed positively. A café owner described her father at the time of his death as "gay but not drunk." The former army sergeant Sébastien Billoir, called "le Décoré," because he always wore his decoration, also used the term *gai*: "I was sometimes gay, this is true, but I never insulted anyone." "Dazed," in contrast, was a stronger term and indicated that the belligerent and destructive side of drink had begun to appear. A café owner described Billoir thus: "I saw him drunk only one time, but I saw him several times dazed [*étourdi*]." A concierge described one of the tenants, an assistant cook, as "not appearing drunk [*ivre*] at the moment that I stopped him in the basement. It is possible that he was a bit dazed [*étourdi*] by drink but he did not appear to be squinting." Additional expressions indicating an intermediate stage of intoxication include: "to have a cup of sun"; "close to drunkenness"; "a little excited by the drink"; "a little launched"; "he could have been drinking but he was far from losing his reason"; and "he was overexcited but did not lose his reason."[123]

The state of abject drunkenness was equally endowed with a vivid and nuanced vocabulary. Terms for this extreme condition included *plein raide, ivrogne, s'enivrer souvent*, and *alcoolique*.[124] In 28 percent of the court cases, witnesses considered one of the defendants to be a drunkard or one who got drunk frequently. This percentage presents a stark contrast to the eighteenth-century court records, which contain virtually no use of the term *ivrogne*.[125] In the late-nineteenth-century working-class lexicon, the great hallmarks of a drunkard were lack of control over behavior—even if after just a few drinks—lack of memory, and change in personality. A disputatious street vendor drew on most of these ideas in his attempt to prove that he was a drunkard (*ivrogne*) rather than an anarchist. While the police insisted he had merely been slightly tipsy (*legèrement pris de boisson*), he responded that he did not need to drink much to become intoxicated, and that once this happened he became "unconscious" of his actions.[126] Her neighbors in the tough 11th arrondissement quarter of Sainte-Marguerite called an irascible woman ragpicker nicknamed the "Turio," who was charged with murdering her lover, an "incorrigible drunkard."[127]

By the mid 1890, Paris workers had started to use the term "alcoholic" (*alcoolise*). Newspapers of that day reported cases of ordinary people who realized that their chronic drinking had turned into a disease. The mass-circulation daily *Le Petit Parisien* reported the case of an "alcoholic" consulting a doctor: "Doctor, I am plagued by interminable attacks, violent spasms and convulsions."[128] The seamstress and maid Elise Sainsaulieux used the term "grand alcoholic" in court testimony to describe chronic drinking.[129] These examples show that popular opinion assimilated the disease concept of alcoholism amazingly quickly considering that Paris doctors and the temperance movement had only recently begun to study French alcoholism systematically and to wage a broad campaign against intemperance.[130] As remarkable as the workers' adoption of the new medical terminology was their perception, noted by many doctors, that habitual and heavy wine consumption could lead to drunkenness. The head of a house-painting firm mentioned that one of his workers became argumentative and disorderly "when he has consumed only two or three glasses of wine." In another case the foreman at a glass factory reported of one of his employees: "He drinks, however, sometimes and cannot even hold a glass of wine." Defendants in a murder case tried to use this new sensitivity to the effects of wine to claim a memory loss: "I lost in the wine the memory of what happened next." By 1914, in short, the popular mentality had become well versed in the differences between sobriety, intoxication, and alcoholism.[131]

The biggest transformation in the working-class conception of drink relates to the question of intentionality. During the eighteenth century, workers were unsure of how drunkenness worked, especially whether the drink or the drinker was most responsible. This is the reason why Brennan's witnesses so often say that a person "seemed" to be drunk. The assimilation of the term *sang-froid* into nineteenth-century usage reflected the growing realization that the drinker himself controlled the consumption process. An equally important indication of this shift is the much greater use in the nineteenth century of the verb "to drink." Rather than saying, as they did in the eighteenth century, that the drink had only slightly affected them, workers now asserted that they had drunk only a little bit (*J'ai bu un peu*). By the 1880s, even a sedate elderly café habitué such as the 64-year-old day laborer "Father Henri" could attribute his uncharacteristic drunken comportment to the fact that an acquaintance had treated him to a liter of wine, explaining that he was not used to drinking so much. Singularly, he did not claim, as he might have had he lived in the eighteenth century, that the wine had "taken him."[132] Workers used this explicit construction, admitting their free-will participation in the act of drinking, in one-third of the cases after 1870.

During the nineteenth century, then, workers came to see the act of drinking as much more volitional. Witnesses in court often determined the degree of a person's inebriation by his or her ability to reason. A café owner in the suburb of Clichy described the state of a glassmaker who had murdered his mother: "He seemed delirious; I saw that he had drunk, but, in my opinion, he was not irrational." Shifts in personality were also noted, and workers often likened inebriated actions to those of an insane person (*fou*). A used furniture salesman, for instance, claimed he was almost insane (*presque fou*) when intoxicated. Not surprisingly, people more often associated drinking and insanity when the drinks consumed had been absinthe or other strong liquors. Many observers also described the actions of intoxicated individuals as bestial. A café owner described the decorated one as emitting "some yelps and shouts like a wild beast."[133]

The concept of the drunkard was thus not simply imposed by the elite on the working class. Rather, the term emerged from society's own growing experience with alcohol.

Drinking Behavior: From Frivolity to Pathology

The behavior of workers while intoxicated represents the most dramatic change in the drinking experience of proletarian Parisians. Between the eighteenth and nineteenth centuries, an unprecedented shift took place both in the manner in which the authorities in government and medicine viewed and regulated drunken behavior and in the way workers themselves acted. The act of drinking steadily lost its connotations of festivity, first among the authorities and eventually among the workers themselves.

This transformation occurred in tandem with a shift from collective weekly drinking binges to individual daily consumption. As drinking became individualized, it became increasingly connected to political dispute and social disorder. Inebriation ceased to be viewed as a group effect and came to be considered an increasingly serious activity that carried heavy political and moral symbolism. Once again, the Second Empire marked a turning point in this evolution.

During the early nineteenth century, drinking behavior and its regulation were still viewed largely within the traditional paradigm of collectivity, festivity, physicality, and irresponsibility. During the first half of the century, drunkenness was commonly noted on Sunday, Monday, or a holiday. It usually occurred in the context of large gatherings, often at the barrière cafés, when various rival groups assaulted each other. After intense in-group convivial drinking, with rounds, clinking of glasses, and passing the cup, the group would search for some physical activity to release their energy. Fights often erupted between competing journeymen's associations (*compagnonnages*), rival trades, neighborhoods, youth, ethnic, or provincial groups, or between soldiers and civilians. For example, a violent struggle broke out in December 1823 between soldiers and a group including both workers and bourgeois on the rue des Arcis. Sometimes these brawls involved hundreds of participants. A large brawl of this type happened on 19 April 1825 at the barrière near the boulevard Montparnasse and involved two hundred youths, including students and clerks.[134] Before 1850, the police were still largely the witnesses rather than the targets of this activity. The areas in which the workers unleashed these passions were also circumscribed: primarily the exterior barrières and boulevards, but also the rookeries and thieves' dens on the Ile de la Cité in the center of Paris.[135] Although often randomly and collectively brutal, the violence surrounding this type of periodic alcoholic excess did not produce the intimate and often personalized aggression that would become common as alcohol consumption became more steady, regular, and intense. In the first half of the century, there are few cases of the sort of alcoholic insanity and fury that became common after 1860.[136]

Because they associated drunken behavior with large groups and extraordinary circumstances, the Old Regime and early nineteenth-century governments did not think it necessary to enact a permanent or systematic set of regulations. Drunkenness was still more associated with festivity than with politics or disease. For this reason, royal authority, under the Old Regime as well as the Restoration and the July Monarchy, sanctioned and encouraged such celebrations as a means of gaining or increasing public approval. Traditionally, the king's entry into a town, his birthday, his marriage, or a military victory justified generous distribution of wine to the populace. Napoléon, the restored Bourbons, and then Louis Philippe all continued these practices.[137] For the first Bastille Day celebration in 1879, during the early years of the Third Republic, this tradition was revived for the poor, who received bread and wine.[138] But by 1900, the French government had put a stop to these handouts, for alcohol consumption had by then become associated more with a chronic problem of daily life than with the rhythm of public holidays.

Judicial practice under the Old Regime and the first half of the nineteenth century also viewed drunken behavior in a festive spirit. In practice, if not in theory, the French judiciary and police apparatus saw drunkenness as a circumstance that lessened the gravity of an infraction. The emphatic and innovative quality of the Napoleonic Court of Cassation pronouncements, on 19 November 1807 and 7 June 1810, that drunkenness could never be an excuse or mitigate a crime, merely underscored the disparity between the strict letter of the law and the lenient decisions of judges and juries, especially in Paris.[139] In court, judges sometimes explicitly admitted that drunkenness, in some circumstances, could be a mitigating circumstance.[140] Through the 1840s, the *Gazette des tribunaux* provides abundant examples that the excuse of drunkenness often worked in a defendant's favor.[141] For this reason the *Gazette* gave a humorous twist to the barrière brawls of Sunday and Monday. One author, describing a Monday incident on 3 February 1831 at "Papa" Tomangeau's establishment on the rue de l'Arbre Sec, felt that the scuffle among old soldiers was a worthy subject for "Walter Scott to make a comedy of at the cabaret." Certainly, both the judge and jury laughed at the testimony of a retiree who recounted how he had shaken the hand of one of his old comrades and then proposed that they go get a shot (*coup de boire*) and clink their glasses together (*trinquer*), for "I am an old one such as you." The court tolerantly acquitted the feisty old inebriate.[142]

Even cases of drunken disorder with political overtones following the July 1830 revolution put the courts in a festive and forgiving mood. During the fall and winter of 1830–31, a series of disturbances fomented by the partisans of the deposed Bourbons erupted around Paris. For example, on the evening of 18 October, agents of Charles X organized a demonstration on the rue des Gres. A courier who was already slightly drunk joined the demonstrators as they headed to the home of one of the leading government ministers, Dupin senior. By 11 P.M., when the crowd arrived at Dupin's house at 5 rue Coq Héron, the courier was completely drunk and shouted for Dupin's death. At his trial, the courier drew laughter when he stated that it was the wine talking, not himself. The fact that he was "as meek as a child" when he was arrested, and that many witnesses testified to his intoxicated state, secured his acquittal. The trial of a metal forger, arrested for his part in disturbances on 23 October, a week later, had a similar conclusion. This 43-year-old caused repeated bursts of hilarity in the courtroom as he recounted the night of continual drinking that resulted in his being "dead drunk" (*ivre mort*) and yelling "Down with Polignac!" and "Long Live Philip I." These cases represent just a few characteristic examples from the rich pages of the *Gazette des tribunaux*.[143]

The *Gazette* continued reporting in this humorous tone even through the 1848 revolution. In January 1848, we still find individuals successfully using the excuse of drunkenness to avoid conviction in public disorder cases. One such individual was the "intrepid" Martin Pécher, who, "when not happy tries to drown his cares in pots of wine, gets drunk, becomes a brawler and searches for the *sergeants de ville*." On this particular occasion, the police arrested him singing at the top of his lungs on the quai des Ormes. The court declared the song exempt of all sedition. The festive atmosphere of the February Revolution's first month reinforced the tolerance of Paris juries and judges toward drunken behavior. An alleged participant in one of the suburban disturbances of March, in this case the fires in Nanterre, provoked laughter and gained his freedom by noting: "I was drunk. They passed the bottle and I could not refuse." The courts viewed with similar humor and indulgence the "Bacchic refrains" that caused a disturbance in the political clubs, such as the one on the rue Enfer on 10 May 1848.[144]

Drunken behavior began to change radically during the Second Empire. During the two-decade imperium that brought an end to the barrières and a doubling in the drinking of alcohol, drunkenness was increasingly manifested by individuals rather than by groups. Gérard Jacquemet has found that in Belleville after 1860, the decade in which the district was incorporated into Paris and ceased to be one of the main centers of barrière sociability, drunkenness no longer ended in "general brawls" but instead in "simple verbal assaults."[145] This transformation was most dramatically registered in the shifting composition of the population incarcerated for insanity during the 1860s. In their study spanning over a century (1801–1912) of public assistance and hospital records, both Dr. M. Magnan and Dr. A. Fillassier discovered that until 1863, women predominated; then, in an ever-increasing proportion, men outnumbered women. The researchers traced the cause of this change to the ravages of alcoholism, especially that caused by the drinking of absinthe and other strong spirits. Their findings correlate almost precisely with the jump in spirit and wine consumption during the 1850s and 1860s.[146] Moreover, the Magnan and Fillassier study is corroborated by a late 1860s inquiry by the British embassy in Paris that also emphasized the excessive drinking of working-class males.[147]

These indications of an intimate connection in the changes between drinking and behavior find further support in Paris newspaper and literary accounts of drunkenness during the Second Empire. These accounts are more serious and provide greater detail than those before 1850 on how the drunken behavior of individuals resulted in accidents or crimes. They focus largely on individual acts of violence and deviance, rather than on the large, collective disturbances and brawls emphasized earlier. For example, the *Gazette des tribunaux* contains many more references in the 1860s to drunken coachmen getting into fights or causing accidents than in the previous decades.[148] The 1860s also saw the emergence of the alcoholic type in literature.[149] The detective novels of Emile Gaboriau introduce some of the first characters whose excessive drinking takes on the characteristics of alcoholism.[150]

Increasingly, during the 1860s, the police became one of the primary targets of drunken rage. Here we confront one of the most interesting and ironic facts of Parisian drunken comportment: as it became more individual, it also became more political. This new connection between drunkenness and politics emerged from the conjuncture of severe political repression and a dramatic increase in alcohol consumption during the 1850s.[151] Deprived of legal and formal means of organization, Parisian workers relied heavily on cafés for their clandestine meetings (see Chapter 8), and showed a growing tendency to use drunkenness as an excuse to hide the political nature of their actions. During this decade, especially in the turbulent final years of the empire when political dissent and labor organizing regained much of their previous momentum, an unprecedented number of workers insulted the police. But charged in court with insulting public authority, the defendants claimed that drunkenness, rather than politics, explained their actions.

The growing number of drunk-and-disorderly cases was not simply an effect of increased working-class political awareness, however, but also of a new official awareness that drunkenness and revolution were often connected. The humorous Balzacian image of barrière drinking as a diversion of and drain on working-class energies gave way to the notion that inspired the 21 December 1851 decree: drunken disorder was seen as the prelude to revolution. The March 1851 proposal in the National Assembly that motivated the decree provides one of the clearest statements of this idea: "Has not experience shown that when a man habitually frequents the cafés, when he is given to the vice of drunkenness, he moves toward his ruin, and that, on this fatal slope, he become a man who is a danger to society? Be assured that when a man becomes debauched and ruins himself, he becomes a demagogue and an anarchist.[152] Following Louis-Napoléon's coup d'état, the new imperial government took a small but significant step to ensure that drunkenness could no longer be used so easily as an excuse for disorderly behavior: it increased the jurisdiction of the correctional tribunal.[153] Because this court had no juries, the empire thus made sure that drunkenness cases could no longer be greeted with humor and sympathy. Despite this change in judicial venue, the Paris populace continued to use drunkenness as an excuse in the vain hope that it would still be a mitigating circumstance.

Following the empire's fall, the Paris Commune fused the festive and contestatory cultures of the café (see Chapter 8). In his study of the Commune as festival, Henri Lefebvre catches much of this flavor, but he provides no analysis of the roles of either café life or drinking. Nevertheless, he unwittingly inverts and gives positive interpretation to old diatribes against the Commune as an "alcoholic orgy." As Susanna Barrows has shown, the Commune gave a vital impetus to the development of the French temperance movement and the emergence of the disease concept of alcoholism in French medical and legal practice. What has not been explored is the social history underlying the connection between the repression of drunkenness following the Commune and the effects of that repression on popular politics.

The Commune left an indelible impression on Parisian drunken comportment for a generation. For almost two decades, the insults directed at the police provide a vivid chronicle of this connection. Naturally, the feeling was most intense in the months and years immediately following the Commune's repression. In August 1871, a homeless day laborer arrested for attempted theft told the police: "Our turn will come again, and this time we will not be drunk."[154] The number of workers insulting the police jumped dramatically. From an average of 800 in the 1860s, the yearly number of court cases leapt to an average of 2,500 during the 1870s, 3,200 in the 1880s, and a peak average of 3,500 during the years 1890–94. In most years between 1870 and 1914, the Department of the Seine accounted for over one-quarter of the entire number of insults to public authority reported. This type of repression was virtually unique to Paris.

Drunkenness usually provided the excuse for these attacks on the police or soldiers. In July 1872, the *Gazette des tribunaux* provided a typical example of the thousands of cases heard before the correctional tribunal. A locksmith had directly and explicitly referred to the Commune and its repression when he called a policeman a "Versaillais" and other similar epithets. The *Gazette* noted that "as happens in all such cases, the accused excused himself due to his drunken state. 'One can suppose,' the judge observed, 'that your drunkard's ideas are the same when you are sober, because an examination of your dossier shows that you are suspected of being part of the armed battalions of the Commune.'"[155] In another insult case, this one involving a wallpaper maker, Léon Galmiche, one of the two arresting officers testified, "The accused appeared not to be truly drunk." The other noted, "He pretended to be drunk [*en curibotte*] more than he really was," and that "the accused was drunk but not to the point that he did not know what he was saying or doing."[156] The tone of the *Gazette des tribunaux* and its descriptions of the Paris courtroom atmosphere is completely different from that of the 1830s and 1840s. No one is laughing anymore.

The *Gazette*'s hopes that the government would get tough with public drunkenness seemed well placed when the law repressing public drunkenness was enacted in March 1873. Inspired by French doctors, the new theory of alcoholism, and the specter of the Commune, this law premised that drunkenness was the first step on the road to alcoholism.[157] But the framers of the law restricted its scope to include only manifest public drunkenness. Drunkenness in the private home or club, the preserve of the middle classes, was exempt, a clear example of class bias. The law also ignored the fact that drunkenness in France had traditionally not included the blatant and overt signs of loss of physical inhibition and control typical of drunkenness in Anglo-Saxon and northern European countries.[158] Even into the early twentieth century, both French and Anglo-American observers asserted that Parisians in general and the working class in particular seldom showed outward physical signs of drunkenness.[159] Thus the law was not well attuned to the particularities of French drunken comportment.

Nevertheless, when the measure became law in March 1873, the *Gazette* was exultant. "The new law on public drunkenness is in full effect, and there are numerous charges brought each day in the police courts," the paper reported at the end of April, two months after the enactment of the law.[160] Initially, certainly, the hopes of the *Gazette* were well placed. The number of arrests in Paris for simple public drunkenness climbed steadily, from 11,825 in 1873 to 17,632 in 1877. Moreover, in over half of the cases of insulting the police, the police also charged the defendant with public drunkenness. Nevertheless, the Paris police and courts were nowhere near as assiduous as their counterparts in Rouen, prosecuting only 37 cases per 1,000 inhabitants to the latter's 60 cases per 1,000.[161] Arrests remained high for another two years—14,350 in 1878 and 10,840 in 1879—but then, with the national government safely and successfully returned to Paris, the numbers fell below 10,000 in 1880 and then declined steadily for the rest of the century. Between 1880 and 1889, the numbers fell from 7,370 to 3,927.

The police, in short, lost interest in strictly enforcing the law. Although the number of arrests for unaggravated cases of public drunkenness declined sharply after the late 1870s, the police continued to apply the law in more serious cases of theft and assault and battery, especially in instances of physical and verbal attacks on themselves. During the 1870s through the 1890s, roughly half of the charges of insulting the police still included the additional charge of public drunkenness. The Paris police thus used this law less to repress working-class drinking—as the legislators had hoped—than as a means of punishing workers for disobedience and disrespect. This selective enforcement of the law focused on drink as a form of dispute but not as a cause of social pathology. The case histories of many murderers prosecuted in the assize courts record protracted heavy drinking and the abuse of family, friends, neighbors, and workmates. In many cases, despite their drunken rampages, these individuals had never been arrested for public drunkenness. Only when their chronic drinking led them to commit murder did they appear in court. In this way, the legislators' grand schemes for social amelioration were undermined by the police's more prosaic concern for public order.[162]

Despite its evident failure to stop the spread of drunkenness and alcoholism, the 1873 law did succeed in changing the climate of opinion about drinking and drunkenness inside Paris courtrooms. By the 1870s, drinking was no longer viewed as frivolous and seldom aroused laughter. Working-class defendants increasingly mentioned drink, not to make light of their actions, but to claim that its effect had been so powerful that it had made them forget all they had said and done. In 57 percent of the court cases examined between 1870 and 1900, the defendants made this claim. Workers used this ruse not only in cases of the disputing police authority but also in cases of assault and battery, sexual seduction, and swindling. At a pretrial deposition, Jean-Marie de Lisle, a clerk arrested for attacking his former wife, said repeatedly, "I never get drunk and I never drink wine." All the other witnesses concurred that he was not drunk. At the trial, however, he revised his stance: "I recognize that I hit my wife, but I was overexcited by anger and a little bit by drink." An affluent entrepreneur in public works tried to mitigate the charge of attempted corruption of minors by blaming absinthe: "I drank some absinthe and lost my head." The two young girls in the case undermined this defense by swearing that at the restaurant they had gone to, he had drunk only wine.[163]

These cases reveal the close interconnection between the physical effect of drink and its symbolic meaning. Clearly absinthe connoted irrational, uncontrollable behavior, and some defendants used this association to absolve themselves. Workers quickly seized upon the concept of alcoholism as another defense. In 1872, the *Gazette des tribunaux* reported a case where Pierre Reines, a coachman accused of murder, attempted to use the medical report stating he was an alcoholic to plead for a light sentence. In this particular case, the tactic backfired, inasmuch as the judge held that such a medical opinion made the individual more rather than less responsible for his crime.[164] By the 1870s, only 14 percent of defendants used the traditional excuse that they had been "taken" or "pushed" by wine or drink, since this no longer seemed sufficiently to stress the power of alcohol. Only a small percentage, 7 percent, flatly denied that they had been drunk. As court officials came to take drunkenness more seriously, so also did defendants. Drink was no longer primarily seen as a stimulant that produced energy and fun, but as a depressant that wiped out memories and caused unpremeditated acts.

After 1900, defendants almost completely abandoned drink as a legal excuse. In this move, workers followed the lead of working-class militants and leftist journalists, who often claimed that the police created the charge of drunkenness to discredit them: "I was not drunk. All of that is the invention of the secretary of the police commissioner," charged Isidore Finance in 1878. A journalist for the *Cri du peuple* made the same accusation in the mid 1880s.[165] A blanket denial of drunkenness became more common during the 1890s and in the first decade of the twentieth century.

M. R., a worker in a print shop, entered a café at the intersection of rue Dussoubs and rue Grenèta in Bagnolet and unleashed a cascade of curses at some workers who had refused to join a strike. In his defense, he said simply that he had been angry and had had no bad intentions.[166] This pattern of courtroom testimony became predominant during the great strike wave between 1909 and 1911. Ditchdiggers and roadworkers in suburban Neuilly used it, as did striking joiners during their 1910 strike.[167] Ironically, in these same years in which working-class militants dropped the excuse of public drunkenness, the Paris police once again rigorously enforced the 1873 law. Between 1908 and 1912, for the first time since the late 1870s, the police made more than ten thousand arrests. By World War I, the link between alcohol consumption and politics, but not that between the café and politics, had weakened. The shift of emphasis in the courtroom testimony of Paris workers after 1900 indicates that the warnings of the temperance movement about drink had begun to influence the working-class mentality.

Paris provides rich confirmation of Didier Nourrisson's idea that the nineteenth-century French population gained "the right to drink."[168] The unprecedented change in drinking, in its symbology, and in the behavior it inspired shows that the people of Paris had indeed annexed a commodity and behavior that had once been restricted to the elite. Although increased production and distilling innovations made alcoholic drinks a mass consumer item, this process did not immediately displace the earlier notion that drink had certain quasi-mystical powers. During the middle decades of the century, while the festive and collective aspects of alcohol consumption were still strong and political repression at its most intense, drink became politicized. The Commune marked the apogee of this convivial disputation and spawned a ritual behavior that linked the café and the courtroom. This comportment remained prevalent well into the 1890s. By 1900, however, growing working-class awareness of the effects of drunkenness, along with increasing legal and medical intervention, greatly reduced the traditional festive and political associations surrounding drinking habits. Only gradually did drink and its effects come to be viewed in instrumental and medical terms. At no point between 1789 and 1914 were physiological effects divorced from cultural perceptions. Nevertheless, by 1900, workers had become aware of the social and economic costs of alcoholism. At least in the courtroom, linkages of drink with frivolous behavior gave way to the recognition of the pathological problems of drunkenness.

No understanding of the drinking experience or of its relation to café-going can be complete without exploring the commercial and social functions of the café owner. These proprietors sold almost 80 percent of all drink consumed in Paris, the vast majority of it, naturally, to the working class.[169] We shall now step up to the counter.

CHAPTER FIVE

Publicans

*From Shopkeepers
to Social
Entrepreneurs*

J
acques Rancière has argued that small merchants were central to
working-class life because, like poets and political activists, they
"talked" with people as they engaged in cash exchanges in
their neighborhoods. This "talk" helped define working-class
community for itself.[1] But neither he nor other historians have yet explored
how café owners—perhaps the preeminent shopkeepers to talk to the
workers—functioned in this capacity. The café owner was not merely another small shopkeeper: customers entering a café went there not simply
to buy a product but also to experience an amiable and sociable ambience.
If the atmosphere was not to their liking, they might not return. As we have
seen, the most perceptive nineteenth-century observers looked upon the
café owner as the workers' priest or social confessor and his establishment
as the church of the working-class. However, none of these commentators
amplified upon this analogy or explored its historical roots, evolution, or
social impact.

Café owners faced a challenge not confronted by other small retailers, because they had simultaneously to be attentive to three strands of social and economic life. First, they had to ensure their own solvency and
prosperity; second, they had to be adept at human relations, because they
not only sold a product (food and drink) but also an experience (sociable
and leisurely intercourse); and third, because their establishments were
the primary meeting places of Paris, they had to regulate the behavior of
their customers in concert or in conflict with the police. In short, the café

owner had to balance the often-conflicting claims of profitability, sociability, and legality.

Although the owner had a vital influence on the mood of a working-class café, the workers had an equally crucial influence on an owner's livelihood. The importance of this influence was magnified by the fact that as competition within the trade increased dramatically over the century, the chances of individual success declined. Paradoxically, we find that as the social influence of the café owner increased, his or her financial position deteriorated.

The Evolution of the Trade

By proclaiming freedom of commerce and abolishing the Old Regime's guild structure and commodity taxes, the French Revolution dramatically altered the retail sale of food and drink. The old distinction between cafés and wine shops vanished at a stroke, because any drinking establishment could now sell whatever drink or food it chose. At the same time, the reading of newspapers, hitherto largely restricted to the elegant upper-class cafés of the fashionable parts of the city, became a common practice in working-class taverns, along with the rise of papers such as Hébert's *Le Père Duchesne* catering to the taste of the populace. As a result, the old distinction between a wine shop and a café ceased to have hard-and-fast legal or commercial meaning.

Although the distinction between a café and a wine shop no longer had any legal basis, governmental accounting and economic competition ensured that a clear line between substantial and modest drinking establishments persisted and, especially after 1850, became accentuated. Bankruptcy reports, the best source on the evolution of café commerce, continued to use the traditional eighteenth-century terms "lemonade seller" (*limonadier*) and "wine merchant" (*marchand de vin*). Across the nineteenth century in the bankruptcy records, the assets and debts of the *limonadier* were consistently, on average, higher than those of wine merchants or of wine merchants also selling food (known as *marchands de vin–traiteurs*). As the century wore on, the assets and debts of the shopkeepers who sold to a proletarian clientele fell behind those of the restaurateurs and limonadiers.

Table 5.1 shows that (1) the average net worth of all varieties of shopkeepers in the retail drink and food trade declined across the century, and

Table 5.1

AVERAGE ASSETS AND DEBTS IN PARIS DRINK AND FOOD TRADE BANKRUPTCY
REPORTS, 1814–1912 *(francs)*

	Restaurateurs		Limonadiers		Marchands de vin		Marchands de vin–traiteurs*	
	Assets	Debts	Assets	Debts	Assets	Debts	Assets	Debts
1814–30	54,197	54,326	36,589	49,134	28,440	48,867	26,819	41,731
1832–46	39,703	45,909	35,708	36,765	22,643	27,857	20,772	25,182
1854–68	29,862	44,388	31,017	35,768	14,429	21,061	14,124	18,647
1876–95	23,628	58,072	59,017	72,220	17,114	30,344	8,261	25,125
1900–1912	24,682	55,559	26,386	77,739	7,009	23,123	3,303	13,234

Sources: As for table 3.1.

Note: The periods reflect political regimes of nineteenth-century France as well as the two primary economic periods of the Third Republic before World War I. Although the periods are not commensurate, they permit extrapolation of the overall trend.

*Wine merchants who also sold food.

(2) there was a growing disparity in the net worth of restaurateurs and limonadiers as opposed to wine merchants. After the Revolution, the retail drink and food trade catering to workers started off on a more or less equal footing with that of the restaurateurs and large café owners catering to the upper classes, but after the Restoration, the workers' establishments fell farther and farther behind. All tradesmen selling drink and food experienced a decline in their average worth, but the drop was much sharper for both classes of wine merchants than for restaurateurs and limonadiers. The one saving grace for all wine merchants was that on average their debts declined sharply, too, which was not the case for their more substantial competitors.

The first half of the nineteenth century has been called the golden age of the small shopkeeper, because Parisians reputedly seldom left their neighborhoods and thus bought what they needed within an extremely small radius of their homes.[2] Certainly, the assets of the drink and food retailers—higher in all four categories during the first half of the century—bear out this stereotype. Indeed, some café owners were able to amass fortunes.

The surest means to prosperity for a café owner was also to own the land upon which the shop stood, which was most often the case in what were then the Paris suburbs. An outstanding example of one who achieved this social ascent was "Papa" Dénoyez, who had inherited both the property and the popularity of the famous eighteenth-century taverner Ramponeau at 4 rue Ménilmontant, in then suburban Belleville. His fame and prosperity helped him to become a commander of the National Guard and in some sense the founder of Belleville. At his death in 1876, Dénoyez was worth 1,546,833 francs, of which land represented 913,000.[3] Another indication of the worth of suburban Belleville real estate is the price of 272,000 francs that the city's administration paid in 1845 for a tavern to make into a new town hall.[4] At the northern and southern ends of Paris, we see similar trends. At the north central barrière, called Rochechouart, "Papa" Nicolet in 1832 opened an imitation of Dénoyez's establishment called the Petit Ramponeau. Twenty years later, Nicolet retired as a millionaire. The new owners, the Lallemand couple, likewise made a fortune. At the southwestern barrière du Maine, one cafe owner was named Desnoyer, "as popular a name as Napoleon."[5] For retailers who started at a higher social level and were lucky enough to own or run one of the smart boulevard cafés, success was virtually assured. Some of these establishments were gold mines. The famous café Tortoni, for example, made a fortune for everyone who owned it right up to the 1880s.[6] Few working-class café owners could hope to run, much less own, one of the elegant upper-class cafés in central Paris, or even one of the suburban establishments as Paris outgrew its old limits and property values increased.

Yet even in this seeming "golden age," the seeds of later decline were already germinating. We can see this in the fact that between the Restoration and the Second Empire, café owners sustained a high rate of bankruptcies: from 13 to virtually 30 percent of the commercial failures each year. The one mitigating factor in the first half of the century was the fact that there were seldom more than 4,500 establishments in the Paris region at any given time. Thus a relatively small number of shops competed for the drink and food trade. This situation changed dramatically after 1850.

The sources of growing competition after 1850 can be found in the innovation of the modern serving counter, which first appeared in 1821. Prior to the Restoration, the counter had been used only as a surface where wine was poured for the customers sitting at tables; it had not been a center of sociability. The new utilization of the counter during the 1820s provided the café owner with a spatial and commercial prop by which to enter and regulate the social world of his or her shop. The modern counter, later dubbed the *zinc* after its constituent material, was developed by the joiner Emile Verrière. His was the inspiration to incorporate the functions of serving drinks and washing glasses all in one space, allowing the owner simultaneously to serve and socialize with shop customers. Verrière's idea was quickly adopted and spread rapidly throughout Paris.[7] An owner could be both economically more efficient, accomplishing more tasks in the same amount of time, and socially more proficient, having more opportunities to get to know the customers.

The counter was adopted by virtually all shops selling food and drink. Grocers (*épiciers*) augmented their trade by selling drink by the bottle and by the glass over the counter.[8] By 1868, the *Gazette des tribunaux* was able to announce that it was every grocer's dream to have a counter.[9] In his novel *Caught in the Net*, Emile Gaboriau indicates that a successful grocer's reputation depended in part on the wine sold.[10] In another novel, the Goncourts' *Germinie Lacerteux*, the heroine's purchase of brandy at a grocer's starts her descent into alcoholism.[11] Alcohol and sociability were available in so many grocer's shops that around 1900 the Bonneff brothers hesitated to restrict the number of cafés, arguing that customers would simply go to a grocer's.[12] Not only grocers but also dairies (*crémeries*), restaurants, and hotels frequently sold alcoholic drinks retail and were often regarded as cafés by their customers (as well as by social critics). In the 1880s, worried observers fretted over the fact that there were 70,000 counters over which alcoholic drinks were being sold in Paris. "One half of the city poisons the other half," Léon Say exclaimed.[13]

The counter emerged and flourished in an age when thousands, perhaps millions, of ordinary French people dreamed of opening their own cafés. The great nineteenth-century historian and man of the people Jules Michelet captured this aspiration in his empathic ethnography *The People* (1846): "Since he used to live in the bistro, he opens a bistro. He opens not far from his old haunts. . . . He flatters himself with the sweet idea that he will ruin his neighbor. In fact he has customers immediately—all those who owe the other and will not pay." Inevitably, Michelet concludes, these "customers" do not pay their debts at the new shop. The aspiring proprietor thus loses money and "what was worth even more— the habit of working."[14] Another product of the 1840s, the *Nouveau tableau de Paris*, quipped that the aspiring café owner needed neither education nor an apprenticeship, but had only to rent a shop, buy coffee, sugar, and wine on credit for 500 francs and then strike a haughty pose behind a counter and wait for customers. Like Michelet, the author noted that it usually took only a few months for the earnest entrepreneur to go bankrupt.[15] The caricaturist and writer Bertall attributed the allure of café proprietorship to the continuation of an aristocratic streak in the French temperament, which preferred inaction to work.[16] Late-nineteenth-century temperance advocates, wishing to strip all traces of romanticism from the café, similarly saw it as a result of laziness, which lured a worker from the workshop and made him "incessantly borrow money because he cannot put his life in order."[17]

Reviewing bankruptcy dossiers for the department of the Seine at the start and the end of the century respectively, Louis Chevalier and Gérard Jacquemet chart the commercial history of the average café owner. Unlike most other tradesmen, café owners came from a few specific provinces and had remarkably similar career trajectories.[18] During the first half of the century, immigrants came predominantly from the regions of Burgundy, Yonne, Côte-d'Or, and Saône-et-Loire, and from the departments of the Massif Central: Cantal, Creuse, and Aveyron, with an important minority from the Languedoc departments. In the second half of the century, these southern areas, especially the Auvergene, were even more dominant. The future café owners were primarily young peasants between the ages of twenty and twenty-five. Usually lacking education or artisanal skills, they were employed in Paris in a diverse number of unskilled occupations that required no apprenticeship: as coachmen, café waiters, floor polishers, water or charcoal carriers, and, in some cases, distillery clerks. Often they worked for a relative or fellow provincial, sometimes in a café. During the first half of the century, there were few similar opportunities for young women, although the situation improved in later decades.[19]

Between five and twelve years after their arrival, they opened shops of their own, investing a sum of money, usually between 500 and 1,000 francs, borrowed from relatives or friends, who might be or might know of a sympathetic wine distributor (*fournisseur*). The operation of a café was relatively inexpensive in comparison with the building trades, for example, and the demand for drink was stable.[20] The first shop was usually in the outer Parisian districts or in the suburbs, where leases were cheap and operating expenses low. The café owner typically moved several times before establishing a shop in a prime location such as the center of Paris on the main boulevards.[21] Another successful ploy was the addition of a restaurant or hotel. The father of the Parisian working-class radical Jean Allemane provides a typical example of a café owner's life. In the late 1840s, the elder Allemane immigrated from the department of Haute-

Garonne in the southwest and, following in the footsteps of many of his fellow provincials, settled in the Latin Quarter. Weathering the troubles of a city in revolution, 1848–49, he opened a café, and by the end of 1850, he was able to add the occupation of lodging-house keeper to his already prospering drink trade at 149 rue Saint-Victor.[22]

As already noted, the Second Empire brought a dramatic increase in the number of cafés.[23] The number of shops jumped fivefold—from 4,500 in the late 1840s to over 22,000 in 1870.[24] This unprecedented increase was part and parcel of a more general, but less dramatic, expansion in the ranks of the small shopkeepers. Indeed, the number of business licenses (*patentes*) increased substantially between 1852 and 1869, from 78,000 to 109,000. The food trade, of which cafés were an integral part, boomed during this era: from 3,673 establishments and receipts of 262 million francs in 1847, the number shot to 29,069 establishments and 1 billion 87 million in receipts by 1860.[25] Cafés flourished on the broad boulevards of the carefully planned bourgeois center, in the murky narrow alleys and passageways of the neglected side streets, and in the uncoordinated peripheral areas inhabited by the working class.

During the reign of Napoléon III, there was not only a spectacular increase in number of cafés but also a diversification in styles. Many of the hastily constructed shacks set up for commercial use on the periphery of Paris added a wine shop. On the side streets of the boulevards, where little renovation took place, the traditional working-class café experienced few changes. This was especially true around the old faubourgs Saint-Denis, Saint-Martin, and the place Maubert. These shops were worth between five and six thousand francs. On Haussmann's gleaming new grands boulevards, especially near the Opéra, a new type of café emerged—lavishly ornamented, opulently furnished, and brightly lighted. The aim, in the words of Louis Hautecoeur, was to transform "the perfumer's shop into a temple of the Graces and a wine shop into a sanctuary of Bacchus."[26] The outside terraces of these cafés became so popular that they continually expanded onto the sidewalk. The glamorous free-standing Grand café on the boulevard Saint-Martin, with a spectacular entrance designed by the Opéra's architect Charles Garnier, was the most fashionable. With thirty billiard tables and more than a hundred waiters, this glittering establishment spawned many imitators, such as the Grand café du XIX siècle.[27] Increasingly, other upper-class cafés became transformed into elegant and expensive restaurants to seduce the most chic clientele.[28] Georges Montorgeuil's comment on the café owners of 1895 can be applied equally well to those of the Second Empire: "100,000 francs to decorate a door is nothing to them; they will spend a million to make their customers feel welcome."[29]

Even some working-class cafés acquired a measure of "elegance."[30] In *Germinie Lacerteux*, the Goncourts describe one of these establishments, the dance hall "Boule Noir": "The room had the modern character of the pleasure resorts of the people. It glittered with false riches and poor luxury . . . the sort of paintings and tables which one sees in wine ships. . . gilded gas-apparatus and glasses for drinking a quart of brandy, velvet and wooden benches, the wretchedness and rusticity of a country inn amid the embellishments of a palace of cardboard . . . crimson velvet valances . . . on the walls in large white panels, pastorals by Boucher surrounded by painted frames, alternated with Proud'hon's 'Seasons' [a painting]."[31]

Despite these glossy flourishes, success was less easily achieved by the end of Haussmann's era (1870). The wealth of many café owners during the first half of the century, as we have seen, depended on their owning not only the shop but also the land upon which it sat. By 1870, small shopkeepers had virtually ceased to be landlords in central Paris and owned less and less land even on its periphery.[32] Café owners during the second half of the century had to rely almost exclusively upon the success of their trade. As table 5.1 shows, the average worth not only of wine merchants but of restaurateurs and limonadiers as well fell dramatically after 1850, in most cases to less than half the peak values.

Success would become even more difficult to achieve with the advent of the Third Republic. With freedom of trade restored in 1880, the number of Parisian cafés began a new ascent. In the summer of 1880, just before the annulment of the harsh 29 December 1851 decree, there were 20,886 cafés in Paris. By 1884, virtually as many declarations of new café openings—18,500—had been sent to the prefect of police. At the 1884 parliamentary inquiry into the economic crisis in Paris, the prefect of police, Jean Camescasse, admitted that he did not know how many of these shops remained in existence, because the law did not require café owners to report closures.[33] The standard directory of Paris commerce, the Didot-Bottin, nevertheless confirms that the number of wine shops in business may well have doubled by 1884: the fifteen pages devoted to cafés in the 1878 edition had expanded to fifty by 1884. Municipal council debates and journalistic testimony from the 1880s indicate that at various times the number of cafés may have been as high as 42,000.[34]

These new cafés were heavily concentrated in working-class districts and the burgeoning proletarian suburbs. Contemporaries noted that in proletarian quarters, one did not have to take more than ten or twenty steps to find a café, and some blocks boasted one in every building.[35] In the suburbs, Ivry, for example, cafés mushroomed from 18 in 1875 to 246 in 1914.[36] Overall, the number of cafés in the suburbs of the department of the Seine skyrocketed from a mere 248 in 1870 to 5,049 in 1910.[37]

The period 1880–1914 set new records not only for the increase in openings but also for the unprecedented number of failures. Between 1881 and 1912, an astonishing 145,972 establishments opened. Tens of thousands of ambitious and affable people tried to tap the vast Parisian demand for sociability. Not surprisingly, bankruptcy figures reveal that the occupations of restaurant and café owner continued to have one of the highest rates of business failure in Paris.[38] In fact, in 1895, one out of every three bankrupt businesses in Paris was a café—in popular slang, a "pickled pothouse."[39] Newspapers advertised about 130 café businesses for sale per week. The typical ad listed a daily income of 70 francs and an asking price of 3,500 francs.[40] During the late 1890s, the department of the Nord had the dubious distinction of having the largest number of annual café bankruptcies: 48,441. The much more populous Seine ranked slightly behind, with 42,529.[41]

The massive migration into the café trade arose partly, of course, from the laborer's traditional dream of becoming a small merchant, but also partly out of desperation arising from a different quarter. The Paris economy underwent a drastic restructuring during a long, worldwide depression from the 1870s through the early 1890s. In this era, the traditional artisanal trades of Paris, especially the luxury goods trades, were decimated by foreign and provincial competition. As a result, unemployed artisans tried their hands in the food and drink trade.[42] In many families, wives installed themselves behind the counter while husbands searched for other jobs. The working people of Paris persisted in thinking that the café trade, despite its rate of failure, was easier than any other.[43]

By 1914, the café trade, although providing employment for tens of thousands more people than it had in 1814, was more precarious. The trade had a larger number of participants but a lower rate of economic success. This shift is epitomized in the supplanting of the sprawling and spacious suburban taverns at the barrières by the densely packed network of small shops in these new working-class slums. As a result, the value of the average small shop was much more modest than in the first half of the century.

The aggregate figures of assets and liabilities shown in table 5.1 illustrate only part of the story of struggle that was the café owner's average lot. In some cases, sudden tragedy or unexpected events might interrupt what had seemed a steady social ascent.[44] The "dead season" in the textile and luxury trades precipitated some bankruptcies. In other cases, the aftershocks of political events triggered business failures. The departure of the French Chamber of Deputies to Versailles after the proclamation of the Commune spelled the ruin of one café owner, whose clientele had consisted almost entirely of government employees and servants. For most, however, the great question seems to have been not so much a matter of success or failure but simply the daily struggle to make ends meet. Café owners often carried on for years, in some cases decades, registering neither losses nor profits and often averaging receipts of 50 francs per day.[45]

The economic instability of the era, combined with the job requirements of continuous sociability, often led owners themselves to become drunkards or alcoholics. The occupations of café owner and hotel keeper were always among those most commonly cited as at risk of alcoholism.[46] In 1895, a temperance journal published a plausible daily drinking profile of an alcoholic wine merchant: 7 A.M., a coffee with brandy; 9 A.M., three glasses of wine; 10 A.M. to 1 P.M., from two to five apéritifs; 1 P.M., lunch with a liter of wine and a coffee with rum; 2 P.M. to 5 P.M., numerous glasses of wine with clients; at the hour of apéritifs, between two and four of those; another liter of wine with dinner at 8 P.M.; and finally, several alcoholic drinks during the evening.[47]

Often an owner's excessive drinking would destroy his family or ruin his business. This happened in the case of Sulpice and his son Jules Dubrac and their establishment at 330 rue Lecourbe in the Javel district. After the death of the wife, father and son waged a battle of biblical proportions over the inheritance of this classic working-class café with its residential quarters just above the shop. While drunk, Jules Dubrac called his father a scoundrel (*canaille*), to which Sulpice rejoined that his son was a Judas. Admitting that he drank "a little," Sulpice explained, "It's the job that makes me do so, but I always keep my sobriety [*sang-froid*]." The one thing on which they agreed was the old saw, "In our job, one is forced to drink."[48]

Social mobility was, in short, only a dream for most café owners who remained in working-class districts.[49] Even though the owner and his clientele stood on opposite sides of the counter, they were destined to social equality by their poor economic prospects and shared drinking habits.

Success, even when achieved, was seldom immediate or dramatic; wealth was for the lucky and enterprising few. The successful owner whose café catered almost exclusively to workers was typified by Louis Petit, whose establishment at 35 rue de la Charbonnière in Paris generally took in more than a hundred francs a day. After twelve years at this location, Petit's fortune totaled at least 30,000 francs, and before his death he talked of selling his business and returning to his native department.[50] The brothers Coudon, in contrast, illustrate the successful operation of a well-situated boulevard café frequented by the influential and the powerful. Natives of the Aisne department, the brothers bought the café Frontin, located on the boulevard Poissonnière, in 1869, paying an annual rent of 1,600 francs. During the 1870s, their café hosted many of the most powerful radicals around Léon Gambetta, including Eugène Spuller. They were able to sell their café in 1877 at a profit of 250,000 francs, a sum that allowed them to retire and return to their native province. Such café fortunes as were realized in the 1880–1900 era tended to be made in areas such as Montmartre, where an active night life provided much opportunity. In some cases, an investment of 25,000 francs to transform a bar into a nightclub, as happened on rue Pigalle, for example, could yield receipts of 150,000 francs in the first year, 180,000 francs in the second, and 260,000 francs in the third.[51] No wonder Montmartre became a Mecca for innovations in café style during the Belle Epoque![52]

Auvergnat immigrants made the most of this difficult trade. They had been an important factor in the café and wine businesses before 1880, but after that date they achieved a true "conquest" of the trade. Improvements in diet, health care, and schooling in the Auvergne made the new immigrants to Paris from the region between 1880 and 1930 healthier, stronger, more literate, and more sophisticated. They could thus assimilate faster into urban society than did their predecessors. Moreover, they could also rely on the already well-established Auvergnat community in Paris.[53] The rise of indoor plumbing caused a decline in the traditional Auvergnat trade of water carrier, making the café business an even more attractive option. Auvergnats often became cab drivers as a stepping-stone to the café business, or first opened a small business selling coal and then added drinks.[54] Auvergnat dominance was first apparent in the suburbs and on the periphery of Paris, where Auvergnat café owners often served their fellow provincials on animated small streets. Slowly over the course of the 1880s and 1890s, some Auvergnats were able to move from their modest wine and charcoal shops into cafés selling a wide diversity of drinks. By

1900, they had taken over most of the substantial Parisian cafés and were now likely to run extremely lucrative café-tobacco shops as well. The only cafés in Paris not operated by Auvergnats were small and medium-sized establishments run by Bretons and native-born non-Auvergnat Parisians. By the Great War, approximately 80 percent of the café owners of the greater Paris region had originated in the Auvergne.[55]

At no time, however, did the growing bankruptcy rate and Auvergnat dominance result in monopolization. Unlike those of England or America, for example, French wholesale wine merchants, distilleries, and breweries never developed a significant network of tied houses. Running a café remained preeminently a family (with the Auvergnats, a provincial) affair. Certainly café owners were beholden to the wine wholesalers, but these brokers never went into the business, as brewers and distillers did in the Anglo-American world, of owning the shops and selecting the people to manage them.[56] Paris café owners tried, but largely failed, to develop a cooperative system of wine purchasing. By 1900, La Parisienne, a cooperative association of café and restaurant owners in Paris and its suburbs, made wholesale purchases of coal, milk, and pâtés, but wine, the most important product, was not included. Three complications frustrated wholesale purchase: storage costs, too great a variety of types and tastes, and the reluctance of wholesalers to surrender control over the wine market. From its founding in the mid 1870s to 1914, La Parisienne faithfully reflected the small shopkeepers' ethos of independence.[57]

Unlike that in the provinces, the environment of post-1850s Paris was not conducive to keeping a shop in one family over several generations. Although the café may have been a fixture in a rapidly changing urban scene, this stability rested more upon the role of the owner than upon the individual. Paradoxically, as the trade become more unstable economically, it also became socially more complex.

Social Functions

In the nineteenth century, the café owner did much more than simply sell drinks. Over the bar, the owner facilitated the development of neighborhood friendships, marriages, and group activities ranging from pleasure to politics, and in some cases including crime. These multiple functions were usually summed up in two complementary images: the priest in the church and the paterfamilias or matron in the home. During moments of personal or social conflict in the café, its owner became an informal neighborhood judge and policeman, whose "law" often complemented but sometimes contradicted the official social sanctions. By the 1870s, in short, the café owner had become not just another shopkeeper but also an intermediary and social entrepreneur.

The accretion of these functions was essentially the result of the installation of the service counter. Before its installation, a café owner simply did not have much contact with his or her clientele and seldom had any intimate knowledge of the drinkers. "The merchant was separated physically ... as well as socially from his customers," Thomas Brennan notes, adding that "tavern keepers were not always the best sources of information about their customers, though they may have been purposefully vague."[58] Even after the Revolution, in which some café owners figured as important members of the popular movement, the people of Paris still did not have much social interaction with café owners. Even in cases involving the newly decreed right of divorce, which of course most good Catholics denounced as "anti-Christian," only 1.9 percent of the petitioners called upon the traditional "antipriest" to support this new option to end unworkable marriages.[59] While the Revolution may have increased the political power of café owners in the neighborhood, it did little to augment their social influence. As we have seen, this situation had changed dramatically at least by 1860, for by then the café owner had become the primary witness, aside from family members, to workers' marriages, the baptisms of their children, and the deaths of their loved ones.

It was therefore not the increase in the number of cafés, which occurred primarily after 1860, but rather the transformation of the café's social and commercial space by the installation of the counter that brought about the rise of the café owner as a neighborhood social arbiter. This transformation coincided with the onset of the massive wave of immigration that inundated Paris between the 1820s and the 1900s. John Merriman has noted that for newly arrived rural and small-town immigrants, the urban neighborhood became a substitute village.[60] In analogous fashion, the café substituted for the town square and village church. Virtually every nineteenth-century commentator on working-class café sociability noted that the counter had become the center of proletarian sociability. "The affluent at the tables, the workers at the zinc," as a nineteenth-century adage succinctly put it.[61] Denis Poulot in *Le Sublime*, Henri Leyret in *En plein faubourg*, and the dossiers of the judicial archives of Paris all underscore the importance of the counter.[62] Unlike the eighteenth-century records that Brennan has explored, nineteenth-century court cases reveal the café owner to have been the most frequently consulted witness in a defendant's neighborhood after the concierge and family members. Nineteenth-century café owners, also unlike their eighteenth-century counterparts, usually gave precise information regarding the customer's character.

The counter, as accounts of the café after the 1830s abundantly confirm, truly made the café and its owner analogous to the church and its priest. The literary imagination was captivated by the elaborate decor of the 1860s working-class café: multicolored bottles, mirrors, and, in some cases, ornamentation framing the counter. The bar's radiance, magic, and mystery appeared to many observers to be the secular equivalent of a church altar: "The metal shone brightly and the bottles of liqueur cast even more dazzling reflections in the mirrors."[63] Even a reporter for the *XIXe siècle*, describing a tawdry Montmartre bar that supposedly sheltered prostitutes, found himself caught up by the spectacle: "a big zinc counter surmounted with numerous many-colored bottles with a broken mirror hidden by paintings of flowers and garlands and an enormous star in the middle with the date 1871."[64] Describing a barroom in the city's central market district in his novel *Le Ventre de Paris* (The Stomach of Paris; 1874), Emile Zola alludes to the semi-religious aura of the counter: "In particular it was the counter . . . that was so sumptuous, with its broad expanse of silver polished bright. The covering of zinc overhung the red and white marble base with a deep wavy border, thus overlaying it with a silky sheen, a cloth of metal, like a high altar spread with its embroideries."[65] Descriptions of turn-of-the-century absinthe dens, such as the following from Gustave Geoffroy's novel *L'Apprentie* (The Apprentice), complement and complete the equation of publican and priest:

> This is neither a café nor a *marchand de vins*, this is a special place where one drinks absinthe—where the green hour sounds in all its solemnity . . . one drinks only absinthe. . . . The row of glasses before the customers is green opaline without transparency, . . . a terrible intoxicating perfume reigns in the room, hitting those who enter. . . . A proprietor perched on a high chair behind the massive counter is the priest and dominates the altar, . . . the rooms are filled with alcoves and the back has the aspect of a church. . . . In one of the four establishments, there was an organ to go with the offices of the drink.[66]

If skeptical and critical journalists and novelists were this impressed by the counters in working-class café counters, consider how the ordinary urban artisan or rural migrant must have felt!

Publicans, like priests, had to have strategies for attracting and holding a clientele. They had to have ways of rewarding regular attendance, such as hearing confessions and presiding over the important rites of passage in the lives of their customers. A cartoon in the *Journal amusant* depicts a café owner raising his hands and pronouncing a wedding vow to a couple on his counter.[67] While the paper undoubtedly intended this scene to prompt a laugh, the high percentage of café owners witnessing marriage and baptismal contracts reveals an underlying truth beneath the joke.

Publican and priest were also similar in that they both had great powers to include or exclude people from important local communities. Naturally, the nature of those communities was radically different, and at this point the publican/priest analogy breaks down. Customers usually went into a café in a mood of playfulness or rowdiness, not piety and reverence. Unlike the priest, the café owner had to be adept at handling countless monetary transactions and be ready to deal with both verbal and physical assaults. Café owners provided an ambience of spontaneous sociability rather than a clearly articulated doctrine of sanctity and salvation. They had to know how to create camaraderie rather than piety, and relaxation rather than salvation.[68] It may be precisely because they lacked any otherworldly symbols or sanctions that male café owners, unlike priests, were usually stereotyped as big and burly, thus able to use physical force, if necessary, to enforce order in their shops.[69]

The rowdy nature of the café required less a priest than a paterfamilias. The male café owner was usually portrayed as big, strong, and imposing, possessing, in particular, broad shoulders, a short, thick neck, and powerful arms, clearly visible below his rolled-up sleeves.[70] The image of a huge machinelike man dispensing half-liters of wine (*strocs* in eighteenth-century popular slang) prompted the popular mind to nickname him the *mastroquet*, perhaps as master of the strocs.[71] He was always busy directing his waiters or clinking glasses with his habitués. If his customers drank too much on Sunday evening and became quarrelsome, folklore had it that he took them to the local police station, then fetched them at dawn the following Monday morning. An 1877 satirical cartoon in *L'Illustration* portrays a large, powerful "Jean Boileau *mastroquet*," captioned, "He had the most wonderful clientele of drunkards in all Paris."[72] The stereotypical café owner did not fear either a "clientele with knives or competition from other shops," and, according to Léon and Maurice Bonneff, was fully prepared to kick out a client if necessary. The strongbox of a successful, "self-satisfied" café owner, it was said, rivaled the size of his stomach.[73] The ability to maintain order in the shop was perhaps the café owner's most important task, for those who failed to do so did not stay in business.

Robberies, violence, and murders quickly discouraged the clientele.[74]

Nevertheless this paterfamilias of the pleasures of daily life actually exercised his power more through a proprietary and domestic right than through physical force. The emergence of the counter strengthened the domestic ambience already suggested by the owner's living quarters above or in back of the shop and the use of the family to wait on customers. The judicial archives reveal that a high percentage of café owners, over 30 percent between 1880 and 1905, had more than two children.[75] Sulpice Dubrac's description of an evening in his Left Bank café at 330 rue Lecourbe sounds more like entertaining at home: "When several friends came to drink, my son continued to drink with them."[76] Although the police were legally entitled to enter a café at any time during business hours, proprietors often viewed an unannounced entry as an invasion of privacy. Following the arrest of her husband in July 1871 for permitting clandestine prostitution in their establishment at 7 rue du Maine, "*femme*" Gombault protested: "It is incredible that a police commissioner and one of his assistants would cavalierly enter my house, in order to make an arrest as if it were a house of prostitution, without telling me the motive of his visit."[77]

The counter permitted café owners to accentuate this feeling of domesticity by softening their paternalism and fostering a sense of intimacy that made intimidation less necessary. Working-class café owners developed an elaborate set of rituals to promote the camaraderie of the counter. The book *Physiologie des cafés de Paris* (1841) catches the blend of informality and intimacy surrounding the customary handshake between the entering customer and the café owner: "Assuredly the *marchand de vin* does not remain without agreeableness. . . . Enter a shop, the interior is not unworthy of the exterior; the master of the house advances toward you with a smiling face, compressing his mouth for an epigram, and if you are a good fellow [*un bon*], he will shake your hand."[78] Other commentators saw the handshake as calculated condescension or a simple ploy to increase business. *L'Illustration*'s Paris observer described the Troquet couple in their "celebrated" small red shop as having a "hypocritical and strutting familiarity that affects the airs of the big toward the small," involving "handshakes and vermouths on the counter and the clinking of glasses."[79] A 1908 description of an Auvergnat bistro owner at 16 place des Fêtes notes sarcastically how, despite his impatience to make a fortune and head back to his native province, he might sometimes shake the hand of someone who was not actively a customer.[80]

Whatever the motive, the next ritual act a café owner might perform with a new customer, often with the help of his regulars, was to give him or her a nickname. Sometimes this referred to military honors, as with "le Décoré" (the Decorated One); to a home province, as with "la Bretonne" (the Breton); to a person's occupation, as with "le Jardinier" (the Gardener); or to a physical characteristic, for instance, "la Patte" (the Paw).[81]

As the owner got to know the customers, he or she often cemented or sustained the relationship with an act of friendship. Often this involved simply talking with a lonely customer. Such solitary moments could occur even at the barrières. The *Nouveau tableau de Paris* reports that on weekdays in the 1840s, the barrières were "as deserted and calm at night as they were noisy and agitated during the day. Here you see people in cafés less to drink than to pass time and talk with the owner of the house."[82] During slack periods, café owners also played cards with the regulars, as Joseph Combe did in his shop at 67 rue de la Glacière with customer M. Gaguebier, resident at 141 or 143 boulevard d'Italie. Frequently the barkeeper offered a free drink, known as a "courtesy" (*une politesse*). This might be inspired by the fact that the customer was from the owner's native province, Alsace in one actual case. In another instance, a birthday celebration would elicit a round of kirsches.[83] The detective novelist Emile Gaboriau depicted one "father cannon" "who did not serve his best wine to casual customers but only to his 'regulars' who were chiefly the servants of noble families."[84] Perhaps the most controversial of all the café owner's "courtesies" was the extension of credit. For many critics, this was merely a Machiavellian ploy to entrap unwitting customers, especially youths, into alcohol dependency.[85] Yet given all the problems connected with collecting on debts, the granting of credit was more likely just another polite gesture toward the clientele. A popular saying had it that the last persons to give up on a worker were his parents, his friends, and his café owner.[86]

Café owners provided other services unconnected with the food-and-drink business for their habitués, such as witnessing passports. The solidarity that these periodic favors inspired made café owners the "person for the licenses"—that is, weddings and baptisms as well as passports.[87] The mastroquet was often "too respectful to miss a funeral," always wearing a tight-fitting black suit that he could never button.[88] Although workers in Belleville, the most proletarian of Paris districts, may have shifted increasingly away from small shopkeepers to workmates for their marriage witnesses during the late nineteenth century, they remained faithful to the café owner.[89] In some cases, owners even helped their favored customers move. One café owner had his waiter pick up laundry and hire a carriage for a habitué on the day this young butcher left the neighborhood. Another owner, Jean Joseph Ganvin, at 70 rue Julien Lacroix, helped his unemployed customer Louis Barrois find a job by writing a letter of introduction to a friend in suburban Bagnolet.[90]

Café owners catered to the collective desires of their clientele for both entertainment and politics. A long-standing feature of Parisian cafés had been a large room for dancing at weddings and other festivities.[91] In the 1860s, with the rise in popularity of the *café-concert*, many café owners added auditoriums to their establishments to take advantage of the popularity of this new form of entertainment.[92] By the 1870s, the café owner also became important in organizing and funding Mardi Gras. During the 1880s, after the consolidation of the Third Republic, owners became the principal hosts and organizers of Bastille Day celebrations.[93] By 1886, *L'Illustration* reported that provincials invaded Paris every 14 July, filling the cafés.[94] In 1909, *Le Figaro* estimated that during these celebrations, which usually spanned the 13th, 14th and 15th, 2,663 cafés staged dances, and the customers consumed a grand total of 40,477,600 beers![95] Suburban café owners, as Lenard Berlanstein and Charles Rearick have shown, pioneered in the purveyance of concerts and other entertainments, rapidly expanding areas after 1880.[96]

The café owner was equally indispensable in neighborhood political life. Sometimes proprietors encouraged political oratory as a way to attract customers. These pub parliamentarians were highly profitable for the establishments they frequented. In one case, sketched by the great chronicler of Montmartre life André Warnod, an alcoholic orator, whose eloquence always surrounded him with admirers, had consumed 65,820 glasses of absinthe in a twelve-year period. This character brought a fortune to the café.[97]

As early as the 1840s, the strategic value of cafés as sites for campaigning during elections was well recognized, but only with the final and definitive triumph of universal manhood suffrage after 1870 did the café owner become known, usually in a disparaging tone, as the "great elector" of Paris. In the decades following 1870, critics increasingly talked of an unholy alliance between "beer and democracy" and of elections being manipulated in cafés.[98] The temperance journal *Les Annales antialcooliques* lamented that the café owner was "one of the essential wheels of democracy," and that "universal suffrage recruited its best agents on the flamboyant zinc." The "great elector" unfurled his "magic propaganda" and "passed the ballots under the corrupted eye" of France's national symbol, Marianne. Thus the voters examined the virtues and vices of a candidate amid the clinking of glasses, banqueting, and intoxication, all under the watchful eye of the café owner, a "great priest of money."[99] Such criticism was not, however, reserved for the right. In a public meeting in February 1885, a socialist orator, after denouncing private property, considered the dilemma faced by all radical candidates vis-à-vis the café owner. On the one hand, because the café owner was the "great elector," his support was essential. On the other hand, a leftist candidate needed to denounce the owner as the "great poisoner of the workers." The orator then detailed the cost of alcoholism and adulterated drinks to the French economy each year (estimated by him to be 400 million francs) and admitted that he had no solution to the problem.[100] During the 1890s, Maurice Talmeyr estimated that over 200,000 citizens, and perhaps as many as 500,000, used the 40,000 meeting places provided by cafés in Parisian elections.[101]

Café owners sometimes also tolerated or even offered illegal services. The line separating legal from criminal activity was often quite fine during the nineteenth century, given the dramatic changes in politics and law. For example, up until 1837, gambling had been allowed in cafés, especially those of the Palais-Royal. After that date, it became officially illegal anywhere in Paris; nevertheless, throughout the rest of the century, there were always dozens of cafés that permitted it. Pawnbrokery was another questionable service that straddled the legal fence. Some café owners, such as Lepetre at 80 rue du Faubourg Montmartre in 1848, got caught for running a pawnshop without authorization. Prostitution could also be a lucrative side business for café owners (see Chapter 7). In 1872, the *Gazette des tribunaux* noted: "The recruitment of young women for prostitution is for many vagrants an easy and lucrative industry. The place used for this shameful commerce is often provided by café owners, who thus find a way to sell their drinks at double or triple their value."[102]

The intimacy encouraged by the counter as the center of sociability in working-class cafés seems to have brought many café owners into much closer contact with the criminal underworld. Unlike their eighteenth-century counterparts, nineteenth-century café owners often had close ties with individual thieves or robber gangs. The thieves' den *cum* café, known as a *tapis franc* and depicted by the novelist Eugène Sue, did indeed exist.[103] Sometimes the bourgeois who searched for them found out this out to their own chagrin. During the late 1840s, the *Gazette des tribunaux* reported on

M. Staal, an avid reader of Sue's *Mysteries of Paris* who set out on the evening of 20 December 1847 to find one of these exotic establishments. Staal, himself a food seller (*traiteur*) on rue Phélippeaux, stopped in at the notorious café of Paul Niquet at 26 rue aux Fers, run at this time by an M. Sallé. Already intoxicated themselves, several of the customers urged Staal to imbibe more—"Go on, drink up, old boy!"—and to treat them to rounds. When Staal became completely drunk, Sallé and his waiter, as usual, took this tourist of the seamy side of life into a separate room (*cabinet particular*) reserved for those who had been duped and robbed and refused to let him go home.[104] In Parisian slang, this criminal custom was called *faire le poivrot* ("rolling the drunk"), the picking of a drunk's pockets on the boulevard or in a shady café.[105] During the first half of the century, these thieves' dens were located in the densely crowded and dilapidated medieval center of Paris and beyond the barrières.[106] After Haussmannization, most were found outside of the city.

By structuring sociability around the acts of drinking and conversing at the counter, the owner could indicate inclusion in or exclusion from the café community. This brings us to the final major social function of the owners of the working-class café: arbitration of the community's social tensions and conflicts. In this role, owners were sometimes the targets of the frustration and anger of individuals or a group. In seeking to maintain order in the shop, the publican functioned more as a policeman than a priest or paterfamilias. Indeed, on a daily basis and given the hundreds of thousands of people they had to serve, café owners, more than the police, regulated popular behavior.

One of the major sources of conflict between a café owner and his customers was refusal, for whatever reason, to serve a particular customer. Both the dossiers of the correctional tribunal and the crime stories (*faits divers*) of the newspapers record numerous instances of attacks on café owners for refusal to serve a drink. In most instances, the café owner refused service because he or she feared an unpleasant incident in the shop; the person in question might have been drunk, a known or seeming troublemaker, or a person of dubious morals.[107]

One café owner refused entry to a blind street musician who had been insulting pedestrians outside his shop.[108] In order to prevent clandestine prostitution in their cafés, some owners required, long before the police ordinance to this effect, that every woman entering their shops be accompanied by a man.[109] Frequently, such exclusions precipitated violence. A worker who had recently been fired by a café owner for wrecking a coach that he operated went back to his former employer's establishment in suburban Saint-Ouen, where the owner served him but refused to drink with him. According to the worker's father, a ragpicker, the café owner taunted him by saying, "I do not drink with thieves." According to the café owner, he had said, "I do not want to drink." In any case, the confrontation quickly grew into an incident when the worker broke his glass on the counter and threw a fragment at the café owner's head. The café owner then led him forcibly to the door.[110] Such attacks could result not only in property damage but also in the drawing of weapons and, in extreme cases, even the death of the owner.[111]

An equally vexing problem for the café owner occurred when someone ordered a drink and then proved unable to pay for it. According to *La Lanterne*, a prominent republican journal of the 1870s and 1880s, "The height of pretension is to enter a wine shop, get drunk, refuse to pay, be obstinate, and then to embrace the owner before leaving."[112] This apparently routine behavior is recorded in the Parisian slang phrase "to block the mastroquet," meaning to withhold payment from the owner.[113] Three strangers practiced this ploy on Joseph Spiess, a café owner in suburban Aubervilliers, in March 1885. After each had drunk a glass of wine, one of them told Spiess, "I forgot my wallet. I will pay you tomorrow." The two others added immediately that they also did not have any money. When the exasperated café owner again demanded payment, one of them shot back: "For payment I will shit on you," and left.[114] *La Lanterne* reported a similar incident in December 1880: "A professional drunk . . . had an absinthe and then began to leave quietly without bothering to pay for his drink. Stopped by the café owner, he said that he would return with the money. The owner let him leave. Five minutes later, he threw a stone through the window."[115] For their own protection, café owners adopted a firm rule that a bottle "was to be paid for from moment it is put on the table." This rule was relaxed in Paris by the end of the century—perhaps because the 1873 law allowed café owners to prosecute non-payers in court for the first time—but was still usually enforced in the suburbs.[116]

Although it might have been good for business, extending credit was a major cause of disputes between café owners and their customers. Parisian argot described the practice with the simple word "wolf" (*loup*) to mean running up credit in a café.[117] The judicial archives contain numerous cases in which the customers and café owners argued over bills. Clients frequently accused the patron of overcharging for a drink. During a police investigation into the life of a café owner charged with having been a tax collector for the Commune, the investigator reported that his neighbors accused him of making them pay twice for their drinks.[118] Social surveys and judicial archives, however, contain especially extended and poignant testimony to the travails of café owners trying to get reimbursed. A study on the beggars of Paris included what might be called "the café owner's lament": "For two months I have already allowed you credit. . . . I prefer losing what you owe me to continuing to have to do with such a customer. The day before yesterday you received a fortnight's wages and instead of coming to settle our account here you spent all your pay at another public house."[119]

Café owners, usually male ones, often tried to diffuse disputes and confrontations themselves. If need be, they would return the verbal and physical assaults of their customers.[120] In September 1823, the prefect reported a café owner assaulting one of the members of a raucous crowd that had gathered in his café.[121] A 28 January 1848 *Gazette des tribunaux* entry, in the section chronicling Parisian crime, described how the owner of the Pont du Jour café ejected three ruffians during a dispute in his shop.[122] Often such quarrels ended on a bloody note, with the café owner using his fists, a club, a knife, or even a gun. At the urging of customers in his shop at 100 Faubourg du Temple, Pierre Calvet, a 23-year-old beginner in the café trade, shot and killed the knife-wielding brother of a costermonger customer with whom the café had a running dispute.[123] If they felt their honor sufficiently impugned, café owners might challenge an aggressor to a duel. This happened in 1831 when Durandin took umbrage at the denigration of his reputation by two cabbies.[124] In severe and intractable cases involving theft, brawls, or murder, owners called the police.[125]

On political matters, café owners usually sided with their customers rather than with the police. Throughout the century, working-class militants such as the memoirist Martin Nadaud, in his section on July Monarchy Paris, and socialist militants such as Maxime Vuillaume, in his recollections of the Left Bank during the Second Empire, include references to café owners who warned their clientele about police agents or spies.[126] Following the June Days of 1848, a limonadier was implicated in the killing of General Brea at the barrière d'Italie and the concealment of fugitives.[127] Following the Commune, the correctional tribunal archives record numerous incidents between the forces of Versailles and the people of Paris that café owners diffused. On the rue de Charone on 9 September 1871, two policemen were making their usual rounds when a group of workers began to taunt them. However, a neighborhood marchand de vin succeeded in persuading the group to reenter his shop. In cases of confrontation inside their shops, café owners either asked their customers to be silent or told the police or soldiers to ignore a customer's insults because he was drunk. However, if an incident could not be prevented, café owners or their waiters frequently offered extenuating circumstances for their customer's behavior, such as "drinking more than usual" or "recent personal problems." Sometimes, the café owners bluntly blamed the police for the disturbances. After police repression of a protest against censorship in the Latin Quarter in 1893, Richer, proprietor of the café d'Hourcourt, testified that "the students met in my place to organize the *monôme* (a procession of students in single file). . . . The agents roughed up the students, and then things were thrown from inside the café."[128]

As this evidence indicates, there is scant evidence that café owners were ever police spies. Nevertheless, the suspicion that the café owner was an agent was common across the century. A Restoration police prefect's report to the king and minister of the interior, listed as confidential, is ambiguous on this matter. The prefect found it "disquieting" that a jury had acquitted a group accused of singing seditious songs in a café because they felt the owner was in the pay of the police. Even assuming the café owner were a police agent, the prefect wondered, why should his testimony "be regarded as biased?"[129] The judicial archives reveal a few café owners reporting workers involved in political cases. For example, during the June Days, one café owner on the rue Saint-Honoré turned in two wounded insurgents passing as National Guards, and after the Commune, a person who had helped to arrest suspected Communards received permission to open a café in repayment for his efforts.[130] Aside from these cases, judicial dossiers and newspapers contain only a few other bits of circumstantial evidence. The wholesale destruction of police reports that documented what went on throughout the century will always leave historians wondering on this and many other points.

Political Actions

The complex social functions of the café owners made their politics equally intricate. The intimacy between owner and clientele, as well as the fact that cafés profited during times of popular festivity, gave the café owner a perspective significantly different from that of other small shopkeepers. Unlike many other small businessmen, café owners did not believe that "all change is crime; all that is, is good."[131] In other words, café owners were not "conservators."[132] Revolutions, elections, even economic crises often proved excellent for business because they brought people out into the street, to public places, and almost invariably into the cafés, which then became centers of information, organization, and celebration.[133] As a result, most Paris café owners up until the 1880s were on the political left. After the consolidation of the Third Republic, however, they often felt themselves deserted or attacked in an era of growing economic consolidation, surging socialism, and rising fears about alcoholism. They thus increasingly turned to pressure-group politics, and, although they failed to gain much advantage for small business, they did help to blunt the French temperance movement.

The summer of 1789 brought a new age of politics as much to café owners as to any other group. In his book *Daily Life in the French Revolution*, Jean Robiquet has called this period "a golden era for cafés," because in the first blush of revolutionary enthusiasm, the cafés of Paris were filled to capacity. At the same time, under the slogan "We will drink wine at 3 sous, not at 12," Parisian café owners and wine producers attacked and frequently sacked and burned the Old Regime's tollhouses: on 11 July they hit the Blanche and Porcherons barrières, and on the 12th, Monceau and Clichy.[134] Café owners also participated in the taking of the Bastille and went on to play central roles in popular mobilization throughout the rest of the Revolution. Although they usually provided important cadres for the sansculottes' direct democracy, some provided havens for the counterrevolution.[135]

After the repressive eras under the Directory, Napoléon, and the Restoration, the July 1830 revolution brought a resurgence of the 1789 tradition of direct action against indirect taxes. In the suburbs of Ivry, Passy, Meudon, Sèvres, and Belleville, café owners refused to pay these taxes. Their protests sometimes turned into "grave disorders" requiring the intervention of the National Guard. Café owners also organized to prevent wholesale wine merchants from reaching an agreement with the new government on taxes.[136] Although order and indirect taxes were restored by the end of 1831, café owners did not lose their newfound activist impulse. They subsidized and encouraged, by their subscriptions, the growth in the reading of newspapers by the working class. By the 1840s, the democratic, republican newspaper *Le Siècle* (founded in 1836) had become known as the "educator of the cabarets," complementing *Le Constitutionnel*, which had achieved a similar status in middle-class cafés.[137] *Le Siècle* attracted a large working-class audience not only for its politics but also for its serial novels, such as those of Alexandre Dumas *père*.[138] Aside from making a political statement with their newspaper subscriptions, most café owners did not blatantly advertise their political beliefs. When café owners did engage in politics, they usually did so clandestinely. For example, the café on the place Belhomme near the Rochechouart tollhouse during the July Monarchy had a clientele composed mainly of conspirators, spies, and double agents. Such notorious figures as Marc Caussidière, Albert Chenu, and Lucien de la Hodde met there twice weekly, on Mondays and Thursdays.[139] The political role of the café owner came to the forefront during the famous banquet campaign of 1847 and 1848 that helped topple Louis Philippe.[140]

During the 1848 revolution, café owners again combined combativity and conviviality. Their most fervent hopes materialized when, on 31 March 1848, the revolutionary government abolished the indirect drink taxes. The reimposition of certain drink taxes in April did not cause too much of a stir, because they were more equitably assessed on the retail wine consumed by the workers and the wholesale wine consumed by the upper classes. But disquiet turned to denunciation on 10 July as the government—increasingly in the grip of the "party of order"—reimposed the July Monarchy's system of indirect taxes. A great deal of grumbling ensued, but only the café owners in suburban Grenelle, led by a "gang of four" refused outright to pay the taxes.[141]

Perhaps even more than in 1789, the festival atmosphere of March 1848, the revolution's first month, brought a bonanza to café owners. While all other work essentially ceased in the city, the cafés remained open and bulging with babbling customers in what seemed the dawn of an era of social peace and fraternity. As the boundaries between public and private life dissolved, the café became the ideal meeting place.[142] Numerous owners stoutly resisted the revolution's reversal during the June Days. Recent research has found that café owners were more prominent among the insurgents than, as Marx thought, among the defenders of property.[143] Unlike other small shopkeepers, café owners catering to the working class saw repression, not revolution, as bad for business.

After the June Days, a pall swept over publicans that had not been seen since the Terror. For the remainder of the Second Republic and during the first decade and a half of Louis-Napoléon Bonaparte's Second Empire, café owners kept a low political profile. Nevertheless, some maintained a sub rosa solidarity with the republican cause. Victor Hugo describes several such sympathizers in his memoir of the 2 December

1851 coup d'état, *The History of a Crime*. Hugo first met Auguste, owner of a café on the rue de la Roquette, during the June Days, when he intervened to save Auguste and three comrades from certain execution as barricade fighters. "If ever you need me, for whatever purpose, come," Auguste said gratefully. After the coup, the great writer availed himself of Auguste's offer to hide him, for as a member of the now outlawed National Assembly, he was a wanted man as well as a potential leader of revolt against the freshly proclaimed empire. Hugo also notes that another deputy, Labrousse, relied upon the owner of the café Cardinal on the rue de Richelieu to help organize resistance. Moreover, Ledouble, whose café near the National Assembly had been the regular eating establishment of four of the resisting representatives, also proved sympathetic. Some of the last street-fighting during this short-lived resistance occurred at a café at the juncture between the rue de Cléry and rue Montorgueil.[144]

Although a few Paris café owners, such as Jean Allemane's father and Zola's fictional Leibgre became imperial party militants or spies, most refused the blandishments and the bullying of the Second Empire authorities.[145] During the Second Empire, café owners remained faithful to the opposition paper *Le Siècle*, and almost all of them subscribed to it.[146] As the street-smart Second Empire detective novelist Emile Gaboriau noted, popular opinion held that the paper a café owner subscribed to reflected the shop's political allegiance.[147] In 1868, when public meetings again became legal, the sites frequently used for these meetings were cafés or café-concerts. For example, in the 1st arrondissement there was the café des Halles centrales, 18 rue Saint Denis; in the 5th, the café du Progrès, at 36 boulevard de l'Hôpital; in the 9th, the café-concert de la Galeté, 15 boulevard Rochechouart; in the 12th, the café Trousseau, 2 place Mazas; and in the 18th, the Reine-Blanche dance hall at 88 boulevard Clichy. This list does not begin to include all the rooms, such as the salle Lévis at 8 rue de Lévis in the 17th arrondissement, attached to cafés.[148] In addition, by the end of the Second Empire, radical writers and activists such as Maxime Vuillaume had found sympathetic café owners who sheltered and protected them from police spies. One of these, named Glasser, opened his modest brasserie on the rue Saint-Séverin, near the boulevard Saint-Michel, during the last months of empire, after having been fired from his teaching post in Alsace for his republican opinions.[149] At this shop, simply called Glasser's, Vuillaume and his friends received the *Tintamarre*, the most distinctively Parisian and original of the small satirical journals of the era.[150]

The harsh restrictions the Second Empire had imposed on café owners were rescinded when military disaster and popular demonstration ushered in the Third Republic. On the day of its proclamation, a police officer passed by Alexandre Rousseau's café in Popincourt. Upon seeing him, the confident café owner gave voice to long-pent-up rage: "He [Rousseau] said that he knew me well, and that I carried a bludgeon, and that neither myself, nor my comrades could torment him in the future."[151] Undoubtedly, Rousseau spoke for his fellow café owners.

The Prussian siege and the Commune represent the apogee of radicalism for working-class café owners. Again the trade's distinctive qualities permitted it to prosper during times of economic and political crisis. During the siege—19 September 1870 to 28 May 1871—Paris suffered a chronic food shortage but was well stocked with wine and spirits.[152] Because alcoholic drinks, unlike food, did not easily or quickly spoil, café owners did not run low on their basic commodity. Consequently, this was an era of particular prosperity for the café. Moreover, the Commune from its inception carefully courted the small shopkeepers, regarding them as workers.[153]

In general, the Commune found a disproportionate number of adherents among café owners. Some actually became officials, such as Andignoux, a member of the Central Committee and a delegate to Finance Administration, and Jean Mauriol, one of the directors of the Bureau of Direct Taxation. Theodore Benoist became the de facto mayor of the quarter of Grenelle on the Left Bank, supervised elections, and commanded a National Guard battalion, as did Boursier, another café owner.[154] Jules Senicourt, a national guardsman and café owner on the avenue Bel Air, worked in the regime's telegraph services and reportedly "did not attend to his business, but instead was known to frequent clubs, associate with people hostile to order, and have an exalted politics whose ideas differ little from the Commune."[155] Others were leaders of their neighborhood clubs, such as a café owner on the rue Cadet who was president of a club that met in the church on the same street.[156] Some sympathetic café owners sold radical literature, such as the one on the corner of the rue Montmartre and the rue du Croissant; he sold placards of the "Declaration of the Rights of Man and Citizen formulated in 1792 by Robespierre."[157] Others had their counters and mirrors redecorated to reflect their political loyalties. One such café at the outer reaches of boulevard Clichy had an "enormous star with the date 1871" fitted above its bar.[158]

Café owners and waiters were arrested and punished in disproportionate numbers. Of the 36,309 apprehended for participation in the Commune, 738 were café owners, and of the 2,253 deported to New Caledonia, 28 were café owners and 22 waiters.[159] In both groups, the café trade was overrepresented in proportion to its numbers in the city's population: roughly 2 percent of those arrested and 2.22 percent of those condemned were in the café trade, although the trade represented only about 1.3 percent of the city as a whole.[160]

Despite the heavy repression of some of its members, the retail drink trade in general continued to prosper through what became known as the "terrible year" of 1871. Even as embers smoldered from the extensive fires that swept Paris as the Commune fell, boulevard and side-street cafés opened for business. Within a matter of weeks, the city's glittering café nightlife was essentially back to normal. In July and December 1871, L'Illustration's chronicler of Paris mores, "Bertall," penned one of the most sustained and sarcastic reflections upon this revival. The café de Madrid, he wrote, "attracts a great number of tourists as the great site of the Commune." At this "pilgrimage site," the curious could hear about "Courbet banging his fists on the table, the demitasses of coffee consumed by Grousset, the proclamations of Vallès, the meetings of Delescluze, and all the other insanities of the people of March 18." Bertall concluded that "troubled times are the land of Cockaigne for the café owner. They look at all futures with serenity; the ministers and the senators come and go, the café owner remains."[161]

There were café owners sympathetic to the plight of the Communards, like Retiveau, who joined in one of the first successful political offensives of the French left during the mid 1870s, a drive to amnesty the Communards that proved to be a vital link between the Commune and the socialist movement of the 1880s. Quite logically, sympathetic café owners helped direct this movement. After all, it was in their shops that the working class of Paris gathered on the first anniversary of the proclamation of the Commune to drink to its revenge. As the drive gathered strength, the leaders of the amnesty campaign frequently met in cafés, such as M. Bergeron's at 91 rue Saint Martin, to organize the campaign. Moreover, café owners such as L. Maurice at 40–42 avenue Saint Mandé also helped to organize banquets to raise funds for the campaign. Finally, cafés provided an ideal spot to obtain signatures for petition drives. A militant often offered a round of drinks for a group that signed the petition. One petition drive in May 1876 canvassed local and boulevard cafés, such as those along the boulevard Saint-Michel and in the faubourg Saint-

Antoine.[162] Once the amnesty had been won, in 1879 and 1880, the café owners fêted the returning heroes.[163]

During the 1870s, a significant number of café owners helped perpetuate the legacy of the Commune by sponsoring labor and socialist movements. Approximately one quarter of the decade's closures (nine of the thirty-seven) under the 1851 decree were retribution for political propaganda.[164] Perhaps the most prominent café owner militant was Ysablin, a longtime sawyer as well as a café owner, who unionized his trade.[165] Numerous other café owners were also involved in radical politics. One of the most influential was Charles Braun at 2 rue de la Bastille. Here Jules Guesde and other leading French socialists encountered such leading expatriate German socialists as Karl Hirsch. Braun's café was also the rallying point of the committee that organized the aborted International Congress of Workers in Paris in 1878.[166] The 20th arrondissement quarter of Belleville had an especially high number of café owners active in working-class politics. M. Varennes on the rue des Panoyaux, for example, was an important figure in the politics of the quarter, organizing numerous banquets. Candidates ran for the municipal council from this workers' stronghold. In 1880, M. Petroulle, marchand de vin at Charonne, "who possesses a certain fortune and controls several hundred voices in the district in which he is liked," was considered as a candidate by the working-class committee of the twenty arrondissements.[167] But neither in Paris nor in the rest of France did left-wing café owners have formal organizations within the socialist movement as did their German counterparts.[168]

The majority of café owners during the 1870s were moderate republicans. When the Chambre syndicale des débitants de vins de la Seine, an association of Parisian café owners, emerged in 1877, its foremost patron was Léon Gambetta. By this date, socialist and working-class leaders often detested this great tribune, who had first won fame as a café orator.[169] The allegiance of the café owners to Gambetta is illustrated by the decorations that Laplace, owner of the brasserie de la Grande-Pinte in the 9th arrondissement, displayed for the first Bastille Day after the return of the amnestied Communards. A banner painted by the famous caricaturist André Gill hung across the rue de Rochechouart with a picture of Gambetta shaking hands with one of the amnestied.[170] In 1881, Gambetta delivered "a simple speech to my friends" at their annual banquet and praised the café owner as part of the "new social strata" that had achieved power under the Republic. During the early 1880s, many other "opportunist" republicans shared Gambetta's hope that café owners could help to solidify a moderate republic. Gambetta's deputy Lockroy echoed his patron's sentiments: "You, the café owners of Paris, have the ear of the workers. When after work they come to take food and drink and talk politics, you instruct them and therefore you host the true salons of liberalism." In short, especially as the decade of the 1880s began with the repeal of the draconian 1851 decree, it seemed as if a new day had dawned for both republicanism and café owners. The subsequent decades, however, brought disillusionment.

Between 1884 and 1914, café owners saw themselves as besieged by economic crises and hampered by the temperance movement. The return of economic freedom with the 1880 law led, as we have seen, to a dramatic increase in the number of shops and to much stiffer competition. In addition, the police became much more aggressive in the prosecution of adulteration and fraud in drink and food products. In response, café owners marched on the National Assembly in 1887 to protest the prison term meted out to shopkeepers for adulterating drink.[171] Surmounting these problems, the economic crisis of the 1880s and 1890s hit small shopkeepers especially hard. Like other petty bourgeois, café owners attributed their plight to growing commercial and financial concentration. Since their trade continued to be decentralized, café owners did not target department stores as a specific cause of their problems, but they did attack regulations that in the name of pedestrian traffic control inhibited their use of the street.[172] Thus they opposed the March 1899 decree that limited the amount of sidewalk devoted to commercial use.[173] Moreover, the social unrest of the period, especially the strikes and demonstrations, often devastated rather than enriched them as in previous decades.[174] As their association paper noted: "When a strike erupts, much violence occurs around the workshops and neighborhood cafés. It is often impossible to prevent the breaking of glasses and dishes, especially if the protesters find strikebreakers eating and drinking. If the owners object to this limitation of their freedom of commerce, then the strike leaders ban all workers from frequenting the shop. The proprietor then has only two options: to close the shop or sell it at a derisory price for lack of customers."[175] Finally, café owners also felt beleaguered by temperance advocates. On this front, as Patricia Prestwich shows, the café owners achieved a measure of success. They had an eloquent advocate in the Chamber of Deputies in the person of Georges Berry. Café owners were also capable of running an astute propaganda campaign. For instance, when the Office of Public Assistance printed and posted posters denouncing spirits and wine in 1903, the café owners responded by placarding Paris with their own poster quoting Louis Pasteur's judgment that wine was the healthiest of all drinks.[176] All in all, the French campaign against drink was a feeble venture compared to the powerful temperance thrusts in England, Scandinavia, and America.

By the 1890s, café owners felt increasingly that the main threat to their business lay on the political left. The rise of various schools of socialism, including Marxism, did, indeed, pose particularly strong intellectual and economic challenges. Many French socialists absorbed Marx's idea that the small shopkeeper would be swept away by the growing concentration of capital. The French Marxist Jules Guesde echoed the master by saying that café owners, like all other small merchants, could survive only if they linked themselves to the working class and fought the monopolists. With their great rise in electoral strength during the 1890s, socialist leaders viewed cooperatives as replacements for the small shopkeeper. Jean Jaurès, for instance, had faith that cooperatives could tame the "commercial anarchy" of Paris. Indeed, the 1890s and 1900s brought extensive growth in socialist-inspired grocery and restaurant cooperatives in the Paris region.[177] By May 1909, Paris had over 260 cooperative societies comprising 85,000 families and 100,000 individual members. Café owners, like other small merchants, believed cooperatives posed a basic threat to their business.[178]

As a result, many café owners steadily shifted to the political right during the 1880s and the 1890s. General Georges Boulanger's rise in 1886 appealed to the populist, anti-capitalist, and anti-collectivist strain deeply embedded in the mentality of the Auvergnat immigrants now so dominant in the café trade. Boulanger and his lieutenants, such as Maurice Barrès, fostered this attitude by attacking socialism, especially its cooperatives, and by favoring a revised form of business license that would diminish the financial burden on the small shopkeeper. These points corresponded exactly with the program supported by Parisian café owners. One of Boulanger's strongest partisans was the Auvergnat journalist Louis Bonnet, recent (1882) founder of *L'Auvergnat de Paris*, a newspaper for his compatriots in the city, which galvanized Auvergnat café owners, waiters, and coachmen in support of Boulanger.[179] Although Boulanger's popularity had dissolved by April 1889, his movement started the café owners on a rightward drift that was sustained by a Parisian shopkeepers' association established the previous year. Uniting support for Boulanger, this Ligue syndicale du travail de l'industrie et du commerce gained great influence in Parisian municipal politics between 1888 and 1896. Working-class café owners never became prominent in this organization.[180] Moreover, café owners primarily serving the workers did not become as prominent as their counterparts in the affluent inner districts. For example, the outstanding nationalist leader Charles Girardin (also head of the Chambre syndicale of the café owners in the early 1900s) had a café in the central 1st arrondissement.[181]

By the end of the 1880s, however, many café owners had become disillusioned with politics in general, and their organization focused increasingly upon commercial survival. The Chambre syndicale's president proclaimed that "our counter is a confessional where we propagandize in favor of our business." Café owners now believed that political neutrality was the best means of gaining and keeping customers. If a café owner vented his political views, he might alienate customers; accordingly, he should have no political opinion and should subscribe to every available paper, covering every shade of political and religious opinion. Clearly, proprietors felt this was as important as carrying every type of wine and liquor.[182] An association newspaper, *Le Défenseur*, reflected this perspective by studiously avoiding any mention of doctrinal politics beyond immediate commercial concerns.[183] The paper portrayed café owners as martyrs to their customers and to the government: they labored long hours serving an impoverished clientele and coped with heavy taxation and police harassment.[184] Perhaps the best evidence for the increasingly apolitical attitude of café owners is the evolution of the newspaper most often found in the cafés: during the 1870s this was the moderately radical *Le Rappel*, but by the end of the century, it was the escapist, mass-circulation daily *Le Petit Parisien*.[185] Complete unity among café owners was achieved only within the trade's narrow interests. Meetings of the Ligue syndicale du travail de l'industrie et du commerce held in Paris periodically after 1905 reflected this philosophy.[186]

CHAPTER SIX

The Etiquette of Café Sociability

Intimate Anonymity

eprived of property and thereby of tangible representations of their identity, the vagrant poor and, above them, a large part of the working class [in nineteenth-century Europe] did not have a materialized civilization, but a culture of sociability and accommodation," the German social historian Lutz Niethammer writes, suggesting that proletarianization possesses a congeniality all its own.[1]

Neither Niethammer nor any other historian has, however, explored how the café fits into this "culture of sociability." Precisely because nineteenth-century workers had little choice or control over their jobs and housing, they wanted at least to exercise control over their associations during their free time. The arbitrary and transitory nature of a laborer's life meant that these relationships might not last long.[2] Nevertheless, these informal social ties could be crucial for survival. Consequently, workers strove to create a type of sociability that would give them freedom and opportunity to form relations quickly, relations that could provide support and solidarity. The café provided an opportune space in which to create relations based on spontaneous solidarity. This fleeting fraternity rested on three values. The first was selectivity—that is, the freedom of participants in café sociability to converse with whomever they wished. The second value was autonomy—the right not to be interrupted by third parties once you had begun to talk with a particular person or group. The third involved the ideal of tolerance—that is, the concept that no one in the café should take offense at the minor irritations and insults that accompanied socializing in a small space amid a dense urban agglomeration. The ethos of the working-class café generated an atmosphere that offered both intimacy and anonymity and proved to be one of the most important ways in which the Parisian milieu reconciled neutrality and sociability.[3]

Nineteenth-Century Theories of Sociability

One of the major ironies of this nineteenth-century Parisian proletarian sociability is that its emphasis on selectivity, autonomy, and tolerance had many affinities with eighteenth-century aristocratic salon sociability. Both sociabilities embodied the traits of "artificiality" and "superficiality" that the great German sociologist Georg Simmel felt were at the heart of sociability. Naturally, working-class sociability was by necessity less structured, rigid, and permanent than that of the rarefied salon society of the Old Regime, because it sprang from the poverty and anonymity of a large city rather than the privilege and opulence of an aristocratic order. Nevertheless, these two forms of sociability both emphasized open, free-form sociability, in contrast to the emerging middle-class ideal of sociability, which stressed the desirability of intense, intimate, and long-term friendships among men in clubs or cafés, exclusive of women.[4] Eighteenth-century critics of salon life and nineteenth-century critics of café life unwittingly mirrored each other in their attacks on the immorality and debauchery that women brought to these non-bourgeois forms of sociability. Even many working-class leaders and left-wing intellectuals criticized the proletarian café on the same grounds as conservative or liberal writers and advocated that workers socialize instead under the auspices of political parties or labor unions.

The idea that the only valid sociability was rooted in formal associations explains why most nineteenth-century observers—running the gamut from tourist-guide writers to doctors to bureaucrats to left-wing labor leaders and intellectuals—dismissed the notion that café life could elaborate an etiquette. Rather, the café appeared a place of unstructured commingling, where the employed picked up the vices of criminals and vagabonds. In 1885, a U.S. government report on labor conditions in France warned: "These restaurants, being the resort of all unemployed men, are a danger alike to public health and morals, being the home of outcasts of society, honest workmen are thrown in contact with them."[5] French doctors voiced a similar concern: "In the long meetings in the café, he becomes familiar with the regular customers of these dens: vagabonds, beggars, pimps, thieves, and swindlers; whose pockets are filled with money they have gained quickly . . . in these shops, especially in Paris, he is almost certainly lost."[6] Labor leaders and leftist intellectuals expressed similar fears. Friedrich Engels in his observations on Manchester during the 1840s provides a most damning critique of life in drinking establishments: "When one considers, apart from the usual consequences of intemperance, that men and women, even children, often mothers with babes in their arms, come into contact in these places with the most degraded victims of the bourgeois regime, with thieves, swindlers, and prostitutes; when one reflects that many a mother gives a baby on her arm gin to drink the demoralizing effects of frequenting such places cannot be denied."[7] This description is remarkably similar to the perception of the conservative psychologist Gustave Le Bon, who viewed café sociability as little more than mob behavior: "The conceptions at present rife among the working classes have been acquired at the public-house as the result of affirmation, repetition, and contagion."[8]

Given these lurid images of unrestrained impulse and indiscriminate mixing, it is no wonder that the guidebooks to Paris advised their middle-class clientele against patronizing working-class cafés. Baedeker recommended that only those cafés south of the boulevards Montmartre and des Italiens be frequented, because to their north, in the working-class districts, the "society . . . is far from select." Bayle Saint John warned his fellow Americans never to make acquaintances in public places. However respectable a stranger might appear, he might still be a thief, a policeman, or an agent provocateur.[9]

Even Henri Leyret, a sympathetic observer of café life, did not deign to explore or delineate why and how the café could function as a haven for the working class. Instead, the focus was almost always upon the general patterns of working-class life. The café appeared more as a metaphor typifying the social mores of working-class life rather than as an institution that existed in time and space. Writers such as Maurice Halbwachs chose other metaphors, in his case the street, to illustrate working-class social life.[10] Virtually no author inquired into the specific relationship between the café, the street, and other recreational facilities and activities in working-class life, much less into how all these spaces evolved and interacted across the nineteenth century.

The Cafe in Relation to Other Public Places

Throughout the eighteenth and nineteenth centuries, as a modern system of social classes emerged, public space in Paris became in general less open to the public. Along with churches and theaters, cafés were among the primary public places where people spent time outside of work and home life. Cafés were in a complex relationship with these other spaces. They were less public than churches, because they required the purchase of a commodity for admission and thus did not permit anyone to stay on their premises. Nevertheless, they were more tolerant than churches, because they offered people a wider range of behavior than churches did. The café did not offer as much entertainment as a theater, but it was cheaper and in some cases provided singing, dancing, and card-playing. Naturally, the relationship between the theater and the café was more complementary than that between the church and the café. Theatergoers, especially in the upper classes, almost ritually retired to the café after a performance. In addition, a synthesis of the theater and the café occurred when the café-concert developed during the Second Empire. By the 1890s, with the receipts of the café-concert steadily rising, there was much fear (groundless as it turned out) that it would replace the theater.

Although in theory a public place open to all comers, the café, like the theater and church, reproduced class distinctions. The great difference between the café and the theater or church is that there was less rigor and formality to these distinctions in the café. In the theater, the pit (*parterre*) and the upper sections of the second tier, called *le paradis* (the gods) because of their height and distance from the stage, were the spaces for the lower classes. In the church, the pews were reserved for the upper classes. In the café, we see similar spatial divisions, such as the tables for the upper classes and the bar for the workers, but the spaces were less formal and could not be as easily policed as was possible in churches and theaters.

By the late nineteenth century, a new public space had opened up that permitted a degree of social mixing not found in any other public places. This institution was the sports stadium and included tracks for horse and bicycle races. Spectator sports, especially horse racing, seemed to contemporaries the only activity that truly brought the classes together. During this period, for example, *L'Illustration* described the Longchamp racecourse as the great "neutral terrain" of Parisians. As they put down their bets and then cheered their favorites on to victory, the observer saw "society in microcosm."[11] The commonality found at the sporting event re-suscitated a public mixing that had previously been the hallmark of the street, the most important public place during the centuries before 1750.

Traditionally, the street had been the preeminent public space be-cause most commercial and social life occurred there. In their detailed studies of the daily life of the eighteenth-century populace of Paris, both Arlette Farge and David Garrioch have found that, in Garrioch's phrase, the street was the "community space *par excellence*." Garrioch notes that on the main streets, there were "semi-permanent stall-keepers," which helped make these places "strategic centers of sociability." He also de-lineates the way in which the Parisian bourgeoisie retreated from street life during the first half of the eighteenth century. Increasingly merchants, entrepreneurs, and financiers did not socialize on the street or allow their children to play there. Instead, they strove for selectivity in their social relations, and consequently socialized almost exclusively within their sa-lons, gardens, or courtyards. For them, the street became a passageway rather than a living room.[12] The street was left to the lower orders.

The street had heavily influenced the popular café during the eigh-teenth century. Most contemporaries, especially such well-known ob-servers as Louis-Sébastien Mercier and Restif de la Bretonne, pictured eighteenth-century tavern life as an extension of the street. Although it may have been more bacchanalian, tavern life seemed to be the human equivalent of Brownian motion: an endlessly changing swirl of gratuitous gregariousness.[13] Although Brennan effectively refutes this view by show-ing that café sociability clearly followed occupational lines and seldom in-volved unfettered commingling with criminals and vagabonds (rare groups in the tavern anyway), he shows (along with Farge) that tavern customers did not enjoy immunity from the intervention of third parties, and that the eighteenth-century tavern provided little sense of privacy. Brennan's work also documents Garrioch's thesis on the comportment of the bourgeoisie by showing that they composed an ever-shrinking percentage of café habitués over the century.[14]

In essence, nineteenth-century Parisian authorities slowly succeeded in taming the anarchic and turbulent eighteenth-century street. During the last decade of the Old Regime, the prefect of police, Jean Lenoir, assigned each street vendor to a particular location, moved the street theaters to the boulevards, and expanded the central market by relocating the cimetière des Innocents outside of the city.[15] In addition, despite popular protest, the police established a system of numbers for each building on every street. During the Revolution, especially after 1793, the Paris police renewed this policy of rationalizing and regularizing street life. As Richard Cobb notes, the police came to regard any large gathering on the streets as a potential riot that could produce another revolution, and increasingly devoted much of their activity to breaking up such gatherings.[16]

Nevertheless, during the first half of the nineteenth century, much street life survived. If only by reason of overcrowding, the streets must have maintained or increased their social function in the ever more densely packed central districts, filled with the immigrants Louis Chevalier has so memorably evoked. Observers in the early nineteenth century continued to see working-class café sociability as diffuse and anarchic. Eugène Sue, for example, equated the café's clientele with the crowd. One of Sue's criminal characters finds himself "suddenly in the thickest of a dense throng of people . . . coming out of the cabarets of the Faubourg de la Glacière" to watch an execution.[17] Newspaper reports of café violence during the first half of the nineteenth century also emphasized unruly groups engaging in uninhibited bellicosity, as in a brawl in October 1827 "at Bobinot's wineshop, 6 quai de Bercy, between 60 and 80 joiners; for no motive except the animosity between workmen of the compagnonnage. . . . The battle was so furious from the start that all the shops shut and everyone fled; the wretches assaulted each other with compasses and cudgels."[18] Similarly, in May 1848, there was a "bloody brawl" involving a dozen disputants in a café on the rue de la Tannerie when Auvergnat coal and water carriers attacked a group of Limousin masons and pavers whose songs drowned out the Auvergnats' dance tunes.[19] Revealingly, although Paris papers were filled with this type of story, the early nineteenth-century café had not yet become the primary focus of moralistic wrath that it would be after 1850. The probable reason is that the turbulence of the café was still largely assimilated into that of the street. Only when violence became more directly tied to excessive drinking did the café appear to be a particularly dangerous place.

A dramatic change in street life resulted from the Haussmannization of Paris. The baron's broad boulevards finally made traffic circulation rather than social interaction the primary function of streets.[20] Indeed, between 1850 and 1870, while the central city's population grew by 25 percent, inner-city traffic jumped by 300 to 400 percent.[21] Between 1891 and 1910, vehicle traffic increased tenfold.[22] Late-nineteenth-century commentators noted that the streets had ceased to be a place to live and were now just places of passage. For example, the Champs-Elysées was merely a route to the Bois de Boulogne.[23] The effects of this shift in the function of Paris streets has still not been fully explored. Jeanne Gaillard is right that Paris ceased to be a closed, medieval city and became an open, modern city because the opening up of streets to traffic eroded the insularity of the old neighborhoods. Gaillard does not, however, sufficiently consider how the decline of the street as a center of sociability contributed to making Paris a much more socially segregated city, and one that was, therefore, less rather than more open.[24]

Haussmannization also accelerated the century-long shift from the street vendor to the shopkeeper. The best index of this shift is the steady rise in the number of business licenses (*patentes*) during the 1850s and 1860s.[25] The growing rationalization of street life forced even beggars and musicians into fixed hours and regular routes.[26] The Second Empire was also the era in which the modern department store developed. Such stores as the Bon Marché benefited from the new boulevards and the increased flow of traffic and began to attract customers from the entire city. Consequently, commerce and its attendant sociability became focused in more centralized and enclosed locations and thus further diminished the ubiquity of Parisian street life. Although the number of street vendors increased from 6,000 to 20,000 during the economic crisis of the 1880s, the police provided only grudging tolerance, and after 1900, they severely cracked down on the street trades.[27] Parisian workers may have gained the ability to consume and circulate, but they lost much of their ability to congregate and converse.

Haussmann's broad boulevards may have facilitated the flow of traffic and goods across the city, but his new housing segregated the classes more completely than ever before. Largely because the new cafés on the first floors of the new buildings were as luxurious as the new apartments on the upper floors, café sociability evolved in the direction of housing rather than that of traffic—that is, it became more segregated and segmented instead of more open and interconnected.[28] These brightly lit and lavishly decorated establishments sprawled onto the sidewalks and created the now famous terraces. The expanding Parisian bourgeoisie used these elegant and expensive cafés as spaces to flaunt their wealth and fashion. In so doing, they effectively intimidated the working class from frequenting, much less loitering in, now-stylish neighborhoods that had once been proletarian.

Baudelaire's prose poem "The Eyes of the Poor" is a classic statement of this new type of sociable segregation. At the prompting of his lover, after they have spent "a long day together," Baudelaire's narrator takes a seat at the front of a "dazzling" just-completed boulevard café. They admire the "blinding whiteness of the walls, the expanse of mirrors, the gold cornices and moldings, fat-checked pages dragged along by hounds on leash, laughing ladies with falcons on their wrists, nymphs and goddesses bearing on their heads piles of fruits, patés and game"—in short, "all mythology pandering to gluttony"—but suddenly they see before them a family in rags. The father is "playing nurse-maid taking the children for an evening stroll," Baudelaire tells us, and adds, "the eyes of the little boy" communicate the sentiment "How beautiful it is! How beautiful it is! But it is a house where only people who are not like us can go." Untouched by this sight, the narrator's lover says, "Those people are insufferable with their great saucer eyes." She then asks, "Can't you tell the proprietor to send them away?"[29] Her expectation is that the café owner will supplement the police as an enforcer of the newly segregated social space. After the 1860s, the western boulevards did become primarily the preserve of the bourgeois, and the police provided an especially close but unobtrusive surveillance of these streets.

Café activities such as drinking, eating, and smoking seldom provided common ground upon which the various social classes could socialize on an equal footing. Although over the course of the century, mores in these respects became increasingly standardized in all drinking establishments, this growing uniformity did not encourage cross-class sociability. The price differential between upper- and lower-class establishments ensured that the classes remained apart. In addition, the bourgeoisie believed that even if workers drank "their" drinks, such as absinthe or an apéritif, the worker's behavior lacked "measure or decorum" and was "in defiance of good sense."[30]

For most of the century, the question of smoking also played a vital role. The "typical" working-class café was often defined as a shop with no gas, few chairs, but a lot of smoke.[31] Such images of "seediness" prompted the belief among the well-to-do that there was a distinctive "smell" to working-class cafés. In Alphonse Daudet's novel *Jack*, we see the protagonist carrying with him this distinctive "scent" during a visit to his middle-class parents.[32] Most cafés catering to the upper classes barred smoking during the early nineteenth century. In this era, it was also considered bad form for upper-class men to smoke on the streets or in gardens.[33] Taverns (*estaminets*) were the primary public places that tolerated the use of tobacco. Such tolerance went well with their general informality: tavern patrons seldom took off their hats upon entering. On the less formal Left Bank, particularly in the Latin Quarter, the prohibition against smoking waned by the 1850s. In contrast, the fashionable Palais-Royal café de Foy retained the ban on all nicotine products into the 1870s; many other luxurious Right Bank cafés continued this policy through the 1890s.[34] Yet even after this date, the spread of smoking could not bridge class differences any more than the drinking of absinthe could in previous decades.

Nineteenth-century Parisian café etiquette was essentially class specific; no space or language developed with which class differences could be transcended.[35] Only a few places and spaces provided exceptions to this rule. During the late eighteenth and the first half of the nineteenth century, the Palais-Royal cafés, as we have seen, provided a venue for class fusion.[36] In general, however, by the 1870s even these old centers of sociability were casualties of Haussmann's fashionable new boulevards.[37] The most social mixing occurred first in the cafés of the Latin Quarter and then in those of Montmartre. The venerable café Procope provides a good example of interclass sociability in the Latin Quarter during the 1860s. On its first floor, "serious types" played dominoes and booksellers discussed their business; on the second floor, students smoked and played billiards amid political harangues from the likes of the young Léon Gambetta. Only in the milieus of marginality haunted by students and bohemians, by definition outside of full bourgeois respectability, did the classes mix.[38]

Paradoxically, although they no longer felt at home in the city, working-class Parisians could now travel around it much more easily. By the late nineteenth century, even the workers were coming to see the street as a passageway rather than a home. "In the street [the worker] feels uneasy, he submits to the ambience of the situation, believing, just like the bourgeoisie, in the necessity of composing a demeanor," Henri Leyret noted in his Belleville café.[39] The English mechanic Henry Steele noted no differences between the classes in their behavior on Paris streets: "In the streets, in the omnibuses, trains, theaters, or in any public places, all Frenchmen and women are practically equal. There is one code of manners for all. The *camelot* selling laces expects the same politeness as the wealthy banker."[40] Certainly, as period photographs abundantly indicate, the side streets of working-class quarters remained filled with animation. Nevertheless, street life on these cramped, narrow streets was a far cry from what it had been in the eighteenth century, when it had dominated Paris life rather than being a vestige of a vanished age.

As Haussmannization increased the distance between a worker's home and his workplace, proletarians came to frequent a number of cafés rather than one predominantly. Drinking at several cafés became ritualized to the extent that the new custom acquired a variety of names: "making a round" (*faire un tour*), "pub crawling," "counter jumping," or "doing the panther (or leopard)."[41] As Alphonse Daudet noted, this last image drew an analogy between a panther pacing back and forth in a zoo and a habitué going back and forth between cafés. The term originated in and was associated with the suburbs.[42] The term "counter jumper" registers the central place that counters had assumed in café life after the 1820s, and to the fact that drinks could be ordered and consumed quickly, allowing rapid movement from shop to shop. The radical republican *La Lanterne* described one such café-to-café spree in 1879: "The young X . . . about 25 years old passed the day in the company of one of his comrades. They had drunk together in a great number of cafés and taverns, leaving at each of these shops a little bit of their reason at the bottom of their glasses."[43]

By the 1860s, consequently, the café was the scene of much of the animation of traditional street life as it became progressively forced off the main thoroughfares. The tremendous vitality and variety that observers found in nineteenth-century cafés sprung from an infusion of street life. Working-class café life grew across the century both to complement and to compensate for the workers' loss of street sociability. Many café owners sublet some of their space to newspaper and chestnut vendors and even to shoemakers, thus encouraging the interconnection between street and café life.[44] Flower sellers, costermongers, toy and trinket sellers, newspaper boys, organ grinders, singers, and musicians all focused on cafés, because these spaces contained concentrations of people.[45] Moralists noted fearfully that thousands of obscene books, pamphlets, toys, and devices were being sold in cafés.[46] Moreover, vagrants and vagabonds regularly collected cigarette butts—nicknamed "orphans"—from the sidewalks in front of cafés.[47] Judicial archives reveal that cafés were also primary sites where police uncovered evidence of counterfeit money and shady financial schemes.[48] The interface between café and street life was thus an unstable boundary between order and disorder, as well as between sociability and marginality.

Working-Class Café Etiquette

Although the working-class cafés assimilated the vitality of street life, they also tamed and reduced much of its anarchy and violence. As workers increasingly did their socializing in cafés, they developed an etiquette to regulate their behavior. This adjustment was necessary because the café was a much more delimited and segmented space than the street or the traditional suburban tavern. Because of their spaciousness and the constant flux of people within and among them, a strict code of conduct had not been as needed on the street or in the tavern. The lack of clearly demarcated spatial boundaries meant that people at one end of the street or tavern did not necessarily feel disturbed if a fight occurred at the other end. In the constricted space of the urban café, however, a fight could immediately disrupt the entire establishment. Customers and café owners thus had to develop various methods of negotiating interpersonal relations and so prevent or contain disputes that were far more disruptive in a café than they would have been on the street.

The rise of the counter is the most striking example of the manner in which café space became more specialized and personalized. Another factor is the increasing spatial differentiation within cafés. Even suburban taverns after 1820 moved away from the traditional undifferentiated space found at such establishments as Desnoyer's shop at the barrière du Maine, where a vast clientele filled an enormous room. Another establishment popular during the 1830s and 1840s, Little Ramponeau's at the sign of the silver lion at the barrière Rochechouart (allegedly this tavern sold the most wine and had the best acrobats), broke up its cavernous space into discrete rooms for different types of customers.[49] Naturally, the incorporation of these suburbs into Paris in 1860 brought the downfall of many of these large taverns. Only a few of the working-class cafés of the city could handle the large crowds that once swarmed around the taverns. The average proletarian tavern served only about fifty customers per day rather than the hundreds or even thousands who often patronized a tavern on weekends.[50] By the 1880s, providing different spaces for different functions had become common in working-class cafés. An October 1886 article in *L'Illustration* featured the plight of the disadvantaged in the midst of the decade's economic crisis and described how the café Munier at 20 rue des Amandiers catered simultaneously and in separate rooms to moderately affluent employed workers, to those on the edge of destitution, and to the down-and-out who had lost all confidence in themselves.[51]

The most dramatic effect of the rationalization, segmentation, and often diminution of space within the café was the decline across the eighteenth and nineteenth centuries in the size of the groups socializing in cafés. Court records provide abundant data on this subject. A comparison between the court records of the eighteenth and nineteenth centuries reveals a steady decline in the number of people involved in disputes. In eighteenth-century archives, Brennan discovered that "the average number of customers drinking together declined steadily over seventy years from 3.8 in 1691 to 3.3 in 1761."[52] Destruction of judicial archives during the fall of the Commune, as already noted, prohibits a continuation of this study for the years between 1789 and 1870. When the records resume, however, we discover that the average number of people involved in café disputes that ended up in the courtroom was 2.7 between 1871 and 1914. These figures, based upon the average number of people involved in judicial incidents, obviously cannot be taken as an objective sociological sample of the size of café interactions. Nevertheless, they reveal a crucial long-term trend: the size of groups socializing in cafés steadily declined between 1700 and 1900. By the 1870s, over 72 percent of the interactions recorded in the judicial dossiers involved four people or fewer.

Café sociability for the working class increasingly meant small groups of two or three, but seldom four or more. Working-class café sociability became progressively smaller-scale during the 1850s through the 1880s, decades in which the number of cafés skyrocketed. In this same era, the separation between café and street sociability became more marked. By the 1880s, proletarian Parisians often had a choice of five or six cafés on almost any street in their districts. If conflict erupted between the habitués and the owner or within groups, this selection allowed the disgruntled to find a new place to socialize. In this behavior, workers were no different from politicians or journalists, who often formed and reformed around various tables at an assortment of cafés.[53] Judging from the testimony in the judicial archives, few of these cafés were so crowded that a group of habitués could not carve out a niche for themselves.[54] The vast number of premises ensured that any group could find an autonomous space.

Contemporary and historical accounts confirm that Parisian workers were indeed socializing in smaller groups. Georges Duveau came to this conclusion in his classic examination of the Second Empire's working class. He felt that by the 1860s, Paris proletarians had lost interest in large gatherings: "If the worker no longer mixes in communal festivals with the same joy as in the past, this is often because, having acquired a more heightened conscience, he has lost his taste for collective enjoyment."[55] An American chronicler of Parisian life of the same era provided a specific example of intimate café groups when he noted that at one café, four people had met regularly for twelve years at the same table to play dominoes.[56] Steele, the English mechanic who lived and worked in Paris in the late 1890s, noted that at quitting time, "Out they come, repeating the hand-shake of the morning and the 'Bonsoir, Paul, *à demain!*' to those who are not going in their direction. Gradually they separate into little groups, often the same groups who dine together, and who go home together the same way."[57] The Pelloutier brothers also noted the tendency of workers to gather in groups of five or six.[58]

As a result, a marvelous mélange of café milieus proliferated across proletarian Paris. By what process did working-class Parisians select café companions? Did they rely primarily upon the network of their neighborhood or their workplace, upon their regional or ethnic group, or upon the casual friendships they made in the café? The wide range of sources on café life, patently more abundant after 1870, reveal that these small groups reflected neighborhood life more than any other factor. A description of the café de Cluny on the boulevard de Sébastopol in 1862 as the place where "the notables of the quarter gather" could apply generally to most cafés.[59] In judicial archives, newspapers, and sociological literature, neighborhood ties are three times more prevalent than work ties, which rate as second. This finding reveals one of the most stable and enduring aspects of popular cafés across the eighteenth and nineteenth centuries.[60] The judicial archives are especially eloquent on this continuity and abound with such testimony as "the whole quarter says," "the whole quarter knows," and even, among the suspicious, "the neighborhood is conspiring against me."[61]

Despite the intimate connection between the café and work, references to the workshop or to strikes are, similarly, only about a third as prevalent as neighborhood references. Very few references occur in archival or literary sources, especially after 1859, to a "shoemaker's café," for instance, or a "mason's café." In fact, café owners regarded people who frequented cafés exclusively with workers of their own occupation as odd. The preponderance of neighborhood over work considerations is also supported by the fact that verbal and physical conflict in cafés usually concerned the former rather than the latter. For example, a feud between the Allaire and LeClerc families on the rue de Lyon lasted for over a year and a half—that is, between 1871 and 1873—and a feud between Isidore Moreau and Eugène Sourdilliat on the boulevard de la Villette continued for over three years—1871–74.[62] The café, in short, was preeminently the theater of neighborhood life.

In fact, in the wake of the decline of the street and the severe housing crisis, the café may have become the most stable and accessible space in many a worker's existence. Contemporaries and historians have noted how often workers would change dwellings yet remain within the same neighborhood.[63] Ann Louise Shapiro notes a well-accepted axiom that the Parisian proletarian "rented the district even more than the individual dwelling."[64] In this circumstance, it would not be surprising to find people more familiar with their favorite café than with their apartments. Indeed, people seem to have been as likely to go to a café to find their relatives, friends, and neighbors as to their homes. One night, in 1894, for example, a traveling salesmen had dinner at a restaurant in the Latin Quarter with a friend, who suggested looking for one of his cousins on the terrace of a boulevard café afterwards.[65] In another case that year, a laundress, Anna de Knaff, naturally looked for her husband in all the town's cafés when he failed to come home one evening.[66]

In some cafés, especially in the artistic Latin Quarter and Montmartre, painters or other habitués graphically depicted neighborhood life on café walls. On the rue des Cordiers in the late 1860s, a café named the "Faithful Pig" had its walls covered with murals painted by its habitués.[67] In 1875, in another Latin Quarter café, the famous Père Lunette, a painter by the name of Lefebvre painted a series of murals on the walls portraying, as the republican journal La Lanterne noted, "the celebrities of the neighborhood." Neighborhood allegiance to a café is also illustrated by the fact that sometimes a large crowd attended its owner's funeral. "Yesterday at 3 P.M. the civil burial of M. Cocquart, retail wine merchant at 19 rue des Noyers, occurred," La Lanterne noted on 11 March 1879, adding that the deceased "was universally esteemed in his neighborhood, and a numerous crowd followed his coffin. He was a member of the Belleville choral group. The entire group sang at his funeral."[68]

Regional and neighborhood ties often overlapped. Auvergnat, Burgundian, and Breton immigrants, in particular, developed distinctive café cultures in their respective neighborhoods.[69] Lodging houses with wineshops—and vice versa—often catered to immigrants in the same trade or from the same province or country.[70] Louis Chevalier has noted that the history of population flows is well preserved in the street names, shop signs, and especially, he emphasizes, in the names of the café and dance halls. He believes cafés played a large role in the survival of the "departmental physiognomies" of Paris.[71] Because of their extensive involvement in the drink trade, the Auvergnats had perhaps the most developed and distinct provincial café subculture, focusing not only on the unique traditions of music and dance but also on business.[72]

Similar patterns developed among many of the foreign immigrant groups. In her study of late-nineteenth- and early-twentieth-century Russian Jewish immigration, Nancy Green argues that the café was a Parisian institution well adapted to immigrant life. Cafés permitted the Russian Jewish immigrants to engage in their customary animated conversations, and the sheer number of shops, moreover, allowed each political faction to have its own forum. Nevertheless, Green notes that this close-knit café life delayed assimilation, and in some cases sparked a desire to return to Russia.[73] Italian immigrants seem to have been less successful in creating an autonomous café culture, judging by the number of times during the 1870s and 1800s when they vandalized cafés that discriminated against them.[74]

The growing autonomy and independence from the street of café life not only facilitated the development of distinctive small-scale sociabilities based upon work, neighborhood, provincial, or ethnic identities but also spurred the emergence of cafés specializing in specific types of leisure activities. Two of the most important pastimes were singing and card-playing. Throughout the century, cafés were the venue for spontaneous, informal group and individual singing that was an integral part of popular life. During the first half of the century, cafés were also the site of singing societies. After 1867, many shopkeepers added stages and turned their shops into café-concerts. Card-playing was a similarly pervasive phenomenon. "Everybody plays at cards from a marquis to the porter to the ragpicker," Bayle Saint John noted.[75] It was often a short step from card-playing to gambling. Again, gamblers of each social class found cafés to suit them. After its prohibition in 1837, all café gambling became, officially at least, clandestine. The abundant judicial dossiers and newspaper accounts of café gambling reveal that along with rentiers and white-collar workers, skilled artisans—jewelers and makers of watches, mirrors, rugs, and artificial flowers—were most often found in police sweeps, which usually picked up between thirty and seventy players.[76] After 1870, the government decided to harness rather than repress this passion and permitted pari-mutuel betting, which quickly found a secure home in cafés.[77]

Gambling was only one of many café activities ambiguously wedged between legality and illegality. The emergence of a distinctive café culture during the nineteenth century has perhaps no better illustration than the rise of "suspicious cafés" (*cabarets borgnes*), which sheltered the activities of pimps, prostitutes, swindlers, vagabonds, and thieves much more frequently and systematically than eighteenth-century taverns had.[78] Unlike the archives Brennan examined, the nineteenth-century judicial archives contain numerous accounts of criminal activities in cafés. For example, during the 1870s, the police commissioner of the Clignancourt district described the Ernest Lecala's establishment at 66 rue Ordener as one where "shady businessmen conduct their affairs." During the same decade, the suburban police of Pantin reported that the café of Pierre Penot and his wife Léonie had a bad reputation because "of the suspect clientele that frequents the establishment; all one sees in the shop are vagabonds and pimps [*souteneurs*]."[79] The growing concern with juvenile delinquency—distilled in the notion of "savage" Parisian youth, dubbed "Apaches" by journalists—focused upon the cafés that the Apache gangs made into their headquarters.[80]

"The cabaret was not so much a place to find fellowship, rather, one went with companions or arranged to meet there," Brennan writes of the eighteenth-century laborers' tavern,[81] but this was no longer true after 1860, when café sociability became much more than the sum of contacts made outside the premises. The emergence of a highly diverse café subculture by the 1880s is indicative of the level of autonomy café sociability had achieved. Workers or anyone else could find almost anything in late-nineteenth-century Paris cafés. The wide range of their activities permitted people to make new contacts inside the café. A measure of this subculture's distinctiveness is found in such common popular expressions as "café friend" and "café talk," according special status to friendships nurtured in cafés.[82]

Evidence of strong café friendships appears as early as the 1830s. Novels of lower-middle- and working-class Parisian life provide vivid elucidation. In tracing the rise and fall of a small merchant in *César Birotteau*, Balzac describes a climactic scene with the lawyers. Birotteau's attorney is able to intimidate his main creditor by referring to café opinion: " 'You did not send for us, I suppose, to tell us that the case was to be transferred to a criminal court,' said Pillerault. 'The whole café David would laugh this evening at your conduct.' The little old man seemed to stand in awe of the opinion of the café David; he gave Pillerault a scared look."[83] A less famous but equally perspicacious Parisian novelist in the first half of the century, Paul de Kock, provides another variation on the theme of café friendship. When the title character in *Monsieur Cherami* is in need of a friend to lend him some money, he turns to the boulevard, "where there is no lack of cafés; for one cannot walk thirty feet without passing [one]." Shortly after ordering lunch, he renews the acquaintance of a person he has met at a party. He is not able to get the loan, but he does get free lunch and dinner.[84] These and other novelists show us the wide range—from influential friendships to casual contacts—that café relations could encompass. Alain-René Le Sage (1668–1747), author of *Gil Blas*, compared café friends to monks and actors, in that "chance brings them together and they see each other without liking each other and quit without regret."[85]

The "café friend" was not, however, merely the invention of novelists. Sociological insight into the concept is offered by courtroom testimony, which had to be plausible to be believed, even if it was often more special pleading than dispassionate description. A pair of assize court cases in 1878 involving café habitués give a good definition of café friendship, and the great demographic, social, and political differences between the defendants indicate the prevalence of the concept.

The first case involved Sébastien Billoir, a 58-year-old retired army sergeant who murdered his lover, Jeanne Bellengé, in a fit of jealous rage and then chopped her body into small pieces in an attempt to hide his crime.[86] "I go to the café to create my relationships," Billoir said when the judge probed the extent of his carousing during a pretrial investigation. A couple who ran a café at 36 rue de Clignancourt, Montmartre, confirmed that he did indeed find his friendships among fellow cafégoers: "Billoir had hardly any comrades; he associated [*faisait sa partie*] with the habitués, I could not indicate to you anyone with whom he had intimate relations." Henri Duprey, a dentist and a regular at the café, noted: "Outside of the café I have never seen Billoir."

Billoir did, however, establish one friendship in the café that transcended the bar and tables. Auguste Métra, a white-collar worker, and his wife became friendly with Billoir and Bellengé at the café. The two couples took an excursion together to Bercy at the end of the winter of 1876 in order to see the flooding of the Seine. Moreover, Madame Métra helped Billoir and his lover move from their apartment at 43 rue de Clignancourt to 14 rue Christiani. But after Billoir showed a tendency to drunken and disorderly conduct, most of the habitués, including Métra, shunned him.

Henri Duprey was one of these fair-weather friends: "His politeness, his age, his decoration made us at first regard him highly. Six months ago he was in a very pronounced state of drunkenness. The opinion about him after that was less favorable; we believed that he was a man lost to absinthe."[87] Billoir clearly formed his relationships in the café; they were essentially fleeting, and he lost them through his bad behavior and failure to follow café etiquette. Following his trial, he was sentenced to death and guillotined.

The second case shows a café habitué discounting the value of café friendships. The defendant, Lucien Lagarde, was accused of belonging to the International Working-Men's Association, a serious crime at the time, because the French "moral order" governments of the 1870s believed it had helped create the Paris Commune. Aside from military service and café relations, he had nothing in common with Billoir. Lagarde was young, well educated (a former student at the Ecole des beaux-arts) and politically motivated, as revealed by his interest in the International.[88] At his pretrial investigation, the judge asked him about his café contacts. "You have said that you only know Jacquin because you have seen him in a café. It appears from the letters we found in your possession that he is one of your friends?" To this Lagarde responded: "Yes, sir, I recognize that this is one of my friends, but I know him only as a café friend." Here we see the reduction of a substantive to a minor relationship. Significantly, the prosecuting attorney did not ask what Lagarde meant by the term "café friend"; presumably being familiar with this excuse, he realized it would be extremely hard to disentangle such a maze of relationships. Certainly, this was the attitude of the prefect of police Jean Camescasse a few years later when he was queried about the nature of grassroots popular politics: "Nothing is more mobile than these associations with no defined purpose, which often form at a café table among five or six workers under the name of social studies groups."[89]

The judicial archives of Paris are filled with similar accounts from the lives of ordinary workers of contacts made in cafés. Witnesses often began their testimony by stating, "I met him either at a theater or at a café." During an investigation of assault and battery, when a prosecuting attorney asked Léon Mathieu, a 34-year-old house-painting contractor, about his relations with Charles Rainot, a 24-year-old commercial agent, Mathieu replied, "I know Rainot only from having encountered him at Tintinger's wine shop at 72 boulevard de la Villette, at whose café I have an account." "Father" Louis Henri, a 64-year-old day laborer, responded similarly when asked about Henri Houdremont, a 41-year-old bookkeeper, "I know Houdremont somewhat, only because I see him in the shops I frequent."[90] In another case, a 36-year-old mechanic in Saint-Denis observed, "I know Fuchs [a rug maker] because he lives maritally with the sister of my wife. I drink with him from time to time at Kobel's." In a further example, an apprentice pastry maker noted, "I have known Chevalier [a butcher] since last winter. I am his neighbor and meet him often in Raynal's café."[91] When the prosecutor interrogated an unemployed mason, Antoin Panchon, for participating in a late-night disturbance, Panchon claimed not to know his accomplices. He said he only drank with them.[92] The diversity in the occupations and ages of the witnesses and defendants talking about café friends—from a young college student to a retired army sergeant—demonstrates the pervasiveness of the concept of the café friend among lower-middle-class and working-class Parisians.

How did people form café friendships? Although much spontaneous interaction did occur between strangers, these contacts were usually neither gratuitous nor promiscuous. Instead, they were based on a set of rituals that created a casual closeness. Paradoxically, a study of the violence and insults in court cases best reveals this code of comportment. Court testimony, by delineating the transgressions of deviants, reveals the pattern of normal life.[93] Witnesses describing café sociability frequently used the expressions "have a party" or "make merry" (*faire une partie; faire la fête*) to portray ordinary drinking and socializing among friends.[94] Theodore Keller, a rentier and habitué of the café Charles at 2 boulevard Orano, measured his friendship with Billoir by the number of times they had had a "party": "I have seen Billoir in the café Charles for about a year. He had a very suitable demeanor. I had maybe one hundred parties with him." Witnesses in other court cases used similar terminology. When questioned about his friend Eugène Gabot, a wood turner, their shared experiences in a favorite café were one of the first things to come into the mind of Auguste Thoyer, a cabinetmaker: "I have known the Gabot family for a long time, but especially Eugène Gabot, who has worked with me as a joiner and turner—I go with him and M. Berteau to the wine merchant's sometimes. We make a party there."[95] This sociable principle found its way onto the Paris stage in Tristan Bernard's classic comedy *Le Petit Café*. The ingenue Isabelle defends her café outings on this principle: "I have come to the café to see some friends with whom I want to have a party [*fais une partie*]. When I make merry [*faire la fête*], it is always with friends and never with people I don't know."[96] Thus the concept of having a "party" indicated the personal and exclusive nature of café sociability.

Counters proved especially conducive to these "parties." The dominance of the table in the eighteenth-century tavern had discouraged the intermixing of strangers and different groups.[97] When the bar emerged as a center of sociability after 1830, it created a more open and informal space, in which groups could constantly form and reform according to their tastes. The counter thus increased the possibility of strangers meeting and interacting. Testimony from the judicial archives indicates that by 1900, bar sociability represented about one-third of working-class café sociability.

The friendships that often developed during these "parties" were codified by the bestowal of nicknames. We have already noted that café owners frequently gave their customers nicknames, and the same was also true of customers. Over a toast, café habitués might receive nicknames from the proprietor or other patrons. Theodore Keller explained how Billoir had received the appellation "le Décoré": "He always wore his decoration in the café, so we called him the Decorated One." Habitué nicknames displaced the person's real name to such a degree that often when the police asked clients about fellow drinkers, the clients could identify them only by their nicknames. Mathias Hermann, a day laborer, knew Ferdinand Christian, also a day laborer, only by his nickname of "the Paw." Marie Ardisson, a registered prostitute (*fille soumise*), referred to two habitués of a café on the rue des Mathurins solely by their café nicknames: "There was the wine merchant, an individual who carried the nickname of the carp [la Volige], lover of a person called the pockmarked one [la Grelée] who sold potatoes." Café habitués employed nicknames to create their own separate world of sociability. Many of the designations—"Turio," "Aglaré," "Charlot," and "Pinsonneau"—have no fully comprehensible meaning outside of the specific café context in which they were coined.[98]

Rituals such as "having a party" or giving nicknames ensured that small groups created a degree of "legitimate intimacy" from the surrounding clientele.[99] Even the poorest and loneliest customers normally maintained their social space. In October 1886, *L'Illustration* ran an article about the café Munier at 20 rue des Amandiers. The author noted that "the totally disadvantaged who have lost all confidence in themselves" might "throw their envious eyes on the food" of workers who were better off, but that "no fights or jostling" occurred as a result.[100] Even the eccentric Sébastien Billoir upheld the idea of discretion in the café. He rebuked Jeanne Bellengé for accompanying another woman to a café on the grounds that she had met the woman only minutes earlier in an employment agency. "I emphasized to her that she was very wrong to associate with people she did not know and especially to go drinking with them." Clearly, Billoir applied what we see now as a sexist double standard: he could go to the café to make friends, but he denied his lover the same right.

Café owners assumed that their customers would respect one another's privacy. For this reason, Dominique Tintinger, a wine merchant at 72 boulevard de la Villette, complained of a habitué, Charles Rainot: "Rainot seems to me to have a mania to mix in all the conversations and to accost men and women equally." In general, habitués did not get involved in other customers' business. If habitués of one café had a fight with the owner or with other habitués, the offended ones could easily find another café where they would not be bothered.[101] In 1868, covering a minor dispute during a café card game, a staff writer for the *Gazette des tribunaux* noted that as a "general rule" one should "never mix in what does not concern you, especially in the case of a bad sport."[102]

An equally important factor guaranteeing that these small groups could socialize with a minimum of disruption was the principle of tolerance. Café customers tried consistently and good-naturedly to ignore the jostling and interruptions that were inevitable in an often noisy and crowded public space. Court testimony clearly demonstrates that café customers usually tried to mitigate rather than exacerbate potential trouble. A court case from March 1878 in the Paris suburb of Fontenay-sous-Bois provides a typical example of a petty café confrontation. Eugène Tellier testified, "I had been there a few minutes with M. Desforges, one of my comrades, when Knaff entered. After being served a small glass [*petit verre*] he insulted me, using terms I do not remember. I was content to make a brief response, [and] shortly thereafter I left with my comrade."[103] Only because the confrontation continued after this initial incident did it reach the attention of the police and later the court. The Billoir case also illuminates this concept of tolerance. Café owners and customers alike considered Billoir strange because he tried to pick a fight at the least affront. One evening in the summer of 1876, when he and his wife were sitting with his friend and fellow shoemaker, the shoemaker Léon Elénore reported,

An individual whom I did not know approached us. He was drunk [*pris de vin*], [and] he uttered some light, even ugly, remarks to my wife. On several occasions I requested him to leave us alone. He paced back and forth in front of us, uttering threats to which I paid no attention because I saw he was drunk. Besides, Erard, who had known him for a long time [not surprisingly, since Billoir had once worked at the same shoe factory as a clerk] told me to pay no attention to his remarks because he was mad when he was drunk. Leaving, he proposed that I come with him to the place Saint-Pierre, saying that he would fix me there.

It is a measure of the tolerance in Paris cafés that despite his attempts, Billoir never succeeded provoking a fight at any one of the eleven cafés he was known to frequent in Paris and its suburbs. Habitués merely avoided him.[104]

What is most remarkable about this etiquette of tolerance is that even policemen and soldiers abided by it, and were often hesitant to create confrontations. A common phrase in police reports was "I did not pay any attention, but the individual continued his invectives."[105] Even in the aftermath of the Commune, when both police and soldiers quickly arrested anyone who insulted them, these upholders of public order were reluctant to respond to provocations in cafés.[106] In August 1871, Sergeant-Major Melchoir Cabanis was in a café on the boulevard des Batignolles when a mason, Jacques Jardinot, entered and began to insult him. "As I did not respond and appeared not to notice him, he continued," the sergeant-major testified. In another incident, a group of officers who frequented the café Moka at the place des Ternes in the summer of 1871 reported that their tolerance and patience toward the seemingly humorous barb "*à Berlin!*" directed at them daily by Auguste Wallard, an elderly bookseller, had undoubtedly provoked his tirade on September 7.[107] A tolerant attitude toward café comportment was even more pronounced in later years when passions over the Commune began to cool.

This tolerance is based on the idea, held also by the police in the above incident and by judges in some court cases, that café life should be seen in terms of humor and play rather than with seriousness and inflexibility.[108] Joking, laughter, and pranks were a large part of café life; across the nineteenth century, habitués and writers invoked the word *rigolo* (meaning funny, amusing, jolly) to convey this playful café spirit.[109] Proprietors sometimes used the word in shop signs and advertisements, or even adopted it as a name (e.g., "café Rigolo").[110] Of course, café humor rarely appears in the archives. However, in newspapers, plays, prose and poetry, innumerable pieces testify to the comic in café life. Almost every Paris newspaper devoted a column to small humorous happenstances of daily life. Often called "Echoes," or by other phrases indicating the ephemeral speech of café and street life, these anecdotes provide an invaluable record of café wit and emphasize that café conflict is always to be taken with a large dose of levity. A good example can be found in a leftist bohemian journal of the 1870s, *La Lune rousse*. The 6 May 1877 issue—in its section "Cancans de partout" ("Cancans everywhere")—told the story of a parliamentary deputy eating on a boulevard café terrace. A dozen steps away on the sidewalk, a big peasant from lower Normandy spotted him and delivered a stream of invective: "Rascal, Crook, Scum, Liar!" A passerby stopped and inquired why this person deserved such treatment. The peasant responded that he objected to his deputy drinking Bordeaux; on the campaign trail, he had drunk only cider with him and his comrades![111]

If humor and tolerance failed to work, café customers might join the owner in trying to prevent disputes from becoming violent and disruptive. In the semi-carnivalesque world of café humor, just as the police might play the fool with a customer, so a customer might assume the role of the police. Lacking a sense of humor or feeling for the ambience of proletarian cafés, prefects of police repeatedly expressed incredulity when working-class café customers solved their own disputes. In March 1823, one prefect believed it was a singular event when groups of laborers and soldiers settled their own dispute at barrière de Fontainebleau.[112] Judicial archives and newspapers show, however, that this case was not unique. Of course, we can never know how many fights were resolved without the aid of the police, because by definition they are not mentioned in police reports. Nevertheless, these sources reveal enough attempts at mediation to show that the conciliation process was an important element in café sociability. Customers often requested help from their relatives or friends when a dispute appeared to be getting out of hand.[113] In a 1905 case, when a belligerent costermonger, Charles Trasi, threatened to disrupt their quiet evening of listening to a new phonograph, a group of habitués—including Adolph Delalte, a 27-year-old street merchant; Ferdinand Lebenzit, a 19-year-old metalworker; Gaston Rouer, a 20-year-old cabinetmaker; Léon Boudet, a 23-year-old mechanic; and Marcel Louvain, an apprentice butcher—helped the café owner expel the troublemaker from the establishment and warned the owner when the enraged street vendor returned toting a revolver.[114] Women also often assumed the role of mediators in café disputes. Moreover, unlike in London, police surveillance was not simply an extension of community methods of conflict resolution in Paris.[115]

The concept of a fun-loving tolerance inhibited the development of an aristocratic or middle-class sense of honor. The proletarian concept of café tolerance was intimately related to the idea that these spaces were neutral ground and represented "time out" from ordinary affairs. Although workers and small shopkeepers cared about their reputations, they seldom talked in terms of "honor." This distinction between reputation and honor may appear to be specious. Nevertheless, it illuminates one of the most persistent and paradoxical facts about working-class café life. In both the eighteenth and nineteenth centuries, proletarian Parisians were much more likely to sue a person who had insulted their "good name" in court than they were to resort to informal or formal physical violence, such as a duel. Based upon judicial records, it appears that café customers were equally likely to take a dispute to civil court as to resort to physical violence. Thus the aristocratic code of honor that Robert Nye shows as moving down into the bourgeoisie during the course of the nineteenth century did not have a noticeable effect on working-class café sociability.[116]

Available evidence indicates that "affairs of honor" and duels declined in working-class cafés across the century, for most of the cases come from the first three decades of the century. In 1826, for instance, the prefect of police reported to the minister of the interior that one of the large "cabaret quarrels" had resulted in a duel.[117] Three years later, the *Gazette des tribunaux* noted the exotic case of a former officer who, following a dispute in the English Tavern at 6 place des Italiens, insisted on a boxing match with an Irishman, who in the course of it killed him with a punch in the stomach. In February 1831, the paper reported a duel between a cabby and a café owner named Durandin in the latter's shop. The following month this judicial newspaper described a drunken fight between "two champions," a barrel maker and a blacksmith, in the suburban village of Dammartin.[118]

By the February 1848 revolution, most stories of duels resulting from café interaction related to the middle and upper classes. For example, in the early days of the following June, an exchange of cards—the personalized address card being a preeminently bourgeois status symbol of the era—occurred after a man caught another staring at his female companion in the café des Mille Colonnes. The duel took place the following day.[119] Court records after 1871 confirm the decline of the working-class duel. One morning in early July 1889, a young officer in uniform showed up at Joseph Robert's café at 14 rue Lecourbe and asked the proprietress about the whereabouts of her son. The proprietor came forward, whereupon the officer suddenly asserted that the son would not be allowed to see his beloved anymore. The café owner then "spoke some conciliatory words and asked him to leave." The officer "offered to drink a bottle" with the café owner. The two drank and talked for the next two hours. To no avail, however, because when the son did arrive, the officer "called my son a coward and demanded a duel with sword or revolver." The son replied that he could not fight a duel with an officer. The café owner then prevailed upon his son to leave.[120]

The decline of the duel or "affair of honor" among working-class café habitués was closely linked with the eclipse of the barroom brawl in incidents involving a small number of individuals. Dossiers from all of the Paris courts—including the correctional tribunal, court of appeals, and assize court—after 1870 reveal only a couple of cases of a classic barroom brawl—that is, one entire group going after another.[121] Naturally, some confrontations still occurred, as the following short bulletin from *La Lanterne* in September 1880 indicates: "Sunday night towards 1 A.M. Monday morning, seven Italians and three ragpickers were in the process of drinking and singing in a *marchand de vin* of the rue Harvey (13th arrondissement). They occupied two neighboring tables. At a given moment, the three ragpickers rose, irritated by the singing of the Italians; they uttered some foolish things and then left. The Italians followed them into the street and a brawl started. The Italians drew their knives and one of the ragpickers . . . received a violent wound in the stomach. He is in critical condition."[122] Nevertheless, by the 1870s, most newspaper reports of café violence described disputes between a few individuals rather than the old-fashioned free-for-all (which the French call a *rixe* or *bagarre*).

The reputation of the late-nineteenth-century working-class café as a violent space comes mostly from these small-scale incidents, which were indeed often extremely brutal. What made them seem so savage to contemporaries is that the violence was often highly idiosyncratic, spontaneous, and unstructured. An 1883 court case illustrates these points. In the Paris suburb of Asnières, a person by the name of Jacques Bordet had become the lover of an older widow of some financial means, enough to allow him to forsake the carpenter's trade. Bordet's new financial and living arrangements caused his fellow carpenters to shun him. One evening in June 1883 at a café, some of these carpenters refused to drink with Bordet. According to one of them, Alexandre Leroux, "I had a drink at Birotte's with some comrades. Logut, who was seated at the next table also wanted to drink with us. Bordet, who shares an apartment with him, wanted to do the same, but, as he is not liked by some workers, Fuzeres refused to let him join the group, saying that he was too lazy." An argument ensued but quickly died down, and Bordet left. A quarter of an hour later, however, he returned. Dressed in his Sunday best and carrying a metal cane and a revolver, Bordet demanded of Leroux "to come with him for a kilometer and discuss matters, because he did not like the remarks made about him." Leroux responded that he was not so naive as to follow him. Bordet then proceeded to address the café as follows: "Here are four people I want to come out on the rue des Carbonnets. I have some lead to wash out their mugs and some steel to make them see the light."[123]

Like so many other cases of late-nineteenth-century café violence, this scene fell in between the rubrics of the brawl and the duel and so lacked any predictable structure or pattern. The judicial archives and newspapers are filled with similar sorts of incidents involving individuals in small groups or alone who suddenly became belligerent and often brutal. By the 1870s, café owners were aware of this distinction between an individual who precipitated small-scale disruptions and one who provoked large-scale disturbances. Sylvian Lacan, who ran a café and an apartment house at 4 rue Montmartre, described his tenant Jean Palat, a coachman, as "a brutal character, he has had some quarrels in my place, but he is not a brawler."[124]

At least three reasons account for this shift away from large-scale brawls to small-scale fights. The first has to do with the growth in the consumption of alcohol, especially spirits such as absinthe, which often led to alcoholic rages erupting over the most minor affairs. The second is connected to the radical changes in the city of Paris itself: the massive increase in population, the housing crisis, and the easy access to all districts as a result of improvements in the streets and mass transportation. A third reason for the growing gratuitousness of much café violence may be the increasing alienation that many lone drinkers experienced. By the 1880s, a new motif had emerged in working-class café descriptions, a motif that would have been virtually inconceivable during the eighteenth century: the idea that it was the isolated worker who went to the café.[125] Impressionist painters in particular drew upon the rich and ironic paradox of alienation being expressed in a place consecrated to social interaction. Although most of their scenes depicted bourgeois or bohemian café anomie,

Degas and Manet in particular, especially in the former's *L'Absinthe* (1877), represent the alienation experienced by the proletariat.[126] Court records shows that some 19 percent of café incidents concerned lone individuals. This percentage may seem low, but it is still virtually double what Brennan found for the 1690–1770 period.[127]

Thus, even though the declining size of café interactions decreased the likelihood of large brawls, small-scale, potentially intimate sociability was no guarantee against violence and disorder. Café sociability was premised on the dynamic of small, selective groups, but the intimacy of spatial scale did not guarantee intimacy of feeling. Not surprisingly, the café was a place where intimacy was more often expressed than created. Relationships that did develop in the café did not necessarily lead to close friendships. The case of the decorated ex-sergeant Sébastien Billoir is again illustrative. One of the habitués who knew Billoir, the shoemaker Joseph Erhard, dismissed the importance of the relationship, saying, "I have known Billoir for about two years. I have never gone to his place; I have only seen him at [the café]."[128] A café contact could launch a friendship, Erhard implies, but if the connection is to become really close, one of the customers has to invite the other to his home or have some other contact outside of the café. In short, although it fostered small-scale and exclusive sorts of social interaction in close proximity—note Madame Raydon's use of the common phrase "to make a party," café socialization did not necessarily lead to intimate or even close relationships.

Despite the numerous instances of violence in cafés, their reputation as disorderly, anarchic places was overstated. The frequent assertion by jurists, doctors, and moralists in the late nineteenth century that café drinking caused 90 percent of Parisian violence was a gross exaggeration.[129] In fact, an examination of the judicial archives reveals that only about 50 percent of such incidents occurred in cafés. Close study of the judicial archives reveals that most cafés had only infrequent violent incidents. For example, until an incident in 1883, a large establishment in the turbulent Latin Quarter, the café-restaurant Bouland at 34 boulevard Saint-Michel, had not had a police intervention for at least fifteen years.[130] If there were a straight correlation between the number of cafés and the level of crime, one would expect dramatic jumps in the crime rate after 1850, again after 1880, and then a leveling off after 1890. The statistical profile of Parisian crime does not at all fit this pattern. As Jean Chesnais, a leading historian of violence, has noted, Parisian violence decreased between 1825 and 1880. For example, the number of murders in Paris declined by half during the period when the number of cafés doubled. Paris, Chesnais also observes, become truly dangerous only around 1900; by 1914, its murder rate was 200 percent higher than that of the rest of country.[131] By 1890, as we have seen, the number of cafés had stabilized.

If anything, café sociability seems to have mitigated violence. By the 1860s, a surprising number of observers, given the accepted elite view that proletarians were semi-savages, emphasized the refinement and gentleness of Parisian workers. One of the most perceptive analysts of French workers, Armand Audigane, noted in the 1860s that "in the industrial population of Paris, sociable instincts are more pronounced than in any other, [and there are] a more open spirit, larger ideas and a certain philanthropic sentiment that engenders the desire to aid one another mutually and develop habits of reciprocal tolerance."[132] The American writer Bayle Saint John echoed Audigane's sentiments, asserting that the capital's workers were "well informed on history and politics," better in fact, "than many middle-class and petit bourgeois types."[133] Although Audigane did not specifically link these manners to the café, like many other English-speaking observers of France,[134] Saint John did; in the bohemian cafés of the Left Bank, he found skilled artisans who had a "certain gentleness of bearing and elegance" and, unlike English workers, did not insult foreigners.[135]

The rise of the café and the decline of street life during the nineteenth century improved both the capacities and the opportunities of the workers. Even as Arlette Farge celebrates the proletarian presence in the Old Regime street, she admits that the people had no other places to go. The proliferation of cafés after the mid nineteenth century presented laborers with a wide selection of spaces and ambiences. Thus workers now had a greater measure of choice in what they did and whom they saw in the public realm. At least in the area of sociability and in the case of Paris, therefore, we see a refutation of the commonly held thesis that proletarianization brought an impoverishment of leisure.

The growing separation between the street and the café permitted a distinctive ethos to emerge. As Robert Nye has recently noted, the concept of ethics derives from the notion of ethos.[136] In the case of the working-class café, we see a close fusion of the ethos and ethics. The increasingly small-scale nature of most groups congregating in cafés permitted individuals to have much more chance of joining in the interaction. The informality and mutability of these groups also permitted café customers to find friends and contacts in the café.

But the ability to be selective in café sociability would have been undermined if there had not also been the principle that each person or group should be as tolerant as possible of the shoves, slights, and other minor irritations that were an inevitable part of interacting within an enclosed space. What did these social principles produce? The answer is a greater sense of the worth and equality of each person and personality. "Social equality is the law of the café," François Fosca concludes his *Histoire des cafés de Paris* (1934). "In a café the rich man who is boring is disdained, [whereas] in a salon who would dare to interrupt him? . . . the café permits personalities to be affirmed."[137]

CHAPTER SEVEN

Women and Gender Politics

Beyond Prudery and Prostitution

afé life evolved more dramatically in gender relations than in any other respect after 1789. The Revolution brought women into cafés in an unprecedented fashion in the areas of both politics and prostitution. Even as the political mobilization and economic depression that increased women's participation in café life waned after 1800, the innovation of the counter and the proliferation of private dining rooms in restaurants and cafés, called *cabinets noirs* ("black rooms"), in the following decades sustained and expanded the role of women in cafés. The Paris Commune marked the peak of women's participation in café politics, and two decades later, the Belle Epoque registered the greatest incidence of café prostitution.

Female cafégoers ranged from the expected large number of prostitutes to an unexpectedly large number of married women and widows. The occupational range of female café customers was almost, with one prominent exception, as diverse as that of the female population of Paris in general. Middle-class observers were more accurate than they realized when they called the café the salon of the working man. In an analogous but less sumptuous fashion to upper-class salon hostesses (*salonières*), working-class women contributed to creating a café etiquette. In the case of women's café politics, their mere presence as much as their actual speech and actions constituted a challenge to the reigning pieties of male politics.

The Evolution of Women's Café Presence

When did working-class women begin to frequent cafés? Historians of eighteenth-century Paris have so far generated more heat than light on this issue. The distinguished eighteenth-century French historians Arlette Farge and Daniel Roche both believe that women were an accepted part of tavern life. But so far rather more evidence has been uncovered to support the thesis that the tavern or wine shop was a male space. "A woman going to a wineshop alone risked being taken for a prostitute, and to say that she 'courait les cafés' (ran around the cafés) was tantamount to calling her a whore," David Garrioch observes. Thomas Brennan reached a similar conclusion: "Few women went to cabarets unescorted, and most went with their husbands. Men acted as protectors and sponsors, providing women with an entree into a male world."[1] The historian Dominique Godineau has argued that after the spring of 1789, seamstresses and other working women composed half of the clientele in political cafés.[2]

An excellent source delineating women's right to engage in political discussion in cafés is the 1791 *La Mère Duchesne* (and its continuation, the *Journal des femmes*), which instructed working-class women in the art of being virtuous republicans. Even though Mère Duchesne defers to the wisdom of her husband, the famous fictional character Père Duchesne of Jacques-René Hébert's influential paper, she is clearly at home in the political arena. In one issue, after arguing that women should devote themselves to raising good citizens until the age of fifty and only then engage in politics in a hypothetical women's parliament, Mère Duchesne concludes by chiding her comrades, "Always the particular interest and never the general interest—come, let us drink."[3] Because workers seldom drank wine with company in their wretched apartments, the action is clearly taking place in a café. The protagonist obviously sees no contradiction between drinking and political discussion in the café, both acts being fully in the public sphere.

After 1791, as the Revolution became more radical, women's participation in café political life provided an apprenticeship in the new rights and duties of the citizen. In December 1793, at a café on the place Maubert, women joined in a debate on the fate of Anacharsis Clootz (guillotined along with Hébert on 24 March 1794). At another café, as a female cosmetics merchant read aloud an article from the newspaper *Père Duchesne* condemning Camille Desmoulins (guillotined with Danton on 5 April 1794 for his opposition to the Terror and the Hébertists), a woman in the audience interjected that all such scum should be hung on lampposts. In January 1794, at a café on the rue de la Montagne-Sainte-Geneviève, a group of laundresses gathered to read and reread the Jacobin Club's article in the paper *Le Créole patriote*. They heartily praised Robespierre and denounced the "English dogs" for spoiling French strategy toward Austria.[4] During a festival on 21 January 1794, a group of women in a shop at the porte Saint-Honoré remarked that "one cannot make better pleasure for the sansculottes than to use the guillotine on a day such as today, because if the guillotine were not in operation, the festival would not be so beautiful."[5] These women's conversations, and they are far from being atypical, undermine the historiographical wisdom that proletarian women were less radical than their upper-class sisters and that they were less "publicly garrulous" than working-class men.[6]

The discourse of revolutionary women did not, however, merely mimic male rhetoric. Proletarian women in Paris articulated a politics that combined the private concerns of their family economy with public concerns about the nature of the government and the role of political participation in it. In February 1794, for example, in a small shop near the Arsenal, a group of market women praised the Paris Commune for its vigorous measures in defense of the *maximum* on prices. In the same month, at Courtille on the outskirts of Paris, "poor women" blessed the Convention for allowing them to regain their effects from the municipal pawnshop (*mont-de-piété*). In another of Courtille's cafés, tripe sellers and hawkers of matches complained about the high cost of green beans.[7] The café allowed working women to combine their traditional public role as family providers with a new role as politically active citizens. The marketplace and the street, traditional spaces for the conversations of working women, remained important, but they were no longer definitive.

Café sociability was as important for women during the early years of the Revolution as their presence in the spectators' galleries of the various parliaments or in the neighborhood sections of the radical Paris Commune. The practice of gathering in public, developed by going to cafés, helped pave the way for the creation of the first female political club in modern European history: the Society of Revolutionary Republican Women. The café provided for working-class women what the salon furnished for upper-class women: an informal institution of political discussion and debate.[8] After the Jacobins outlawed women's societies and clubs in late October 1793, and then at the end of the year banned all female political participation in public—effectively removing women from the

Convention's galleries and the sections of the Paris Commune—one would expect women to have also been banned from cafés, but this did not happen.[9] Judging from the reports of police spies, the number of women in cafés increased after these fall decrees. It would appear that after being chased out of their own clubs and societies, women gathered in cafés in order to continue their political activity.[10] As long as the women praised the Committee of Public Safety and other revolutionary institutions, Jacobin police spies did not view such activity as threatening. Police reports after October 1793 often described women's conversations and opinions as "very revolutionary" (a sign of approbation until the Thermidorians brought the Terror to a close with the execution of Robespierre and his adherents on 28 July 1794).[11] Political correctness was clearly more important than gender.

Women's participation in café politics waned only after Thermidor, when popular political mobilization was systematically dismantled. Proletarian women did not, however, abandon political activity without resistance. Female sansculottes tried to prevent the reactionary *jeunesse dorée* ("gilded youth") who roamed Paris cafés from smashing busts of the radical journalist Jean-Paul Marat. Only after the unsuccessful popular rising of May 1795, largely inspired by women, did the police start to label café women "furies."[12] Significantly, café women were never accused of being drunkards.[13] At the end of July 1796, the police reported that the cafés were once again male spaces, where drunkenness and quarreling occurred, and churches were female places in which concern for "general affairs"—that is, the political sphere—was absent.[14] Subsequent reports show, however, that women did indeed continue to frequent cafés during the Directory and Napoleonic periods.

Despite this attempted repression, proletarian women in cafés initiated an important political precedent. In each succeeding revolution during the nineteenth century, women would be integral to café life, a consistent attribute of revolutionary mobilization. The café in 1789 revealed that the new political "public sphere" could transcend the traditional gender distinctions embedded in daily life. A truly inclusive notion of a public sphere, open equally to men and women, developed in the cafés at the height of the Revolution. Here, even if only for a limited amount of time, men and women confronted one another in new ways, as concerned citizens who put aside personal disputes to consider the "public good." When they used revolutionary language, even ordinary working women caught the ear of the male political establishment. Women's votes may not have counted, but their opinions registered. Café sociability was one of the primary means by which women became involved in political life before they were allowed the formal attributes of citizenship.[15]

The tumultuous 1790s, however, brought women into cafés not only as revolutionaries but also as prostitutes. The economic dislocations of the late 1780s, followed by the collapse of the luxury trades when aristocrats disappeared in the early 1790s, brought severe unemployment to Paris. In such dire circumstances, women, as they had done before, turned to prostitution as the fastest and surest means of earning a living. Not surprisingly, the incidence of café prostitution jumped dramatically during this decade. In her meticulous work on prostitution during the Revolution, Susan Conner has found that nearly a quarter of women arrested listed their occupation as *femme publique* ("public woman") or admitted that they supplemented their earnings in this way. During this same decade, *femme publique* replaced earlier terms for the prostitute. Thus, the public attention paid to the availability of the prostitute in the new world of the Revolution, as much as, if not more than, her morality, was now the element that stigmatized her. One would think that revolutionary authorities would immediately have conflated the women who engaged in politics with those who pursued prostitution in cafés. But this did not happen until the Directory. The Thermidorian police reports, like those of the previous revolutionary forces, made a clear distinction between women engaged in politics and those pursuing prostitution. Only during 1796 did the police automatically connect women in cafés to prostitution rather than to politics.[16]

Following the revolutionary and Napoleonic periods, the presence of women in cafés was sustained by innovations in the café's architecture and economic functions. The creation of the serving counter had a vital impact on gender relations in the café. Women at the counter, either as owner or as server, were at the very heart of café sociability. An equally important innovation was the proliferation of private dining rooms.[17] Both of these innovations, as we shall see, would have profound implications for the café's gender relations.

The proprietress at her counter sparked a series of stories and myths. Indeed, one legend holds that a female café owner initiated the custom of drinking at the counter: Mother Moreaux at her eponymous shop in the place des Ecoles supposedly started the practice of "perpendicular drinking" at her zinc counter.[18] At an even more modest establishment on the rue Saint Honoré-Bosquet, a demure and beautiful woman with a an ugly and calculating husband held court at the counter. Her looks and charm attracted such crowds that by 1817 the couple were able to purchase a grand café in the fashionable Palais-Royal, the café des Mille-Colonnes. Here the wife became famous as the lovely lady café owner (*la belle limonadière*) whose large counter "scarcely suffices to contain all her tributes."[19] Sometimes shrewd café owners deliberately hired comely or famous young women for their counters. A few days after Giuseppe Fieschi's attempted assassination of Louis Philippe with his "infernal machine" in 1834, his young girlfriend Nina was hired as *dame de comptoir* for the café de la Renaissance on the place de la Bourse. Outfitted in a flame-colored satin dress, and with her hair richly ornamented, she was paid 1,000 francs per month and attracted "a daily throng of unfeeling idlers."[20]

By the 1840s, almost all writers concerned with Parisian mores commented on the desirability, if not the necessity, of a pretty woman behind the counter. An attractive woman was generally believed, as in the case of La Belle Limonadière, to be able to increase a shop's clientele greatly.[21] The *Nouveau tableau de Paris au XIXe siècle*, a multivolume compendium of Paris life that appeared in this decade, simultaneously honoring and updating Louis-Sébastien Mercier, provides one of the fullest descriptions of the ideal woman behind the counter:

> Almost all cafés [operate] under the presidency of a *demoiselle de comptoir*. The shop's success rest upon her. She must be cute, personable, always smile at the customer who pays for one drink or the gourmet with 20 francs in his pocket. Her eye must be nowhere and everywhere, and she must not notice the bad language and come-ons. She must repay compliments after the fashion of Madame Maintenon, who knew how to replace a roast with an anecdote. By her grace of manners, charm of figure, and good taste in dress, she must draw the customer away from the illicit marriage of coffee and chicory and adulterated cream.[22]

For the most part, the predominantly male clientele of the working-class café were reassured to have a woman behind the counter. Not only did she provide a bit of feminine beauty, she also filled the traditional female role of serving food and drink. The woman café owner was only slightly more of a professional than those proletarian women who, when the cost of wine rose, made their family an imitation wine out of raisins.[23] At other times, working-class women, especially those who lived near the barrières (before 1860), would go out beyond them in the morning to buy as much of the cheaper suburban wine as the city guards would allow for the family dinner that night.[24] Thus working-class men could comfortably expect women to serve them drinks.

In many cafés, a woman was valued behind the counter for more than just a pretty face. In the case of couples who ran cafés, the wife often also played the roles of financier, cashier, and accountant. The mother of the Communard and Third Republic labor leader Jean Allemane took this sort of active role in the family café on the Left Bank.[25] The dowry or savings of the wife or lover were often decisive in purchasing the shop in the first place. In the daily running of the shop, the wife often provided the clear and sober head for business, while her husband or lover drank and socialized with the customers.[26] The proprietress often retired from the bar after 8 P.M. to count the day's earnings and to ensure that the bar was well stocked for the evening rush. She was customarily still on call until the closing hour, which by the end of the nineteenth century was usually midnight.[27] In addition, the wife was frequently required to take over the management of the shop when excessive drinking led to a decline in her husband's health (the reason why so many female café owners were widows). The Paris bankruptcy archives are rich, especially for the 1870s, 1880s, and 1890s, with examples of female café owners indispensable to their businesses.[28]

This female presence behind the bar ensured that Paris cafés were not ordinary patriarchal spaces. Unlike the eighteenth-century sources, those for the nineteenth reveal virtually no incidents of women being insulted or asked to leave solely because of their gender. Moreover, there are few occurrences in the sources after 1789 of male workers spending much time with their buddies criticizing their wives or lovers.

The rise of the female proprietress facilitated the growth of a female clientele in the café. The husband usually had his own circle of habitués, who were also his friends, and the wife likewise had her own circle.[29] From the early nineteenth century on, laundresses and female concierges were regulars at the bar. Aristide Bruant immortalized this relationship in his songs about small bistros.[30] But women from other occupations also frequently talked and drank with the proprietress at the bar. In the early 1880s, for example, Marie Houdremont, a day laborer, would usually *prendre un bouillon* at dame Lefebvre's shop at 39 rue des Amandiers in Belleville to celebrate their long-standing friendship. The large number of civil insult cases between women café owners and female concierges, hotel keepers, and other women testify to the female networks surrounding the woman behind the counter.[31] Perhaps the most dramatic example of the solidarity of these female networks happened on the avenue Raspail in the suburb of Gentilly shortly after 1900. One morning a brutal husband refused to let his wife back into their shop (and home) so she could take her medicine. Moreover, he publicly cursed the weeping woman from the café's terrace: "Go on, woman! Wash your dirty mug!" A crowd of 150 female clothing workers from an adjacent bullet-making workshop watched this incident as they returned from lunch, at around 12:45 P.M. Several women threw clay at the husband, who in turn threw stones at them, injuring one woman in the face. At the trial, this 25-year-old worker explained why she had become involved: "I saw the wife in tears. The husband's attitude provoked me and my comrades." The group then escorted the wife to another café, where she could be attended to. Subsequently they took up a collection for her.[32] Running a small business, probably the most powerful position to which a working-class woman of these times could aspire, gave the female café owner behind her counter a great deal of status with other women in the neighborhood.[33]

A diverse set of sources reveal the regular presence of women in cafés by the 1850s. Throughout the first half of the century, numerous observers reported that wives accompanied their husbands to the barrière cafés as they had done in the eighteenth century.[34] The reports of the prefect of police to the minister of the interior during the 1820s indicate that women were present at many of the large taverns brawls of the era. In May 1823, for instance, women were listed among the injured when a fight erupted at a wine shop on the rue Saint-Denis between water carriers and porters.[35] The judicial newspaper Gazette des tribunaux also frequently noted café incidents involving men and women. An entry in its November 1828 chronicles of Parisian life recounted a story of vengeance and honor that erupted in a café when a drunk carter and a female vendor of potatoes fought over whether he had a right to drink from her glass.[36] The autobiography of the artisan Jacques-Etienne Bédé reveals that women, as wives and workers, participated actively in both the talk and the toasts at the banquets of workers' associations in the 1820s.[37] In November 1830, the Gazette reported a case involving a prostitute who had been living with a market porter for three years and was now reproaching him for infidelity.[38] In July 1848, the Gazette noted the peregrinations of a confidence man, trading on the recent revolution, who always claimed to women in cafés that he did not have to pay for drinks anymore because "the new republic will pay for them."[39] Later, in December, the paper recounted the story of a woman being swindled by a crooked costermonger in a café who gave her counterfeit money in change for the purchase of potatoes.[40] These are just a few of the myriad examples of working women in the thick of café life.

The rise and fall of the Commune reveals the entire spectrum of behavior of working-class women in cafés. In the late 1860s, Nathalie Le Mel, a seasoned labor organizer and member of the First International, ran its cooperative restaurant and meeting place, La Marmite, thus politicizing the role of the Belle Limonadière.[41] This era also saw the radicalization of the *grisette* (young working-class woman) and the *lorette* (courtesan). At the parliamentary inquiry into the causes of the Commune, several witnesses claimed that "loose women" and female café owners had seduced and brainwashed much of the army, the police, and the National Guard. The former head of the Paris Police Detective Service, Gustave Macé, provided specific details. One sergeant in the National Guard, who also ran a café on the rue Saint-Paul, had enlisted the aid of streetwalkers (*filles galantes*) and street vendors in January 1871 in his successful bid to replace the regular police with National Guards. A Captain Garcin at the inquiry believed that the stipend, 1 franc 50 centimes for the National Guards and 75 centimes for their wives, had been the cause of the "flirting and dancing" that had taken guardsmen from the cafés into the clubs. The former prefect of police Ernest Cresson reported that police agents—in other words, spies—had been carefully watched by female café owners. These proprietresses supposedly took notes and passed them on to the militants, who then knew the identity of the police spies.[42]

The drunken female Communard was an important stereotypical brick in the edifice constructed by the anti-Communard press. Two of the most rabid members of this school, Maxime Du Camp and Alexandre Dumas *fils*, elaborated upon this theme. They were even occupationally specific, alleging that seamstresses were at the forefront of these intoxicated "furies." The few contemporary voices that spoke in defense of the Commune, including the photographic pioneer Nadar, emphatically denied seeing any women, even errant ones, in the cafés. One of the few working-class Parisian women of the period to write her autobiography, Victorine Brocher, provides a much more nuanced view than either the prosecutors or the defenders of the Commune. Although clearly unsympathetic to cafés (she is one of the few proletarian observers to portray cafés as anti-female spaces), she nevertheless shows that women, including herself, frequented them. Especially during the "bloody week" that followed the fall of the Commune, Brocher notes, women found in cafés a place where they could share their experiences and misery at seeing their husbands and sons shot by the Versailles forces. She also records some of the epithets, such as "bunch of pigs and murderers," that women hurled at police and soldiers.[43]

The crushing of the Commune halted the creative political synergy that women had developed in the café since 1789. Working-class women continued to go to cafés, and militants such as Louise Michel and some of the female anarchists continued to use cafés as venues for propaganda and organizing. One female café owner sympathetic to the anarchist cause was Louise Pioger, a 46-year-old widow who lived maritally with a former tailor. During the decade 1895 to 1905, some of the most important Paris anarchists—such as Sébastien Fauré and Paul Bernard—frequented her establishment, along with their wives, lovers, and relatives. Pioger freely admitted to anarchist sentiments and an anarchist clientele, but she asserted that anarchism would triumph by persuasion and talk rather than by violence.[44] The café politics of working women did not extend beyond the example of such individual militants to encompass women's organizations in the cafés.

Instead, the decades after 1870 witnessed an elaborate efflorescence of café prostitution. The ambiguous status of working-class women in cafés and the informal and spontaneous nature of its sociability facilitated this development. As we have already seen, it was often difficult to demarcate clearly between "lewd" and "respectable" behavior, as in the case of the prostitute who rebuked her cohabitant for infidelity. A police report from a Paris suburb in the early 1870s provides another variation on the ambiguity of women's sexuality in the café. The report noted of two female café frequenters: "Paquet and her friend lived at Arcuil, 6 Grand rue, above Lucien Drier's café. He has let them stay there free for five or six weeks. . . . The two women live together. They have drunken habits and drink with the first comer. No one reproaches them with regard to their honesty or their morals."[45] The police usually reserved the phrase "with the first comer" to describe the behavior of prostitutes.[46] Nevertheless, in this case, the police considered neither woman morally suspect. Instead, these women, like the "Decorated One" encountered in previous chapters, probably preferred to form their relationships in cafés. Numerous other cases in the judicial archives after 1870 also reveal that the café comportment of women contained all possible shadings between promiscuity and respectability. The same ambiguity is naturally found in the literature on Bohemian Paris. In the Latin Quarter cafés popular with students and artists throughout the century, the distinctions among prostitute, model, étudiante, and demi-mondaine (these last two categories comprising women bohemians) were unclear. By the 1890s, even upper-class women began to frequent this world, often with pen and ink at hand.[47]

The difficulty of isolating café prostitution as a distinct phenomenon is the reason why historians of prostitution in nineteenth-century Paris, ever since the landmark work of Alexandre Parent-Duchâtelet during the 1830s, have minimized the role of the café. During the first half of the century, these historians concentrate on the rise of the system of tolerated and licensed bordellos rather than on the growth and use of the cabinet noir in cafés and restaurants. For the second half of the century, they chart the fall of this regulated system of tolerated houses and the diffusion of prostitution into rented rooms and hotels. In both eras, they have underestimated the continuing centrality of the café in Parisian prostitution. Jill Harsin and Alain Corbin, the leading contemporary historians of Parisian prostitution, realize that the café assumed a major role after the decline of the tolerated houses, but they overlook the rituals and behavior surrounding café prostitution. Consequently, they focus more on the act of prostitution than on the ambience. Corbin's failure in this respect weakens one of his most brilliant points: that prostitution in Paris steadily eschewed the "mercantile" atmosphere of the bordello for the more "romantic" milieu of Parisian life.[48]

Even though café prostitution had been pervasive since at least the 1790s, police and public opinion focused on this activity only after 1860. When the last Restoration prefect, Jean Mangin, made what Harsin calls "the century's most radical pronouncement on the subject of prostitution," he mentioned by name virtually every public place—streets, thoroughfares, boulevards, and gardens—in which it occurred, but not cafés.[49] Like all his counterparts between 1789 and 1861, he enacted no ordinance directed against café prostitution or even against cabinets noirs. After the 1778 and 1780 ordinances, in fact, until the 1860s, the only augmentation of the arsenal of laws against café prostitution was the promulgation of the December 1851 decree. Nevertheless, the essential point about the regulation of Parisian café prostitution was not lack of laws but lack of enforcement. Throughout the first half of the century, the number of infractions prosecuted under the 1778 and 1780 ordinances never exceeded a hundred. After 1850, however, both ordinances were used more regularly. For example, the number of infractions under the 1778 decree went from 30 in 1855 to 126 in 1860 and 175 in 1862. For the 1780 decree, we see a similar pattern: from 35 infractions in 1855 to 171 in 1861.

This flurry of ordinances concerning café prostitution after 1860 reflects the dramatic decline of the tolerated house system and the rise of rented rooms and cafés as primary sites of venal sex.[50] Statistics on the number of registered prostitutes in tolerated houses, and to a lesser extent also the number of tolerated houses, reveal the abruptness of the transition. From a peak of 2,008 women and 235 houses during the 1850s, we see a leveling off during the 1860s and 1870s at around 1,500 women, and then a reduction to 976 in 1882 and to 387 in 1903. The number of houses did not fall so precipitously, declining from 202 in 1856 to 133 in 1880 and below 100 in 1885; then, during the late 1890s and early 1900s, the figure rose to 123 in 1903.[51] As Harsin notes, the police had come to favor a more informal prostitution system.[52] This regime was best symbolized by the certificate of tolerance, which the police issued to the individual women, rather than to the bordello.[53] By the mid 1880s, Harsin finds, running a tolerated house no longer had any advantages.[54]

Conducting prostitution in a café had significant benefits: shelter from the gaze of the police and the protective cover of the usual male-female café interaction. Anecdotal writers deftly caught the moral indeterminacy of café customers. In the 1880s, the cabaret Arabi in Montmartre was a preserve of "the most heterogeneous and bizarre clientele, . . . a tower of babel of debauchery of the nocturnal type." The "real workers," whether male or female, "looked askance at the women and the men who finished the night in this smoky place."[55] The weekly magazine L'Illustration in April 1892 noted a heterogeneous café clientele that included "women of good life," "girls of bad life," and some "timid" ones too.[56] Café owners turned these secluded and sociable features of café life to good advantage in their running battle with the police. "Cafés and lodging houses" were the refuges during police sweeps of the prostitutes "who swarm in the Latin Quarter," the Gazette des tribunaux noted.[57] Other papers declared that streets densely populated with cafés, such as Montmartre's rue de Clichy, were "sacred havens" for the pimps of the neighborhood.[58]

Whenever confronted with police repression, café owners turned these benefits into excuses, citing "freedom of commerce" or "private property" and claiming that the police had no right to enter their establishments. Naturally, the police brushed aside such specious assertions, but they had more trouble with the excuse that the women in the shop were customers, not prostitutes, because this was often true. In 1901, a café owner who claimed that the women on his premises were not prostitutes but laborers from the neighboring workshops almost succeeded with this alibi, losing only on appeal.[59]

Café owners often encouraged behavior patterns conducive to prostitution. In some cases, observers claimed, they even recruited young women at the doors of their shops and then gave them free food and drinks if their looks enticed customers in.[60] The *Gazette des tribunaux* in 1868 publicized the case of a deceptively philanthropic café owner who repeatedly provided "free soup" for the needy, but in reality did so in order "to attract young women and tempt them into a life of debauchery."[61] In other cases, certain café owners, who were also landlords engaging in clandestine prostitution, provided a free room for the purpose.[62] Occasionally, too, the building's concierge would be brought into the system to serve as a procuress.[63] The opportunities for prostitution increased during the 1860s, when, as we have seen, café owners started to hire large numbers of female waitresses.[64] By this time, it had become common for pimps and prostitutes to strike deals with a café owner and thus to turn the shop, for all intents and purposes, into a house of prostitution.[65]

Café prostitutes had two basic strategies, both immortalized in Parisian slang. On the one hand, the term "boulevard women" (*femmes des boulevards*) applied to women who lured men into cafés for a couple of drinks and perhaps an evening together. On the other hand, "fun girls" (*filles de joie*) let themselves be picked up by customers already in the café.[66] The *Gazette des tribunaux* provides some especially vivid examples of these *femmes des boulevards*. During the late 1860s, Marguerite Durand, nicknamed Camille Le Blanc, a 28-year-old lodger on the rue des Martyrs, sent her female lodgers every night to recruit on the streets and in the cafés. The next morning she made the rounds of the rooms and collected the earnings. In another case, dating from early February 1868, a woman picked up a man as he left a café on the boulevard Montmartre. She asked if he wanted to go to the Bal de Casino, and after dancing, she persuaded him to come back to a room above a café. When he awoke the following morning, he found that both the woman and his wallet had disappeared. A few days later, in a similar incident, a petty manufacturer met two girls on the place du Château-d'Eau. A conversation ensued, and the two girls accepted his offer of refreshments. They took him to a café on rue des Fossés du Temple and into a cabinet noir, where thieves robbed him.[67]

Late-nineteenth-century novelists and the researcher Alain Corbin have meditated long and fruitfully on the meaning of café prostitution, but they have not fully grasped its power over the male imagination, because they have not placed it fully within the history of the café's gender relations. Following the lead of Joris-Karl Huysmans and Maurice Barrès, Corbin sees the rise of beer halls with women waitresses (*brasseries à femmes*) as representing a male desire for a less mercenary form of venal sex than that of the bordello.[68] In the café, an artisan, clerk, or day laborer could foster the illusion that he was making love rather than buying sex. The novelists and Corbin fail equally to note the most important ingredient that sustained this café fantasy: genuine and sincere men and women did court and make love in cafés. For the very reason that the café was not an exclusively male space, the women one met in a café could not be presumed to be prostitutes. Thus the line between commercial sexuality and true romantic love became blurred, allowing for the free play of the imagination.

The diversity of café relationships served a double purpose. On the one hand, prostitution was shielded from the gaze of the police—how could an officer know which were the genuine couples? On the other hand, the illusion was upheld that this was a space where ordinary people could fall in love. Huysmans intuitively grasped this dichotomy in his novel *A rebours* (1884): "Monstrous as this might appear, the tavern satisfied an ideal . . . a vague, stale, old-fashioned ideal of love . . . to court a girl in a tavern was to avoid wounding all these amorous susceptibilities." However, he then noted the "stupid and mercenary" nature of the tavern staff and the fact that like "the staff of a brothel," the women in such places "drank without being thirsty, laughed without being amused, drooled over the caresses of the filthiest workman, and went for each other hammer and tongs at the slightest provocation."[69]

What Huysmans failed to add is that the clients of these filles de joie probably took heart from the honest acts of affection between actual lovers in the café.[70] Léon and Maurice Bonneff lamented young male workers' habit of frequenting "loose" cafés in order to find a woman and usually winding up with a prostitute.[71] These authors do not consider the feelings of the women. Did they hope, too, that they could find a man who could take them out of their miserable economic conditions and prevent them from falling into alcoholism? Although some women may have been able to find husbands in this way, most who became trapped in the trade of café prostitution probably felt like the compulsive absinthe drinker who, after she was arrested for scandal and seditious outcries, confessed, "I suffer so much. The sadness makes me crazy. Please be indulgent, I would hardly dream of attacking the government. I have totally destroyed myself."[72]

Occupations

Is it possible to make an accurate composite sketch of women in nineteenth-century Paris cafés? What were their occupations, their ages, and what proportions were single, married, or widowed? No nineteenth-century observer has provided a systematic outline. Police reports during the 1789–1815 period often noted "some women" or "the women" or "a group of women" in a café, but they never attempted to enumerate their occupational or civil status.[73] Opponents of the Paris Commune created the myth of the radical female Communard as a drunken incendiary (*pétroleuse*) who set Paris aflame. Maxime du Camp and Dumas *fils*, two of the most vehement anti-Communard polemicists, asserted that the majority of these "furies" were seamstresses and other clothing workers.[74] Neither author, however, presented any quantitative evidence.

Because of the destruction of judicial archives, we have no source from the first seventy years of the nineteenth century for more than an anecdotal or impressionistic sense of which women went to cafés. From marriage contracts after 1860 and from judicial archives dating from 1873, the historian is provided with four sources: wives who had café owners witness their marriages, women who brought civil insult cases against café owners, and women who were charged with public drunkenness in either the police courts or the correctional tribunal. Data from these four discrete populations offer different but equally illuminating insights into female cafégoing and the way in which questions of honor, publicity, politics, and sexuality intersected in Paris cafés (see tables 7.1 and 7.2).

In criminal matters, women constituted decided minorities: 12 percent of the defendants in cases involving aggravated public drunkenness and a mere 5.3 percent in cases of the misdemeanor of simple intoxication. In the case of marriage contracts, they naturally formed half of the population, and they also constituted a substantial percentage of those who brought suit for slander. In civil insult and defamation cases involving café owners, they represent over a third (35.5%) of the defendants or plaintiffs.[75] These various percentages provide the approximate proportion of women in various café activities. Women were much more involved in conversation than in drinking. This fact is borne out by the substantial percentages of women defending their reputations or insulting the police as compared to the minuscule percentage of those arrested simply for public drunkenness. The role women played in Parisian café life naturally varied from time to time and from place to place. Nevertheless, these

Table 7.1

OCCUPATIONS OF CAFÉGOING PARISIENNES WHO SUED FOR SLANDER, CHOSE CAFÉ OWNERS TO WITNESS THEIR WEDDINGS, OR WERE PROSECUTED FOR PROSTITUTION OR PUBLIC DRUNKENNESS, 1873–1902 *(percentages in parentheses)*

				Public Drunkenness	
Occupation	Sued for Slander	Cafe Owner as Wedding Witness	Charged with Prostitution	Police Court	Correctional Tribunal
Garment trade	42 (13.7)	2,930 (27.6)	1,816 (26.5)	85 (22.8)	175 (19.2)
Housewife	113 (36.8)	1,932 (18.2)	0 (0)	71 (19.3)	105 (11.5)
Day laborer	12 (3.9)	669 (6.3)	312 (4.5)	47 (12.7)	143 (15.6)
Concierge	24 (7.8)	25 (0.2)	0 (0)	2 (0.5)	0 (0)
Prostitute	0 (0)	0 (0)	0 (0)	9 (2.4)	138 (15.1)
Streetvendor	24 (7.8)	106 (1.0)	49 (0.7)	34 (9.2)	50 (5.5)
Domestic	20 (6.5)	987 (9.3)	2,681 (39.2)	15 (4.1)	74 (8.1)
Laundress	10 (3.2)	541 (5.1)	622 (9.0)	31 (8.4)	80 (8.7)
Rentier/ Landlady	10 (3.2)	180 (1.7)	0 (0)	3 (0.5)	8 (0.8)
Cook	5 (1.6)	1,253 (11.8)	2 (0)	12 (3.2)	35 (3.8)
Articles de Paris (luxury trade)	9 (2.9)	276 (2.6)	472 (6.9)	3 (0.5)	17 (1.8)
Metalworker	4 (1.3)	265 (2.6)	246 (3.6)	11 (3.2)	25 (2.7)
Shopkeeper	18 (5.8)	42 (0.4)	29 (0.4)	8 (2.4)	23 (2.5)
Furniture maker	4 (1.1)	64 (0.6)	234 (3.4)	10 (3.1)	18 (1.9)
Employee/ Clerk / Teacher	6 (1.9)	307 (2.9)	88 (1.3)	4 (1.2)	2 (0.2)
Ragpicker	0 (0)	2 (0.01)	5 (0)	14 (4.0)	14 (1.5)
Food preparer	0 (0)	106 (1.0)	0 (0)	0 (0)	0 (0)
Entertainer	0 (0)	138 (1.4)	54 (0.08)	1 (0.2)	5 (0.5)
Small manufacturer	2 (0.6)	11 (0.1)	1 (0)	0 (0)	0 (0)
Construction	3 (0.9)	106 (1.0)	0 (0)	0 (0)	3 (0.3)
Printing	0 (0)	53 (0.5)	124 (1.8)	0 (0)	1 (0.1)
Service and Commerce	4 (1.1)	605 (5.7)	107 (1.6)	9 (3.0)	6 (0.6)
Total	307	10,616	6,842	368	913

Sources: Data for prostitution arrests derived from O. Commenge, *Hygiène sociale: La Prostitution clandestine à Paris* (Paris: Schleicher, 1897), 336; other data from sources cited in table 3.1.

percentages give an idea of the proportion of cafégoers who were female, fluctuating in a high range of from 35.5 percent (civil insult cases) to 50 percent (those seeking a marriage witness), and in a low range of from 5.3 percent (simple intoxication) to 12 percent (aggravated public drunkenness).

Table 7.2

CIVIL STATUS OF PARISIENNES INVOLVED IN PROSECUTIONS FOR SLANDER AND
PUBLIC DRUNKENNESS, 1873–1902 *(percentages in parentheses)*

Status	Prosecutions for Slander		Public Drunkenness			
			Police Court		Correctional Tribunal	
Married	210	(68.2)	86	(50.4)	277	(30.3)
Single	59	(19.3)	120	(32.5)	479	(52.5)
Widowed	35	(11.6)	63	(17.1)	152	(16.7)
Not stated	3	(0.9)	0	(0)	5	(0.5)

Sources: As for table 3.1.

These statistics lend quantitative credence to the idea that café behavior encompassed the whole spectrum of women's comportment from the
"virtuous and respectable" to the "vicious" and the "debauched." The
mere fact of women bringing suit against café owners for besmirching their
reputations demonstrates that the Parisian lower classes in general viewed
the café as a respectable place. At the same time, the prominent number
of prostitutes confirms that much prostitution did indeed occur in cafés.
The data dramatically illustrate the wide range of women's café behavior:
from the wife willingly defending her reputation in court to the prostitute
dragged into court after insulting the police. Café comportment was as diverse as the concubinage observed in Paris by H. A. Frégier.[76] In short,
there is no simple dichotomy between married women defending their
virtue and young, unattached single women getting drunk and insulting
the police. Rather, the overlap in occupations among the various female
populations reveals that women who defended their reputations against
neighborhood slights might be equally disposed to decry police injustice.
Working women who engaged in café life were not marginal to their communities.

Female cafégoers as a group did not have the same occupational profile as the prostitute population. O. Commenge's *Hygiène sociale: La Prostitution clandestine à Paris* (1897) highlights the differences. This detailed
and systematic study covers the same era (1878–87) as tables 7.1 and 7.2.
Moreover, the size of Commenge's sample—6,842 prostitutes—is roughly
equivalent to the civil (brides) and court (defendants) figures.[77] A comparison finds two crucial discontinuities. First, domestics composed the
largest category—with 2,681 women (39.3%)—of the clandestine prosti-

tutes listed by Commenge, but totaled only 74 women (8.1%) of the women brought before the correctional tribunal and only 9.3 percent of the brides. Second, the category of those without a listed occupation, which may very well include housewives along with day laborers, was vastly larger among those arrested for public drunkenness than for prostitution: 306 women (4.48%) as opposed to 105 women (27.1%) in the correctional tribunal and 18.2 percent among the brides. This comparison between women arrested for prostitution and those involved in café life does, however, show continuity with respect to two important occupations. Both the garment workers and the laundresses have virtually the same numbers and percentages in these sets of data. The garment workers total 1,326 women (19.38%) among Commenge's clandestine prostitutes and 175 women (19.2%) in the correctional tribunal. Among those women getting married, however, garment workers did form a much higher percentage (27.6%). The laundresses totaled 614 (8.97%) among clandestine prostitutes, as opposed to 80 (8.7%) in the correctional tribunal. Among the women getting married, the percentage of laundresses was lower, only 5.1 percent.

One implication of these statistics is that the sexual relations of Parisian domestics must have occurred largely, if not almost entirely, in garrets, apartments, or private houses, and only seldom in cafés. In short, two routes led to prostitution: one public and one private. The private route led through intrigues in homes and apartments, and the public way ran through liaisons in cafés. Domestics took the former road, whereas garment workers and laundresses took the latter. Many other groups active in café life—such as housewives, day laborers, street vendors, petty merchants, and artisans—were, however, unlikely to engage in prostitution.

These statistics thus furnish additional proof that cafégoing by women was not always connected to venal sexuality. The three factors most influential in female cafégoing were, rather, women's earnings, the labor discipline imposed upon them, and their local business and social relations.

Judging from the statistics, well-paid late-nineteenth-century working Parisiennes were not likely to marry café habitués or indulge in heavy drinking and disorderly behavior. The percentages of the two highest-paid groups—women engaged in the manufacture of luxury goods (known as *articles de Paris*), such as artificial flowers, jewelry, umbrellas, and toys, and those in white-collar jobs, such as saleswomen or clerks—are much lower in these categories than is the case with men (see Chapter 2). The most surprising fact about the café behavior of this upper stratum of working women is the virtual absence of women in white-collar occupations. This certainly cannot be explained by the fact that they did not go to cafés, for Theresa McBride and Charles Rearick, in particular, have shown that white-collar women helped spawn a "new leisure culture" at the end of the century, of which cafés, music halls, bicycles, and amusement parks were an integral part. The presence of these women became so ubiquitous and predictable that some establishments catered especially to them.[78] Perhaps the best way to explain the scarcity of female clerks among those arrested for public drunkenness and disorderly behavior is that even more than their male counterparts, they sought to uphold their reputations as white-collar workers, especially in comparison with artisans and industrial workers, for restraint and sobriety. Female department-store employees in particular sought to impress their employers with how serious and hardworking they were.[79] White-collar women's low political consciousness or lack of social ties in their neighborhoods may also help explain their low numbers in these statistics.

If good wages and abundant leisure time did not translate among women, as they did among men, into disorderly or disputatious café behavior, what can we expect in the way of café behavior among women who were poorly paid and had little free time? In the case of domestics, on the one hand, the answer is a minimal presence in the statistics, not much greater than that of white-collar workers, given the fact that domestics were the largest occupational group among Parisian women.[80] Garment workers, on the other hand, are relatively strongly represented, but nevertheless less so in the case of drunken and disorderly behavior than in the general Parisian female population, of which they composed the second-largest group.[81]

The dramatic difference between these top two occupational categories stemmed from their very different working conditions. The statistics demonstrate the rigorous surveillance of their servants that families maintained, which made café life simply out of the question for domestics. In contrast, garment workers, who often toiled endlessly in their apartments for pitifully low salaries, with little time or money to go out to eat, do seem to have constituted a sizable café clientele by the 1870s, consisting especially of women who had married café habitués. The development of textile and garment factories and large workshops after 1870 forced thousands of clothing workers into jobs outside their apartments, which probably increased the importance of cafés in their lives. Leaders of the dressmakers' union, as well as other observers, noted the prevalence of garment workers eating their meals in cafés after 1870.[82] The few female artisans in other trades—such as metal, furniture, construction, and printing—faithfully reflect their small numbers in these sectors. But the numbers also show that these female artisans often engaged in the same raucous café behavior as their male shopmates.

Although it may not appear obvious, most of the other occupational groups do have something in common in terms of their labor processes that explains their participation in café life: easy access to cafés during their working hours. We have already noted that street vendors who plied their trades in or around cafés had numerous drinking opportunities during the day.[83] Such visible public professions naturally resulted in numerous civil and criminal insults, as well as a prominent percentage—5.7 percent—of the women who married café habitués. Laundresses were another group constantly exposed to public life, for their shops were one of the principal places where women socialized. Yet the sociability of laundresses extended to cafés, too; their rank as fifth-largest category among the public drunkenness cases confirms contemporary observations that they were frequent cafégoers and, in fact, received daily rations of wine as part of their wages.[84] The same observation is also true of cooks who worked in restaurants and cafés. Although evidence for this café presence is slight in the case of aggravated public drunkenness cases, it is strong in the case of the marriages, in which they represent the third-highest percentage—11.8 percent—of women marrying café habitués.

Naturally, prostitution is the primary example of a female occupation correlated with cafégoing. Among women charged with drunken and disorderly conduct, prostitutes constituted the third-largest group, making them the most overrepresented group among all women for these infractions. Moreover, female prostitutes arrested for public drunkenness were also much more likely to be charged with insulting or assaulting a police officer than other female inebriates. Conversely, intoxicated females who were not prostitutes were much more likely to be involved in some other correctional offense, such as theft or begging.[85] Prostitutes clearly resented being arrested and often created scenes in cafés when the police moved against them. The police, in turn, were often reluctant to persist in doing so, because pedestrians and café habitués, moved by the prostitutes' wails and woes, often protected them. To prevent bad publicity for the police department, Prefect Albert Gigot decreed on 15 October 1878 that only officers in civilian dress should arrest prostitutes in such circumstances, and that they must always act tactfully. Subsequent incidents and the attendant press attacks on the police, especially during the early 1880s under the regimes of the prefects Andrieux and Camescasse, reveal the failure of these approaches. The best solution, the police found, was to be indulgent.[86] Even though the police did clearly target prostitutes more than other women when repressing female public drunkenness, they nevertheless did not use drink as a pretext to arrest prostitutes to anywhere near the same degree they did with male workers.

The civil cases heard by the correctional tribunal reveal another integral aspect of cafégoing by working-class females: the question of honor. The primary reality that these cases measure is not the labor process but the social networks that bound female neighborhood life together. In the still tightly knit communities of proletarian Paris, insults, innuendoes, and rumors could be fatal to anyone's reputation and/or business. Thus it is not surprising that the main groups bringing civil suits were shopkeepers, hotel keepers, street vendors, concierges, merchants, entrepreneurs, landlords, property owners, and married women.[87] These women tended to be much more established in a neighborhood than an unattached or rootless single woman. The proportion of these neighborhood notables involved in civil disputes, 94 out of 307, or virtually one-third of the total, is significantly higher than their number among the brides (27.1%), and higher still than their minimal representation among those charged with drunken and disorderly conduct (17.8%). Examining the upper strata of this group—concierges, hotel keepers, merchants, and small manufacturers—we see an even greater disparity: 17.5 percent among the civil cases, a paltry 3.4 percent among the criminal cases, and even fewer among the brides.

Housewives, the other major group to bring suit for defamation, were also far more likely to seek redress for the besmirching of their honor in café conversation (36.8%) than to engage in disorderly behavior in cafés (11.5%). A similar gap is also found in the civil status of the two groups in the courtroom: married and widowed women made up 79.8 percent of those bringing civil suits and only 47.0 percent of those charged with drunken and disorderly conduct (see table 7.2).

Mentality, Behavior, and Meaning

There is little evidence that either proprietors or customers during the nineteenth century assumed that every woman who entered a café was a prostitute. No explicit statements along this line can be found in judicial archives or newspapers, which much more eloquently support the contrary proposition: unless proven otherwise, a woman accompanying a man to a café was considered to be his wife, a relative, a friend, or a neighbor. Male witnesses often referred to the women in the café as "neighborhood women" (dames du quartier).[88] Sébastien Billoir was not challenged in Montmartre cafés during the mid 1870s when he and his girlfriend Jeanne Bellengé claimed that they were married. Theodore Keller, a rentier habitué of the café Charles, summed up the opinion of that establishment: "Billoir sometimes brought a woman to the café, [and] we considered her his legitimate wife." Jean Devin, a used goods dealer and client of Raydon's, had the same opinion: "I believed they were married." The café owner himself, Jean Raydon, agreed: "He was almost always in the company of a woman, who we thought at first in the house was his legitimate wife; only later did we suspect the truth."[89] The same lack of suspicion is exhibited by cafégoers at that other great center of café life, the Latin Quarter. When the young butcher Joseph Delest met the seamstress Marie Sabre in a café one Christmas Eve, he did not suspect (and perhaps did not care) that she had been a registered prostitute in Vichy. In Paris she was simply another seamstress frequenting the cafés and hoping to find a permanent relationship.[90] These two examples clearly refute the notion that women and prostitution were easily or automatically equated in café life.

Because the café had become one of the main spaces of male-female interaction, nineteenth-century working women were not afraid to go to a café even when they were alone. "Sunday, May 21, I went in the evening to get a cup of coffee in the neighborhood," a female day laborer remembered of the time when the "bloody week" of the repression of the Paris Commune was getting under way.[91] The behavior of Marie Morel, one of the rare cafégoing domestics, illustrates the casualness with which women used cafés. While out for a walk in 1886, she met Louise Montginaux, the new lover of her former beau, and invited the couple up to her apartment. "A short time afterwards, . . . Marie said, 'Do you want to take something below at the wine merchant's?'" Montginaux later recalled.[92] Novelists also portrayed working women as having no compunction about entering a café alone. In Emile Gaboriau's Other People's Money, a female character going home alone after the theater walks for five or six minutes and then enters an establishment that is "half eating-house, half wine-shop."[93] The ambience of these cafés is a radical departure from that found by Brennan in the eighteenth century.

Another indication of the acceptance nineteenth-century working women found in cafés is that grandmothers, aunts, or mothers—not just fathers or brothers—would chaperone young women. Describing a typical working-class café, the American observer Alvan Sanborn noted: "In a distant corner a dark-skinned beauty of not more than eighteen is engaged in an exciting game of dominoes with an elderly woman evidently her mother. . . . Other women are sewing and chatting busily."[94] The correctional tribunal cases also supply numerous examples of men who showed no hesitation whatsoever in taking their female relatives and friends to the café.[95]

Although women may have felt free to go to cafés, it has been the assumption of many historians that they could not have played much of a role there. This thesis finds some support in Zola's novels, especially *Le Ventre de Paris*, which contains a detailed description of café life with a focus on the role of women. Zola provides an elaborate description of a small band of conspirators who regularly meet at a café in the central market district. Among them are a couple named Charvet and Clémence. "Clémence . . . hardly ever spoke. . . . Lost in the midst of all these men . . . and . . . smoke . . . she knew her place as a woman . . . keeping her opinion to herself in not being carried away as the men were." Her husband, Charvet, periodically takes potshots at her, at one point dubbing her an "aristo" because she drinks grog.[96] This profile of a café couple consisting of an abusive male and a demure female had a real-life parallel in Billoir and Bellengé. When she asked to go home after a long night in the café, he responded by barking, "Shut up! You do not have the right to talk before midnight." Indeed, she seems seldom to have uttered a word. Some witnesses went so far as to describe her as being "like a sheep," and all agreed that she was extremely submissive.[97] The most significant fact about this couple is that both male and female witnesses agreed that they were completely eccentric. Clerks, shoemakers, dentists, and female café owners unanimously agreed that Bellengé's docility and slavish attention to Billoir were bizarre. In fact, in no other case in the judicial archives is female café behavior shown to be even remotely so submissive.

The vast bulk of all the primary judicial and social evidence indicates not only that women felt comfortable in cafés but also that they participated actively in café sociability. In short, most female café habitués were far from *soumise*. Even Zola's novels, upon closer examination, provide evidence of female initiative. In *Le Ventre de Paris*, a fishmonger notices the café owner on his way to the police to report on the conspiracy being hatched in the back room of his shop. She does everything in her power to tell the conspirators, but they ignore her, and so "the trap slowly closed."[98] In actual incidents, women often got more respect from male habitués. In January 1848, at 11 P.M. a man claiming to be a policemen entered a café at 28 rue aux Fèves, next to the Palais de justice, and demanded that one of the customers come with him. A woman customer indignantly intervened, saying: "If you are a police inspector, show us your card." The impostor then hit the woman, but he was wrestled to the ground by a street vendor and a typesetter and taken to police headquarters.[99] This woman's actions were far from exceptional. During the Prussian occupation of suburban Rosny-sous-Bois in May 1871, a woman diffused a potential incident between a local farmer and a Prussian officer in a café. As the town's secretary noted: "Without the composure [*sang-froid*] of a young woman who was present, there would have been a brawl among all the men in the shop."[100] In June 1883, in suburban Asniers, a seamstress warned a carpenter about the threats made against him by an unemployed man in a neighborhood café.[101]

But did active participation in café life mean that women's conduct in cafés was virtually indistinguishable from that of men? "Women take the roles of men and are left to easy vices," one of Le Play's students in the series *Ouvriers des deux mondes* commented ominously.[102] The assumption underpinning this theory of female degradation was that women needed to be separated from men during their leisure time; otherwise, a woman might go to a café, forget all about her home life and her children, and thus lose her feminine domestic qualities. Based on this shaky logic, moralists on both the right and the left—Denis Poulot, Jules Simon, Victorine Brochet, and the Confédération general du travail—made heroines of the women waiting meekly outside cafés for their husbands.[103] In this perception, a woman could retain her nurturing and familial sense only if she remained outside the café.

In fact, the actions of women, including many mothers, in cafés indicate that they certainly did not become "masculinized" there. The documents—especially the judicial archives—reveal numerous female café habitués battling with their husbands over money and moral issues inside cafés, but no instances of women waiting outside cafés. The average working woman may have found it much more effective to confront her man inside the café rather than waiting until he went outside or came home. Marie Houdremont ran into her estranged husband in a café at 39 rue des Amandiers one morning in 1885 while she was taking her usual *bouillon* and chatting with the proprietress, for example, and rebuked him for not visiting his children and for squandering his money on drink—he had come into the place dead drunk after a night of carousing—rather than on supporting his family.[104] A similar argument arose in 1874 when a clerk accosted his former wife, who had obtained a *séparation de corps* and custody of their children, as she sat on the terrace of the café de la Rotonde at 50 boulevard de Courcelles.[105] What these couples fought over was not the legitimacy of going to a café but rather the amount of money or time spent on drink or debauchery. Just because working-class women did not honor the notion of separate spheres as it applied to the café does not mean that they failed to defend the interests of their families.

By diminishing confrontations and by promoting the interests of the family and the home, working women ensured that the upper-class masculine code of honor, whose ultimate recourse was the duel, did not gain much of a foothold in the working-class cafés of Paris. The fact that café life synthesized rather than separated the public and the private was often very disconcerting to members of the upper class, especially the military officers who periodically frequented these establishments. When a student at the Ecole des mines made what the army officer Mesnier de Méricourt considered a pass at his dinner companion at a café in the Latin Quarter, Méricourt handed the student his card and demanded a duel. He subsequently suffered the double indignity of losing and of having the affair come before the court when the youth and his friends were charged with aggravated assault and battery. Méricourt drew the scorn of the prosecuting attorney when he asserted that "when a woman is with me I do not allow anyone to insult her." The prosecuting attorney dismissed such gallantry because it was inapplicable to such a woman in a café, saying: "Have you forgotten that you were in a Latin Quarter café and that the woman who was with you belongs to everyone?" In the eyes of the prosecutor there was a direct connection between a public place and a "public woman."[106] Like so many of her sisters, the woman seems to have been alternately seamstress and prostitute: the court docket showed her to be a seamstress by occupation, but the prosecutor categorized her as a prostitute on the strength of the police report: "She indiscriminately receives visits from a great number of men and even seems to solicit on the street."[107]

The testimony that the prosecuting attorney gathered among the habitués supported this ethic of tolerance and acceptance. Jeanne Rigaud, a nineteen-year-old flower-maker, a member of the most skilled women's trade in Paris, indicated clearly that this incident was not a question of prostitution and bourgeois respectability: "Mesnier de Méricourt was very wrong to take the remark as an insult, because everybody knows each other in the Latin Quarter and a man who is with a woman has no reason to get angry when someone speaks to her. The café Bouland is where the most proper [*comme il faut*] women go."[108] This complex testimony seems to have had no effect on the course of the trial, but it does illuminate the subtle blend of informality and respectability found among working women in cafés. For the judge, any woman who went to a café was a prostitute, but for Rigaud, women who went to the café Bouland were part of a neighborhood community. A free-floating sociability was part of this convivial space, and anyone who participated in it should have realized that leisure, not honor, was its central value. Support for the flower-maker's idea comes from, of all places, the police report on this café, which substantiates her perception of it as a peaceable establishment. The local *commissaire* considered this an exceptionally well-run café and noted that there had been no previous incidents in it. Additional confirmation comes from *A Woman's Guide to Paris*, which also appeared in the 1880s: "Needless to say, a woman alone [in the cafés of the Latin Quarter] is the commonest of sights and you would not hesitate to enter any of these establishments."[109]

Perhaps the most important "feminine" influence that women brought to cafés, the one that helped them to maintain their sangfroid and promote a spirit of tolerance, was moderation in the consumption of alcohol. In their temperate habits, female customers followed the lead of the proprietress. Just as she kept a clear head while her husband reveled in boozy sociability with his buddies, so her female customers seem to have looked after their husbands, lovers, friends, or children.

During the first half of the century, no writer gathered any systematic evidence on the alcohol consumption of working women,[110] but the growing concern about drink produced numerous data after 1870. A government-sanctioned study of seamstresses working at home—seamstresses and other women in the clothing industry comprising one of the two largest female occupations—reveals that most of these grossly underpaid workers had barely enough to spend on food, much less on drink. For example, among the dozens of individual and family profiles, many of these seamstresses budgeted no money for wine or other alcoholic drink. In the cases of women who did drink wine, consumption ranged widely: one bought a liter every ten days; another drank half a liter a day with her husband; one bought 52 liters annually; and an exceptional seamstress drank a liter daily.[111]

Although working women may or may not have been restrained in their café drinking, their political conversations and disputes with the police seem to have been quite uninhibited. Whereas Parisian women represented exactly the national average (5.5%) in police court charges of simple public drunkenness, they were more than twice as prominent (more than 12%) among those charged with aggravated public drunkenness, which commonly involved insulting a police officer. On a statistical basis, indeed, women charged with public drunkenness were just as likely to insult a police officer as men.[112] If working women did turn the working-class café into a salon, as claimed, this was done by interjecting their own political voice, not simply by bringing "feminine" refinement and restraint to café life.

As the correctional tribunal cases show, this women's political voice in cafés crossed moral, civil, and occupational boundaries. The top four groups were garment workers (175 cases), day laborers (143 cases), prostitutes (138 cases), and housewives (105 cases). Unmarried women made up 52.7 percent, a slight majority; 30.4 percent were married and 16.8 percent were widows. Thus whores and housewives alike—single, married, or widowed—contested governmental and police authority in cafés. If Parisian working-class women or the police watching their activities in cafés worked under a strict code of respectability, one would expect to find few housewives on record as insulting the police. In fact, working-class women in Paris saw no contradiction between feminine respectability and confrontation with the police.

Proletarian life in Paris was simply not rigidly compartmentalized along gender or spatial lines. Cutting across and uniting the spheres of work, neighborhood, and leisure, café life fulfilled a wide variety of proletarian needs, dooming to failure attempts to enlist working women in a struggle to get working-class men out of the cafés.[113] This is why the period 1860–1914 simultaneously experienced a steady fall in the rate of illegitimacy and a dramatic rise in café prostitution. The openness and tolerance of café space permitted women a facile adjustment of moral behavior to economic conditions: they could engage in prostitution if necessary and relinquish it when expedient. Even though this might make a woman in a café a "public woman" in the eyes of the bourgeoisie, the women themselves demanded that the "private" virtues of relaxation, peace, and acceptance be a part of café life. A widely divergent group of women thus expressed diverse attitudes in the thousands of cafés in the Paris area, with a series of subtle gradations separating, yet connecting, the housewife and the prostitute. Domestic servants aside, women in cafés were a roughly representative sample of the female working population of the city.

CHAPTER EIGHT

Behavioral Politics

s the crossroads of work, neighborhood, family, and leisure activities, café sociability permitted people to integrate the various strands of their lives and situate themselves and their fellow citizens in a broad social context. The café was thus a space of latent class consciousness, which, when properly utilized, could help create and sustain political action. Successive waves of popular political action, from the sansculottes of the 1790s to the anarcho-syndicalists of the 1900s, emerged from working-class cafés between 1789 and 1914. The greatest success of this café culture was the implantation of republicanism in the mores of the people of Paris. The most conspicuous failure was the inability of the Paris proletariat to establish the socialist democracy that they were among the first to articulate. The café also played an important role in the first attempt to do so, during the June Days of the 1848 revolution, and an utterly decisive role in the second attempt, the Paris Commune. The crushing of the Commune during the "bloody week" of late May 1871, rather than destroying this café culture of contestation, invigorated it. Unlike during the first eighty years of the 1789–1914 period, however, the café politics of the late nineteenth century did not precipitate a revolution, although it helped to generate a wide range of new radical movements, in politics as in art and literature. The guns of August 1914 muted but did not extinguish this café culture.

The vitality of café politics stemmed from its ability to reconcile the seemingly opposite poles of social life: the individual and the collective, talk and action, spontaneity and organization. The repertoire of strategies

207

one could employ in the café included discussion, speeches, and insults, which could be addressed to small groups or large assemblies. Whether spontaneously or deliberately, such talk and gatherings could result in social action running the gamut from peaceful demonstrations to bloody riots. In addition, café life could produce formal organizations such as associations, clubs, or even political parties. Inasmuch as one of the most important outcomes of café sociability was the shaping of public opinion, the history of the café also provides one of the best windows on the diffusion and circulation of political ideas and ideologies, as well as on the role of the press, journals, and books in social life. (This history also points to an intriguing new field: the history of conversation.) As a result, the historian can much more easily discern periods of growing politicization and depoliticization.

Because of its durability, adaptability, and mutability, café politics escapes easy analysis. As we have seen, this politics disconcerted every French government from Robespierre's Terror to Clemenceau's radical coalition. It also challenges the standard categories by which historians distinguish between "traditional" and "modern" forms of protest. Fluctuating between banality and sedition, café conversation seemed important only after it resulted in a concrete crime or a revolution.[1] Sadly, the seeming lack of connection to the "great" events of French history produced a great tragedy for French social history: deciding that police reports of café conversations were, indeed, unimportant, the Archives nationales destroyed its holdings.[2] Nevertheless, the ubiquity of the café in political life ensures that a superabundance of source material remains.

Incubator of Revolution: The Working-Class Café, 1689–1794

Louis XIV's interest in conversations in the first Paris cafés shows that these spaces became politicized almost from the first cup of coffee consumed in the late seventeenth century.[3] What worried the king was the sight of his upper classes gathering in public to discuss the events of the day. Royal anxiety was no doubt further raised when the first French newspapers, also a product of the Sun King's reign, became a staple of café life.[4] Throughout most of the century, however, working-class taverns seemed immune from contemporary political concerns. Thomas Brennan's study of the eighteenth-century tavern from the 1690s to the 1760s confirms eighteenth-century police reports on this point.[5] Perhaps the greatest moment in the intellectual history of eighteenth-century upper-class cafés arrived when Denis Diderot developed his concept of the *Encyclopédie, ou dictionnaire raisonné des sciences, des arts et des métiers* on the marble-topped tables of the café Procope in the 1750s.[6]

By the 1780s, when both coffee as a beverage and the institution of the café had been adopted by the lower classes, the ambience of Paris cafés had changed dramatically. The social status of the intellectuals frequenting cafés had also declined. The Voltaires, Rousseaus, and Diderots at the café Procope had been supplanted by "grub street" intellectuals. Louis-Sébastien Mercier pours scorn on these marginal writers who "just made noise" and were "merciless critics." They "arrived at 10 A.M. and stayed until 11 P.M.," he declares, engaging in "idle talk that was always boring, and revolved incessantly around the newspaper and ministerial pamphlets."[7] P. J. G. Gerbier, an Old Regime loyalist, nonetheless stresses the decisive role of café habitués in precipitating the French Revolution: "Where does so much mad agitation come from? From a crowd of minor clerks and lawyers, from unknown writers, starving scribblers, who go about rabble rousing in clubs and cafés. These are the hotbeds that have forged the weapons with which the masses are armed today."[8]

The epicenter of the Paris cafés during the 1780s was the Palais-Royal. After its construction in 1781, entrepreneurs found its enclosed arcades a perfect site for cafés. On the eve of the Revolution, some twenty-five cafés—including the prominent café de Foy, café des Mille-Colonnes, café Italien, café de Caveau, and café de la Régence—had displaced the café Procope and other Left Bank establishments as the most dynamic in Paris. As James Billington and Robert Isherwood have noted, what gave these cafés their especially powerful energy was the "convergence between popular and elite culture."[9] The resulting sociable egalitarianism is what struck Théroigne de Méricourt most forcefully about the Palais-Royal at the start of the fateful summer of 1789: "What most impressed me was the atmosphere of general benevolence; egoism seemed to have been banished, so that everyone spoke to each other, irrespective of distinctions [of rank]; during this moment of upheaval, the rich mixed with the poor and did not disdain to speak to them as equals."[10]

Billington has argued that "the verb 'to politic' [*politiquer*] may even have originated from discussion in the Palais' cafés."[11] In any case, what is certain is that in Palais-Royal cafés, unprecedented fusion between philosophic, political, and popular speech occurred. "No Molière comedy could have done justice to the variety of scenes I witnessed," the young marquis of Ferrières remarked of the Palais-Royal's cafés in the first blush of revolution, illustrating this fusion of literate and oral cultures. "Here a man is drafting a reform of the Constitution; another is reading a pamphlet aloud; at another table, someone is taking the ministers to task; everybody is talking; each person has his own little audience that listens very attentively to him. . . . In the cafés, one is half-suffocated by the press of people."[12] A plethora of firsthand accounts reveals the marvelous mélange of philosophic and pornographic works. In the café de Foy, for example, they read and discussed such pamphlets as *The Eaters of the People Go to the Devil* and a "shocking" brochure on Lafayette's private life.[13]

The events of 1789 brought the Palais-Royal's spontaneous political sociability to cafés throughout the city. In front of the coffeehouses, "those who have stentorian lungs relieve each other every evening," Camille Desmoulins wrote to his father. "The coffee-houses . . . present astonishing spectacles . . . expectant crowds are at the doors and windows, listening . . . to certain orators, who from chairs or tables harangue each his little audience; the eagerness with which they are heard, and the thunder of applause they receive for every sentiment of more than common hardiness or violence against the present Government, cannot easily be imagined," noted Montjoie in his account of the Revolution.[14] Not only did workers listen in rapt attention to the latest news and ideas, they read and discussed newspapers and books on an unprecedented scale. Police reports often noted that cafés were "full of reading material." In October, the new municipal government of Paris requested that the police committee of the Saint-André-des-Arts district seize "all the libelous manuscripts and published material in the *marchands d'eau de vie* and *marchands de vin* and *cabarets* and send them to the Hôtel de ville."[15]

This revolutionary proletarian café sensibility found a series of former grub street writers ready and willing to articulate it. The most famous of these writer-agitators were Jean-Paul Marat, with his paper *L'Ami du peuple*, and Jacques-René Hébert, with his *Père Duchesne*, but several other papers, such as the *Tailleur patriotique* (Patriotic Tailor), followed the same formula. These newspapers, Simon Schama has argued, "contrived to reproduce the authentic voice of the *bon bougre*—the foul-mouthed plain-talking man of the wineshops and the markets, his head enveloped by the fumes of alcohol and tobacco and his tongue hot with expletives directed at the Autri-Chienne (the Austrian bitch a.k.a. the Queen). Their appeal was verbal violence."[16] Schama's point is perceptive but unsubstantiated. He does not analyze the nature or content of this militant language.

A study of the "verbal violence" of these papers reveals that journalists such as Hébert and Marat assimilated much of the bawdy, ribald, combative vocabulary of the Parisian laboring population. The insults, stock and repetitive in nature, hurled at "aristos" and counterrevolutionaries were an ideal means by which to fuse popular language with revolutionary politics. By the constant use of such abusive terms as "scum" (canaille), "robber" (brigand), "knave" (coquin), and "murderer" (assassin), these journalists transformed their insults into political statements. These epithets on the lips of proletarian café habitués became the staple terms of scorn for the police and other agents of governmental authority throughout the nineteenth century. Marat, Hébert, and other radical journalists thus launched a dialogue with radical café sociability—with its mixture of oral and written cultures—that endured throughout the century.[17]

Given the centrality of the working-class café ambience to popular political mobilization, it is no wonder that the idea of the sansculottes emerged from them.[18] The first bonnet rouge, the distinctive headgear of the movement, was donned in the café Procope, and the December 1792 massacre that helped to sustain the preeminence they had won earlier in August also started in the Procope.[19] The petition, another element of popular democracy, was a staple of working-class café life.[20]

The main political activities in cafés during the flowering of participatory democracy, 1789–93, involved an ongoing dispute between the various factions of the emerging political spectrum. Sometimes these conflicts were overt, with "café orators," at other times they were covert, with "spies." The pages of L'Ami du peuple, for example, provide a running commentary on the battles between revolutionaries and counterrevolutionaries in cafés. Marat's paper warns constantly of spies in cafés and provides examples of revolutionaries, including café owners, who reported on the machinations of royalists, Girondists, and Lafayettists.[21] After Marat's assassination, many of these cafés prominently displayed busts of their hero.[22] Although by the Napoleonic era, plebeian café politics was essentially dead, a small cadre of the faithful fondly recalled the sansculotte legacy.[23] Thus, after 1794, cafés changed from incubators to shelters as café politics went into full retreat.

After 1793, ever-mounting repression brought about the abrupt decline of this vibrant "proletarian public sphere," to use Jürgen Habermas's phrase. The Jacobin-inspired Terror during the first half of 1794 dealt the first blow. Political repression and economic depression cut the number of cafés virtually to half—1,685—of their 1789 figure.[24] Nevertheless, when Gracchus Babeuf tried to launch his conspiracy of equals in 1795, he did so from a café connected with the Chinese Baths at 27 boulevard des Italiens.[25] Now, however, police repression had become sophisticated enough to nip this revolutionary move in the bud.

By the time Napoléon came to power in 1799, the political nature of working-class cafés had essentially been eradicated. The soon-to-be emperor ended the decade that had seen the emergence of modern café politics by purging its place of origin, the Palais-Royal, of all overt political expression.[26] Although political discussion in upper-class cafés reemerged after 1805 in such places as the café Lemblin, it had little impact on the working class. Aside from a few *enragés*, virtually all the "café orators" who came to the attention of the authorities in the latter part of the First Empire were middle class—professionals and former government officials, called *exclusifs*—and police reports noted that they were no longer able to politicize workers' cabarets and wine shops.[27]

Strategies in the Shelter: Café Politics Refashioned, 1814–1830

During most of the Restoration, politics seemed to remain the preserve of bourgeois cafés, while habitués of working-class cafés appeared engrossed in their traditional popular pursuits. Only slowly did both the police and the people realize that a new type of politics was being created in these working-class cafés. As early as December 1819, proletarians returned to the practice, prevalent during the Revolution, of drafting and circulating petitions in the old sansculotte stronghold of the faubourg Saint-Antoine and suburban cafés.[28] Mirroring the same impetus to associational life as the middle class, workers began during the 1820s to create their own clubs.[29] The better to avoid police surveillance and harassment, they often met at or beyond the barrières. For example, in 1822, the "shady" tavern at 4 barrière de Rochechouart had become a veritable working-class club.[30] As noted in Chapter 1, the decrees and ordinances of the prefect reveal that during the 1820s, goguettes (cafés where workers sang) were multiplying rapidly, as were the number of street singers around the city's cafés and in the rural taverns beyond the barrières.[31] Even more serious in the eyes of the Bourbon prefects was the spread of newspaper-reading in cafés. Complementing, and perhaps contesting, police harassment of these new forms of association and communication was the growing tendency of workers during the 1820s to attack the police who investigated cafés verbally, or even physically. The prefect of police started to cover them closely in his daily reports to the crown in 1823, and the *Gazette des tribunaux* commenced copious coverage by 1828. In one report, the prefect wondered whether the workers were insulting the police as part of "a strategy to excite the people against the soldiers and the authorities."[32] By May 1829, at a time of unprecedentedly high bread prices, the prefect complained in a confidential circular that the alarmed population had contracted the bad habit of believing that they had a right to get daily bread and that they uttered such reprehensible and seditious talk in their cafés and other public places.[33] Yet the prefect was caught completely unawares by the revolution in the following year.

The fermentation of this mixture—a concern for bread, the consumption of drink, the singing of political songs, and the shouting of insults—helped produce the proletarian mobilization during the 1830 revolution. The workers who fought on the barricades during the three glorious days of the July Revolution and in subsequent revolts during the early 1830s sang songs of Pierre Jean Béranger's that had been made popular in the goguettes.[34] The cauldron of café politics continued to bubble until the massacre on the rue Transnonain in 1834 removed some of the heat, but this was only a momentary setback. A movement so closely rooted in daily life could not easily be defeated. The center of traditional popular café life, the barrières, became one of the primary focuses of the new labor and socialist movements. As Alain Faure has noted, use of these barrière cafés was probably a transformation of the traditional *compagnonnage* tactic of deserting a city when confronted with recalcitrant employers. But it can also be seen as an entirely rational response to governmental prohibition of working-class organizations.[35] Café life at the barrières and in the city proper steadily elaborated workers' strategies across the 1830s and 1840s.

To the dismay of conservatives and to the joy of radicals, as noted in Chapter 1, café politics became central to the development of the new republic in 1848. Festive aspects of café life came to the fore and were transformed. References to drink in the revolutionary songs that appeared after the February Days—such as Pierre Dupont's "Song of the Workers" ("Chant des ouvriers")—evoked proletarian solidarity through the image of comrades drinking together and toasting to the unity of the world. In his songs, Eugène Chatelain prophesied a time when everyone would have "bread, work, and good wine."[36] To this end, workers formed cooperative restaurants designed to provide cheap and nourishing meals, with the profit going to the collective rather than to the shopkeeper. Some observers saw these establishments as "better than filthy eating houses," a reference to the cafés that workers usually frequented.[37] Yet rather than being a contradiction to the working-class café, such cooperatives merely made this sociability more truly proletarian by removing the venality of the small shopkeeper.

During the opening months of the revolution, February and March, Parisian workers transformed café politics into club politics. In fact, some cafés actually had their back rooms appropriated as clubs.[38] This was as true of modest cafés on the rue Jean-Jacques-Rousseau as of the great boulevard café Tortoni, which now hosted the likes of Armand Barbès and Louis Blanc.[39] The result, as Marx noted, was that these clubs bridged the gap between the "parliaments of the people" (the cafés) and the new National Assembly: "The struggle of the orators on the platform evokes the struggle of the scribblers of the press; the debating club in parliament is necessarily supplemented by debating clubs in the salons and the pothouses."[40] As universal male suffrage took effect, many orators who had previously had only café customers for their audiences now gained the National Assembly as their forum. An appalled member of the assembly, Alexis de Tocqueville, provided a telling portrait in his *Récollections*:

> I felt I was seeing these Montagnards for the first time, so greatly did their way of speaking and mores surprise me. They spoke a jargon that was not quite the language of the people, nor was it that of the literate, but that had the defects of both, it was full of coarse words and ambitious expressions. A constant jet of insulting or jocular interruptions poured down from the benches of the Mountain; they were continually making jokes or sententious comments; and they shifted from a very ribald tone of voice to one of great haughtiness. Obviously these people belong neither in a tavern nor in a drawing room; I think they must have polished their mores in the cafés and fed their minds on no literature but the newspapers.[41]

To the relief of the right and the chagrin of the left, such politicians did not constitute a majority in the National Assembly. The failure of café politicians to transform parliament ensured that these parliaments of the people would quickly feel the heavy hand of repression with the rise of the party of order. The party made its first move against Paris workers in June 1848.

Café life quite logically played a dramatic role in the June Days. When the government dissolved the National Workshops (established to guarantee work for all citizens) on 22 June and ordered all unmarried workers either to join the army or to return to their native provinces, one of its moves that precipitated the revolt, agitators in cafés fanned the flames of resentment. The next day, café militants in the faubourg Saint-Antoine and at the Trône barrière announced a meeting at the place du Panthéon, on the Left Bank, for the following day to discuss workers' demands and formulate a petition. At the same time, as cries of "Work!" and "Down with Lamartine and the mayor!" reverberated from cafés in epithets and songs, agitators entreated workers not to leave the city but to stay and fight for their interests. Simultaneously, unemployed masons, street pavers, and ditchdiggers were being arrested for physical and verbal assaults on the police.[42] When the barricades went up on the 23d, the cafés stayed open to serve the combatants.[43] In some cases, the National Guard took their wounded to cafés.[44] But behind the barricades most café owners helped the insurgents. A café owner was implicated in the killing of General Brea at the barrière d'Italie and of sheltering some of the fighters at the barricades. Almost a month later, on July 5, the police picked up François Manchon, assistant to a grocer, from Lenseille's café at 92 rue de Charonne in the faubourg Saint-Antoine after he was overheard bragging that he had killed the archbishop.[45]

Café life helped sustain the working-class movement even as it faced the mounting repression following the June Days. Café owners played a vital role in the development of the workers' associations that flowered in 1849. By 1851, 28 of the 190 associations of socialist inspiration in Paris were solely for café owners.[46] Nevertheless, café life did not then pose a serious threat to the government. Following Louis-Napoléon Bonaparte's coup d'état on 2 December 1851, the police closed few cafés in Paris, because workers in the capital did not put much effort into defending a republic that already seemed to have betrayed them. Nevertheless, as Victor Hugo, an eyewitness, observed, cafés were often the target of the fiercest repression. In his *History of a Crime*, Hugo records a massacre at the café Tortoni, the pillaging of the café Leblond, and the bombardment of the café de Paris and the café des Anglais. A modest establishment owned by one Billecoq took so many shells that it had to be demolished the following day.[47] Moreover, workers around the rue Sainte-Marguerite, a center of café dispute throughout the century, were among the few proletarians to erect barricades.[48] Finally, two wine shops stayed open and helped sustain some of last street warfare and barricades on the rue de Cléry and the rue Montorgueil.[49]

Like those in the provinces, the military commissions set up in Paris to prosecute those who had risen against Louis-Napoléon's coup treated any connection with café life as tantamount to a suspect's guilt. According to Hugo, judges "would often convict people with accusations as brief as 'name. Christian name, profession, a sharp fellow. Goes to the café. Reads the papers. Speaks, dangerous.'" Hugo then provided an actual interrogation to prove his point:

> "I can think of nothing." "What! You have not been to the café?" "Yes, I have breakfasted there." "Have you not chatted there?" "Yes, perhaps?" "Have you not laughed?" "Perhaps I have laughed." "At whom? At what?" "At what is going on. It is true I was wrong to laugh." "At the same time you talked?" "Yes" "Of whom?" "Of the President." "What did you say?" "Indeed, what may be said with justice, that he had broken his oath." "And then?" "That he had not the right to arrest the Representatives." "You said that?" "Yes. And I added that he had not the right to kill people on the boulevard."[50]

The new empire complemented the overt repression of the military commissions with covert repression by police spies and agents provocateurs, who swarmed in the capital after December.[51] An American observer in Paris at the time believed that there was a good chance any café customer might run into one of them.[52] And, indeed, Parisians from all walks of life who frequented cafés did have this fear.[53] Several writers noted that police spies approached them in cafés shortly after the coup and invited them to dinner.[54] The imperial secret agents focused especially on cafés such as the Divan Lepelletier, at 20 rue Neuve des Petits-Champs, famous for literary and political gatherings. One night in December 1851, the police arrested many of the ordinary customers. This action intimidated most of the café's clientele, except for the newspaper editors and writers, who afterwards had the café almost to themselves.[55] Spies and provocateurs used these same techniques on workers, too. They tried to draw unwitting proletarians into a discussion of politics to trap them or, in some cases, let them go on the condition that the workers would incriminate their comrades on the job, their employers, or their families.[56] Unfortunately, only random expressions of this repression have been preserved; the meticulous reports of the undercover agents have, for one reason or another, been destroyed. Thus the strategies of discussion and dissimulation can only be projected rather than systematically studied.

Given the intense repression, subterfuge logically became one of the main strategies in café sociability. Customers developed a wide repertoire of tactics to subvert police surveillance. The simplest technique involved finding an empty, or almost empty, room in a café or a completely empty shop. Then members of the group might keep watch at the front and back doors to watch for spies or patrols.[57] If they were unsure of the sympathies of the owners and the servers, the customers might discuss forbidden topics only when they were sure of not being overheard.[58] On other occasions, they might follow the example of the writer and future Communard Maxime Vuillaume and his friends, who discovered a small shop, the brasserie de la rue Saint-Séverin, where they knew the owner and all the habitués. "It was not easy for the police to adventure into our small brasserie. Every one knew each other. Outside of our group, hardly any other habitués, besides a half-dozen shopkeepers of the quarter who came for a billiard game after dinner, came to the café."[59] Although this strategy may have facilitated privacy, it did so at the expense of secrecy. Gathering regularly as a group in the same spot could easily result in a police raid. We have seen this happen to the fictional conspirators at Lebigre's café in Zola's novel *Le Ventre de Paris*. A real-life case, for example, was Bellemare's conspiracy at the cabaret Aveugle near the théâtre Italien.[60]

Some habitués preferred the completely opposite strategy of blending into the crowd of busy cafés. They believed that anonymity was a safer cover than isolation. As one contemporary noted, if Napoléon III arrested everyone who criticized him, he would have had to arrest half of Paris.[61] A wide range of observers—from French experts on industrial life such as Armand Audigane to Parisian workers and journalists such as Anthime Corbon to American travelers to London workers—all noted how working-class sociability, although seemingly spontaneous, had developed a distinct and coherent political attitude.[62] In June 1871, even after the fall of the Commune, the *Bee Hive*, a London workers' journal, admired the way Paris proletarians had been able to build a movement over the previous twenty years without the freedom to organize a political society, much less to march in a procession. The "ground was prepared," the paper declared, "by talk at workshops and cabarets."[63] There were simply too many people discussing too many topics in too many cafés for the emperor's police to control or even to keep track of café conversation. Jeanne Gaillard, in her study of the 1863 elections, was struck by the inability of the police to penetrate the working-class world. In the 5th arrondissement, for example, agents could furnish the addresses of only four cafés in which groups of workers met.[64]

During the 1860s, the proliferating counters, tables, and terraces of Haussmann's new city helped undermine the empire and stimulate the reemergence of a republican movement. Edmond Lepelletier believed that "the great movement of ideas which occurred in France under the silent reign of Napoleon III, when the people were mute, the press muzzled, and right of assembly confiscated, had for its stage the brasseries of the Latin Quarter."[65] As in previous decades, these shops contained a mixture of students and workers.[66] After the dramatic success of the republican "list" in Paris in the 1863 elections, the writer Ludovic Halévy exclaimed, "The cafés have triumphed. The bourgeoisie would not have succeeded without the admirable cafés."[67] In the 1869 elections, a wealthy Belleville café owner by the name of Braleret helped fund Léon Gambetta's successful electoral effort in this workers' district.[68] What Alphonse Daudet said of the Latin Quarter cafés—"in sum these discussions around beer and the smoke of pipes prepared a generation and awoke France from its deadened state"—can be applied to the proletarian cafés too.[69]

The years 1869 and 1870 saw the return of the overtly political café and an unprecedented amount of attendant disputation.[70] At a diverse number of cafés near Montmartre on the grands boulevards and in the Latin Quarter, radical militants brazenly gathered and organized for the coming conflagrations, which they hoped and planned for but could not realistically have predicted. At the cafés de Suède and de Madrid on the boulevard Montmartre, the café Huber on the rue Monsieur le Prince, the brasserie Saint-Séverin, the café d'Harcourt, and the Cochon fidèle on the rue des Cordiers, Andler's on the rue de l'Ecole de médecine, the café Saint-Roch (nicknamed café Robespierre) on the rue Neuve Saint-Roch, cafés on the rue Guy Lessuc, and countless others in the 20th arrondissement (Ménilmontant), the militants who would staff the Commune and speak for republicanism during the 1870s and 1880s met and plotted.[71]

Napoléon III's disastrous war against Prussia in July and August 1870 brought a swift return to café disputation.[72] The chaos produced by a defeated army and a defunct empire proved highly conducive to a revival of revolutionary activity in cafés. Freed again from jail and back in Paris, Auguste Blanqui, the great symbol of Paris radicalism, opened a club at the café des Halles centrales, 20 rue Saint Denis. He also frequented a café on the avenue Victoria where the National Guard met.[73] The Prussian siege of Paris, starting on 18 September 1870, gave added impetus to café disputation. Both contemporary observers and historians have noted this fact, but they provide diametrically opposed assessments. On the one hand, army generals, police officials, and conservative historians after the Commune believed the blockade brought an enforced idleness to the army and National Guard that permitted the "undisciplined" and "degraded" Paris workers to "debauch" themselves in cafés with wine and women.[74] On the other hand, leftist historians have emphasized that the deprivations of the siege developed a deep solidarity among the soldiers and citizens of Paris.[75] Ted Margadant has speculated about the likelihood that "a diffuse pattern of sociability—in workshops and cafés—preceded and sustained this formal network of republican organizations."[76] Yet cafés were very much part of the formal associations as well. The café de Strasbourg, for instance, on the boulevard of the same name, served as headquarters for the 31 October 1870 march on the Hôtel de ville. Precipitated by news of the surrender of the French army at Metz, this march led to the proclamation of a new government.[77] Later, in early March 1871, after Thiers had made peace with Prussia and relocated the national government at Versailles, he conducted negotiations with the disgruntled National Guard and republican radicals at the café de Suède in Paris.[78]

Working-Class Café Culture at Its Apogee: The Commune

The proclamation of the Commune on 28 March brought the working-class café culture to its zenith. From the outset, conservatives stressed the vital role the café had played throughout the tumultuous two months of the Commune's existence, because such an influence validated their theory of the Commune as an "alcoholic orgy," the term applied to it by Maxime du Camp, the leading right-wing historian of the Commune, who also asserted that every café had become a political club.[79] In response to this caricature, the surviving Communards and their partisans steadfastly denied any drunkenness and minimized the role of cafés.[80] Even during the 1960s, when the Commune was being reappraised by writers like Henri Lefebvre, the Situationists, and Jacques Rougerie, who saw it as a "festival of the oppressed" and a "free city," none of them connected cafés to this "festivity."[81] However, Kristen Ross has suggested that Arthur Rimbaud's *Le Bateau ivre* ("The Drunken Boat") is a tribute to working-class cafés, and that Rimbaud linked drinking and socializing in cafés to revolution and the Commune.[82]

The café's informality and spontaneity animated much of the Commune's political culture and even its governmental operations. The café de Madrid was rightfully called "the cradle of the Commune."[83] Nightly, there, "the politicians overthrew the empire in their imaginations and in their saucers; later they overturned kiosks," Henri d'Aleméras observes.[84] The future leaders of the Commune also congregated at cafés on and around the rue du Château-d'Eau in the faubourg du Temple, including the café de l'Independence, the café des 20 Billiards, and the Rat mort, and at the café de la Renaissance, the café Voltaire, the café de Serpente, the brasseries Saint-Séverin and Glaser, and the café Procope in the Latin Quarter.[85] A list of the habitués of these cafés reads almost like a Who's Who of the Commune: Raoul Rigault, head of the "Ex-Prefecture of Police" (so entitled to distinguish it from the hated imperial one), Theophile Ferré, second in command at the ex-prefecture and member of the vigilance committee of the 18th arrondissement; Emile Duval, a commander of the National Guard and member of the Commune for the 13th arrondissement; Frédéric Cournet, another member of the Commune; Gabriel Ranvier, officer and member of the Committee of Public Safety; Gustave Tridon, member of the Commune from the 5th arrondissement; Eugène Vermersch, Maxime Vuillaume, and Alphonse Humbert, editors of the influential *Père Duchêne*, a paper that revived Hébert's practice of using café slang; Jules Vallès, member of the Commune for the 15th arrondissement and founder of the *Cri du peuple*; the artists André Gill and Gustave Courbet, the latter a member of the Commune for the 6th arrondissement and president of the Artist's Foundation; Jean-Baptiste Clément, member of the Commune for the 18th arrondissement and famous in the tavern world for his song "Les Petites Bonnes de Chez Duval"; and, finally, the notoriously temperate Eugène Varlin, a militant in the First International as well as a member of the Central Committee of the National Guard and of the Commune.[86]

In cafés, government offices, and other public places, these leaders incorporated the traditional symbols of café camaraderie as part of their administrative style. When drinking, they followed the proletarian rituals of clinking glasses at the counter and paying for rounds of drinks. These practices were part of the populism integral to the Commune's ideology. Naturally, conservative critics, once again with du Camp in the lead, accused the Communards of turning the Hôtel de ville into a *gargote* (greasy spoon). Du Camp alleged that Eugène Protot, one of the Commune's judges, sat in the Guard of the Seals office "as in the room of a café."[87] At the parliamentary investigation of the Commune, Admiral Saisset elaborated on this motif of the Communards turning government offices into cafés, charging that they had "greatly abused spirits and had sung the

Marseillaise in the Grand Hôtel" at Passy (16th arrondissement) "around tables arranged as in a café." Tirard, mayor of the 2d arrondissement, who fled after the proclamation of the Commune, claimed that for all intents and purposes, the Grand Hôtel had been turned into a café: the Communards had eaten in all the rooms, and there was a prevailing odor of tobacco, wine, and food. Rounding out this picture, Cresson, prefect of police after 31 October 1870, portrayed the Communards as "people without a domicile. They live in a cabaret one day and a furnished hotel room [hôtel garni] the next."[88] If we look past the obvious bias, we can see that this evidence provides further support for the idea of the Commune as festival, its government being one large "drunken boat."

When the Versailles government's troops reentered the city on 22 May 1871, cafés once again switched from being incubators of the revolution to become shelters. Vuillaume's memoirs of the "bloody week" of repression that followed show Communards forging their solidarity in cafés as their dream shattered. The onset of street-to-street and house-to-house fighting found the Communard commanders distributing their men among neighborhood cafés where they could find easy protection and quick cover from oncoming invaders, as well as drink to give them courage. Vuillaume describes how, amid the sound of rifle fire, both leaders and rank-and-file partisans at the café de la Salamanderie on the place Saint-Michel, for instance, shook hands, treated one another to drinks, and clinked glasses at the counter. He also mentions meetings between military leaders—Louis Rossel, for example—and journalists at "our habitual marchand de vins at the angle of the place des Victoires and the rue des Petits-Champs." As they lost the center of the city and retreated into the eastern districts, Communard leaders and journalists, among them Prosper Lissagary and Alphonse Humbert, found lodging above cafés such as the one at 78 rue Haxo.[89] Fittingly, the last headquarters of the Commune to fall was at the Belleville town hall, which had been the famous Ile-d'Amour restaurant celebrated in Paul de Kock's novels. The final barricade to go down was on the street named after the great eighteenth-century tavern owner Ramponeau.[90] After the last defenders died in Père Lachaise cemetery, Communards such as Vermersch, like their fellow revolutionaries after the June Days of 1848, found safety in cafés.[91]

Remarkably, during and after the "bloody week," the freedom of speech, including defamatory invective and gestures, that had been one of the hallmarks of the Commune continued unabated in cafés.[92] Parisians remained remarkably bold in their allegiance to the Commune, despite the ferocity of the Versailles troops, their itchy trigger fingers, and their often drunken propensity to flaunt their victory—indeed, one soldier entering a café remarked, "Hey there! Won't you give something to those who have delivered Paris?"[93] As the Versailles troops entered Paris, Ludovic Halévy observes, crowds congregated at neighborhood marchands de vin.[94] Halévy, as well as du Camp and Brocher, among others, recorded the epithets that the Communards and their sympathizers hurled at the soldiers and police. In fact, the jet of proletarian vituperation unleashed by the crushing of the Commune did not abate until the mid 1890s. Despite the fact that approximately 25,000 Parisians had died and another 50,000 had been arrested as suspects, the number of cases of insult to public authority was the second-highest ever in the last six months of 1871. Visiting Belleville a few days after the "bloody week," Edmond de Goncourt noted "people drinking in cabarets with faces of ugly silence" and "the appearance of a vanquished but unsubjugated district."[95]

Clearly the embers of the fires that accompanied the Commune's destruction still smoldered in the hearts of the workers. After 1871, insults to the police, especially in this district and other predominantly proletarian ones, registered an unprecedented increase, jumping to a yearly total of 3,000, after having on average increased only 800 per year during the already-turbulent 1860s. The 1880s witnessed a continued upward progression to 3,467 per year. The first half of the 1890s, the apogee of Parisian anarchism, saw an astonishing average of 4,329 per year. After 1896, however, the average declined to fewer than 3,000 per year for the remaining pre-1914 years. Even so, this figure is far above those of the pre-Commune era. This extraordinary pattern raises questions of causation and context, and definitely reflects the increased sensitivity of the Paris police to any slight to their authority. The figures do not, however, mirror an increase in the number of police officers; their numbers remained virtually constant across these decades.[96] How closely do these increases correlate with the growth in the number of cafés during the 1870s and 1880s and then their decline in the 1890s? Unfortunately, that question cannot be answered with precision, because the correctional tribunal registers do not list the place of the infraction. Nevertheless, assuming that the few hundred surviving dossiers of insult cases do provide a representative sample, roughly 60 percent of all these cases took place in or around cafés.

The continued insults hurled at the police during the 1870s and 1880s kept the Commune in the forefront of the proletarian mind. For over two years after "bloody week," approximately 20 percent of these epithets were similar to, though often shorter than, the following explicit remembrance: "Do not be so proud! We know that you have fled before the Prussians; you are cowards, because if you have conquered Paris, it's because you were thirty to one."[97] After 1874, Commune references became less precise: workers shouted only "scum" or "murderer," for example, and did not add "Versailles." Nevertheless, these epithets continued to make up roughly one-third of all the insults directed at the police until the mid 1880s. From that date forward, the Commune slowly began to lose its immediacy in the proletarian imagination. This process is most tellingly traced in the decline of the epithet *canaille* (scum) and the rise to prominence of a new term of abuse, *vache* (cow). *Canaille* remained the most popular epithet, by a margin of two to one, over *fainéant* (idler) until the mid 1880s, when *vache* overtook it in workers' utterances (18% to 16%). During the 1890s and the early twentieth century, *vache*, which synthesizes animal and sexual imagery, took first place, and *canaille* dropped out of use. *Fainéant* remained the second-most-popular term of abuse throughout the entire period.

One of the best indications that there was indeed a political intention behind this vocabulary of insult is that workers used a very different set of terms to abuse their fellow workers or café owners. In civil insult cases in which individuals took each other to court for besmirching their names or reputations, "thief," "whore," "pimp," and other terms relating to finances or sexual affairs outnumber *canaille* by a ratio of almost four to one. Other terms used for insulting the police, such as *assassin*, *lâche* (coward), and *fainéant*, are even less frequent. Not surprisingly, no instance of the adjective "Versailles" being applied to a fellow worker is recorded in the months and years after May 1871. However, "Communard" was sometimes used as a term of abuse.[98] In light of the torrent of denunciations—a total of 400,000, 95 percent of them anonymous—that streamed into the police department after "bloody week," this is to be expected.[99]

Moreover, the same occupations and the same districts that most fervently supported the Commune were also the ones that supplied the most defendants in insult cases and, after the enactment of the February 1873 law on public drunkenness, in cases of defaming public officials while intoxicated. Metal and construction workers and day laborers—the three occupations most prominent in these infractions during the 1870s and 1880s—had also suffered most arrests for participation in the Commune.

These three groups composed 43 percent of the insurgents and 40 percent of the intoxicated insulters appearing before the correctional tribunal.[100] Furthermore, 55 percent of the defendants were from the six most militant arrondissements of Paris under the Commune (the 4th, 5th, 11th, 18th, 19th, and 20th). In contrast, only 22 percent of the defendants were from the seven predominantly bourgeois arrondissements (the 1st, 2d, 6th, 7th, 8th, 13th, and 16th). The remaining 23 percent lived in the other predominantly working-class arrondissements of Paris, such as the 14th and 15th in the south and southwest, which had not been as active during this "festival of the oppressed."

Given this deep identification of the people of Paris with the Commune, as well as the fact that the right to hold political meetings remained highly restricted under the 1870s regime of "moral order," it was predictable that the first mass movement to energize Parisian proletarians after the Commune focused upon the amnesty of its deported members. Starting in 1875, café owners and their establishments played an important part in all stages in the amnesty movement. Leaders of the movement met, sponsored petition drives, and collected donations in cafés.[101] On 3 June 1876, for instance, thirty friends of Gabriel Deville, editor of the newspaper *Droits de l'homme*, which figured prominently in the amnesty drive, met in the venerable café Procope in the Latin Quarter to bid him farewell before he began a six-month prison term for having published articles deemed "insulting" to the French nation. The presenter of one of the toasts used the favorite epithet of workers in cafés, *canaille*, urging Deville to struggle against the "government scum and to defend with passion the oppressed, the brothers in New Caledonia [islands in the southwestern Pacific to which the convicted Communards had been deported], and the Republic."[102] Thus we see the café again functioning as a site where the oral culture of workers and the literary culture of journalists intersected.

The Commune remained a major motif in the resurgent political meetings held in cafés or their annexes during the 1880s. At one meeting in November 1881, the slaughter of "bloody week" was again evoked. Amid lively applause and the refrain "Vive le Commune!" Pierre Girault, a piano maker, denounced the government as a bunch of assassins.[103] During a June 1884 meeting of the Paris section of the Marxist Parti ouvrier, one of its principal leaders, the housepainter Georges Crespin, alluded to the Commune, declaring, "We shall shoot those who shot our fathers, brothers, mothers, sisters."[104] In February 1885, at a meeting to organize the unemployed of Paris, Frederic Boulé, a jobbing (*tâcheron*) stonecutter and one of the leaders of the commission of the unemployed workers, invoked the memory of the Commune, brooding that the city might become a bourgeois stronghold: "The workers of Paris must stand guard at their places. If not, then Paris will become a reactionary city. The forts and barracks surrounding the city will be turned against us and we shall be machine-gunned."[105]

In the 1880s, resurgent radical groups borrowed not only their slogans from the Commune—"Vive la Commune!" for example would remain a staple at meetings for decades—but also the Commune's belief that Paris must once again be a "free city" (*ville libre*).[106] During the same era, Jules Guesde also worried that social and economic change would force workers out of the city.[107] At some unconscious level, the desire to protect the café as a special working-class space in Paris may have been an unconscious motive for the epithets hurled at the police and for resentment of their surveillance. Café sociability serves here as a means of asserting what Henri Lefebvre has called "the right to the city."[108]

The most lasting link between the Commune and the café proved, most appropriately, to be the annual celebration at the Père Lachaise cemetery wall where the last *fédérés* had fought. Born during "bloody week," this ritual was initially celebrated in cafés on the first anniversary of the Commune's demise because the government banned all public demonstrations. The prefect of police scoffed at these small-scale anniversary remembrances: "At most, if one can take any notice at all, workers surround themselves with precaution and mystery and drink to revenge."[109] Little did the prefect know that these furtive toasts to the memory of the Commune would blossom subsequently into a consummate leftist ritual celebrated annually with great fanfare. Police reports from the 1870s through the 1910s show that the café remained the central organizing site for this ritual.[110]

Between Spontaneity and Organization: Café Politics, 1877–1914

The end of the Parisian revolutionary cycle—1789, 1830, 1848, 1871—after the Commune might lead one to conclude that working-class café culture played some part in the decline of Paris as the leading center of radicalism in France.[111] Although eminently plausible, this theory does not fit the facts. Neither the increase in the amount of alcohol consumed nor the expansion in the number of cafés can account for the apparent slackening in the revolutionary drive of the Paris proletariat. Café consumables did not suddenly become the "opium of the people." The one negative impact of the proliferation of cafés after 1880 is that their sheer numbers helped to fragment Parisian radicalism. Each sect or faction among the socialists, anarchists, Boulangists, and nationalists could find a café to be their headquarters, just as literary and artistic groups were doing.[112] During this so-called "golden age" of the café, any small group could congregate and formulate their distinctive qualities in café life. Nonetheless, despite their ideological differences, their common comportment in cafés gave the various radical groups of the era a distinctive cultural coherence.

Working-class café sociability should be considered one of the "small-scale informal collective practices" that Alain Cottereau has postulated explain how the French working class has simultaneously been one of the least organized and most revolutionary of industrial proletariats: "least organized" in terms of membership in unions and other workers' associations and "most revolutionary" in terms of periodic moments of great action and solidarity, when rates of unionization and strikes dramatically swell.[113] Although Cottereau has not explored the role of the café in general or the role of the Paris proletariat in particular, the working-class café culture of Paris provides one of the best illustrations of his thesis. The ongoing casual conversation and small-scale controversy in cafés illuminates how, after decades of seeming lassitude and organizational inertia dating from the crushing of the Commune, the workers of Paris were able to mount a sustained challenge to the Third Republic during the years 1903–11. This high tide of anarcho-syndicalism never sparked a revolution, however, and has been called the "last gasp" of the Parisian artisan. Even so, the strike wave marks the most important upheaval in Paris between the Commune and the Popular Front of 1938. More important for our purposes, working-class café culture is shown to maintain its potential for turning small-scale resistance into revolution.

A diverse number of observers during the 1880s and 1890s provide insights into the mechanisms that gave working-class cafés a political rather than merely social culture. The American observer Eliot Gregory was greatly impressed how "after dinner habitués come grouping themselves about small tables," engaging in political discussion that was "passionate in a way unknown in Anglo-Saxon countries." He also noted how "someone amidst these discussions may stand up and orate." The "lady at the desk" he reported was "happy if the debates were brilliant," because then "many new customers will come." "Hardly an orator at the bar today or in the Senate," he concluded," "did not start out this way."[114] During the 1884 parliamentary investigation into the industrial crisis in Paris, Prefect of Police Jean Camescasse noted the presence of informal social groups: "Nothing is more mobile than these associations with no defined purpose, which often form at a café table among five or six workers under the name of social studies groups."[115] Gustave Le Bon, an influential writer on crowd theory in late nineteenth-century Paris, believed café life performed a didactic function: "The conceptions at present rife among the working class have been acquired at the public-house as the result of affirmation, repetition, and contagion."[116]

Police repression continued to lend coherence to café culture by providing a handy target. Although workers by the mid 1880s had formally won the right to assemble and associate, the police contested their actual right to do so through intrusive surveillance of workers' gatherings.[117] In short, police practice had changed little from the dark days of the empire and the moral order.[118] During the 1890s, Henry Steele, an English mechanic who lived and worked in Paris, noted the omnipresence of police surveillance of cafés and other workers' institutions: "You may go into the genuine workmen's quarters where life and property are safe and crime unknown, and you will find the police hanging around the café doors, lounging about the '*Universités Populaires*' or workmen's clubs, ready to pounce on any unfortunate who might utter somewhat too loudly any revolutionary sentiment, or speak in uncomplimentary terms of the powers that be."[119] Thus, although the workers might have "won" these rights in the Chamber of Deputies, they had to fight for them repeatedly in the cafés and at meetings. This daily contestation of the right to assemble and associate explains in part why charges of insulting the police continued to increase in number during the 1880s and early 1890s, and why that number returned to pre-Commune levels before 1914. As one social scientist noted at the turn of the century, the "eternal hatred of the people for the police" was "worse now than ever."[120]

Continuing police repression is one reason why the café remained important for the working class, strategically as well as emotionally. Another important reason is that until the mid 1880s, the café was virtually the only space where workers could meet. The meeting halls they used during the period 1875 to 1900 were almost always annexes of cafés: the *salles* Favié, Chaynes, Rivoli, Lévis, Palais-Bourbon, and Renaudin, to mention only a few of the most famous. Following the fall of the moral order government in May 1877, the "Opportunist Republicans" returned to the liberal days of the late empire and permitted public meetings. By October 1877, the chronicler of Parisian life for the weekly magazine *L'Illustration* noted that on the nights they were held, these meetings generated 3,453 harangues between 8 P.M. and midnight and cut down on the number of people attending private parties, concerts, dances, and theaters. Significantly, he did not mention any loss of patronage at cafés during these meetings.[121] By the 1890s, cafés had become primary sites for the new style of grassroots electoral politics.[122] At the same time a new type of café gathering emerged. Entitled "punches" or "soups," these meetings provided any attendee willing to support a particular cause with the added incentive of food or drink.[123] Virtually all left-wing groups held their own versions of these.[124] In addition, during these decades, workers also used cafés to continue the tradition of the goguettes, which managed to hold their own against the newer and more commercial café-concerts.[125] There were still approximately three hundred such singing societies in the peripheral districts of Paris in 1900, and although they often sang the new songs of the café-concerts, they remained communal and participatory.[126] Indeed, with Aristide Bruant a prime example, some of the great commercial singers drew inspiration for their cabaret shows from their experiences in proletarian cafés and goguettes.[127]

The rise of new workers' institutions after 1885 did not pose a challenge to the café's central role. As noted in Chapter 3, the establishment of the Paris labor exchange (Bourse du travail) after 1887 proved a complement to the café, but it was not as important to the workers' movement in Paris as it was in other cities, because municipal government maintained a strong voice in its operation and did not permit it to become a truly working-class space.[128] The emergence by 1900 of a network of cooperatives, popular universities, and "people's houses" (*maisons du peuple*) did not pose a serious threat either.[129] In general, workers used these spaces to complement rather than to supplant café sociability, thus fulfilling neither the hopes of the temperance reformers nor the fears of the café owners.[130] Only at the very end of the era, just before World War I, did the café start to decline as a meeting place, with the growing centralization of the working-class movement and the emergence of the Confédération general du travail.[131] Nevertheless, as we shall see, cafés retained their primacy as sites of agitation and confrontation.

Four interconnected events show how working-class café culture was able to transcend the narrow sectarian differences in the labor and socialist movements: first, the role of the café in the rise of a Marxist socialist movement; second, its place within renewed public meetings of the 1880s and 1890s; third, its role in the emergence of anarchism; and, fourth, its influence in the rise of anarcho-syndicalism. These events helped sustain and then launch the new outburst of proletarian militance on the eve of World War I. In short, café life sustained political consciousness throughout the 1880s and 1890s, decades of seeming fragmentation and alienation in working-class Paris.

The events surrounding the founding of the first French Marxist group in 1872 at the café Soufflet, one of the traditional intellectual and political cafés of the Latin Quarter, reveal the wider ramifications of café sociability. The story of a group of young students and radicals (the most prominent being Jules Guesde) and how they learned about Marxism from a German journalist by the name of Karl Hirsch is briefly covered in most histories of labor and socialism.[132] Not as widely known is the way this café and others provided both context and pretext for dissemination of this new philosophy to the working class.[133] By 1878, the original group had expanded in numbers and was using a wide variety of cafés. The most important was the one owned by Charles Braun at 2 rue de la Bastille. This café functioned as headquarters for the committee, including Hirsch and Guesde, that organized an international workers' convention to coincide with the 1878 Paris International Exposition. But the organizers also rented café rooms for their more "private meetings"—that is, meetings open only to invited guests with tickets. Throughout August 1878, the prefect of police threatened to prohibit private meetings concerned with the Congress. A confrontation between the police and a working-class leader, Isidore Finance, in a rented café room on the rue des Entrepreneurs in September has justly become one of the most famous and important chapters in the early years of French socialism.[134] At their trial, Guesde and the other defendants dramatized the plight of workers trying to exercise their civil liberties.[135]

From the 1880s through the 1900s, following the lead of Guesde, leftist Parisian politicians and journalists conspicuously publicized and denounced police abuses of workers' civil rights, including those in and around cafés. Between 1881 and 1887, Edouard Vaillant and Jules Joffrin of the Paris municipal council were dogged and caustic critics of police actions, including those around cafés.[136] This agitation on the municipal council complemented the campaigns by such leftist papers as *La*

Lanterne and Vallès's *Le Cri du peuple* exposing these abuses.[137] In fact, some writers for these journals, such as Emile Odin, and many of the street vendors who sold them, directly participated in challenging the authority of the police around cafés.[138] Indeed, large numbers of workers in both Paris and the suburbs read and were emboldened by these exposés. In September 1879, the housepainter Edme Baudin, after harassing police agents in Harang's café and on the way to the police station, gave his brother a franc to tell *La Lanterne* his story.[139] In another case, in February 1885, a day laborer by the name of Catherine Andrieux, calling the police "dirty cows, a bunch of rotten pigs, and venereal scum [*canaille*]," concluded her tirade by threatening to report them to the *Cri du peuple* so that they would be dismissed.[140]

Café-based public meetings proliferated after 1877, providing another means by which the café molded the various leftist parties and the people of Paris into a common culture. The amalgamating ambience of the café tempered, fused, and transcended the clashing ideologies and invectives of anarchists, socialists, Blanquists, and even Boulangists. Reports of these meetings and assemblies reveal that both the "rowdy" and "respectable" elements of the working-class movement still found common ground in the café.[141] In fact, a distinction often could not accurately be made between the two elements. Paul Brousse, Jean Allemane, Simon Brunet, and the many less prominent leaders who attended these meetings were regarded by the police as sober and hard-working, but all of them were nonetheless charged for various infractions of public assembly and the laws of association.[142] The comportment of many café habitués straddled a complex and often contradictory middle position between "sober" and "drunk." Police reports frequently termed workers—in two recorded cases, for instance, a cabinetmaker and a machine driller—not only "hardworking and sober" but also "easily led."[143] The phrase "easily led," often associated with cafégoing or heavy drinking, was seldom used in these police cases. On the "rowdy" side of the spectrum, militants such as Hippolyte Prades, general secretary of the railroad worker's union and a strike leader in the 1880s, were noted as assiduous cafégoers, and in Prades's case also for debts contracted but never paid.[144] Evidence of this kind undermines the notion, current among temperance writers during the 1890s, that working-class militants no longer drank.[145]

Anarchists, more than any other group, put the café at the center of their politics, a course consistent with their stress on the struggles—or liberation—inherent in daily life. Pyotr Kropotkin noted the role the café played in the emergence of anarchism. In the beginning, it had been "ridiculously small," with half a dozen people meeting in Paris cafés, but then "in some mysterious way, by a sort of invisible infiltration of ideas," the movement expanded.[146] Given the nature of Parisian proletarian café sociability, this process does not seem as "mysterious" or "invisible" as he thought. In 1895, this expansion was mentioned by the widow Louise Pioger, who had operated "anarchist" cafés in the suburb of Courbevoie and in Paris at 13 rue Mousigny, at 6 rue Joquelet, and at 11 rue Ramey. From her observations of the leaders who ate and drank at her cafés, she believed anarchism would "triumph through persuasion and talk" rather than through violence.[147] Such prominent anarchists as Paul Martinet, Emile Pouget, Emile Henry, and Sébastien Faure frequented cafés assiduously and participated fully in their songs and invective, as did Gustave Mayence, manager of the highly influential anarchist journal *Le Père Peinard* and possessor of an excellent ear for café slang.[148]

The growth of Parisian anarchism indeed exemplified the proliferation of small groups so characteristic of the city's working-class life after 1880. The hundred or more grassroots anarchist organizations that mushroomed between 1885 and 1900 included "the Insurgents," "Anarchist Vengeance," "the Equals," "the Undisciplined," "the Black Hand," "the Young Anti-Patriots," "the Ça Ira" (named after the great 1789 revolutionary anthem), "the Committee of the General Strike," and various groups that took their names from their home districts.[149] The overwhelming majority of these groups met in cafés.[150] Moreover, in the neighborhood wine shops and cabarets of the peripheral faubourgs, anarchists also helped sustain the goguettes. During their evening meetings, "everyone was expected to take their turn" at singing.[151]

Although anarchism was on the wane by 1900, the new century witnessed the resurgence of working-class militance. Not since the Commune had the Paris proletariat been so mobilized. The decade or so after 1902 has become known as the "heroic age of syndicalism."[152] Revolutionary syndicalists, in their emphasis on an immediate, face-to-face struggle between workers and capitalists, continued the anarchist emphasis on daily confrontations, many of which occurred in cafés.[153] Anarcho-syndicalist militants often had a profile similar to that of the anarchists. For example, M. R., a mason living in the suburb of Asnières, who had a reputation as a "dangerous organizer," had a mistress, moved frequently, contracted bad debts in cafés, and "advocated sabotage and anarchism."[154] Syndicalists also continued their efforts to intimidate the police watching their cafés.

When two policemen entered a café in suburban Saint-Denis in June 1910 in order to keep track of a tramway employees' union meeting, some of the group rebuked the officers as spies whose treacherous behavior made them lower than dirt.[155] When the government closed the Bourse du travail in October 1903 and January 1907, thus denying the workers their official headquarters, cafés again became informal organizational centers. Anarcho-syndicalists or their sympathizers, in short, continued the traditions of café agitation and propaganda.

Anarcho-syndicalists also added an innovation: the use of cafés as strategic points of struggle during mass demonstrations. Indeed, during these *grandes mêlées*, cafés became veritable forts and ammunition depots. During the "monster" demonstrations on 20 January 1907 in support of an officially mandated day of rest, "serious tussles" broke out on café terraces among the workers and the police and army, which had been called out. On the terraces of the café Balthazard on the corner of boulevard Magenta and rue du Château-d'Eau and the nearby bar Chatel, for instance, workers transformed tables, chairs, carafes, and crockery into projectiles and shouted, "Long live the day of rest!" In other cases, demonstrators detached the metal shutters of cafés to use as shields and barricades. In response, the police forced customers out of cafés.[156] Similar sorts of incidents multiplied two years later, in the early months of 1909, when the strike wave reached its maximum intensity. For example, during one of the demonstrations connected with the electricians' strike, a wedding at the nearby church of Saint-Paul et Saint-Louis prevented the demonstrators from taking the rue de Turenne as planned. A struggle ensued, at which many demonstrators and café customers threw chairs or glasses at the police. One of the offenders was the 19-year-old J. B., previously convicted of physically assaulting police officers, who had been sitting with friends at a café on the corner of the rue de Turenne and the rue d'Ormesson.[157] Another individual arrested in the same row was the striking ditchdigger J. H.; at a café on the nearby rue Saint-Antoine, he had thrown a beer glass at a policeman's head.[158]

Instead of throwing up barricades, the Belle Epoque Paris worker thus engaged in a form of urban guerrilla warfare in the cafés. Perhaps the Paris working class intuitively learned from the experience of "bloody week" the same lesson that Friedrich Engels deduced from studying the improvements in armaments: that barricade fighting was now obsolete. Certainly, old-fashioned street-fighting would have been foolhardy, considering that during this supposedly tranquil interlude before "the Great

War," Paris was the most fortified city in the world.[159] Georges Clemenceau in his years as head of the government, 1906–9, had no hesitation in bringing out the army at the least hint of trouble in Paris. Historians may minimize the potential of the agitation between 1903 and 1911, but contemporaries certainly did not. If there had been a fissure in the upper classes during this period as there had been during other revolutionary periods, perhaps the workers in their cafés would again have been at the forefront of a revolution.

What we have seen across the long nineteenth century in terms of working-class café politics is the development and elaboration of a unique culture that often bridged the distinction between conversation and agitation.[160] The café, where workers rested and reflected upon their common sufferings, fears, and hopes, was a vital asset to their political capacities and strategies. Families and friends were not the only groups to take advantage of the privacy and intimacy of the working-class café, for now political clubs and labor unions did too. Through their occupation of these sites, workers were able to acquire space for self-expression. In times of political freedom, cafés became incubators of new ideas, organizations, and actions; in times of political repression, they served as shelters—under the mantle of humanity's need for food, drink, rest, and relaxation—in which the embers of class consciousness could find protection, even if only in the form of insults directed at the powers-that-be. French workers might join or leave unions depending on whether they felt militant or quiescent, but few ever interrupted their café lives.[161]

A study of the insults hurled and returned in cafés illuminates how class struggle occurs not only through language but also within language. The various tides of revolutionary upheaval in the café confirm the argument of the Russian Marxist language scholar who used the name Volosinov that "sign becomes an arena of class struggle," in which "any current curse word can become a word of praise, any current truth must inevitably sound to many people as the greatest lie."[162] As we have seen, the police and the people battled over the meanings of words daily before café audiences. Working-class café sociability may not always have been overtly political, but the public and collective nature of this sociability always endowed it with great strategic potential. Through their ritual of insulting the police, workers disrupted the routines of everyday life and thereby created outrageous situations in which café customers faced the reality of repression and surveillance in their lives. One hundred years later, the Situationist International might have marveled at this tactic.[163]

Conclusion

The houses in which Jane Austen set her novels, Raymond Williams remarks, are "places where events prepared elsewhere, continued elsewhere, transiently and intricately occur."[1] Nineteenth-century Parisian working-class cafés did not, however, similarly serve merely as an annex to the world of plantations, factories, parliaments, and battlefields. Rather, cafés were a vital venue, a "third place," that both shaped and articulated the sentiments, attitudes, and actions of work, family, and neighborhood life. "I go to the café to create my relationships," Sébastien Billoir told a Paris police court to justify his behavior, substantiating Vernon Lidke's thesis that a proletarian's identity rested on the three pillars of work, family, and social relations.[2] The study of cafés, clubs, and other associational venues shows why, to use the language of the sociologists, a worker's social relations represent an independent, rather than a dependent, variable.

The myriad tactics used by workers to negotiate the space of the café can be summed up in three images: shelter, incubator, and stage. The shelter image well describes the defensive uses of the café's space. Between the 1789 Revolution and the 1914–18 war, Parisian workers confronted a series of wrenching dislocations in all facets of economic, social, and political life. Whether in the form of political repression, housing deterioration or dislocation, or workplace discipline and constraints, workers found few places in which to exercise their initiative or express their feelings. In terms of politics, the "unserious" and banal nature of the café—that is, as a place of drink and leisure—served as a cover for seri-

234

ous discussion. In terms of housing, workers created in the cafés the living rooms they lacked in their own cramped quarters. As a result, café habitués developed an elaborate etiquette that allowed family life to flourish. In terms of work, laborers used these spaces for breaks and fraternization, and in so doing they reduced the amount of work time and retained a measure of control over the labor process.

The incubator image covers the organizational impetus that the café facilitated. This could take numerous forms: secret political or labor societies, political factions or parties, labor unions or strikes. The actions café sociability precipitated were also wide-ranging: verbal insults and physical assaults, petition and collection drives, demonstrations and riots. These small-group tactics helped the workers fight for their grand strategic goal of economic, social, and political emancipation. Cafés, in short, substituted for the parliaments, clubs, and salons of the upper classes.

The stage metaphor is appropriate, because at the café a complex social drama occurred between workers, employers, publicans, and the police. Each of these players evolved a role to negotiate and orchestrate behavior in these spaces. Power relations thus not only surrounded the café but also were imbricated within it. The café owners, the police and the bosses each had their own scripts. The café owner was the most imaginative and in the 1820s introduced the zinc serving counter, a social and commercial prop allowing direct and continuous contact with customers. The role of the owner became that of social entrepreneur, with the goal of developing a large and loyal clientele. Like any good host or hostess, café owners were solicitous of their guests, but only to the point where customers did not hurt business. Owners proved to be more tolerant than the police of "debauchery" and "sedition," just so long as customers were not frightened away by disorder or violence. Although café owners might cooperate with the police, especially in murder cases and other types of nonpolitical crime—indeed, might in some cases become informers—in general their sympathies were with the workers.

The employers' role atrophied over the course of the century. The distance between boss and worker grew, until they finally ceased drinking together, and the café was no longer a place for recruitment and hiring. Café sociability increasingly had no role for managers who emphasized production above all else. By the 1890s, café owners derived more benefit out of employment agencies in their shops than did employers. The best bourgeois tactics against the café had to await the emergence of a wholesale shift in strategy during the twentieth century. With the development of a consumer society during the 1950s, when the lure of consumption in a well-furnished home outweighed the fear of labor discipline, café indiscipline ceased to be a worry.

Governmental response to café life was an incongruous amalgam of alternately lenient and repressive laws balanced by increasingly subtle police surveillance. After the Terror, the Paris police never engaged in the wholesale closures or mass repression periodically suffered by cafés in other parts of the country, especially in 1851–55 and 1877. Even after the repeal of the draconian December 1851 decree and the promulgation of the lenient July 1880 law, the Paris police continued to be less repressive than their counterparts in Lyon, France's second largest city, for example. Instead of employing naked force, the police contented themselves with mapping the geography of café disputation and repressing only its most conspicuous results. In Michel Foucault's terminology, the police relied on the power of the "gaze" to regulate cafés.[3] These tactics worked best in cases of "ordinary crime," when the police could gain the assistance of the café owners and the clientele, but largely failed in cases covering political and labor issues. On the question of drunkenness and alcoholism, the tension between governmental strategy and police tactics was most acute. While the framers of the March 1873 law punishing public drunkenness intended it as a public health measure, the police used it to maintain public order. Cops on the beat were thus more likely to arrest abrasive artisans than alcoholic ragpickers.

The failures and limitations of the tactics used by employers and governments ensured a culture of contestation in Paris cafés. Paris workers, much more successfully than their English counterparts in London, were able to maintain connections among work, family, and leisure in such a manner that all three spheres remained politicized. The nineteenth-century Paris café was a transitional space between the essentially public world of early-modern lower-class life, epitomized by the street and the marketplace, and the essentially private world of late-twentieth-century workers, usually living in high-rise apartment complexes. As an informal institution that bridged the distance between public and private life, leisure and work, the individual and the family, the café provided a unique space in which the tensions arising from such juxtapositions could be articulated. One of the most unique and creative aspects of working-class café sociability was that privacy assumed class, rather than personal, attributes. In the café, workers felt at home among themselves and resented any outside interruptions.

By fusing the voices of thousands of customers through common rituals, reading matter, and conversations, the café made possible the growth of a proletarian public sphere. The phenomenon of individuals gathering to discuss public issues, which Jürgen Habermas has noted among the bourgeoisie in their salons and coffeehouses, also occurred among groups in proletarian establishments. Poverty, desperation, and police repression may not have allowed them to attain the same level of "objectivity" as their upper-class counterparts; nevertheless, a true climate of opinion emerged in these places that facilitated the development of proletarian politics from the sansculotte era through the revolutions of the nineteenth century, the labor unrest of the early twentieth, and the Popular Front of the 1930s, right up to the "Events" of May 1968. In Parisian suburban development during the first half of the twentieth century, as Tyler Stovall has shown, this interweaving of public and private life in the café continued.[4]

The class consciousness that developed in Paris working-class cafés does not fit the traditional dichotomy of working-class consciousness as either reformist or revolutionary. Rather, the café provided not only a terrain upon which organizations could meet but also the stage for an entire spectrum of comportment and discourse for ordinary people. As we have seen, the cafés were not the center of some united working class that opposed the enemies of a just society. Drink and the attendant rituals often caused conflict, especially among groups during the first half of the century and more among individuals in the second half. Café sociability, without extinguishing conflict, generally tended to promote intimacy, tolerance, and fraternity. These are necessary building blocks for any public sphere and for the emergence of a class consciousness.

The universe created in the café by the Paris working class reveals the great creativity with which that class coped with poverty and proletarianization. The café was a threat to the bourgeoisie because it was "betwixt and between" the worlds of work and leisure, public and private, promiscuity and sociability, male and female, political and nonpolitical, drunk and sober.[5] If mass demonstrations can be called "the symbolic capturing of a capital," then the pervasive and persistent peopling of cafés by groups outside established institutions of power must be seen as another form of collective assertion.[6] The café was always a potential bridge between the ordinary world and the festival time of carnival and revolution. This being the case, it makes little sense to view nineteenth-century working-class Parisians through the lens of the "culture of poverty" thesis. A growing literature rejects the "misérablist" label so often attached to nineteenth-century Parisian workers,[7] who should be seen as the sociable or connected class rather than as a segment of the *classes dangereuses*. Collective mobilization, rather than social disintegration, was after all what most frightened the bourgeoisie.

Just as the question of class consciousness in the café cannot be put in terms of the traditional revolutionary/reformist dichotomy, so the question of a working-class café culture cannot be put into the standard distinction between tradition and modernity. To reformulate a fruitful reflection by Peter Stearns, one of the most systematic social historians on this very distinction, we may say that precisely because the café's functions changed, it permitted continuity in Parisian popular culture. When bosses progressively banned drink from the workplace, for example, rituals uniting work and drink could still flourish in cafés. Consequently, workers could continue the tradition of synthesizing their work and leisure lives, as well as maintain an element of communal participation in an age, particularly after 1850, when leisure became increasingly commercialized. "Drink was the lubricant that helped [the] working class shift from customary community to the new gregariousness with workmates and neighbors," Stearns notes.[8]

Embodied in the notion of the "café friend," this process helped acculturate the burgeoning white-collar sector into working-class café culture after 1860. Few proletariats were as culturally creative as the workers of Paris, who were the first working class to embrace modern socialism during the 1830s and 1840s, and fought for it in the 1848 revolution, precisely because they were able to mesh traditional notions of community life with modern political and technological change. Only since 1945, with the radical transformation of Parisian and French life, has "modernity" outpaced the Paris café.

Finally, the question naturally arises of whether working classes in other French cities or in other nations have relied on cafés or public drinking establishments to the same degree. An exhaustive answer is not yet available. Nevertheless, some cautious generalizations may be offered. Workers in Latin Catholic countries seem to have used cafés more fully than those in predominantly Protestant countries such as England, the United States, and Germany. In general, working-class café culture has been least evident in the Scandinavian nations, where it has been displaced by powerful temperance movements. The closely supervised rural taverns that serviced the Polish and Russian peasantries, where stupefaction rather than sedition was the norm, provide perhaps the most radical contrast to the Paris working-class café. There the drinking establishment truly seems to have been an "opiate of the masses."

As this book has shown, drinking-establishment life is more closely tied to historical contingency than to sociological regularity. Despite historical differences, up until our "postmodern" era, virtually every society has had need of some type of drinking establishment where people could gather for informal relaxation and conversation. In a world facing ecological limitations to the continued expansion of consumer societies, the sociable ethic of the nineteenth-century Paris café suggests an alternative way to spend time.[9] Conceivably, too, the proliferating electronic bulletin boards of the information superhighway may constitute a new, technological type of tavern that will help recreate a true "public sphere."

Appendix

Historiography and Methodology

lthough the world of Paris cafés has always attracted Parisians and foreign observers, it has not, at least until the past decade, attracted historians. This oversight was not unique to Paris or France. In general, the history of drinking establishments has only recently become a subject of serious study.[1] Peter Clark's *The English Alehouse: A Social History, 1200–1830* and Perry Duis's *The Saloon: Public Drinking in Chicago and Boston, 1880–1920*, the first substantial works on this topic covering England and the United States, were completed only in 1983. Three years later, Roy Rosenzweig's *Eight Hours for What We Will: Workers & Leisure in an Industrial City, 1870–1920* situated the drinking establishment within the context of family, work, and the labor movement in Worcester, Massachusetts. The systematic study of French establishments commenced with Thomas Brennan's *Public Drinking and Popular Culture in Eighteenth-Century Paris* (1988), followed two years later by Henri-Melchior de Langle's *Le Petit Monde des cafés et débits parisiens au XIXe siècle*.[2] Historians are currently working on diverse establishments in a wide number of eras: eighteenth-century middle-class English coffeehouses, taverns in early modern Augsburg, early-twentieth-century English pubs, working-class bars in the United States in the late nineteenth and early twentieth centuries, and urban and rural cafés in nineteenth-century France. The importance of cafés, bars, and taverns in social history is thus well established.

These historians of the drinking establishment have uncovered a dazzling array of data, comparable in range to the babble at the counters or tables of their subject institutions. Nevertheless, their work can be grouped within three basic frameworks. The most popular thesis, so far, considers bars, taverns, and cafés in the context of the "modernization" of society. Duis, especially in his chapter "The Long, Slow Death of the Saloon," and Rosenzweig, particularly in his chapter

241

"From Rum Shop to the Rialto," typify this perspective. They argue that improvements in housing, the arrival of the telephone and the automobile, the development of new types of entertainment, and the advent of bottled beer and other efficient forms of wholesale liquor distribution killed the nineteenth-century version of the public drinking establishment.[3] De Langle and Clark provide variations on the theme of cafés helping people to cope with urban and industrial change. Clark demonstrates the adaptability of the English alehouse by following its evolution from the thirteenth through the sixteenth centuries, when it served as a refuge for the poor and the migratory, through its growing respectability in the eighteenth century, to the changes brought by the Industrial Revolution in the early nineteenth century.[4] De Langle emphasizes the plasticity of the café and stresses the means by which the occupations of owner and server helped acculturate rural workers to urban life and diffused new drinks into the modern diet. All these studies are emplotted, to use Hayden White's term, along a story line that essentially traces the rise and fall of the café.[5]

The work of Brennan, Lawrence Klein, and Beverly Ann Tlusty provides variations on this theory of historical evolution. Both Brennan and Tlusty place their studies of tavern behavior, its rituals of drinking and upholding honor, in the context of early-modern "popular culture."[6] Brennan and Tlusty also show how the tavern functioned within small-scale, face-to-face communities as a vital space of "social exchange." Klein's work complements theirs by showing how the English elite, much like their counterparts in France and probably Germany, separated themselves from "the people" by developing the café. Using Norbert Elias's notion of the civilizing process, he shows how these upper-class drinking establishments helped inculcate the ethic of self-control and social restraint at the heart of modern society.[7]

The biggest problem with these historical studies is that their theory of historical change is too limited. Most postulate, either implicitly or explicitly, that modern social and economic forces are rendering public drinking establishments obsolete. Although in contemporary developed societies, their numbers may be reduced, taverns, bars and cafés have not disappeared. Recently, in fact, they have played a vital role in the emergence of the gay and lesbian culture and movement.[8] Given the dramatic changes that have rocked the modern nuclear family over the past generation, there is a possibility that the public drinking establishment will outlast the current family structure.

A stream of historical writing is emerging that stresses the legitimate and constant social needs served by drinking establishments. Maurice Agulhon's study of the assimilation of republican politics in the southern French department of the Var provides one important model. Through meticulous archival research, he shows how "sociability"—the habit and practice of gathering in clubs, cafés, and public squares—played a central role in the implantation of the contemporary democratic political system.[9] Surprisingly, as Peter Burke has noted, none of the many scholars influenced by Agulhon has yet studied the café.[10] Susanna Barrows is, however, applying Agulhon's insights in a nationwide study of cafés in France under the early Third Republic,[11] and although Iain McCalman devotes only a few chapters to tavern life in his *Radical Underworld: Prophets, Revolutionaries, and Pornographers in London, 1795–1840*, he nevertheless demonstrates how these spaces facilitated cultural and political insurgency in England.[12] David Gutzke has explored how British workers fought to preserve their pubs in a later period. In their eyes, he points out, the pub was much more than just a transitional institution on the road to extinction.[13] The same sense that bars contribute to community cohesion informs the work of Madelon Powers on American workingman's bars between 1870 and 1920.[14]

This new historical trend finds inspiration in the recent work of sociologists, anthropologists, and urban planners. For example, the American sociologist Ray Oldenburg and the French socialist bureaucrat Roland Castro have argued that bars, taverns, and cafés play an essential role as "third places" (Oldenburg's term) that allow a population to spend time outside of the workplace and the home and thereby produce more balanced lives and personalities.[15] In his recent study of the history and sociology of resistance—the "powerless" against the "powerful"— the American anthropologist James Scott views drinking establishments as one of the primary spaces in which protest and dissent develop.[16]

The historical study of bars, taverns, and cafés requires both of these perspectives. While the evolutionary view reveals the historical specificity of drinking-establishment sociability, the essentialist view guards against viewing these sociabilities as somehow merely "transitional" to some "higher" stage of historical evolution, and hence trivial. Combing both approaches confers dignity upon the diverse manifestations of café life.

Having discovered the importance of the nineteenth-century working-class café and seen that its study fits within a burgeoning field of social history, the researcher must determine which sources offer the best entry into this social world. Because café sociability has been subject to sweeping stereotypes, my goal is to uncover sources that provide detailed descriptions of particular individuals and their actions in specific spaces. When do individuals act as members of a family, as friends, as neighbors, or as members of a social class? What were the customs and rituals that governed their speech and actions? For all his brilliance, Agulhon never examined these interpersonal aspects of sociability. I believe that the history of social interaction can be advanced by shifting the focus from abstract notions of social interaction to actual analysis of concrete encounters, fusing the insights of such microsociologists as Erving Goffman with the work of such microhistorians as Carlo Ginzburg and Natalie Z. Davis. Michel Foucault's interest in "micropowers" makes his work useful too.[17] By focusing on the words, actions, and attitudes of ordinary individuals in this study, I have sought to lower the "threshold of individuality," enabling us to see how general historical forces influence ordinary people.

The primary sources that best detail the thoughts and actions of cafégoers are, in order of importance and abundance, court cases, marriage records, bankruptcy records, police reports, and autobiographies. Brennan's deft use of the files of eighteenth-century district police commissioners and bankruptcy records has so far provided the most detailed study of tavern sociability. These records furnish cases, not only of public disturbances handled by the police, but also of petty disputes that customers brought to police stations on their own initiative. Inasmuch as these disputes arose from conversation, Brennan is able to explore the ages and occupational statuses as well as the conversational themes of tavern habitués. His nuanced portraits rival those of Restif de la Bretonne and Louis-Sébastien Mercier in color and excel them in accuracy, and he has provided a model for future histories of drinking establishments. As may be seen throughout this study, his work also establishes an invaluable point of comparison with nineteenth-century café life.

Unfortunately, the historian of nineteenth-century Paris cafés cannot simply pick up where Brennan left off. The bloody and fiery aftermath of the Paris Commune of 1871, the apogee of the Parisian café political culture, saw the judicial and police records of all the years since the 1789 Revolution go up in smoke. The Commune thus casts a large shadow over the subject, not only politically but also archivally. The copious commentary on café life found in judicial archives begins only after 1871. Despite these losses, the nineteenth-century researcher still has over six hundred cartons of judicial dossiers as well as thousands of bound volumes of court decisions for the four Paris courts: the police court (*tribunal de simple police*); the court of petty sessions, or correctional tribunal (*tribunal de police correctionnelle*); the assize court (*cour d'assise*), and the appeals court (*cour d'appel*). In addition, the Paris judicial archives contain over one hundred and fifty cartons of cases that were dropped for lack of evidence (called *non-lieu* cases). These stillborn investigations reveal a less "deviant" side to Paris life, because the individuals involved were in general found to be law-abiding citizens, and hence were released. The use of these dossiers permits the historian to gain valuable insight into two usually opaque areas of the judicial process: determination of whom to prosecute and on what grounds.[18]

Despite the proliferation of judicial documentation during the nineteenth century, these records are often not as suitable for the study of café sociability as the eighteenth-century records Brennan examined. The nineteenth-century police commissioners did not collect data on petty café disputes with the same zeal as their eighteenth-century counterparts. Later prefects concentrated rather on more serious offenses, and they wrote reports more narrowly focused on the victim, the assailant, and a cogent account of the incident. They had less, rather than more, of an anthropologist's eye. The dramatic growth in the size and complexity of the city probably accounts for the decreased police attention to the homely details of daily life. Commissioners often complained that if they gave their attention to café cases, they would have little time left for more important ones.[19] As a result, it has been impossible, for example, to replicate Brennan's quantitative series on the occupational composition of café groups for the nineteenth century.

Nevertheless, nineteenth-century historians have a much richer and more varied set of sources than their eighteenth-century counterparts. The police, judicial, and civil bureaucracies that emerged from the Revolution generated a much greater quantity of information than had their predecessors. After 1789, the government, rather than the Church, controlled the registration of marriages, birth, and deaths. The secular bureaucrats at local town halls who now administered these records of passage required four witnesses to sign each marriage contract and two witnesses for each baptismal and death certificate, witnesses in all cases defined as family or friends. A study of these marriage, baptismal, and death registers in 1860 (the first year available), 1880, and 1900 reveals that café owners witnessed 23 percent of the marriages in 1860, 23 percent in 1880, and 17 percent in 1900; they also witnessed approximately 10 percent of the baptisms and deaths. The occupational profile of those who appeared before the civil authorities with a café owner as witness provides an illuminating contrast to the groups brought before the courts for disturbances in or around cafés. We thus have an opportunity to measure the seemingly normal and "healthy" side of café life against the deviant and "pathological" face that criminal and medical literature present. Complementing these civil and judicial records are the numerous mid- and late-nineteenth-century government studies of working-class life. These abundant sources all testify to the increased ambition and reach of the nineteenth-century bureaucratic state.

Moreover, the student of the nineteenth century can also exploit the forest of journalistic, literary, moralistic, and even a few sociological accounts of café life. These dense sources provide richer and more colorful documentation than any comparable eighteenth-century sources. In particular, the reports on café incidents, especially after 1827, in the great judicial newspaper of nineteenth-century Paris, the *Gazette des tribunaux*, permit the historian to compensate for the major gap in the judicial archives created by the 1871 fire. This source well complements the highly detailed reports of Restoration police prefects (1815–30) to the king and the minister of the interior. During the Restoration, the "social question" emerged and led to a proliferating number of studies of proletarian poverty and vice across the century. In the 1840s, Eugène Sue popularized the serial novel dealing with the social question. His example helped inspire Victor Hugo, Alphonse Daudet, and Emile Zola, among others, to contribute ever-more-discerning fictional depictions of actual social conditions.

The emergence of the democratic voice after 1789 produced more Parisian working-class autobiographies and some excellent sociological studies. Whereas Brennan had to rely primarily on Jacques-Louis Ménétra's *Journal of My Life*, I have been able to use the memoirs of Jacques-Etienne Bédé, covering the early Restoration, Martin Nadaud's account spanning the 1830s and 1840s, Denis Poulot's study for the Second Empire, and the recollections of Jeanne Bouvier and René Michaud for the turn of the century. In addition, Paris workers produced a surprisingly large, eloquent, and diverse amount of poetry and song, which, as we see in Jacques Rancière's analysis, can illuminate the workers' mentality. The working-class press that emerged during the 1830s and the labor and socialist movements in subsequent decades provide more documents of proletarian articulation. These accounts contain some invaluable insights into café life and provide a welcome contrast to the alternate condescension and derision so often found in middle-class accounts.[20] Frédéric Le Play's team of social investigators in the series *Les Ouvriers des deux mondes* provides in-depth profiles of eighteen Paris-area workers.

Like police and judicial records, these sources have their own specific shortcomings. Newspaper reports, in particular, must be used with caution. A careful comparison between judicial and newspaper accounts during the 1870s and 1880s provides one example of journalistic bias. As one would expect, newspapers tended to report the more sensational and exotic cases; murders were more likely than café arguments to make the headlines. Moreover, the incidents cited in newspapers usually occurred outside of peak cafégoing hours. Most of the café incidents reported in the *Gazette des tribunaux* between 1871 and 1873, as well as in *La Lanterne* between 1879 and 1881, for instance, occurred after ten o'clock at night. By contrast, barely a quarter of the cases in the judicial dossiers during the 1870s occurred after that hour. The press also often placed assertion ahead of investigation. Thus in January 1873, *L'Evénement* alleged that a music society using a café in the La Chapelle quarter of the 18th arrondissement was really a front for a cell of the recently outlawed International Working-Men's Association. After an investigation, the police concluded that the story was based on rumor and had been printed to boost *L'Evénement*'s circulation.[21]

The quest for dramatic stories and the consequent distortions also bedevil much of the literary output concerning the café. Just as Brennan's meticulous mining of the archives has shown the distortions and exaggerations in Louis-Sébastien Mercier's *Tableau de Paris*, so Alain Cottereau's "counterreading" of Denis Poulot's *Le Sublime* (1870) revealed Emile Zola's subordination of social fact to story line in his "realist" classic *L'Assomoir*.[22] In other novels, such as *The Stomach of Paris* and *The Ladies' Paradise*, Zola provides more accurate detail. Like most nineteenth-century novelists, he furnishes the most reliable descriptions of café life when it is part of the setting rather than the main subject of the story.[23]

The same tendency to the lurid and the macabre is also true, sadly, of much medical literature on the café. Doctors often rivaled dramatists in their portrayal of the violence, madness, and degeneration that could be the result of excessive cafégoing and the alcoholism that seemed to be a natural consequence. As a result, these supposedly sober and dispassionate scientific treatises often framed and selected their evidence to fit a predetermined model of the café's pathological social function. As Patricia Prestwich has cogently argued in her pioneering *Drink and the Politics of Social Reform*, after the emergence of the disease theory of drunkenness (alcoholism) in the early 1850s, French psychiatrists dominated the study and treatment of alcoholism in France for over a century, linking the study of alcoholism to Bénédict Morel's theory of biological determinism and mental illness, embodied in his highly influential study *Dégénération* (1857). In the 1860s, in a series of significant studies, Valentin Magnan seemed to confirm the pathological effects of alcohol consumption in laboratory experiments in which he injected rats with large doses of alcohol. Such laboratory studies, as well as examinations of alcoholics in insane asylums, led Magnan's most eminent pupil, Paul-Maurice Legrain, to conclude, in his compelling *Hérédité et alcoolisme* (1889), that alcoholism was hereditary and degenerative. This bleak prognostication, as Prestwich notes, inhibited exploration of the social factors that might have caused alcoholism. As a result, many medical treatises on alcoholism are not as useful as they might have been if a more socially grounded theory had been considered. There are two conspicuous exceptions: dissertations by Henri Imbert (1897) and Charles Bonnet (1913), based upon hospital records, on the occupational pattern of alcoholism in Paris.[24] These two sources, along with the Le Play team's studies, come closer to contemporary standards of objectivity.

It is only fitting that the café, an informal institution that touched so many areas of social life, should be explored through so many different types of sources. References to the café, like the place itself, cut across public and private documentation as well as political, economic, and demographic sources. Almost any novel, police report, social account, or government bulletin might contain pertinent material. The café is as ubiquitous in social literature as indeed it was in social life. It would be foolhardy to think that one study could discover, much less digest, all this material. What can be done, however, is to provide a road map of the terrain to allow future researchers to explore the routes thus opened up more deeply and more quickly. The quantitative and serial sources of the judicial, civil, and police archives allow the historian an alternative to the traditional anecdotal approach to the study of the café. At the center of the present study are over twenty thousand court cases and over ten thousand marriage and baptismal contracts, spelling out the class, gender, and age dynamics of café life, supplemented by court testimony, memoirs, novels, poems, and newspaper accounts. The quantitative material reveals the representativeness of the stories and incidents, and, conversely, by hinting at human faces, the slices of café life enliven the dry factual data.

Into which paradigm will all these data be squeezed? I intend this work to be a synthesis: not only of the two divergent schools of drinking-establishment history already elaborated, but also of the two seemingly contradictory perspectives propounded by Foucault, famous as the great theorist of discipline and social control, and Jürgen Habermas, who has become equally noted as a theorist of social communication, especially for his notion of the "public sphere." Combined, their two perspectives illuminate the two strong forces that vied for the café: the discipline imposed by the government, bosses, landlords, or concierges on café customers, as opposed to the customer's self-expression.

Foucault's work sensitizes us to the relationship between the imposition of discipline in schools, the military (with universal conscription), hospitals, prisons, and factories, on the one hand, and attempts to extend this surveillance and order to places of leisure and diversion such as streets and cafés, on the other. At the end of the eighteenth century, as Foucault's colleague Arlette Farge has shown, the Paris police attempted to impose greater order on these public places. Like their counterparts across France and Europe, they posted the name of each street and put a number on each building; they required licenses of each street vendor and open-air merchant. Their goal was to turn the street into a space of orderly traffic rather than a place where groups socialized and sometimes rioted.[25] Much of the sociable function of the street was thus taken up by the emergent culture of stores and shops and, in particular, the working-class café,[26] which, lacking the decorum, distance, and deference of bourgeois cafés, can be seen as an inversion of the enclosed, segmented, and hierarchical space of the prison and the hospital. The café was a place where a network of multiple exchanges and individualities embodying egalitarian rather than hierarchical contacts could develop.[27] Foucault postulated that the application of power always elicits resistance, but he never elaborated on the tactics and strategies of contention.[28] James Scott's work fills an important gap with its significant analysis of resistance. This book seeks to build upon Scott's insights while contextualizing them in regard to two questions that have not received sufficient attention in the literature on social movements: "how new groups oriented to new world-views come into being, and under what conditions ill-defined sets of people, such as passersby or friendship networks, become important collective actors."[29]

In his watershed book *The Structural Transformation of the Public Sphere*, Habermas locates the resistance and communications of the café within the broader questions of politics and public opinion. The public sphere, briefly summarized, permits private individuals to come together in a public space to participate in matters of common concern according to the rules of rational and critical inquiry and discussion. Habermas discusses the bourgeois public sphere almost exclusively. However, he does allude briefly to the French Revolution: "In the stage of the French Revolution associated with Robespierre, for just one moment, a public sphere stripped of its literary garb began to function—its subject was no longer the 'educated strata' but the uneducated 'people.'"[30] Habermas has little more to say on the matter of a "proletarian public sphere," other than that it "remains oriented toward the intentions of the bourgeois public sphere." The proletarian public sphere did not decline in Paris after the Jacobin era; instead, it steadily gained ground through the nineteenth century. Like the bourgeois public sphere, it articulated public opinion, but it did so in a different fashion. Government surveillance and repression led to its expression often being couched in carnivalesque invective rather than dispassionate discussion.[31] But this did not deprive the proletarian public sphere of its own logic and rules.

The ideas of Foucault and Habermas highlight the asymmetries in the access of the working class to expression of public opinion. The impediments placed in the way of discussion, assembly, and association in the café did not, however, make workers' efforts to express themselves any less important. Understanding the working-class café is a key to understanding the evolution of working-class public opinion across the nineteenth century. Only with this key in hand can we begin to rethink and nuance our notion of class consciousness and class action.

Bibliographic Essay

y main concern in studying the Paris café was to discover the heart of its life and its appeal: its sociability. To this end, I concentrated on finding sources that would provide the actual voices of café habitués. Yet I did not wish to write just another a chatty, anecdotal book about café life. To overcome this barrier, I searched for serial sources that would supply a continuous view of café life, in terms both of statistics and of voices. I found three different types of sources well suited to this quest: judicial and civil records and newspaper accounts of horrible and humorous doings in cafés. All these sources were rich either in voices or in statistics.

Concerning the court records, I used the records for the Paris region at the Archives départementales de la Seine et de la Ville de Paris. For my purposes, examining sociability amid daily life, the registers and dossiers (D1U6 and D2U6 respectively) of the correctional tribunals, or courts of petty sessions (*tribunal de police correctionnelle*), were especially important, because these courts handled the insults, brawls, and disputes of daily life. The registers contain a complete list of all defendants, their occupations, places of birth, and residences, as well as a list of the epithets employed in the case of insults to the police. I examined the registers systematically for the years 1873, 1880, 1885, 1890, and 1899, and more randomly for other years. The dossiers (containing all the material gathered by the examining magistrates—*juges d'instruction*) are but a tiny fraction of all the court cases. I examined the correctional tribunal cartons from 1870 up to 1911 (nos. 1 to 169). I also examined the dossiers of the court handling felonies, the assize court (*cour d'assise*), in particular, the cartons for the 1870s (series D2U8, nos. 50 to 70). The dossiers of the appeals court (*cour d'appel*) for the 1870s and 1880s were also very useful (series D4U9, cartons 1 to 30). Finally, I also examined the judgments (there are no extant dossiers) of the police courts (*tribunal de simple police*) (series D22U1, cartons 81 to 89: 1874 to 1902). An especially rich source, finally, is in the series D3U6, correctional tribunal and assize court cases dropped for lack of incriminating evidence, which I examined for the years 1870 to 1895 (cartons 1 to 105).

The civil archives I examined were both at the Archives départementales de la Seine et de la Ville de Paris (series V4E) and the archives of the twenty district mayoralties of Paris (series M). Much more work could be done with these records than I have been able to accomplish so far. The researcher could record the addresses of all the café owners, married couples, and the other witnesses to map the spatial locations and interrelations between cafés and their clienteles. Or one could explore the extent to which the population of Paris café owners was tapped over time to witness marriages, births, and deaths.

The Archives départementales de la Seine et de la Ville de Paris also contain one of my other major primary sources: bankruptcy records for the drink and food trade. I have examined the registers (series D10U3) containing the assets and debits of all business failures for the following years: 1814–19, 1820–23, 1824–25, 1826, 1827, 1828, 1829, 1830, 1832, 1836, 1841, 1844, 1846, 1854, 1858–59, 1863, 1868, 1876, 1879, 1895, 1900, 1905, 1910, and 1912. In addition, I have consulted individual dossiers of bankruptcies (series D11U3), especially for the period after 1871. I have thus complemented Louis Chevalier's work in this series for the first two-thirds of the century and Gérard Jacquemet's work on Belleville's commercial failures. These two series are monumental and would be worth a book in and of themselves. I did not, however, find the individual dossiers after 1871 to be terribly profitable, because they were often sketchy and irregular in the supply of both quantitative and qualitative information. Moreover, the material was usually not as rich, especially in personal testimony, as the judicial dossiers. For my purposes, the bankruptcy archives were best for quantitative rather than qualitative data.

As far as newspaper sources are concerned, the historian has many options. First, and easiest, one can tap the bulging cartons of series 77 ("Actualités") at the Bibliothèque historique de la Ville de Paris, which contain thousands of newspaper clippings about cafés. Especially important are the brief histories of various cafés that were published when they closed. Although they did a fine job, the assiduous clippers at the Bibliothèque historique did not, however, exhaust the materials on cafés that appeared in the Paris press. In a wide variety of papers across the century, between 1840 and 1940, French journalists developed a rubric that went under the various names of "Notes," "Notules," "Billets," "Cancans de partout," "Propos," "Echos à travers Paris," "Echos et nouvelles," or simply "Echos." These chatty, humorous, anecdotal stories, often culled at café tables and counters, provide a continuous commentary on café life—its humor and horrors—across the nineteenth century. I have included material from such papers as *La Lanterne, La Gazette des tribunaux, Le Cri du peuple, La Lune rousse,*

Le Père Duchesne, *L'Ami du peuple*, *Le Petit Parisien*, *Le Figaro*, and *XIX*ᵉ *siècle*.
Books on café life could be written based upon the material on the café in these
journals, as well as in *L'Aurore*, *L'Eclair*, *L'Echo de Paris*, *Le Gaulois*, *L'Intran-
sigeant*, *Le Populaire*, *Le Temps*, and other Paris periodicals.

Because I sought personal testimony rather than bureaucratic reports on café
life, I did not exhaust the research possibilities of the Archives de la Préfecture
de police or the Archives nationales. At the former, however, I found the following series and cartons vital:

BA 28	Congrès divers ouvrier socialiste
DB 173–75	Débits de boissons
BA 884	Débits de boissons, auberges (décrets et coupures de journaux)
BA 494	Mariages et enterrements civils 1876–92
BA 1502	Propaganda anarchiste
BA 1545	Anniversaire de la semaine sanglante
BA 1547	Semaine sanglante
BA 86–90	Rapports du préfet de police au ministre de l'intérieur, 1871–73; 1876–81
BA 115	Rapports quotidiens du préfet de police, 1906

In addition, unmarked series of cartons containing police ordinances and decrees
across the nineteenth century were also indispensible, because some of them are
not found in the published collections. Series F7 at the Archives nationales, containing reports of the Paris prefect of police to the minister of the interior for the
first half of the nineteenth century (nos. 3774–88, for the years 1819–36), was
the most important of these for my purposes. Naturally, the Archives nationales
also contain a wealth of materials on café cultures across France, but these were
outside the scope of my research.

Notes

Abbreviations

ADS   Archives départementales de la Seine et de la Ville de Paris

APP   Archives de la Préfecture de police

AN   Archives nationales

Gdt   *La Gazette des tribunaux*

PV   "Procès-verbaux de la commission chargée de faire une enquête sur la situation des ouvriers de l'industrie et de l'agriculture en France et de présenter un premier rapport sur le crise industrielle à Paris," *Annales de la Chambre des députés*, n.s., *Documents parlementaires* (1884)

Rdm   *Revue des deux mondes*

Citation of Cases

Some court cases are identified in citations by the initial of their last name. This has been done to comply with the conditions of an authorization provided by the Archives départementales de la Seine et de la Ville de Paris intended to protect the names of defendants and their families for a hundred years. The notes list the series and cartons within which these cases can be found. In court cases found in newspapers, I cite the full names or the abbreviations according to the text.

Preface

1. Robert J. Holton, "The Crowd in History: Some Problems of Theory and Method," *Social History* 3, 2 (May 1978): 221.

2. On the relation between existence and space, see Martin Heidegger, "Building Dwelling Thinking," in *Basic Writings*, ed. David F. Krell (New York: Harper & Row, 1977), 319–40.

3. See Holton, "Crowd in History," esp. 223, for a good overview of these historians.

4. Gerhard Haupt cited in Ellen Ross, "*Sociabilité* of Workers and the Working Class in Comparative Perspective, 1850–1950," *International Labor and Working Class History*, no. 29 (Spring 1986): 104–7.

5. This term is Howard Becker's concept of "moral entrepreneurs" in *Outsiders: Studies in the Sociology of Deviance* (New York: Free Press, 1963), 147–63.

Chapter 1.
Regulation and Constraint

1. Emerson quoted in Ray Oldenburg, *The Great Good Place: Cafés, Coffee Shops, Community Centers, Beauty Parlors, General Stores, Bars, Hangouts and How They Get You through the Day* (New York: Paragon House, 1989), 27.

2. *Karl Marx: Early Writings*, ed. and trans. T. B. Bottomore, with a foreword by Erich Fromm (New York: McGraw-Hill, 1964), 176.

3. David McLellan, *Karl Marx: His Life and Thought* (New York: Harper & Row, 1973), 131.

4. Jules Janin, *The American in Paris during the Summer* (New York: Burgess, Stringer, 1844), 39.

5. Victor Hugo, *Les Misérables*, trans. Charles E. Wilbour (New York: Modern Library, n.d.), 718–19.

6. Walter Benjamin, *Reflections: Essays, Aphorisms, Autobiographical Writings*, trans. Edmund Jephcott (New York: Harcourt Brace Jovanovich, 1979), 146–62. ›

7. Henri Leyret, *En plein faubourg: Moeurs ouvrières* (Paris: Charpentier, 1895), 17.

8. Thomas Pynchon, *Gravity's Rainbow* (New York: Viking, 1973), 262.

9. Louis Lazare, *Etudes municipales: Les Quartiers pauvres de Paris* (Paris: Bureau de la Bibliothèque municipale, 1869), 45, 92.

10. "Alcoolisme comparée," *L'Illustration*, 18 January 1908, 47; Louis Jacquet, *L'Alcool* (Paris: Masson, 1912), 757. The paper *L'Eclair* ran this same statistic under the title on 10 July 1910.

11. See such dictionaries of slang as Alfred Delvau's *Dictionnaire de la langue verte*, new ed., supplemented by Gustave Fustier (Paris: C. Marpont &

E. Flammarion, 1883), 47, 53–54, 68, 77; and Lorédan Larchey, *Dictionnaire de l'argot parisien* (1872; Paris: Editions de Paris, 1985), 3, 16, 30, 36, 46, 50, 59. Altogether I have counted one thousand terms in these two dictionaries.

12. Theodore Child, "Characteristic Parisian Cafés," *Harper's New Monthly Magazine* 78, no. 467 (April 1889): 687.

13. James D. McCabe, Jr., *Paris by Sunlight and Gaslight* (Boston: National Publishing Co., 1869), 70–71.

14. Alvan Sanborn, "Paris Workingmen's Cafés," *North American Review* 158 (February 1894): 252.

15. Bénigno Cacèrés, *Loisirs et travail du moyen âge à nos jours* (Paris: Seuil, 1973), 172.

16. Joseph Barberet, *Le Travail en France: Monographies professionnelles* (Paris: Berger-Levrault, 1890), 8: 3.

17. Thomas Brennan, *Public Drinking and Popular Culture in Eighteenth-Century Paris* (Princeton: Princeton University Press, 1988), 288–97.

18. Frantz Funck-Brentano, *Les Nouvellistes*, with the collaboration of Paul d'Estree, 3d ed. (Paris: Hachette, 1923), 329–30.

19. Louis-Sébastien Mercier, *Tableau de Paris* (Amsterdam, 1782–88), 7: 227–30.

20. James Billington, *Fire in the Minds of Men: Origins of the Revolutionary Faith* (New York: Basic Books, 1980), 25–33.

21. William Coleman, *Death Is a Social Disease: Public Health and Political Economy in Early Industrial France* (Madison: University of Wisconsin Press, 1982), 178.

22. Katherine A. Lynch, *Family, Class, and Ideology in Early Industrial France: Social Policy and the Working-Class Family, 1825–1848* (Madison: University of Wisconsin Press, 1988), 33–34.

23. Coleman, *Death Is a Social Disease*, 235.

24. H. A. Frégier, *Des classes dangereuses de la population dans les grandes villes et des moyens de les rendre meilleurs* (Brussels: Meline, Cans, 1840), 430.

25. Louis Chevalier, *Laboring Classes and Dangerous Classes in Paris during the First Half of the Nineteenth Century*, trans. Frank Jellinek (Princeton: Princeton University Press, 1981), 489.

26. Flora Tristan, *The Worker's Union*, trans. Beverly Livingston (Urbana: University of Illinois Press, 1983), 93–94.

27. *Compte rendu des séances de l'Assemblée nationale législatif* (Paris: Panckoucke, 1849–51), 12: 445–47, 452–60.

28. Barberet, *Travail en France*, 280–82.

29. Lenard Berlanstein, *The Working People of Paris, 1871–1914* (Baltimore: Johns Hopkins University Press, 1984), 136.

30. *Parti socialiste, section française de l'internationale ouvrière, 9ᵉ Con-*

grès national tenu à Lyons, les 18, 19, 20, et 21 février 1912 (Paris: n.d.),
275–93.

31. Brennan, *Public Drinking and Popular Culture*, 13, 69–73.

32. J. J. Clamagern, *Histoire de l'impôt en France* (Paris: Guillaumin, 1876),
2: 381, 593–94; 3: 363, 402–3, 408; L. Dupleix, *Réglementation des débits de
boissons* (Poitiers: Société française d'imprimerie et de libraire, 1908), 9.

33. Philip John Stead, *The Police of Paris* (London: Staples Press, 1957),
23–33.

34. David Bayley, "The Police and Political Development in Europe," in
The Formation of Nation States in Western Europe, ed. Charles Tilly (Princeton:
Princeton University Press, 1975), 344.

35. Nicolas Delamare, *Traité de la police* (1694; Paris: Brunet, 1772), 4:
222–25.

36. Stead, *Police of Paris*, 28, 31; Alan Williams, *The Police of Paris*
(Baton Rouge: Louisiana State University Press, 1979), 67–94, 104–11.

37. Funck-Brentano, *Nouvellistes*, 245; Alfred Franklin, *La Vie privée
d'autrefois: Le Café, le thé, et le chocolat* (Paris: Plon, 1893), 100.

38. J.-B. Sirey, *Recueil général des lois et des arrêts* (Paris: Bureau de l'administration, 1840–43), 1: 54–55.

39. Barberet, *Travail en France*, 17.

40. See *Instruction sur la police des cafés, cabarets, auberges et des tous les
lieux publiques, avec la jurisprudence de la Cour de cassation sur tous les cas
particuliers* (Paris: Leautey, 1896). The police also had a running commentary
on judicial decisions by maintaining a newspaper file on court decisions.

41. APP, ordinance of 4 August 1810, and *Table analytique des arrêts de la
Cour de cassation rendues en matière criminelle, 1789–1856*, ed. Emile Duchesne (Paris: Imprimerie impériale, 1857), 2: 256.

42. APP, ordinance of 14 July 1814.

43. Barberet, *Travail en France*, 207.

44. "La Préfet de la police a proclamé . . . ," *Gazette des tribunaux* (hereafter cited as *Gdt*), 27 May 1848, 737.

45. E. Guerlin de Guer, "Les Débits de boissons," *Revue générale d'administration*, no. 2 (November 1880): 286–89, and Leon Bequet, *Répertoire de
droit administratif* (Paris: Du Pont, 1885), 3: 555.

46. Henri d'Aleméras, *La Vie parisienne sous le Second Empire* (Paris:
Albin Michel, 1933), 355.

47. See, respectively, M. D. Dalloz, *Jurisprudence générale, recueil péri-
odique et critique*, 1859, sec. 1, 190; ibid., 1855, sec. 5, 45; APP BA 884,
dossier 1, draft of letter, 3 June 1876, to the minister of the interior; Dalloz,
Jurisprudence générale, 1829, sec. 1, 397, and 1861, sec. 1, 454; *Table analytique*, ed. Emile Duchesne, 2: 242; Dalloz, *Jurisprudence générale*, 1860, sec. 5,
221; and ibid., 1865, sec. 1, 313–16.

48. Stewart Edwards, *The Paris Commune, 1871* (New York: Quadrangle, 1977), 290. For actions of the 11th arrondissement, see C. J. Lecour, *La Prostitution à Paris et à Londres* (Paris: P. Asselin, 1877), 322, and François Fosca, *Histoire des cafés de Paris* (Paris: Firmin-Didot, 1934), 181.

49. Edith Thomas, *The Women Incendiaries*, trans. James and Starr Atkinson (New York: George Braziller, 1966), 105–6.

50. Eugene Schulkind, "Socialist Women during the 1871 Paris Commune," *Past and Present*, no. 106 (February 1985): 134.

51. Fosca, *Histoire des cafés de Paris*, 181.

52. Barberet, *Travail en France*, 7: 212–13.

53. Susanna Barrows, "After the Commune: Alcoholism, Temperance, and Literature in the Early Third Republic," in *Consciousness and Class Experience in Nineteenth-Century Europe*, ed. John M. Merriman (New York: Holmes & Meier, 1979), 205–18.

54. *Annales de l'Assemblée nationale*, 1871–76, 3, app.: 279; 4: 278, 351–52; 6, app.: 306–7; 7, app.: 611–12; 19: 26–28, 475–76.

55. See, respectively, Dalloz, *Jurisprudence générale*, 1874, sec. 1, 92, and ibid., 1876, sec. 1, 286.

56. Dalloz, *Jurisprudence générale*, 1880, sec. 4, 93.

57. Testimony of M. Camescasse in "Procès-verbaux de la commission chargée de faire une enquête sur la situation des ouvriers de l'industrie et de l'agriculture en France et de présenter un premier rapport sur la crise industrielle à Paris," *Annales de la Chambre des députés*, n.s., *Documents parlementaires*, 12 (March–April 1884), app., 328.

58. Dalloz, *Jurisprudence générale*, 1881, sec. 4, 93.

59. APP BA 884, dossier 1, letter of mayor of the 11th arrondissement requesting the prefect of police to decree a radius around all schools to prevent the opening of a beer shop at 122 rue des Amelot next to a school for girls. Henri Vidal, *Le Cabaret: Etude de droit administrif et de législation financière* (Paris: Girard & Briére, 1916), 66, notes that article 9 of the 1880 law was applied only in a few large cities, among which Paris was not included.

60. *Annales d'hygiène publique et médecine légale*, 4th ser., 2, no. 3 (July 1904): 285.

61. BA 884 dossier 1, reports of 12 April, 13 May, and 3 July 1878. F. Mironneau, *Nouveau manuel de police* (Paris: Fayard, 1877), 525–26, notes that in Paris it had become customary to let cafés stay open till midnight, but that the 11 P.M. closing time was still law, unless a special permit were obtained from the prefect of police.

62. Louis Andrieux, *Souvenirs d'un préfet de police*, 2 vols. (Paris: J. Rouff, 1885), 1: 152–53.

63. Stead, *Police of Paris*, 146.

64. Maxime du Camp, *Paris: Ses organes, ses fonctions et sa vie dans la deuxième moitié du XIXeme siècle* (Paris: Hachette, 1870), 2: 132.

65. ADS D.2T1, carton 16, folder on "Ligue et concours contre l'alcoolisme, 1909–1923."

66. Elisabeth Hausser, *Paris au jour le jour: Les Evénements vus par la presse, 1900–1919* (Paris: Minuit, 1968), 119.

67. *Circulaires émanées du préfet de police* (Paris: Imprimerie Chaix, 1907), 11.

68. Dupleix, *Réglementation des débitants de boissons*, 123.

69. *Enquête parlementaire sur l'insurrection du 18 mars*, vol. 2: *Dépositions des témoins*, app. no. 740 (Versailles: Cerf, 1872), 107.

70. Emile Gaboriau, *Monsieur Lecoq* (1908; New York: Dover, 1975), 84.

71. Frégier, *Des classes dangereuses*, 22; Louis Paulian, *Beggars in Paris*, trans. Lady Herschell (New York: Edward Arnold, 1897), 152.

72. "Night Rambles in Paris," I, "At the Prefecture and among the Chiffoniers," *Every Saturday*, 22–24 July 1868, 35.

73. APP BA 1545, semaine sanglante.

74. Bayle Saint John, *Purple Tints of Paris: Character and Manners in the New Empire* (New York: Riker, Thorne, 1854), 185.

75. Emile Gaboriau, *Other People's Money* (New York: Charles Scribner's Sons, 1900), 70; and *Monsieur Lecoq*, 169.

76. Charles Tilly, "Reflection on the History of European State-Making," in *The Formation of National States in Western Europe*, ed. id., Studies in Political Development 8 (Princeton: Princeton University Press, 1975), 60; Andrieux quoted in Benjamin Martin, *Crime and Criminal Justice under the Third Republic: The Shame of Marianne* (Baton Rouge: Louisiana State University Press, 1990), 76.

77. Gaboriau, *Monsieur Lecoq*, 15; Saint John, *Purple Tints*, 184–85.

78. Gaboriau, *Monsieur Lecoq*, 100; *L'Illustration*, 12 July 1890, 30, 35; *Mémoires de Rossignol, ex-inspecteur de la Sûreté* (Paris: Société d'éditions littéraires et artistiques, 1900), passim.

79. "The French Police," *Every Saturday*, 2 February 1897, 150.

80. Saint John, *Purple Tints*, 185

81. Emile Gaboriau, *Monsieur Lecoq*, 115.

82. AN F7 3877, report of 18 April 1823.

83. AN F7 3874, reports of 17 May, 23 May, 8 June, 29 October, and 17 July 1819.

84. AN F7 3884, report of 10 November 1830.

85. See, e.g., the reports of 6 Messidor AN XIII (25 June 1805) and 21 January 1806 in *Paris pendant l'Empire*, ed. Alphonse Aulard (Paris: Cerf & Noblet, 1912), 21–22, and 2: 400.

86. AN F7 3879, report of 8 January 1825.

87. AN F7 3877, reports of 23 January 1823, and F7 3875, report of 18 April 1820.

88. AN F7 3877, report of 26 June 1823.

89. AN F7 3874, reports of 26 May and of 26 and 27 January 1819.

90. AN F7 3874, report of 25 May 1819.

91. See also AN F7 3874, reports of 25 January, 10 February, 21 and 27 April, 25 May, and 4 August 1819, and 17 April 1820; F7 3877, reports of 7 April 1823, 16 and 29 March 1819, 3, 19, and 25 January 1819, 27 April 1819, 25 May 1819, and 1 January 1820; F7 3877, report of 30 August 1823; F7 3884, report of 30 August 1830.

92. APP, ordinances of 25 March 1820 and 5 January, 28 February, and 2 September 1822.

93. Patricia O'Brien, "Urban Growth and Public Order: The Development of a Modern Police in Paris, 1829–1854" (diss., Columbia University, 1973), 301–24.

94. ADS D2U6, no. 27, affaire Marié de Lisle, and D2U6, no. 40, affaire Rainot.

95. See David Pinkney, *Napoléon III and the Rebuilding of Paris* (Princeton: Princeton University Press, 1958), 32–40; Jeanne Gaillard, *Paris, la ville, 1852–1870* (Paris: Champion, 1976); Emile Zola, *La Curée*, trans. Alexander T. Mattos (New York: Boni & Liveright, 1924), 197.

96. "Courrier de Paris," *L'Illustration*, 19 June 1869, 386.

97. ADS D2U6, no. 87, affaire Tournois et al.

98. Gaboriau, *Other People's Money*, 3.

99. "Night Rambles in Paris," III, "The Italian Colony—The Bal du Vieux Chene," *Every Saturday*, 18 July 1868, 70.

100. ADS D3U6, no. 1, affaires Lefevre, Galoyer, and Barrois.

101. Vincent Wright, "La Préfecture de la police pendant le XIXe siècle," in *L'Administration de Paris, 1789–1977*, Centre de recherches d'histoire et de philologie de la IVe section de l'Ecole practique des hautes études (Paris: Champion, 1979), 115.

102. For August 1871 decree, see Léon Bequet, *Répertoire de droit administratif* (Paris: Du Pont, 1885), 24: 7; for June 1873 decree, see Guerlin de Guer, "Débits de boissons," 289; for October 1877 decree, see *Bulletin officiel du ministère de l'intérieur* (Paris: Paul Dupont, 1877), 450.

103. *Annales de l'assemblée nationale, 1871–1876*, app. 1873, 309; APP BA 884, dossier 1, "Etat des débits de boissons."

104. APP BA 884, dossier 1, "Etat des débits de boissons"; *La Tempérance* 5, no. 1 (1887): 202, cites the following figures for 1875 in the department of the Seine: total number 24,809; closed for infractions to regulations, 19; closed for reasons of general security, 9; reopened after closing, 7; demands for reopening rejected, 2,354.

105. APP BA 884, dossier 1, minister of the interior's letter of 14 November 1877 to prefect of police.

106. Maurice Block, *Dictionnaire de l'administration française*, 2d ed. (Paris: Berger-Levrault, 1881), 229.

107. Fernand and Maurice Pelloutier, *La Vie ouvrière en France* (Paris: Schlecher frères, 1900), 309, say there were 27,000 cafés in 1892; Paul Griveau, *L'Alcoolisme: Fléau social, moeurs, législation, droit comparé* (Paris: Marcel & Billard, 1906), 227, says there were 33,000 cafés in Paris; *L'Illustration*'s "Faits divers," 9 January 1909, 35, says 43,300 cafés in the department of the Seine; Alfred Fouillée in "Les Jeunes Criminels: L'Ecole et la presse," *Revue des deux mondes* (hereafter cited as *Rdm*), 15 January 1897, counts 30,000 cafés, 445; Jules Siegfried, quoted in Dupleix, *Réglementation des débitants des boissons*, 27, says 30,000 in Paris; Maurice Talmeyr, "Moeurs electorales: Les Marchands de vins," *Rdm*, 4th ser., 148 (15 August 1898): 879, lists 40,000 cafés.

108. As Léon and Maurice Bonneff note, the police led the drunken rich person home and arrested the intoxicated proletarian (*Marchands de folie*, 2d ed. [Paris: Rivière, 1913], 75).

109. "Faits divers . . . justice correctionnelle," *L'Illustration*, 11 September 1875, 175.

110. "Chronique, Paris," *Gdt*, 2 September 1871, 496.

111. Othenin d'Haussonville, "La Vie et les salariés à Paris," *Rdm*, 3d ser., 56 (15 April 1883): 815–67.

112. Stead, *Police of Paris*, 151.

113. *Recueil officiel des circulaires émanées de la Préfecture de la police, 1849–1880* (Paris: Chaix, 1883), vol. 2, 16 January 1879, no. 972, and 18 June 1879, no. 984.

114. J. G. Alger, "Thirty Years in Paris," *Fortnightly Review* 79 (March 1903): 436–37.

115. ADS D3U6, no. 20, affaire Mainiel et al.

Chapter 2.
Privacy in Public

1. On the left, see Flora Tristan, *The Worker's Union*, trans. Beverly Livingston (Urbana: University of Illinois Press, 1983), and Désiré Verhaeghe, *De l'alcoolisation, effet, causes, remèdes: Etude des pathologies sociales*, Thèse refusée par la censure décanale et rectorale (Paris: Société d'éditions scientifiques, 1900), 74, 496. Among Catholic thinkers, see Othenin d'Haussonville, "La Vie et les salariés à Paris," *Revue des deux mondes* (hereafter cited as *Rdm*), 3d ser., 56 (15 April 1883): 823. For the republican view, see Jules Siegfried, *La Misère: Son histoire, ses causes, ses remèdes*, 3d ed. (Paris: G. Baillière, 1879), 211.

2. Louis Albanel, *La Crime dans la famille* (Paris: J. Rueff, 1900), 12.

3. Siegfried, *Misère*, 204.

4. Philippe Ariès, *Centuries of Childhood: A Social History of Family Life*, trans. Robert Baldick (New York: Random House, Vintage Books, 1962), 398–403; David Garrioch, *Neighborhood and Community in Paris, 1740–1790* (Cambridge: Cambridge University Press, 1986), 56–95; Thomas E. Brennan, *Public Drinking and Popular Culture in Eighteenth-Century Paris* (Princeton: Princeton University Press, 1988), 246–49; Arlette Farge, *Vivre dans la rue à Paris au XVIIIe siècle* (Paris: Gallimard-Archives, 1979), 18–21.

5. Louis Girard, *La Deuxième République et le Second Empire, 1848–1870* (Paris: Association pour la publication d'une histoire de Paris, distrib. Hachette, 1981), 188; Roger Guerrard, *Les Origines du logement social en France au XIXe siècle, 1850–1894* (Paris: Editions ouvrières, 1966), 22.

6. Jeanne Gaillard, *Paris, la ville, 1852–1870* (Paris: Champion, 1976), 525–31.

7. "Faits Divers. . . . Les maisons d'habitations à Paris et à Londres," *L'Illustration*, 6 June 1903, 386.

8. Louis Jacquet, *L'Alcool* (Paris: Masson, 1912), 757.

9. Matilda Bentham-Edwards, *Home Life in France*, 6th ed. (London: Methuen, 1913), 87.

10. Eliot Gregory, "The Poetic Cabarets of Paris," *Scribner's Magazine* 27, no. 10 (January 1900): 93.

11. Edmond and Jules de Goncourt, *Pages from the Goncourt Journal*, ed. and trans. Robert Baldick (New York: Oxford University Press, 1962), 53.

12. Girard, *La Deuxième République et le Second Empire*, 328.

13. Theodore Child, "Characteristic Parisian Cafes," *Harper's New Monthly Magazine* 78, no. 467 (April 1889): 688.

14. David W. Bartlett, *Paris with Pen and Pencil* (New York: C. M. Sexton, 1858), 22.

15. Emile Zola, *La Curée*, trans. Alexander T. Mattos (New York: Boni & Liveright, 1924), 137, 148–49.

16. "Perdican," "Courrier de Paris," *L'Illustration*, 9 August 1884, 86.

17. Joanna Richardson, *The Bohemians: La Vie de Bohème in Paris, 1830–1914* (London: Macmillan, 1969), 88.

18. Emile Zola, *L'Assommoir*, trans. Leonard Tancock (Baltimore: Penguin Books, 1970), 248.

19. Brennan, *Public Drinking and Popular Culture*, 45 n. 21.

20. Roger H. Guerrand, *Les Origines du logement social en France* (Paris: Editions ouvrières, 1967), 31–38.

21. Louis Chevalier in *Laboring Classes and Dangerous Classes in Paris during the First Half of the Nineteenth Century*, trans. Frank Jellinek (Princeton: Princeton University Press, 1981), 187.

22. Othenin d'Haussonville, " 'L'Enfance à Paris,' I, La Criminalité.— L'Abandon," *Rdm*, 3d ser., 17 (October 1876): 847.

23. Tristan, *Worker's Union*, 94.

24. See Chevalier, *Laboring Classes and Dangerous Classes*, 188.

25. Guerrand, *Origines du logement*, 96; Louis Chevalier, *La Formation de la population parisienne au XIXe siècle*, Institut national d'études démographiques, Travaux et documents, cahier no. 10 (Paris, 1950), 45–60; Ann Louise Shapiro, *Housing the Poor of Paris, 1850–1902* (Madison: University of Wisconsin Press, 1985), 101–12.

26. Louis Lazare, *Les Quartiers pauvres de Paris: Le XXe arrondissement* (Paris: Au bureau de la Bibliothèque municipale, 1868), 106–7.

27. Michelle Perrot, "La Ménagère dans l'espace parisien au XIXe siècle," *Annales de la recherche urbaine*, no. 9 (1980): 11; Shapiro, *Housing the Poor of Paris*, 143.

28. Theodore Child, *The Praise of Paris* (New York: Harper Brothers, 1893), 188; Fernand and Maurice Pelloutier, *La Vie ouvrière en France* (Paris: Schlecher frères, 1900), 233–34; Georges Picot, *Les Garnis d'ouvriers de Paris* (Paris: F. Levé, 1900), 8–11; Haussonville, "L'Enfance à Paris," 583.

29. Shapiro, *Housing the Poor of Paris*, 63, 123–24, 223, 113–23; Michelle Perrot, *Les Ouvriers en grève, France, 1871–1890* (Paris: Mouton, 1974), 1: 216–23.

30. Perrot, *Ouvriers en grève*, 1: 224.

31. ADS D2U8, no. 53, affaire Palat.

32. ADS D3U6, no. 46, affaire Parra, and no. 20 affaire Rouyer . . . Chastanet.

33. Clément-Eugène Louis, "Cantonnier-poseur de voie de Chemin de fer du nord," *Ouvriers des deux mondes*, 3d ser., 1, no. 99 (1904): 453.

34. ADS D2U6, no. 45, affaire Tellier.

35. But Shapiro, *Housing the Poor of Paris*, 231, argues that the housing crisis eased in the 1890s.

36. Adeline Daumard, "Conditions de logement et position sociale," in *Le Parisien chez lui aux XIXe siècle, 1814–1914* (Paris: Archives nationales, 1977), 17.

37. See, e.g., Edmond Demolins, cited by Shapiro in "Housing Reform in Paris: Social Space and Social Control," *French Historical Studies* 12, no. 4 (Fall 1982): 491.

38. Georges Picot, *Les Garnis d'ouvriers à Paris* (Paris: F. Levé, 1900), 8.

39. William Coleman, *Death Is a Social Disease: Public Health and Political Economy in Early Industrial France* (Madison: University of Wisconsin Press, 1982), 175.

40. *L'Illustration*, 3 October 1896, 274.

41. Adolphe Guillot, *Les Prisons et les prisonniers de Paris* (Paris: E. Dentu, 1890), 125.

42. Georges Picot, *Un Devoir social et les logements d'ouvriers* (Paris: Levy, 1885), 8–9, 11.

43. Léon and Maurice Bonneff, *Marchands de folie*, 2d ed. (Paris: Rivière, 1913).

44. "Chronique," *Gazette des tribunaux* (hereafter cited as *Gdt*), 28 January 1868, 95.

45. Marcel Edant, "La Misère à Paris," *L'Illustration*, 13 November 1886, 332.

46. H. A. Frégier, *Des classes dangereuses de la population dans les grandes villes et des moyens de les rendre meilleurs* (Brussels: Meline, Cans, 1840), 1: 22–23.

47. Chevalier, *Laboring Classes and Dangerous Classes*, 230.

48. Anthony Sutcliff, *The Autumn of Central Paris* (London: Edwin Arnold, 1970), 138.

49. Ibid. and Chevalier, *Laboring Classes and Dangerous Classes*, 230.

50. For 1876 estimates, see *L'Illustration*, 3 October 1896, 274; for 1882 figures, see Shapiro, *Housing the Poor of Paris*, 137.

51. "Etat du nombre de garnis et de locataires au 1er janvier et au 31 décembre," in Ville de Paris, *Annuaire statistique* (Paris: Imprimerie municipale, 1890–1910).

52. Albanel, *Crime dans la famille*, 11.

53. In the 1870s, fewer than 5 percent of cases involved teenagers, with a slight increase to roughly 8 percent during the 1880s, and to approximately 10 percent in the 1890s. For the age group 21 to 25, also frequently associated with "youth," the percentages do not show such a steady increase: 11 percent in the 1870s, over 15 percent in the 1880s, and 12.5 percent in the 1890s.

54. A frequency run on the computer program SPSS (Statistical Package for the Social Sciences) revealed a correlation among the ages of 2,019 defendants. The statistical significance of this tabulation was .0003. The differences in frequency were evaluated with a p value of less than .01 at the 1 percent confidence level.

55. Emile Garçon, *Code penal annoté* (Paris: Sirey, 1952), 2: 811, and *Annales de l'Assemblée nationale, 1871–1876*, 2: 26–28, 49, 475–76.

56. ADS D1U6, correctional tribunal register for December 1880.

57. ADS D2U6, no. 85, affaire Grosselin and Linasset.

58. R. Benon, "L'Alcoolisme à Paris," *Annales d'hygiène publique et médecine légale*, 4th ser., 8, no. 4 (1907): 291.

59. Richard Cobb, *Paris and Its Provinces, 1792–1802* (London: Oxford University Press, 1975), 243–44.

60. Toussaint Loua, *Atlas statistique de la population de Paris* (Paris: Dejey, 1873), 68.

61. Cited in Louise Tilly and Joan W. Scott, *Women, Work, and Family* (New York: Holt, Rinehart & Winston, 1978), 97.

62. Chevalier, *Formation de la population parisienne*, 207.

63. "L'Origine des habitants de Paris," *L'Illustration*, 16 November 1895, 406. During the 1870s, the figure stood at around 34.71 percent; see Chevalier, *Formation de la population parisienne*, 46.

64. "Faits divers," *L'Illustration*, 2 March 1878, 147.

65. Louis-Sébastien Mercier, *Tableau de Paris* (1782; Paris: Mercure de France, 1994), 1: 820–23; Maxime du Camp, *Paris: Ses organes, ses fonctions et sa vie dans la deuxième moitié du XIXème siècle* (Paris: Hachette, 1870), 6: 111.

66. For a good description of the difference between the status and work conditions of a clerk and a day laborer, see Ronald Aminzade, *Class, Politics, and Early Industrial Capitalism* (Albany, N.Y.: State University of New York Press, 1981), 29–31.

67. See Tristan Bernard's play *Le Petit Café*, in *L'Illustration théatrale*, 18 May 1912, 14.

68. Gérard Jacquemet, *Belleville au XIXe siecle: Du faubourg à la ville*, ed. Jean Touzot (Paris: Editions de l'Ecole des hautes études en sciences sociales, 1984), 342.

69. Garrioch, *Neighborhood and Community in Paris*, 26. For a very detailed description of a wedding celebration in a working-class café, see Honoré de Balzac, "Facino Cane," in his *Selected Short Stories*, trans. Sylvia Raphel (New York: Penguin Books, 1977), 237–42.

70. *Paris pendant la terreur: Rapports des agents secrets du ministre de l'interieur*, ed. Pierre Caron, in 6 vols. (Paris: Société de l'histoire contemporaine et Société de l'histoire de France, 1919–58), 3: 188.

71. See circular of 11 January 1837, quoted by F. Mironneau, *Nouveau manuel de police* (Paris: Fayard, 1877), 525–26.

72. "Chronique . . . Paris," *Gdt*, 3 January 1829, 216; Joanna Richardson, *The Bohemians: La Vie de Bohème in Paris, 1830–1914* (London: Macmillan, 1969), 34.

73. Peter de Polnay, "Belleville and Ménilmontant," in *Aspects of Paris* (London: W. H. Allen, 1968), 117.

74. Louis Lazare, *Les Quartiers de l'est de Paris* (Paris: Au bureau de la Bibliothèque municipale, 1870), 125.

75. Du Camp, *Paris*, 6: 121; Theodore Child, "Proletarian Paris," *Harper's New Monthly Magazine* 86, no. 512 (January 1893): 191–92.

76. Lazare, *Quartiers de l'est*, 125.

77. Rachel G. Fuchs, *Abandoned Children: Foundlings and Child Welfare in Nineteenth-Century France* (Albany: State University of New York Press,

1984), 276; Lenard Berlanstein, *The Working People of Paris, 1871–1914* (Baltimore: Johns Hopkins University Press, 1984), 37–147; A. F. Badier, "Compositeur-typographe de Paris," *Ouvriers des deux mondes*, 1st ser., 4, no. 33 (1863): 254.

78. Girard, *La Deuxième République et le Second Empire*, 167; Fuchs, *Abandoned Children*, 264; Berlanstein, *Working People of Paris*, 141–45; Michelle Perrot, "Fin des vagabonds," *L'Histoire*, 3 July 1978; Jean-Claude Beaune, *Le Vagabond et la machine* (Seyssel: Champ Vallon, 1983), 338.

79. Charles Rearick, *Pleasures of the Belle Epoque: Entertainment and Festivity in Turn-of-the-Century France* (New Haven: Yale University Press, 1985), 182.

80. Georges Duveau, *La Vie ouvrière sous le Second Empire* (Paris: Gallimard, 1946), 246.

81. De Polnay, "Belleville and Ménilmontant," 405.

82. *Jack*, vol. 21 of *The Works of Alphonse Daudet*, trans. Marian McIntyre (Boston: Little, Brown, 1899–1906), 322.

83. "La Journée," *Cri du peuple*, 4 January 1884, 2.

84. Gaillard, *Paris, la ville*, 249.

85. E. F. Herbert and E. Delbert, "Tisseur en chales," *Ouvriers des deux mondes*, 1st ser., 1, no. 7 (1858): 318–19.

86. Alvan Sanborn, "Paris Workingmen's Cafes," *North American Review* 158 (February 1894): 252.

87. "Les Premiers Beaux Dimanches—Le Retour au logis par les grands boulevards," *L'Illustration*, 18 March 1911, 199.

88. Victor Hugo, *Les Misérables*, trans. Charles E. Wilbour (New York: Modern Library, n.d.).

89. Maurice Yvernès, "L'Alcoolisme et la criminalité," *Journal de la Société de statistique de Paris* (49 vols.) 2 (1908): 412.

90. Arnold van Gennep, *Manuel de folklore français contemporain* (Paris: Auguste Picard, 1943), 1: 166, 198. In *Marchands de folie*, the brothers Bonneff provide only one example of a café owner tempting working-class youth (13–14).

91. Francois Gasnault, *Guinguettes et lorettes: Bals publics à Paris au XIXe siècle* (Paris: Aubier, 1986), 39.

92. P. du Maroussem, "Ebéniste parisien de haut luxe," *Ouvriers des deux mondes*, 2d ser., 4, no. 74 (1892): 69, 60.

93. See, e.g., Garrioch, *Neighborhood and Community in Paris*, 77–80.

94. Brennan, *Public Drinking and Popular Culture*, 302. Garrioch finds the same thing: "Domestic quarrels usually took place in the relative privacy of the room or apartment and few came before the commissaire" (*Neighborhood and Community in Paris*, 78).

95. Farge, *Vivre dans la rue à Paris*, 42–45, 123–63.

96. Jacques-Louis Ménétra, *Journal of My Life*, with an introduction and

commentary by Daniel Roche, trans. Arthur Goldhammer (New York: Columbia University Press, 1986).

97. James Rousseau, "Les Barrières et les guinguettes," in *Nouveau tableau de Paris aux XIXᵉ siècle* (Paris: Librairie de Madame Charles Béchet, 1834), 5: 302–4.

98. Emile Zola, *Savage Paris*, trans. David Hughes and Marie J. Mason (London: Elek Books, 1955), 245.

99. ADS D2U6, no. 5, affaire Fabre.

100. Georges Rivière, *Renoir et ses amis* (Paris: H. Floury, 1921), 173–76.

101. Ruth Harris, *Murders and Madness: Medicine, Law, and Society in the Fin de siècle* (Oxford: Oxford University Press, 1989), 243–85.

102. "Chronique," *Gdt*, 3 November 1830, 8.

103. ADS D2U6, no. 27, affaire Marié de Lisle. See also "Chronique," *Gdt*, 13 February 1873, 147.

104. Respectively, ADS D2U8, no. 56, affaire Billoir, and D2U6, no. 73, affaire Houdremont.

105. Farge, *Vivre dans la rue à Paris*, 74.

106. Nancy Tomes, "A 'Torrent Of Abuse': Crimes of Violence between Working-Class Men and Women in London, 1840–1875," *Journal of Social History* 12 (1978): 341–42.

107. Henry Steele, *The Working Classes in France* (London: Twentieth Century Press, 1904), 37.

108. Ibid., 101.

109. Jill Harsin, *Policing Prostitution in Nineteenth-Century Paris* (Princeton: Princeton University Press, 1985), 187, 243.

110. Respectively ADS D1U6, register for August 1871, affaire Van der Speck; register for May 1872, affaire Houbert; register for February 1885, affaire Bugnard; and register for April 1885, affaires Jeandin and Barbier.

111. "Tribunaux," *Lanterne*, 10 June 1880, 3.

112. Paris, Conseil municipal *Procès-verbaux/débats* (Paris: Imprimerie municipale, 1885–86). For Joffrin's views, see 1885, pt. 1, 470–81; for Vaillant, see 1886, pt. 1, 632–42, 1093.

113. "Nos graveurs: Les Baptêmes révolutionnaires," *L'Illustration*, 15 November 1890, 414, 426.

114. APP BA 494, "Marriages et enterrements"; "Les Baptêmes révolutionnaires," *L'Illustration*, 23 July 1892, 74.

115. Jacques Donzelot, *The Policing of Families*, trans. Robert Hurley (New York: Pantheon Books, 1979), 45.

116. Fuchs, *Abandoned Children*, 279.

117. Michelle Perrot, "Comment les ouvriers parisiens voyaient la crise d'après l'enquête parlementaire de 1884," in *Hommage à Ernest Labrousse* (Paris: Den Haag, 1974), 189; id., *Ouvriers en grève*, 1: 223.

Chapter 3.
Work and the Café

1. The classic and still best essay on the question of indiscipline is E. P. Thompson, "Time, Work-Discipline and Industrial Capitalism," *Past and Present*, no. 38 (December 1967): 56–97.

2. D. A. Reed has called for this in "The Decline of Saint Monday, 1766–1876," *Past and Present*, no. 71 (1976): 76–101.

3. See esp. Michael P. Hanagan, *The Logic of Solidarity: Artisans and Industrial Workers in Three French Towns, 1817–1914* (Urbana: University of Illinois Press, 1980), esp. 102–42.

4. Alain Cottereau, "The Distinctiveness of Working-Class Cultures in France, 1848–1900," in *Working-Class Formation: Nineteenth-Century Patterns in Western Europe and the United States*, ed. Ira Katznelson and Aristide R. Zolberg (Princeton: Princeton University Press, 1986), 143–44; David Garrioch, *Neighborhood and Community in Paris, 1740–1790* (Cambridge: Cambridge University Press, 1986), 169–204.

5. Stuart L. Campbell, *The Second Empire Revisited: A Study in French Historiography* (New Brunswick, N.J.: Rutgers University Press, 1978), 178.

6. Francisque Michel and Edouard Fournier, *Les Hôtelleries et les cabarets en France depuis la fin du XVIᵉ siecle à nos jours* (Paris: Delahys, 1859), 399.

7. Charles Paul de Kock, "Les Restaurants et les cartes de restaurant," *Nouveau tableau de Paris aux XIXᵉ siècle* (Paris: Librairie de Madame Charles Béchet, 1834), 4: 74.

8. Lenard Berlanstein, *The Working People of Paris* (Baltimore: Johns Hopkins University Press, 1984), 100.

9. Ibid., passim; and see esp. *Moeurs parisiennes, ou lundi à la barrière du Mont-Parnasse: Scène populaire* (Paris: Herhau, 1831).

10. Honoré de Balzac, *The History of the Thirteen*, trans. Herbert J. Hunt (New York: Penguin Books, 1974), 311. The binges of Sunday and Monday increased admissions to Paris hospitals on Tuesdays and Wednesdays, notes Louis Chevalier, *Laboring Classes and Dangerous Classes in Paris during the First Half of the Nineteenth Century*, trans. Frank Jellinek (Princeton: Princeton University Press, 1981), 308.

11. James Rousseau, "Les Barrières et les guinguettes," *Nouveau tableau de Paris* (Paris: Librairie de Madame Charles-Béchet, 1834), 5: 288.

12. Peter Stearns, "Patterns of Industrial Strike Activity in France during the July Monarchy," *American Historical Review* 70, no. 2 (January 1965): 374, 389.

13. *Un Ouvrier en 1820: Manuscrit inédit de Jacques-Etienne Bédé*, ed. Rémi Gossez (Paris: Presses universitaires de France, 1984), 275, 284, 299n.

14. Michael D. Sibalis, "The Paris Carpenters: 1789–1848" (paper delivered at the 33d annual conference of the Society for French Historical Studies, Minneapolis, 19–21 March 1987), 8, 13.

15. *Les Associations professionnelles ouvrières* (Paris: Office du travail, 1894–1904), 4: 320.

16. Agnes Mathilde Wergeland, *History of the Working Classes in France: A Review of Levasseur's "Histoire des classes ouvrières avant 1789"* (Chicago: University of Chicago Press, 1916), 130.

17. Sibalis, "Paris Carpenters," 11.

18. Alain Faure, "Mouvements populaires et mouvement ouvrier à Paris (1830–1834)," *Mouvement social*, no. 88 (July–September 1974): 63.

19. *Associations professionnelles ouvrières*, 1: 708–12.

20. Faure, "Mouvements populaires et mouvement ouvrier," 63.

21. Gérard Jacquemet, *Belleville au XIXᵉ siecle: Du faubourg à la ville*, ed. Jean Touzot (Paris: Editions de l'Ecole des hautes études en sciences sociales, 1984), 349.

22. Raymond Rudorff, *The Belle Epoque: Paris in the Nineties* (New York: Saturday Review Press, 1972), 31; Yves-Marie Bercé, *History of Peasant Revolts: The Social Origins of Rebellion in Early Modern France*, trans. Amanda Whitmore (Ithaca, N.Y.: Cornell University Press, 1990).

23. Charles Rearick, *Pleasures of the Belle Epoque: Entertainment and Festivity in Turn-of-the-Century France* (New Haven: Yale University Press, 1985), 153.

24. Georges Duveau, *La Vie ouvrière sous le Second Empire* (Paris: Gallimard, 1946), 501.

25. See Joseph Barberet, *Le Travail en France: Monographies professionnelles*, in 8 vols. (Paris: Berger-Levrault, 1886–90), 1: 53.

26. Ibid., 1: 53; 2: 138; 5: 265. Marilyn Boxer, "Women in Industrial Homework: The Flowermakers of Paris in the Belle Epoque," *French Historical Studies* 12, no. 3 (Spring 1982): 416–17.

27. Michele Perrot, *Les Ouvriers en grève, France, 1871–1890* (Paris: Mouton, 1974), 1: 392.

28. Lee Shai Weissbach, "Artisanal Response to Artistic Decline: The Cabinetmakers of Paris in the Era of Industrialization," *Journal of Social History* 16, no. 2 (Winter 1982): 67–79.

29. Berlanstein, *Working People of Paris*, 103.

30. Philip G. Nord, *Paris Shopkeepers and the Politics of Resentment* (Princeton: Princeton University Press, 1986), 388–89; picture in Antoine Prost, "Public and Private Spheres in France," in *A History of Private Life*, vol. 5: *Riddles of Identity in Modern Times*, ed. Antoine Prost and Gerard Vincent, trans. Arthur Goldhammer (Cambridge, Mass.: Harvard University Press, Belknap Press, 1991), 38.

31. A. Lailler, "De l'influence de l'alimentation pour prévenir et combattre l'abus des boissons alcooliques," *La Tempérance* 6, no. 1 (1878): 38; L. Laboulais, *L'Ouvrier: Considérations sur le travail* (Paris: Paul Dupont, 1890), 229; Paul Griveau, *L'Alcoolisme: Fléau social, moeurs, législation, droit comparé* (Paris: Marcel & Billard, 1906), 220; Michael Miller, *The Bon Marché: Bourgeois Culture and the Department Store, 1896–1920* (Princeton: Princeton University Press, 1981), 93, 107–10.

32. *Associations professionnelles ouvrières*, 1: 476; 4: 387.

33. Léon and Maurice Bonneff, *Marchands de folie*, 2d ed. (Paris: Rivière, 1913), 48.

34. Ibid., 21–15, 37, 55, 61.

35. Bédé, *Un Ouvrier en 1820*; Louis René Villermé quoted in Duveau, *Vie ouvrière sous le Second Empire*, 510.

36. Denis Poulot, *Le Sublime, ou le travailleur comme il est en 1870, et ce qu'il peut être* (1870; Paris; François Maspero, 1880). In his introduction to the 1980 Maspero edition of *Le Sublime*, Alain Cottereau provides a wonderful summary of these points. See a translation of his introduction in *Voices of the People: The Social Life of "La Sociale" at the End of the Second Empire*, ed. Adrian Rifkin and Roger Thomas, trans. John More (London: Routledge & Kegan Paul, 1988), 104–5.

37. P. Meyer, *The Child and the State: The Intervention of the State in French Family Life*, trans. J. Ennew and J. Lloyd (Cambridge: Cambridge University Press, 1983), 9; Guillaume L. Duprat, *La Criminalité dans l'adolescence* (Paris: F. Alcan, 1909), 138; Berlanstein, *Working People of Paris*, 136.

38. E. Levasseur, *Histoire des classes ouvrières et l'industie en France de 1789 à 1870*, 2d ed. (Paris: Rousseau, 1904), 773–74.

39. This conclusion is based on a series of cross-tabulations comparing the frequency with which metalworkers, construction workers, and day laborers insulted the police. The differences in frequency were evaluated with the chi-square measure of the SPSS (Statistical Package for the Social Sciences) program and found to be significant with a p value of less than .01 at the 1 percent confidence level. The actual chi-square degree of significance between day laborers and metalworkers is .0019 and .0016, and between construction workers and day laborers, .0004 and .0003.

40. Perrot, *Ouvriers en grève*, 1: 469.

41. The ADS series D3U6 records an abundance of cases involving socialist and working-class militants; see, e.g., no. 20, affaire Rouyer et al., no. 30, affaire Tortelier et al., and no. 24, affaire Girault et al.

42. Othenin d'Haussonville, "La Vie et les salariés à Paris," *Revue des deux mondes*, 3d ser., 56 (15 April 1883): 861, noted that day laborers had never formed a labor union nor gone on strike.

43. Alain Faure, "Classe malpropre, classe dangereuse? Quelques remarques à propos des chiffoniers parisiens aux XIXᵉ siècle et de leurs cités," *Recherches*, no. 31, *L'Haleine des faubourgs* (February 1977): 82.

44. "Stan," "Notes," *L'Illustration*, 2 February 1889, 91.

45. Barberet, *Travail en France*, 1: 420. See also Paris Chambre de commerce, *Statistique de l'industrie à Paris . . . pour les années 1847–1848* (Paris: Au dépôt des documents officiels publiés par le ministère du commerce et l'administration des douanes, 1851), 71; Henri Imbert, *L'Alcoolisme chronique dans ses rapports avec les professions* (Paris: Société d'éditions scientifiques, 1897), 25, 27; and Charles Bonnet, *L'Alcoolisation dans différents professions de la région parisienne* (Paris: Jouvet, 1914), 61–64.

46. "Chronique," *Gazette des tribunaux* (hereafter cited as *Gdt*), 1–2 July, 1872, 641; Imbert, *L'Alcoolisme chronique*, 23.

47. Henry Steele, *The Working Classes in France* (London: Twentieth Century Press, 1904), 106; "After the Insurrection," *The Times* (London), 1 June 1871, 5.

48. "Chronique," *Gdt*, 22 February 1872, 179, 31; ibid., 31 January 1872, 102.

49. Eric Hobsbawm and Joan W. Scott, "Political Shoemakers," in *Workers: Worlds of Labor* (New York: Pantheon Books, 1984), 103–30; Perrot, *Ouvriers en grève*, 1: 388–91; and Christopher H. Johnson, "Economic Change and Artisan Discontent: The Tailors' History, 1800–48," in *Revolution and Reaction*, ed. Roger Price (London: Croom Helm, 1975), 87–114.

50. In 1873, tailors and shoemakers respectively accounted for only 27 and 70 out of a total of 2,060 defendants brought before the correctional tribunal for public drunkenness. In 1880, tailors and shoemakers respectively accounted for only 34 and 85 out of a total of 3,397 defendants.

51. This idea is found in Friedrich Engels, *The Condition of the Working Class in England* (1845; London: Granada, 1969 [introduction by Eric Hobsbawm]), 128–29, and Richard Cobb, *Paris and Its Provinces, 1792–1802* (London: Oxford University Press, 1975), 118. A similar sentiment is also found in Paul Leroy-Beaulieu, *Le Travail des femmes au XIXᵉ siècle* (Paris: Charpentier, 1873), 234.

52. Perrot, *Ouvriers en grève*, 1: 155, 387.

53. AN F7 3879, reports of 8 March 1825.

54. H. A. Frégier, *Des classes dangereuses de la population dans les grandes villes et des moyens de les rendre meilleurs* (Brussels: Meline, Cans, 1840), 1: 59–60.

55. Wergeland, *History of the Working Classes in France*, 130.

56. M. A. Focillon, "Tailleur d'habits," in *Ouvriers des deux mondes*, 1st ser., 2 (1859), no. 13, 189; and Bonnet, *L'Alcoolisation*, 109; William Reddy, "The *Batteurs* and the Informer's Eye: A Labour Dispute under the French Sec-

ond Empire," *History Workshop Journal*, no. 7 (Spring 1979): 30–44; Barberet, *Travail en France*, 2: 318; 4: 189–90.

57. Berlanstein, *Working People of Paris*, 134; Alain Cottereau, "Les Jeunes contre le boulot: Une Histoire vieille comme le capitalisme industriel," *Autrement*, no. 21 (October 1979): 204–5.

58. Barberet, *Travail en France*, 4: 189–90.

59. Maxime du Camp, *Paris: Ses organes, ses fonctions et sa vie dans la deuxieme moitié du XIXeme siècle* (Paris: Hachette, 1870), 2: 328.

60. Rousseau, "Barrières," 283.

61. Emile Zola, *Savage Paris*, trans. David Hughes and Marie T. Mason (London: Elek Books, 1955), 25–26.

62. Lazar Sainéan, *Le Langage parisien au XIXe siècle* (Paris: E. De Boccard, 1920), 270.

63. Ibid., 270, 191.

64. Rousseau, "Barrières," 283–85.

65. *Casser la croûte* is now one of the rubrics in the *Annuaire statistique de la France*; see *Résultats de 1986*, n.s., no. 34 (Paris: INSEE, 1987), 198, table D.01-6, "Repas pris à l'extérieur selon le type de repas."

66. Respectively, Bonnet, *Alcoolisation*, 49; Sainéan, *Langage parisien*, 270; Bonnet, *Alcoolisation*, 62, 86–87.

67. "Procès-verbaux de la commission chargée de faire une enquête sur la situation des ouvriers de l'industrie et de l'agriculture en France et de présenter un premier rapport sur la crise industrielle à Paris," *Annales de la Chambre des députés*, n.s., *Documents parlementaires* (hereafter cited as PV), 12 (March–April 1884), app., 221.

68. Bonnet, *Alcoolisation* 50, 104–8. See also *Associations professionnelles ouvrières*, 4: 324.

69. Bonnet, *Alcoolisation*, 99.

70. Alfred Delvau, *Les Heures parisiennes* (Paris: C. Marpon & E. Flammarion, 1882), 131; Fernand and Maurice Pelloutier, *La Vie ouvrière* (Paris: Schlecher frères, 1900), 311.

71. Theodore Child, "Characteristic Parisian Cafes," *Harper's New Monthly Magazine* 78, no. 467 (April 1889): 692.

72. Thomas E. Brennan, "Cabarets and Laboring Class Communities in Eighteenth Century Paris" (Ph.D. diss., Johns Hopkins University, 1981), 119.

73. See Duveau, *Vie ouvrière sous le Second Empire*, 245; and Jeffrey Kaplow, "La Fin de saint-lundi," *Temps libre*, no. 2 (1981): 107–8.

74. Brennan, "Cabarets and Laboring Class Communities," 129.

75. Thomas E. Brennan, *Public Drinking and Popular Culture in Eighteenth-Century Paris* (Princeton: Princeton University Press, 1988), 159.

76. Rearick, *Pleasures of the Belle Epoque*, 155.

77. AN F7 3880, report of 29 January 1826.

78. Du Camp, *Paris*, 327.

79. *Jack*, in *The Works of Alphonse Daudet*, trans. Marian McIntyre (Boston: Little, Brown, 1899–1906), 21: 392; "Arthur," in ibid., 20: 218; and see Edmond and Jules de Goncourt, *Germinie Lacerteux* (1869), trans. Ernest Boyd (New York: Knopf, 1922), 252.

80. Rearick, *Pleasures of the Belle Epoque*, 155.

81. Kaplow, "Fin de saint-lundi," 115, notes that factory bosses were the first to succeed in eradicating Holy Monday. For persistence of Holy Monday, see Berlanstein, *Working People of Paris*, 137.

82. Berlanstein, *Working People of Paris*, 125–26.

83. "Au Conseil des prud'hommes," *L'Illustration*, 7 November 1903, 307.

84. "L'Alcoolisme et les accidents du travail," *Annales antialcooliques*, no. 3 (March 1908): 43–47, and no. 4 (April 1908), 62.

85. Rearick, *Pleasures of the Belle Epoque*, esp. 81–197.

86. Pierre Aubéry, "Poésies et chansons populaires de la Commune," in *Images of the Commune / Images de la Commune*, ed. James A. Leith (Montreal: McGill-Queens University Press, 1978), 49–51; 57, 63.

87. See ADS D1U6 register, May 1872, affaire Clermontet and affaire Deliard et Noel, respectively. Fist shaking was noted in affaires Bringuer, Delaplace, Savreau, and Bulte, in D1U6 register for May 1872. On the fist as a symbol of the working class, see Eric Hobsbawm, "Man and Woman in Socialist Iconography," *History Workshop Journal*, no. 6 (Autumn 1978): 121–38, and Maurice Agulhon's response, "On Political Allegory: A Reply to Eric Hobsbawm," in ibid., no. 8 (Autumn 1979): 167–73.

88. Sainéan, *Langage parisien*, 267.

89. "The population's daily routines matter because they affect the ease with which one or another of the possible forms of action can actually be carried out," notes Charles Tilly in *From Mobilization to Revolution* (Reading, Mass.: Addison-Wesley, 1978), 156.

90. ADS D2U6, no. 179, affaire B. et al.

91. ADS D3U6, no. 101, records seventeen cases involving strikes, six of which involve scenes in cafés and eleven of which do not.

92. On the philosophical basis of these strategies, see F. F. Ridley, *Revolutionary Syndicalism in France: The Direct Action of Its Times* (Cambridge: Cambridge University Press, 1970), 110–16, 122–124, but he does not provide any concrete examples and certainly none concerning the café.

93. APP BA 86, report of 3 December 1871, 1–2.

94. Perrot, *Ouvriers en grève*, 1: 109; Sibalis, "Paris Carpenters," 29; *L'Illustration*, 20 March 1909, 188.

95. Berlanstein, *Working People of Paris*, 170–72.

96. Louis Girard, *La Deuxième République et le Second Empire, 1848–1870* (Paris: Association pour la publication d'une histoire de Paris,

distrib. Hachette, 1981), 401; *L'Illustration*, 30 October 1869; Nicolas Papyanis, *The Coachmen of Nineteenth-Century Paris: Service Worker and Class Consciousness* (Baton Rouge: Louisiana State University Press, 1993), 165–70.

97. ADS D3U6, no. 46, affaire Ribouillard et al.

98. ADS D3U6, no. 101, affaire Jules Brantgen.

99. Respectively, APP BA 115, reports of 3 February, 18 February, 25 February, 3 April, and 12 May 1906.

100. Article on the Salon of 1895 in *L'Illustration*, 27 April 1895, 10.

101. ADS D3U6, no. 30, affaire Hubé.

102. ADS D2U6, no. 75, affaire Desvignes, Aubertin, et Denis.

103. ADS D3U6, no. 101, affaire Perchet. He is called a *meneur*.

104. APP BA 87, daily report of the prefect of police to the minister of the interior, 8 July 1876, 3.

105. APP BA 88, daily report of the prefect of police to the minister of the interior, 21 October 1879, 3.

106. ADS D3U6, no. 24, affaire Fumat et al.; ibid., affaire Louiche et Roucette; no. 28 affaire Toussaint.

107. ADS D3U6, no. 30, affaire Hube et al.

108. ADS D3U6, no. 28, affaire Toussaint.

109. ADS D3U6, no. 33, affaire Pintenat et al.

110. ADS D2U6, no. 162, affaire P.

111. ADS D2U6, no. 169, affaire Gallois.

112. *Annales antialcooliques*, April 1912, 247.

113. ADS D3U6, no. 87, affaire Humbert and Kolten, no. 99, affaire Delahay, and no. 28, affaire Toussaint.

114. ADS D3U6, no. 46, affaire Ribouillard.

115. ADS D2U6, no. 28, affaire Barbier et Fontrobert.

116. ADS D3U6, no. 26, affaire Gibrat et al.

117. Elisabeth Hausser, *Paris au jour le jour: Les Evénements vus par la presse, 1900–1919* (Paris: Editions de minuit, 1968), 103, 266.

118. APP BA 115, reports of 29 April, 30 April, 6 May, 17 June, and 29 August 1906; Berlanstein, *Working People of Paris*, 185–87.

119. "La Manifestation du 20 Janvier," *L'Illustration*, 26 January 1907, 51.

120. APP BA 115, rapports quotidiens du Préfecture de la police, 1906.

121. ADS D2U6, no. 28, affaire Barbier et Fontrobert.

122. Perrot, *Ouvriers en grève*, 1: 262–63.

123. Steele, *Working Classes of France*, 16–17.

124. Berlanstein, *Working People of Paris*, 79.

125. *Statistique de l'industrie à Paris résultant de l'enquête faite par la Chambre de commerce pour l'année 1860* (Paris: Chambre de commerce, 1864), xiii–xiv.

126. Barberet, *Travail en France*, 2: 269–70.

127. PV, 324 and 156 respectively.

128. Michelle Perrot, "The Three Ages of Industrial Discipline in Nine-teenth-Century France," trans. Micheline Nilsen, in *Consciousness and Class Experience in Nineteenth-Century Europe*, ed. John M. Merriman (New York: Holmes & Meier, 1979), 160–63.

129. Berlanstein, *Working People of Paris*, 171–73, 178, 184.

130. Gary S. Cross, "The Quest for Leisure: Reassessing the Eight-Hour Day in France," *Journal of Social History* 17 (Winter 1984): 195–216, 56.

131. Robert Garric, *Belleville: Scènes de la vie populaire* (Paris: Rougerie, 1971), 34.

132. Berlanstein, *Working People of Paris*, 122; Tony Judt, *Marxism and the French Left: Studies in Labour and Politics in France, 1830–1981* (Oxford: Clarendon Press, 1986), 101, 105.

133. Berlanstein, *Working People of Paris*, 6, 21, 137; his observation is accurate that workers' leisure did not reconcile them to their hard lives because it was too closely tied to their daily toil. Timothy J. Clark, "The Bar at the Folies-Bergères," in *The Wolf and the Lamb: Popular Culture in France, from the Old Régime to the Twentieth Century*, ed. Jacques Beauroy, Marc Bertrand, and E. T. Gargan (Saratoga, Calif.: Anma Libri, 1978), 233–52.

Chapter 4.
The Social Construction of the Drinking Experience

1. Stephen Mennell, *All Manner of Food: Eating and Taste in England and France from the Middle Ages to the Present* (Oxford: Basil Blackwell, 1985), 134–44.

2. Roger Dion, *Histoire de la vigne et du vin en France des origines aux XIXᵉ siècle* (1959; Paris: Flammarion, 1977).

3. Michael R. Marrus, "Social Drinking in the Belle Epoque," *Journal of Social History* 8 (Winter 1974): 133–34.

4. Thomas Brennan, "Towards the Cultural History of Alcohol in France," *Journal of Social History* 23, no. 1 (Fall 1989): 71–92. See also Herbert Fingarette, *Heavy Drinking: The Myth of Alcoholism as a Disease* (Berkeley and Los Angeles: University of California Press, 1988), 99–113.

5. Fernand and Maurice Pelloutier, *La Vie ouvrière en France* (Paris: Schlecher frères, 1900), 212.

6. Maurice Halbwachs, *La Classe ouvrière et les niveaux de vie* (Paris: F. Alcan, 1912), 420, 443–44.

7. Marcel Edant, "La Misère à Paris," *L'Illustration*, 9 October 1886, 248.

8. ADS D3U6, no. 25, affaire Glémont.

9. Bernard Moss, *The Origins of the French Labor Movement: The Social-*

ism of Skilled Workers, 1830–1914 (Berkeley and Los Angeles: University of California Press 1976), 14.

10. Halbwachs, *Classe ouvrière*, 402.

11. Louis François Benoiston de Châteauneuf, *Recherches sur les consommations de tout genre de la ville de Paris en 1817 comparées à ce qu'elles étaient en 1789*, Mémoires des academie des sciences (Paris: L'Auteur, 1820), 90; Jeanne Gaillard, *Paris, la ville, 1852–1870* (Paris: Champion, 1976), 238.

12. Siminand cited by Maurice Halbwachs, *The Psychology of Social Class*, trans. Claire Delavenay (Glencoe, Ill.: Free Press, 1958), 95.

13. "Nos graveurs. . . . Le congrès ouvrier du Havre," *L'Illustration*, 4 December 1880, 364.

14. Thomas E. Brennan, "Cabarets and Laboring Class Communities in Eighteenth-Century Paris" (Ph.D diss., Johns Hopkins University, 1981), 252; Michelle Perrot, *Les Ouvriers en grève, France, 1871–1890* (Paris: Mouton, 1974), 1: 234–35.

15. "Procès-verbaux de la commission chargée de faire une enquête sur la situation des ouvriers de l'industrie et de l'agriculture en France et de présenter un premier rapport sur le crise industrielle à Paris," *Annales de la Chambre des députés*, n.s., *Documents parlementaires* (hereafter cited as PV), 12 (March–April 1884), app., 107. A few studies asserted a much higher figure, between 30 and 33 percent. For example, Louis Buis, "L'Enquête sur l'alcoolisme et sur la class ouvrière," *Mouvement socialiste*, no. 242 (June 1912), 56; Jules Simon quoted in Louis Girard, *La Deuxième République et le Second Empire, 1848–1870* (Paris: Association pour la publication d'une histoire de Paris, distrib. Hachette, 1981), 304.

16. Armand Husson, *Les Consommations de Paris* (1856), 2d ed. (Paris: Hachette, 1875), 265–83.

17. Girard, *Deuxième République et le Second Empire*, 221; James Rousseau, "Les Barrières et les guinguettes," in *Nouveau tableau de Paris aux XIXe siècle* (Paris: Librairie de Madame Charles Béchet, 1834), 5: 288; Gaillard, *Paris, la ville*, 239.

18. Benoiston de Châteauneuf, *Recherches*, 85; Pelloutiers, *Vie ouvrière*, 238–40. Ernest Monin, *L'Alcoolisme: Etude médico-sociale* (Paris: O. Doin, 1889), 83; George Rudé, "Prices, Wages and Popular Movements in Paris during the French Revolution," *Economic History Review* 6, no. 3 (1954): 249.

19. Monin, *Alcoolisme*, 83.

20. Georges Duveau, *La Vie ouvrière sous le Second Empire* (Paris: Gallimard, 1946), 513; Girard, *Deuxième République et le Second Empire*, 221; Lenard Berlanstein, *The Working People of Paris, 1871–1914* (Baltimore: Johns Hopkins University Press, 1984), 46.

21. A. Lailler, "De l'influence de l'alimentation pour prévenir et combattre

l'abus des boissons alcooliques," *Tempérance* 6, no. 1 (1878): 30–31.

22. Benoiston de Châteauneuf, *Recherches*, 85; Pelloutiers, *Vie ouvrière*, 305; Gaillard, *Paris, la ville*, 238–40; Monin, *Alcoolisme*, 83.

23. Husson, *Consommations de Paris*, 216.

24. "G," "Faits divers," *L'Illustration*, 27 October 1883.

25. Henri d'Aleméras, *La Vie parisienne sous le Second Empire* (Paris: Albin Michel, 1933), 330.

26. Peter de Polnay, "Cabarets, Restaurants, Cafés and Brasseries," in *Aspects of Paris* (London: W. H. Allen, 1968), 56.

27. "Faits divers," *L'Illustration*, 22 August 1885, 130.

28. Gaillard, *Paris, la ville*, 239, 57.

29. Othenin d'Haussonville, "La Vie et salariés à Paris," *Revue des deux mondes*, 3d ser., 56 (15 April 1883): 830; L. Laboulais, *L'Ouvrier: Considérations sur le travail* (Paris: Paul Dupont, 1890), 224; Girard, *Deuxième République et le Second Empire*, 261.

30. PV, 47, 47–49, 70, 72.

31. Lailler, "De l'influence," 38.

32. Jacques de Riviers, "Serrurier-Forgeron," *Ouvriers de deux mondes*, 1st ser., 5, no. 42 (1875), 252.

33. PV, 225.

34. Baedeker, *Paris and Its Environs* (Leipzig: Karl Baedeker, 1878), 19; (1888), 16; (1896), 16.

35. Paris, Conseil municipal, *Procès-verbaux/débats* (Paris: Imprimerie municipale, 1885–86), 1885, pt. 2, 694–95.

36. Girard, *Deuxième République et le Second Empire*, 248; Lailler, "De l'influence," 38.

37. Lailler, "De l'influence," 45.

38. Maxime du Camp, *Paris: Ses organes, ses fonctions et sa vie dans la deuxième moitié du XIXème siècle* (Paris: Hachette, 1875), 6: 248; Girard, *La Deuxième République et le Second Empire*, 221.

39. Lazar Sainéan, *Le Langage parisien au XIXe siècle* (Paris: E. de Boccard, 1920), 270.

40. Lailler, "De l'influence," 35; L. Landouzy, Henri Labbé, and Marcel Labbé, *Hygiène sociale: Enquête sur l'alimentation d'une centaine d'ouvriers et d'employés parisiens*, Enquête presenté à la IVe section du Congrès internationale de la tuberculos, 2–7 October 1905 (Paris: Masson, 1905), 4.

41. Ann Louise Shapiro, *Housing the Poor of Paris, 1850–1902* (Madison: University of Wisconsin Press, 1985).

42. PV, 105, 305.

43. Pelloutiers, *Vie ouvrière*, 194, 305.

44. Berlanstein, *Working People of Paris*, 46.

45. AN F7 3888, report of 24 December 1835.

46. Pelloutiers, *Vie ouvrière*, 191, 199; Paris, Conseil municipal, *Procès-verbaux/débats* (cited in n. 35 above), vol. 2, 9 December, 695; PV, 21; "Faits divers," *L'Illustration*, 4 December 1875, 36; Duveau, *Vie ouvrière*, 337, 40; "Faits divers," *L'Illustration*, 16 March 1895, 222.

47. See PV, 47, 51, 98. For Italian wine in Paris, see "G," "Faits divers," *L'Illustration*, 10 March 1883, 160.

48. "P. A.," "Courrier de Paris," *L'Illustration*, 10 March 1877, 147.

49. Paris, Conseil municipal, *Procès-verbaux/débats* (cited in n. 35 above), 694, and Joseph Barberet, *Le Travail en France*, vol. 7: *Débitants de boissons* (Paris: Berger-Levrault, 1890).

50. Othenin d'Haussonville, "La Vie et salariés à Paris," 831.

51. "Faits divers," *L'Illustration*, 23 February 1895, 162.

52. "Documents et informations," *L'Illustration*, 15 May 1909, 347.

53. E. Philbert, "Compte rendu annuel," in Ligue nationale contre l'alcoolisme, *Bulletin de la société française de tempérance*, 3d ser., 3 (1897): 85; Patricia Prestwich, "Temperance in France: The Curious Case of Absinthe," *Historical Reflections / Réflexions historiques* 6, no. 2 (Winter/Hiver 1979): 302; "P. A.," "Courrier de Paris," *L'Illustration*, 31 March 1877.

54. *Jack*, vol. 21 of *The Works of Alphonse Daudet*, trans. Marian McIntyre (Boston: Little, Brown, 1899–1906), 344.

55. Philbert, "Compte rendu," 85.

56. Octave Mirbeau, "Courrier de Paris," *L'Illustration*, 8 January 1881, 58.

57. Urbain Guérin, "Ouvrier Cordonnier de Malakoff," in *Ouvriers des deux mondes*, 1st ser., 5, no. 41 (1878): 189.

58. See, e.g., Edmond and Jules de Goncourt, *Germinie Lacerteux* (1869), trans. Ernest Boyd (New York: Knopf, 1922), 181.

59. Jules Simon, "Sauvetage de l'enfance," *Revue de famille* 5, no. 1 (January 1892): esp. 11; Paul Garnier, *La Folie à Paris* (Paris: J. B. Ballière et fils, 1890), 305, 307, 312, 316.

60. Raoul Vimard, "L'Alcoolisme et les accidents du travail," *Annales antialcooliques* 6, no. 4 (April 1908): 61.

61. Gustave Geoffroy, *L'Apprentie* (Paris: Georges Crès, 1919), 267–311.

62. Paul Raymond, "L'Alcoolisme à Paris," in Ligue nationale contre l'alcoolisme, *Bulletin de la société française de tempérance*, 3d ser., 2 (1896): 162; Philbert, "Compte rendu," 87.

63. "Chronique," *Gazette des tribunaux* (hereafter cited as *Gdt*), 1 January 1868, 3.

64. Charles Rearick, *Pleasures of the Belle Epoque: Entertainment and Festivity in Turn-of-the-Century France* (New Haven: Yale University Press, 1985), 183.

65. "Faits divers," *L'Illustration*, 23 March 1895, 242, and same in ibid., 28 May 1892, 478.

66. Marrus, "Social Drinking," 128–29.

67. ADS D2U6, no. 54, affaire Saillant, and no. 68, affaire de Lichtenberg.

68. Baedeker, *Paris and Its Environs*, 1877, 1888, 1877, 1878, and 1888, ADS D2U6, no. 72, affaire Muller, Denul, et Henry; Prestwich, "Temperance in France," 302.

69. Adolphe Coste, *Alcoolisme ou épargne: Le Dilemme social*, 6th ed. (Paris: Alcan, 1892), 18–19.

70. Dr. Legrain, "Paris buveur (simple silhouette)," *Annales antial-cooliques* 3, no. 7 (July 1905): 119, 120, 122.

71. Pelloutiers, *Vie ouvrière*, 224.

72. PV, 49, 51, 79, 133–34. Joseph Reinarch, *Contre l'alcoolisme* (Paris: Fasquelle, 1911), 240–43.

73. Elisabeth Hausser, *Paris au jour le jour: Les Evénements vus par la presse, 1900–1919* (Paris: Editions de minuit, 1968), 50.

74. Léon and Maurice Bonneff, *Marchands de folie*, 2d ed. (Paris: Rivière, 1913), 12.

75. "La Consommation de l'alcool en France pour 1904," *Annales antial-cooliques* 3, no. 8 (August 1905): 140.

76. Legrain, "Paris buveur," 121.

77. Gaillard, *Paris, la ville*, 245.

78. Landouzy, Labbé, and Labbé, *Hygiène sociale*, 4.

79. François Corson, *Etude sur les causes de l'alcoolisme* (Paris: Bonvalot-Jouve, 1907), 31; H. Leroy, *De l'alcoolisme au point de vue de sa prévention et de sa répression sur le terrain du droit pénal* (Paris: A. Rousseau, 1900), 64; Lailler, "De l'influence," 29.

80. ADS D2U6, no. 11, Orieux, no. 31, affaire Akermann et Depot, and no. 79, affaire Schweicher; "Chronique," *Gdt*, 31 January 1872, 3–4.

81. Flora Tristan, *The Worker's Union*, trans. Beverly Livingston (Urbana: University of Illinois Press, 1983), 81, 94; Emile Gaboriau, *Monsieur Lecoq* (1908; New York: Dover, 1975), 66, 42, 94.

82. "Night Rambles in Paris," II, "The Cité Tournier—Cabaret Balls," *Every Saturday*, 11 July 1868, 34.

83. Maxime du Camp, *Paris: Ses organes, ses fonctions et sa vie dans la deuxième moitié du XIX*^ème *siècle* (Paris: Hachette, 1870), 2: 131.

84. Lailler, "De l'influence," 37.

85. William F. Apthorp, "Paris Theatres and Concerts," *Scribner's Magazine* 11 (January–June 1892): 631; de Polnay, "Cabarets, Restaurants, Cafés and Brasseries," 56.

86. Jules Bergeron, "Rapport sur la répression de l'alcoolisme," *Annales d'hygiène publique et de médecine légale*, 2d ser., 38 (July 1872): 50.

87. Henri Leyret quoted in Pelloutiers, *Vie ouvrière*, 310; PV, 100, 106.

88. Gérard Jacquemet, *Belleville au XIX*^e *siècle: Du faubourg à la ville*, ed.

Jean Touzot (Paris: Editions de l'Ecole des hautes études en sciences sociales, 1984), 256.

89. Landouzy, Labbé, and Labbé, *Hygiène sociale*, 4; Jacquemet, *Belleville*, 256.

90. Paul Gaultier, *L'Adolescent* (Paris: Blond & Gay, 1914), 91.

91. Alfred Delveau, *Dictionnaire de la langue verte* (Paris: Dentu, 1866), passim.

92. Thomas E. Brennan, *Public Drinking and Popular Culture in Eighteenth-Century Paris* (Princeton: Princeton University Press, 1988), 187–227; Marc Alexander, "The Administration of Madness and Attitudes towards the Insane in Nineteenth-Century Paris" (Ph.D. diss., Johns Hopkins University, 1976), 82–91.

93. Corson, *Etude sur les causes de l'alcoolisme*, 40.

94. H. A. Frégier, *Des classes dangereuses de la population dans les grandes villes et des moyens de les rendre meilleurs* (Brussels: Meline, Cans, 1840), 1: 38.

95. Eugène Sue, *The Mysteries of Paris* (London: Chapman & Hall, 1845–46), 1: 213.

96. Bonneff and Bonneff, *Marchands de folie*, 21–25.

97. "Clairvoyance," *Annales antialcooliques* 6, no. 3 (March 1908): 47.

98. "P. A.," "Nos gravures. . . . les réservistes la tournée d'adieu," *L'Illustration*, 18 September 1875, 182.

99. Sue, *Mysteries*, 188, 208.

100. ADS D2U6, no. 53, affaire Huot, Chrétien, et Benoit; N. Cornevin, *Les Marchands de vin de Paris* (Paris: Principales Librairies, 1869), 135.

101. Perrot, *Ouvriers en grève*, 1: 236–37; PV, 134.

102. "De la politesse et de quelques des usages mondains," *L'Illustration*, 5 September 1874, 154.

103. L. Dupleix, *Réglementation des débitants de boissons* (Paris: Société française d'imprimerie et de libraire, 1908), 147–49; *Mass Observation: The Pub and the People* (London: Gollancz, 1938), passim.

104. Sue, *Mysteries*, 31.

105. P. Audebrand, "Courier de Paris," *L'Illustration*, 17 February 1872, 99.

106. ADS D2U6, no. 11, affaire Linden.

107. Respectively, ADS D2U6, no. 58, affaire Lebigre et Ferrus; no. 17, affaire Ponsinet et Gaillard; no. 56, affaire de Perceval et Missottin; no. 70, affaire Blanchard de la Bretesche; D2U8 no. 51, affaire Palat, and no. 59, affaire Georgel.

108. Guillaume de Bertier de Sauvigny, *La Restauration, 1815–1830* (Paris: Association pour la publication d'une histoire de Paris, distrib. Hachette, 1977), 116.

109. Doctor Véron, *Mémoires d'un bourgeois de Paris*, ed. Gabriel de Gonet (Paris: Gabriel de Gonet, 1853), 2: 32.

110. ADS D2U6, no. 13, affaire Lagoguet.

111. Gaboriau, *Monsieur Lecoq*, 17.

112. *Jack*, vol. 21 of *The Works of Alphonse Daudet*, trans. Marian McIntyre (Boston: Little, Brown, 1899–1906), 212.

113. Brennan, *Public Drinking and Popular Culture*, 217–42.

114. Véron, *Mémoires*, 2: 28–30, 31.

115. Tristan Bernard, *Le Petit Café*, in *L'Illustration théâtrale*, 18 May 1912, 8.

116. Respectively, ADS D2U6, no. 87, affaire Dubrac; no. 46, affaire Révardeau.

117. Monin, *Alcoolisme*, 104; Leroy, *De l'alcoolisme*, 91; C. Goubran, *L'Influence de l'ivresse sur la responsabilité pénale: Etude de la doctrine et de la jurisprudence française* (Paris: Dalloz, 1925).

118. ADS D2U8, no. 56, affaire Billoir, and no. 57, affaire Perdriat.

119. Respectively, ADS D2U6, no. 15, affaire Grosjean et Renaud; no. 4, affaire Chaix.

120. ADS D2U6, no. 80, affaire Morel, and no. 68, affaire de Lichtenberg; D2U8, no. 51, affaire Palat.

121. "Chronique," *Gdt*, 26–27 June 1871, 269.

122. Respectively, ADS D2U6, no. 56, affaire de Perceval et Missottin; no. 15, affaire Grosjean et Renaud; no. 51, affaire Finance et al; no. 46, affaire Tellier.

123. Respectively, see ADS D2U6, no. 11, affaire Glanzmann; D2U8, no. 56, affaire Billoir; D2U6, no. 11, affaire Linden; no. 6, affaire Rousseau; no. 40, affaire Rainor; no. 46, affaire Tellier; no. 70, affaire Blanchard de la Bretesche; no. 65, affaire Mounier; Sainéan, *Langage parisien*, 271.

124. Sainéan, *Langage parisien*, 272; and see, e.g., ADS D2U6, no. 90, affaire Lavie, and D3U6, no. 48, affaire Nivet.

125. Brennan, *Public Drinking and Popular Culture*, 237.

126. ADS D3U6, no. 46, affaire Goulard; see, too, no. 46, affaire Parra, and no. 48, affiarie Nivet.

127. ADS D3U6, no. 25, affaire Glémot.

128. "Echos et nouvelles," *Petit Parisien*, 6 January 1895.

129. ADS D2U6, no. 87, affaire Dubrac; P. du Maroussem, "Ouvrière mouleuse en cartonnage d'une fabrique collective de jouets parisiens," *Ouvriers des deux mondes*, 2d ser., 4, no. 76 (1892): 178–79, 182.

130. E. Levasseur, *Questions ouvrières et industrielles en France sous la Troisième République* (Paris: Arthur Rousseau, 1907), 909.

131. Respectively, ADS D2U6, no. 17, affaire Ponsinet et Gaillard; D2U8, no. 57, affaire Perdriat; D4U9, no. 9, affaire Costa et al.

132. ADS D2U6, no. 73, affaire Marin et van Overbeck.

133. Respectively, ADS D2U6, no. 59, affaire Moch, no. 13, affaire Galmiche, no. 13, affaire Galmiche, no. 46, affaire Tellier, no. 68, affaire de Lichtenberg; U8, no. 57, affaire Perdriat, no. 59, affaire Georgel; D2U6, no. 56, affaire de Perceval.

134. Respectively, AN F7 3877, reports of 30 December 1823; F7 3879, report of 19 April 1825.

135. Frégier, *Des classes dangereuses*, 1: 126, 430.

136. Jacquemet, *Belleville*, 88.

137. Pierre de Carnac, "Des distributions de vin dans les réjouissances publiques," *Annales antialcooliques* 4, no. 6 (June 1906): 130; AN F7 3888, report of 1 May 1835.

138. Rearick, *Pleasures of the Belle Epoque*, 11.

139. Joseph Reinarch, *Contra l'alcoolisme* (Paris: Fasquelle, 1911), 102; see also Leroy, *De l'alcoolisme*, 49–50.

140. "Chronique," *Gdt*, 8 January 1848, 243; Joseph Marie, baron de Gérando, *De la bienfaisance publique* (Paris: Jules Renouard, 1839), 398.

141. Leroy, *De l'alcoolisme*, 55.

142. "Chronique," *Gdt*, 2 February 1831, 316.

143. "Justice criminelle . . . Cour d'Assis," *Gdt*, 4–5 April 1831, 521.

144. Respectively, "Chronique," *Gdt*, 8 January 1848, 243; "Cour d'Assis," ibid., 29 March 1848, 536; "Chronique," ibid., 10 June 1848, 781.

145. Jacquemet, *Belleville*, 343–44.

146. Drs. M. Magnan and A. Fillassier, "Alcoholism and Degeneracy: Statistics of the Central Service of the Admission of the Insane of the City of Paris and of the Department of the Seine from 1867 to 1912" (London: C. Knight, n.d.), 368.

147. Duveau, *Vie ouvrière*, 521–22.

148. "Chronique," *Gdt*, 2 January 1868, 7.

149. Louis Chevalier, *La Formation de la population parisienne aux XIXe siècle*, Institut national d'études démographiques, Travaux et documents, cahier no. 10 (Paris, 1950), 279–80.

150. Gaboriau, *Monsieur Lecoq*, 17.

151. Richard Sennett, *The Fall of Public Man* (New York: Random House, Vintage Books, 1978), 214; William Reddy, "The *Batteurs* and the Informer's Eye: A Labour Dispute under the French Second Empire," *History Workshop*, no. 7 (Spring 1979): 31–44.

152. Jacqueline LaLouette, "Les Débits de boissons en France, 1871–1919," in vols (thesis, University of Paris, 1979), 1: 2.

153. Jacques Bonzon, *Le Crime et l'école* (Paris: Guillaumin, 1896), 19.

154. ADS D1U6, register for August 1871, affaire Jean Louis Cosa.

155. "Chronique," *Gdt*, 3 July 1872, 653; 6 August 1871, 409; 2 September 1871, 496.

156. ADS D2U6, no. 13, affaire Lagoguet.

157. *Annales de l'assemblée nationale, 1871–1876*, 3, app., 307–10.

158. Prestwich, "Temperance in France," 380.

159. Bayle Saint John, *Purple Tints of Paris: Character and Manners in the New Empire* (New York: Riker, Thorne, 1854), 178; James D. McCabe, Jr., *Paris by Sunlight and Gaslight* (Boston: National Publishing Co., 1869), 71; Theodore Child, "Characteristic Parisian Cafes," *Harper's New Monthly Magazine* 78, no. 467 (April 1889): 688; *L'Illustration*, 2 February 1903, 126; Louis Jacquet, *L'Alcool* (Paris: Masson, 1912), 720.

160. "Chronique," *Gdt*, April 26, 1873, 400.

161. "L. L.," "Discours d'ouverture," *Tempérance* 2, no. 2 (1874): 125.

162. Jules Simon, *The Government of Thiers* (London: Sampson, Low, Marsten, Searle, & Rivington, 1879), 2: 472.

163. Respectively, ADS D2U6, no. 27, affaire Marie de Lisle, and no. 39, affaire Gibert.

164. "Chronique," *Gdt*, July 1–2 1872, 641.

165. Respectively, ADS D2U6 no. 51, affaire Finance; no. 70, affaire Blanchard de la Bretesche; *Cri du peuple*, 3 July 1884, 2.

166. ADS D3U6, no. 101 affaire R.

167. ADS D2U6, no. 169, affaire L. and affaire G.

168. Didier Nourrisson, *Le Buveur du XIXe siècle* (Paris: Albin Michel, 1990), esp. 7–10.

169. Jacquet, *Alcool*, 743–44.

Chapter 5.
Publicans

1. Jacques Rancière quoted in Ellen Ross, "*Sociabilité* of Workers and the Working Class in Comparative Perspective, 1850–1950," *International Labor and Working Class History*, no. 29 (Spring 1986): 107.

2. Philip Nord, *Paris Shopkeepers and the Politics of Resentment* (Princeton: Princeton University Press, 1986), 97.

3. Gérard Jacquemet, *Belleville au XIXe siecle: Du faubourg à la ville*, ed. Jean Touzot (Paris: Editions de l'Ecole des hautes études en sciences sociales, 1984), 134.

4. Ibid., 65.

5. Henri d'Aleméras, *La Vie parisienne sous le Second Empire* (Paris: Albin Michel, 1933), 328; James Rousseau, "Les Barrières et les guinguettes," in *Nouveau tableau de Paris aux XIXe siècle* (Paris: Librairie de Madame Charles Béchet, 1834), 5: 292–97.

6. Doctor Véron, *Memoires d'un bourgeois de Paris*, ed. Gabriel de Gonet (Paris: Gabriel de Gonet, 1853), 2: 18–19; "The Great Paris Cafés," *Putnam's Monthly* 13 (April 1854): 392.

7. Odette Pannetier, *Plaisirs forcés à perpétuité*, cited in Robert Giraud, *L'Argot du bistrot* (Paris: Editions Marval, 1989), 147–48; for England, see Peter Clark, *The English Alehouse: A Social History, 1200–1830* (London: Longman, 1983), 276.

8. Patricia Prestwich, "Temperance in France: The Curious Case of Absinthe," *Historical Reflections / Réflections historiques* 6, no. 2 (Winter 1979): 304.

9. "Chronique," *Gazette des tribunaux* (hereafter cited as *Gdt*), 16 January 1868, 55.

10. Emile Gaboriau, *Caught in the Net* (New York: Charles Scribner's Sons, 1900), 20.

11. Edmond and Jules de Goncourt, *Germinie Lacerteux* (1869), trans. Ernest Boyd (New York: Knopf, 1922), 182.

12. Léon and Maurice Bonneff, *Marchands de folie*, 2d ed. (Paris: Rivière, 1913), 12.

13. Léon Say quoted in Paul Griveau, *L'Alcoolisme: Fléau social, moeurs, législation, droit comparé* (Paris: Marcel & Billard, 1906), 218.

14. Jules Michelet, *The People*, trans. with an introduction by John P. McKay (Urbana: University of Illinois Press, 1973), 71.

15. James Rousseau, "Les Cafés et les estaminets," *Nouveau tableau de Paris au XIXe siècle* (Paris: Librairie de Madame Charles Béchet, 1834), 4: 62.

16. Bertall, "Courrier de la semaine," *L'Illustration*, 29 July 1871, 67.

17. Stephen Mac-Say, "Messieurs les débitants," *Annales antialcooliques* 7, no. 4 (April 1909): 63.

18. Jacquemet, *Belleville au XIXe siècle*, 81–100; Louis Chevalier, *La Formation de la population parisienne aux XIXe siècle*, Institut national d'études démographiques, Travaux et documents, cahier no. 10 (Paris, 1950), 227–32.

19. Maurice Talmeyr, "Moeurs électorales: Les Marchands de vins," *Revue des deux mondes*, 15 August 1898, 878–79.

20. Chevalier, *Formation de la population parisienne*, 229–31; Louis Girard, *La Deuxième République et le Second Empire, 1848–1870* (Paris: Association pour la publication d'une histoire de Paris, distrib. Hachette, 1981), 221.

21. See, respectively, Jacquemet, *Belleville au XIXe siècle*, 134; Chevalier, *Formation de la population parisienne*, 230–31.

22. Sîan Reynolds, "Allemane avant l'allemanisme: Jeunesse d'un militant," *Mouvement social*, no. 126 (January–March 1984): 5–7.

23. Véron, *Mémoires d'un bourgeois*, 2: 37.

24. See Girard, *La Deuxième République et le Second Empire*, 221, for the

figure in the 1840s. The figure for the number of Paris cafés in 1873 is in the Archives de la Préfecture de police, series BA, carton number 884, dossier 1, "Tableau comparatif du recensement des débits de boissons au 31 decembre 1872 et au 31 decembre 1873."

25. See, respectively, Nord, *Paris Shopkeepers*, 94; Girard, *La Deuxième République et le Second Empire*, 217; Georges Duveau, *La Vie ouvrière sous le Second Empire* (Paris: Gallimard, 1946), 209.

26. See, respectively, Ann Louise Shapiro, *Housing the Poor of Paris, 1850–1902* (Madison: University of Wisconsin Press, 1985), 72; Francisque Michel and Edouard Fournier, *Les Hôtelleries et les cabarets en France depuis la fin du XVIe siècle à nos jours* (Paris: Delahys, 1859), 399; Roger Vaultier, *Les Fêtes populaires à Paris* (Paris: Myrte, 1946), 246; Anthony Sutcliff, *The Autumn of Central Paris* (London: Edwin Arnold, 1970), 155; Girard, *La Deuxième République et le Second Empire*, 199; and Louis Hautecoeur quoted by Nord, *Paris Shopkeepers*, 91–92.

27. See, respectively, Charles Rearick, *Pleasures of the Belle Epoque: Entertainment and Festivity in Turn-of-the-Century France* (New Haven: Yale University Press, 1985), 173; "The Cafes of Paris," *Every Saturday*, May 4, 1867, 573; and Alfred Delvau, *Histoire anecdotique des cafés et cabarets de Paris* (Paris: Dentu, 1862), 295.

28. D'Aleméras, *Vie parisienne*, 344; Michel and Fournier, *Hôtelleries et les cabarets*, 399.

29. Georges Montorgueil quoted in Nord, *Paris Shopkeepers*, 94.

30. Baedeker, *Paris and Its Environs* (Leipzig: Karl Baedeker, 1878), 20.

31. Edmond and Jules de Goncourt, *Germinie Lacerteux*, 103.

32. Adeline Daumard, *Maisons de Paris et propriétaires parisiens aux XIXe siècle, 1809–1880* (Paris: CUJAS, 1965), 275.

33. Testimony of M. Camescasse, prefect of police, in *Procès-verbaux de la commission chargée de faire une enquête sur la situation des ouvriers de l'industrie et de l'agriculture en France et de présenter un premier rapport sur la crise industrielle à Paris, Annales de la Chambre des députés*, n.s., *Documents parlementaires* (hereafter cited as PV), 12 (March–April 1884), app., 328.

34. See, respectively, Nord, *Paris Shopkeepers*, 198; Talmeyr, "Moeurs électorales," 879.

35. PV, 363; Charles Bonnet, *L'Alcoolisation dans differents professions de la région parisienne* (Paris: Jouvet, 1914), 47–48; and see Shapiro, *Housing the Poor*, 127, and Victor Fournel, *Ce qu'on voit dans les rues de Paris* (Paris: E. Dentu, 1865), 378.

36. Lenard Berlanstein, *The Working People of Paris, 1871–1914* (Baltimore: Johns Hopkins University Press, 1984), 52.

37. *Annuaire du commerce Didot-Bottin* (Paris: Bottin, 1870, 1911).

38. "Industries et professions surveillées," in *Annuaire statistique de la*

ville de Paris (Paris: Imprimerie municipale, 1880–1914); Talmeyr, "Moeurs électorales," 884; Jacquemet, *Belleville au XIXe siècle*, 96.

39. Statistics from H. F. Mascret, *Dictionnaire des faillites d'apres les journaux judiciaires* (Paris: L'Auteur, 1876–1900); Adrien Timmermans, *L'Argot parisien: Etude d'étymologie comparée, suivie du vocabulaire* (Paris: C. Klincksieck, 1892), 78.

40. Talmeyr, "Moeurs électorales," 884.

41. Griveau, *Alcoolisme*, 213–14.

42. Nord, *Paris Shopkeepers*, 158, 198; E. Avalle and A. Focillon, "Carrier des environs de Paris," *Ouvriers des deux mondes*, 1st ser., 2, no. 11 (1859): 93.

43. See, respectively, Jacquemet, *Belleville au XIXe siècle*, 184; Nord, *Paris Shopkeepers*, 200.

44. ADS D11U3, no. 79336, an extremely rich bankruptcy report.

45. ADS D11U3, nos. 17114, 14395, 795125, and 795130.

46. Fernand and Maurice Pelloutier, *La Vie ouvrière en France* (Paris: Schlecher frères, 1900), 168. Mortality in these professions was, however, lower than in Switzerland or England.

47. Paul Raymond, "L'Alcoolisme à Paris," *Ligue nationale contre l'alcoolisme*, 3d ser., 2, nos. 1–2 (1896): 168–69.

48. ADS D2U6, no. 87, affaire Dubrac. See also D3U6, no. 50, affaire Falachon.

49. Jacquemet, *Belleville au XIXe siècle*, 313.

50. APP BA 497, report of 27 February 1876, and ADS D2U6, no. 53, affaire Huot, Chretien, et Benoit.

51. Bonneffs, *Marchands de folie*, 104.

52. André Warnod, *Bals, cafés et cabarets*, 5th ed. (Paris: E. Figuière, 1913).

53. Roger Girard, *Quand les Auvergnats partaient conquérir Paris* (Paris: Fayard, 1979), 93.

54. Nicholas Papayanis, *The Coachmen of Nineteenth-Century Paris: Service Workers and Class Consciousness* (Baton Rouge: Louisiana State University Press, 1993), 64–66.

55. Girard, *La Deuxième République et le Second Empire*, 98–106.

56. ADS D11U3, no. 805589; others with *fournisseur*: 18042 and 17114.

57. Etienne Martin Saint-Léon, *Le Petit Commerce français: Sa lutte pour la vie* (Paris: J. Gabalda, 1911), 55, 207, 57.

58. Thomas E. Brennan, *Public Drinking and Popular Culture in Eighteenth-Century Paris* (Princeton: Princeton University Press, 1988), 117; id., "Cabarets and Laboring Class Communities in Eighteenth Century Paris" (Ph.D. diss., Johns Hopkins University, 1981), 261–62.

59. Elaine Kruse, "Men in Support of Women's Rights: Witnesses for Divorces in Revolutionary Paris" (paper delivered at the Ninth Annual Meeting of

the Social Science History Association, 25–28 October 1984, Toronto), 7–10.

60. John M. Merriman, "Introduction," in *French Cities in the Nineteenth Century*, ed. id. (New York: Holmes & Meier, 1981), 33.

61. *Histoire de la France urbaine*, ed. Maurice Crubellier and Maurice Agulhon (Paris: Seuil, 1983), 4: 436.

62. Henri Leyret, *En plein faubourg: Moeurs ouvrières* (Paris: Charpentier, 1895), 23.

63. Emile Zola, *Savage Paris*, trans. David Hughes and Marie T. Mason (London: Elek Books, 1955), 295; see also Michel and Fournier, *Hôtelleries et les cabarets*, 399–400.

64. ADS D2U6, no. 87, Blanchouin v. Tournois.

65. Zola, *Savage Paris*, 112–13.

66. Gustave Geoffroy, *L'Apprentie* (Paris: Georges Crès, 1919), 271–72.

67. "Les Quartiers de Paris," drawings by G. Randon, *Journal amusant*, no. 334 (24 May 1862).

68. A. Lailler, "De l'influence de l'alimentation pour prévenir et combattre l'abus des boissons alcooliques," *Tempérance* 6, no. 1 (1878): 39.

69. ADS D3U6, no. 29, affaire Dejour et al.

70. "Gravers . . . L'Armée de salut," *L'Illustration*, 26 March 1887, 208–9, 216; picture in 19 March 1887 issue between p. 192 and p. 193.

71. Lazar Sainéan, *Le Langage parisien au XIXᵉ siècle* (Paris: E. de Boccard, 1920), 268

72. "Les Expropriations et les expropriés," cartoons by Bertall, *L'Illustration*, 6 January 1877, 13.

73. See, respectively, Talmeyr, "Moeurs électorales," 880; Bonneffs, *Marchands de folie*, 6; Fournel, *Ce qu'on voit*, 379.

74. *Un Ouvrier en 1820: Manuscrit inédit de Jacques-Etienne Bédé*, ed. Rémi Gossez (Paris: Presses universitaires de France, 1984), 301; and ADS D3U6, no. 105, affaire Calvet.

75. See D1U6 registers 702 and 880; Talmeyr, "Moeurs électorales," 881. As Michelle Perrot and Anne Martin-Fugier note in "The Actors," in *The History of Private Life*, vol. 4, ed. Michelle Perrot, trans. Arthur Goldhammer (Cambridge, Mass.: Harvard University Press, 1990), 320–30, the one-child family had become common in this era.

76. ADS D2U687, no. 87, affaire Dubrac.

77. ADS D2U6, no. 5, affaire Gombault.

78. *Physiologie des cafés de Paris* (Paris: Desloges, 1841), 27–28; Bonneffs, *Marchands de folie*, 6.

79. Fernand Vandéren, "Un Garçon chez Véry," *L'Illustration*, 9 April 1892, 300–301.

80. "Le Bistrot de la place des Fêtes," *Paris des hommes de bonne volonté:*

Choix et présentations des lise Jules Romains (Paris: Flammarion, 1949), 228–29.

81. For "Bretonne," "Jardinier," and "Décoré," see ADS D2U8, no. 56, affaire Billoir; for "la Patte," see D2U6, no. 53, affaire Huot et al.

82. Rousseau, "Barrières," 286.

83. See, respectively, ADS D3U6, no. 46, affaire Ribouillard et al.; D2U6 no. 11, affaire Provost, and no. 79, affaire Bourré.

84. Gaboriau, *Caught in the Net*, 54.

85. L. Dupleix, *Réglementation des débitants des boissons* (Paris: Société française d'imprimerie et de libraire, 1908), quoting the prominent politician Jules Siegfried and the eminent economist Charles Gide, 30, 114.

86. Louis Paulian, *Beggars in Paris*, trans. Lady Herschell (New York: Edward Arnold, 1897), 20.

87. Paul de Kock, "Restaurants et cartes de restaurants," in *Nouveau tableau de Paris aux XIX*ᵉ *siècle* (Paris: Librairie de Madame Charles Béchet, 1834), 4: 78.

88. Michel and Fournier, *Hôtelleries et les cabarets*, 400.

89. Jacquemet, *Belleville au XIX*ᵉ *siècle*, 108.

90. ADS D2U8, no. 53, affaire Palat; ADS D3U6, no. 1, affaire Barrois.

91. "Facino Cane," in Honoré de Balzac, *Selected Short Stories*, trans. Sylvia Raphel (New York: Penguin Books, 1977), 237–42, contains a detailed description of a laborer's wedding celebration in a café.

92. "The café-concert was on the Boulevard de Rochechouart. It had been a small café and had been enlarged by adding a wooden extension built out into the back yard," Zola writes of such a case in *L'Assommoir*, trans. Leonard Tancock (New York: Penguin Books, 1970), 265.

93. Alain Faure, *Paris carême-prenant: Du carnaval à Paris au XIX*ᵉ *siècle* (Paris: Hachette, 1978), 146–50; Rearick, *Pleasures of the Belle Epoque*, 23.

94. "Courrier de Paris," *L'Illustration*, 17 July 1886, 43.

95. "Echos à travers Paris," *Figaro*, 14 Juillet 1909.

96. Berlanstein, *Working People of Paris*, 127–29; Rearick, *Pleasures of the Belle Epoque*, 201.

97. Warnod, *Bals, cafés et cabarets*, 285.

98. "Courrier de Paris," *L'Illustration*, 20 August 1881, 118; Nord, *Paris Shopkeepers*, 456; Henri Vidal, *Le Cabaret: Etude de droit administrif et de législation financiére* (Paris: Girard & Briére, 1916), 55; Talmeyr, "Moeurs électorales," 877.

99. Stephen Mac-Say, "Messieurs les débitants," *Annales antialcooliques*, 7, no. 4 (April 1909): 64.

100. "Perdican," "Courrier de Paris," *L'Illustration*, 14 February 1885, 102.

101. Talmeyr, "Moeurs électorales," 882–883.

102. "Chronique," *Gdt*, 6 May 1848, 666, and 21 February 1872, 175.

103. Eugène Sue, *The Mysteries of Paris* (London: Chapman & Hall, 1845–46), 1–6.

104. "Chronique," *Gdt*, 13 May 1848, 688; "Night Rambles in Paris," I, "At the Prefecture of Police and among the Chiffoniers," *Every Saturday*, 4 July 1868, 31–32.

105. Louis Latzarus, "Malfaiteurs parisiens," *Revue de Paris*, no. 11 (1 June 1912): 532.

106. "Night Rambles in Paris," III, "The Italian Colony—The Bal du Vieux Chêne," *Every Saturday*, 18 July 1868, 71.

107. "Chronique," *Gdt*, 18–19 September 1871, 557, and "Paris," *Lanterne*, 28 December 1879, 2; 8 August 1880, 3; 17 October 1880, 3.

108. ADS D2U6, no. 4, affaire Chesnel.

109. Maxim Rude, *Tout Paris au café* (Paris: Dreyfous, 1877), 159.

110. ADS D2U6, no. 90, affaire Ferré et al.

111. "Paris," *Lanterne*, 9 September 1879, 3.

112. Ibid., 14 August 1879, 3.

113. Sainéan, *Langage parisien*, 194.

114. ADS D2U6, no. 72, affaire Muller, Denul, et Henry.

115. "Paris," *Lanterne*, 20 December 1880, 3.

116. Michel and Fournier, *Hôtelleries et les cabarets*, 402.

117. Sainéan, *Langage parisien*, 193.

118. See, respectively, ADS D2U6, no. 13, affaire Lagoguet, and no. 10, affaire Mauriol.

119. Paulian, *Beggars in Paris*, 19; in real life, ADS D2U6, no. 32, affaire Patou et al.

120. "Chronique," *Gdt*, 21 March 1873, 485.

121. AN F7 3877, report of 1 September 1823.

122. "Chronique," *Gdt*, 28 January 1848, 1.

123. See, respectively, ADS D2U6, no. 72, affaire Muller, Denul, et Henry; "Paris," *Lanterne*, 19 December 1879, 3; ADS D2U6, no. 105, affaire Calvet.

124. "Chronique," *Gdt*, 4 February 1831, 4.

125. ADS D2U6, no. 90, affaire Ferré et al.; "Chronique," *Gdt*, 29 January 1868, 30, and 18–19 September 1871, 557; "Paris," *Lanterne*, 28 December 1879, 2.

126. Martin Nadaud, *Mémoires de Léonard ancien garcon maçon* (Paris: Hachette, 1976), 198.

127. "Chronique," *Gdt*, 8 July 1848, 868.

128. See, respectively, ADS D2U6, no. 13, affaire Galmiche; no. 22, affaire Perreau; no. 9, affaire Gansia; no. 15, affaire Grosjean; no. 46 affaire Révardeau.

129. AN F7 3875, report of 13 April 1820.

130. "Chronique," *Gdt*, 2 July 1848, 853.

131. Michel Masson, "Le Boutiquier," in *Nouveau tableau de Paris aux XIXᵉ siècle* (Paris: Librairie de Madame Charles Béchet, 1834), 2: 227.

132. Talmeyr, "Moeurs électorales," 881.

133. François Fosca, *Histoire des cafés de Paris* (Paris: Firmin-Didot, 1934), 170–81.

134. Jean Robiquet, *Daily Life in the French Revolution*, trans. James Kirkup (New York: Macmillan, 1964), 39.

135. See esp. Richard Cobb, *The People's Armies*, trans. Marianne Elliot (New Haven: Yale University Press, 1987), 108, 115; George Rudé, *The Crowd in the French Revolution* (Oxford: Oxford University Press, 1959), 181, 185, 215, 217–18; Augustin Challamel, *Les Clubs contre-révolutionnaires, cercles, comités, sociétés, salons, réunions, cafés, restaurants, et librairies* (1895; New York: AMS Press, 1974).

136. AN F7 3884, reports of 24 September, 28 August, 22 September, and 3 October 1830.

137. Duveau, *Vie ouvrière*, 498–99.

138. Girard, *La Deuxième République et le Second Empire*, 302; Bénigno Cacérés, *Loisirs et travail du moyen âge à nos jours* (Paris: Seuil, 1973), 169.

139. Auguste Lepage, *Les Cafés artistiques et littéraires de Paris* (Paris: Martin Boursin, 1882), 243.

140. De Kock, "Restaurants et cartes," 78.

141. "Tribunal correctionnel de Paris," *Gdt*, 15 July 1848, 896; "Chronique," ibid., 6 May 1848, 662; government measure on wine taxes, ibid., 19 April 1848, 607; "Chronique," ibid., 12 July 1848, 882; "Chronique," ibid., 14 July 1848, 890.

142. Girard, *La Deuxième République et le Second Empire*, 16.

143. Roger Magraw, *France, 1815–1914: The Bourgeois Century* (Oxford: Fontana, 1983), 129.

144. Victor Hugo, *The History of a Crime* (New York: Peter Fenelon Collier, n.d.), 3: 193–204, 296, 339; 4: 67, 95–96, 50, 148–57, 177, 253.

145. Reynolds, "Allemane avant l'allemanisme," 249, 263, 295.

146. Fournel, *Ce qu'on voit*, 378; Joseph Barberet, *Le Travail en France: Monographies professionnels* (Paris: Berger-Levrault, 1886–90), 7: 19.

147. Gaboriau, *Monsieur Lecoq*, 174.

148. Alain Dalotel, Alain Faure, and Jean-Claude Freiermuth, *Aux origines de la Commune: Le Mouvement des réunions publiques à Paris, 1868–1870* (Paris: Maspero, 1980), 60–61.

149. Maxime Vuillaume, *Mes Cahiers rouges au temps de la Commune* (Paris: Société d'éditions littéraires et artistiques, Libraire Paul Ollendorff, 1971), 219–22.

150. Philibert Audebrand, *Un Café sous Napoléon III* (Paris: E. Dentu, 1888), 258.

151. ADS D2U6, no. 7, affaire Rousseau.

152. Melvin Kranzberg, *The Siege of Paris, 1870–1871* (Ithaca, N.Y.: Cornell University Press, 1950), 106–9.

153. Fosca, *Histoire des cafés*, 179; Roger Price, "Ideology and Motivation in the Paris Commune of 1871," *Historical Journal* 15, no. 1 (1972): 77–81.

154. Maxime du Camp, *Les Convulsions de Paris* (1881; repr., New York: AMS Press, n.d.), 3: 130; ADS D2U6, no. 10, affaire Mauriol; du Camp, *Convulsions* 2: 83; ibid., 3: 265.

155. ADS D3U6, no. 1, affaire Sénicourt.

156. Paul Fontoulieu, *Les Eglises de Paris sous la Commune* (Paris: Dentu, 1873), 81.

157. Firmin Maillard, *Affiches, professions de foi, documents officiels, clubs et comités pendant la Commune* (Paris, 1871), 44, no. 116.

158. ADS D2U6, no. 87, affaire Blanchouin v. Tournois.

159. *Rapport d'ensemble de M. le general Appert sur les opérations de la justice militaire relative a l'insurrection de 1871* (Versailles: Cerf, 1875), 264; for second figure, see *Prolétaire*, 22 January 1879, 8.

160. *Prolétaire*, 22 March 1879, 6–7.

161. Bertall, "Courrier de la semaine," *L'Illustration*, 22 July 1871, 50–51; id., "Revue de fin d'année," ibid., 30 December 1871, 425.

162. APP BA 86, daily reports of the prefect of police to the minister of the interior, reports of 18 March 1872, 23 May 1879, 1 December 1879, 15 December 1872, 9, 11, and 18 May 1876.

163. "L'Arrivée des amnistiés," *Lanterne*, 15 September 1879, 1; and *Lanterne* columns "Pour ceux qui reviennent," 7 September 1879, 2; 8 September 1879, 2; 11 September 1879, 2; 26 September 1879, 3; 4 November 1879, 4.

164. APP BA 884, dossier 1, "Etat des débits de boissons."

165. Aimee Moutet, "Le Mouvement ouvrier à Paris du lendemain de la Commune au premier congrès syndical en 1876," *Mouvement social*, January–March 1967, 36.

166. See Braun deposition in affaire Finance et al., ADS D2U6, no. 51, and police report on Braun of 24–25 January 1879 in APP BA 459, no. 4865. Furthermore, the prefect of police often mentioned Braun's café in his reports to the minister of the interior; see reports of 4 August 1879, 1; 20 August 1879, 1; 29 October 1879, 2; 11 November 1879, 1, in APP BA 88, and report of 4 January 1880, 2, in APP BA 89.

167. APP BA 87, reports of 9 September 1876, 1, and 12 May 1880.

168. Robert Michels, *Political Parties* (New York: Free Press, 1962), 271.

169. For the left's scorn of Gambetta for his opportunism on the amnesty

question, see Jean T. Joughin, *The Paris Commune and French Politics, 1871–1880* (Baltimore: Johns Hopkins Press, 1955).

170. "La Fête dans les arrondissements," *Lanterne*, 16 July 1880, 1.

171. For an invaluable firsthand account, see A. Taillard, *Mémoires d'un homme du peuple: Une Page d'histoire électorale, étude de moeurs politiques, 1880–1910* (Bois-Colombes: Imprimerie modern, n.d.), 53–66.

172. Nord, *Paris Shopkeepers*, 313, 100, 120.

173. Saint-Léon, *Petit Commerce français*, 270.

174. Nord, *Paris Shopkeepers*, 430.

175. *Annales antialcooliques* 10, no. 4 (April 1912), quoting *Revue vinicole* (a café owners' journal), 247.

176. Prestwich, "Temperance in France," 301–19; Elisabeth Hausser, *Paris au jour le jour: Les Evénements vus par la presse, 1900–1919* (Paris: Editions de minuit, 1968), 119.

177. See, respectively, Girard, *La Deuxième République et le Second Empire*, 164; Nord, *Paris Shopkeepers*, 362–3, 425; Talmeyr, "Moeurs électorales," 886; Girard, *La Deuxième République et le Second Empire*, 165.

178. See, respectively, Saint-Léon, *Le Petit Commerce français*, 267, 268; "La Reforme des boissons," *Ligue nationale contre l'alcoolisme*, 3d ser., 7, no. 1 (1901): 29; Saint-Léon, *Le Petit Commerce français*, 268.

179. See, respectively, Girard, *La Deuxième République et le Second Empire*, 160–66; Nord, *Paris Shopkeepers*, 313, 326; "Rastignac," "Courrier de Paris," *L'Illustration*, 26 January 1889, 70; Nord, *Paris Shopkeepers*, 315.

180. Nord, *Paris Shopkeepers*, 314, 45, 7, 50–51.

181. Ibid., 50–51, 422; Saint-Léon, *Le Petit Commerce français*, 269–70.

182. Girard, *Quand les Auvergnats partaient conquérir Paris*, 165, 161.

183. Talmeyr, "Moeurs électorales," 881.

184. *Le Défenseur*, 11 June 1882, 6; 18 June 1882, 6.

185. Berlanstein, *Working People of Paris*, 168.

186. See, e.g., APP BA 115, 9 November 1906.

Chapter 6.
The Etiquette of Café Sociability

1. Lutz Niethammer, "Some Elements of the Housing Reform Debate in Nineteenth-Century Europe; or, On the Making of a New Paradigm of Social Control," in *Modern Industrial Cities: History, Policy, and Survival*, ed. Bruce M. Stave (Beverly Hills, Calif.: Sage Publications, 1981), 134.

2. "Sociability (an Example of Pure, of Formal, Sociology)," in *The Sociology of Georg Simmel*, trans. and ed. Kurt H. Wolff (New York: Free Press, 1950), 55.

3. Louis Girard, *La Deuxième République et le Second Empire, 1848–*

1870 (Paris: Association pour la publication d'une histoire de Paris, distrib. Hachette, 1981), 359–60

4. See esp. Maurice Agulhon, *Le Cercle dans la France bourgeoise, 1810–1848* (Paris: Armand Colin, 1977).

5. U.S. Consular Reports, *Labor in Europe* (Washington, D.C.: Government Printing Office, 1885), 1022. See also Jeffrey Kaplow, "La Fin de la saint-lundi," *Temps libre*, no. 2 (1981): 115, for a quotation to similar effect.

6. H. Leroy, *De l'alcoolisme au point de vue de sa prévention et de sa répression sur le terrain du droit pénal* (Paris: A. Rousseau, 1900), 26–28.

7. Frederick Engels, *The Condition of the Working Class in England* (1845; repr., London: Granada, 1969 [introduction by Eric Hobsbawm]), 156–57.

8. Gustave Le Bon, *The Crowd: A Study of the Popular Mind* (trans. 1897; New York: Viking, 1960), 128.

9. See, e.g., Baedeker, *Paris and Its Environs* (Leipzig: Karl Baedeker, 1888), 17; Bayle Saint John, *Purple Tints of Paris: Character and Manners in the New Empire* (New York: Riker, Thorne, 1854), 184.

10. Henri Leyret, *En plein faubourg: Moeurs ouvrières* (Paris: Charpentier, 1895), passim; Maurice Halbwachs, *La Classe ouvrière et les niveaux de vie* (Paris: F. Alcan, 1912), 425.

11. "Courrier du sport," *L'Illustration*, 9 May 1874.

12. Arlette Farge, *Vivre dans la rue à Paris au XVIIIᵉ siècle* (Paris: Editions Gallimard/Julliard, 1979), 13–88; David Garrioch, *Neighborhood and Community in Paris, 1740–1790* (Cambridge: Cambridge University Press, 1986), 24, 98, 127, 121, 121, 123.

13. Thomas Brennan, *Public Drinking and Popular Culture in Eighteenth-Century Paris* (Princeton: Princeton University Press, 1988), 21, 23.

14. Farge, *Vivre dans la rue à Paris*, 72–76; Brennan, *Public Drinking*, 69–70.

15. Garrioch, *Neighborhood and Community*, 214–15.

16. Richard Cobb, *The Police and the People* (Oxford: Oxford University Press, 1972), 7–8.

17. Louis Chevalier, *Laboring Classes and Dangerous Classes in Paris during the First Half of the Nineteenth Century*, trans. Frank Jellinek (Princeton: Princeton University Press, 1981), 161–85; Eugène Sue, *The Mysteries of Paris* (London: Chapman & Hall, 1845–46), 3: 384.

18. *Journal des débats*, 25 October 1827, quoted by Chevalier, *Laboring Classes and Dangerous Classes*, 493.

19. "Chronique," *Gazette des tribunaux* (hereafter cited as *Gdt*), 9 May 1848, 674.

20. François Bédarida and Anthony Sutcliff, "The Street in the Structure and Life of the City: Reflections on Nineteenth-Century London and Paris," *Journal of Urban History* 6, no. 4 (August 1980): 379–96.

21. Marshall Berman, *All That Is Solid Melts into Air: The Experience of Modernity* (New York: Simon & Schuster, 1982), 158.

22. Charles Rearick, *Pleasures of the Belle Epoque: Entertainment and Festivity in Turn-of-the-Century France* (New Haven: Yale University Press, 1985), 169.

23. "The Streets of Paris Forty Years Ago," *Blackwood's Edinburgh Magazine*, 156, no. 848 (October 1894): 465

24. Jeanne Gaillard, *Paris, la ville, 1852–1870* (Paris: Champion, 1977), 525–31.

25. Girard, *La Deuxième République et le Second Empire*, 219.

26. W. C. Morrow, with notes from Edouard Cocuel, *Bohemian Paris of Today* (London: Chatto & Windus, 1899), 33.

27. Nord, *Paris Shopkeepers*, 75, 199, and see police court (*tribunal de simple police*) records in ADS D22U1, no. 87, and other cartons after 1900.

28. "Streets of Paris Forty Years Ago," 454, 466; Sennett, *Fall*, 215; David Pinckney, *Napoleon III and the Rebuilding of Paris* (Princeton: Princeton University Press, 1958), 88; "Procès-verbaux de la commission chargée de faire une enquête sur la situation des ouvriers de l'industrie et de l'agriculture en France et de présenter un premier rapport sur le crise industrielle à Paris," *Annales de la Chambre des députés*, n.s., *Documents parlementaires* (hereafter cited as PV) 12 (March–April 1884), app., 50.

29. Charles Baudelaire, *Paris Spleen*, trans. Louise Varèse (New York: New Directions, 1947), 52–53.

30. Dr. Legrain, "Paris buveur (Simple silhouette)," *Annales antialcooliques*, no. 7 (July 1905): 120.

31. "Notes sur une élection," *L'Illustration*, 2 February 1889, 91; Saint John, *Purple Tints*, 177.

32. *Jack*, vol. 21 of *The Works of Alphonse Daudet*, trans. Marian McIntyre (Boston: Little, Brown, 1899–1906), 185.

33. James Rousseau, "Les Cafés et les estaminets," in *Nouveau tableau de Paris au XIXᵉ siècle* (Paris: Librairie de Madame Charles Béchet, 1834), 4: 57–60.

34. See, respectively, Peter de Polnay, *Aspects of Paris* (London: W. H. Allen, 1968), 56–57; *Plummer's Guide to Paris: A New Handbook* (London: Plummer, 1842), 154; Henri d'Aleméras, *La Vie parisienne sous le Second Empire* (Paris: Albin Michel, 1933), 356; Auguste Lepage, *Les Cafés artistiques et littéraires de Paris* (Paris: Martin Boursin, 1882), 89.

35. I take issue with Theodore Child, "Characteristic Parisian Cafés," *Harper's New Monthly Magazine* 78, no. 467 (April 1889): 692, who argues that café life was much the same throughout the city.

36. James D. McCabe, Jr., *Paris by Sunlight and Gaslight* (Boston: National Publishing Co., 1869), 75.

37. Nord, *Paris Shopkeepers*, esp. 238–40.

38. D'Aleméras, *Vie parisienne*, 344, 330, and Rearick, *Pleasures of the Belle Epoque*, 97, respectively.

39. Leyret, *En plein faubourg*, 17.

40. Henry Steele, *The Working Classes of France* (London: Twentieth Century Press, 1904), 78.

41. See ADS D2U6, no. 1, affaire Treijenin et Marchand, and no. 73, affaire Houdremont.

42. Daudet, *Jack*, 312.

43. "Paris," *Lanterne*, 29 October 1879, 2.

44. ADS D3U6, no. 48, affaire Nivet.

45. Jean Borreil, "Circulations et rassemblements," *Révoltes logiques*, no. 7 (Spring–Summer 1978); Louis Paulian, *Beggars in Paris*, trans. Lady Herschell (New York: Edward Arnold, 1897), 52, 80.

46. Paul Bureau, *Towards Moral Bankruptcy* (London: Constable, 1925), 41.

47. Paulian, *Beggars*, 120.

48. "Chronique," *Gdt*, 9 December 1848, 877.

49. James Rousseau, "Les Barrières et les guinguettes," in *Nouveau tableau de Paris* (Paris: Librairie de Madame Charles Béchet, 1834), 5: 304.

50. Joseph Barberet, *Le Travail en France: Monographies professionnelles* (Paris: Berger-Levrault, 1886–90), 7: 20.

51. "La Misère à Paris," *L'Illustration*, 9 October 1886, 248.

52. Thomas E. Brennan, "Cabarets and Laboring Class Communities in Eighteenth Century Paris" (Ph.D. diss., Johns Hopkins University, 1981), 173.

53. APP BA 497, "Réunions . . . au café Frontin," report of *indicateur* no. 6, 10 June 1873; Emile Zola, *Savage Paris*, trans. David Hughes and Marie J. Mason (London: Elek Books, 1955), 249; d'Aleméras, *Vie parisienne*, 339.

54. ADS D2U8, no. 56, affaire Billoir.

55. Georges Duveau, *La Vie ouvrière sous le Second Empire* (Paris: Gallimard, 1946), 498.

56. Saint John, *Purple Tints*, 181.

57. Steele, *Working Classes of France*, 23.

58. Fernand and Maurice Pelloutier, *La Vie ouvrière en France* (Paris: Schlecher frères, 1900), 310.

59. Alfred Delvau, *Histoire anecdotique des cafés et cabarets de Paris* (Paris: Dentu, 1862), 293.

60. Brennan, *Public Drinking and Popular Culture*, 239–41, 245–46; Garrioch, *Neighborhood and Community*, esp. 81.

61. See ADS D2U6, no. 9, affaire Monjaret, no. 14, affaire Sevestre, no. 53, affaire Huot; D3U6, no. 1, affaire Tarbourich; D3U6, no. 1, affaire Renard.

62. See, respectively, ADS D2U8, no. 53, affaire Palat; no. 10, affaire Allaire contre Leclerc, and no. 11, affaire Moreau contre Sourdillat.

63. Gérard Jacquemet, *Belleville au XIXe siècle: Du faubourg à la ville*, ed. Jean Touzot (Paris: Editions de l'Ecole des hautes études en sciences sociales, 1984), 186.

64. Ann Louise Shapiro, *Housing the Poor of Paris, 1850–1902* (Madison: University of Wisconsin Press, 1985), 38.

65. ADS D3U6, no. 46, affaire Révardeau.

66. ADS D2U6, no. 46, affaire Tellier.

67. Maxime Vuillaume, *Mes Cahiers rouges au temps de la Commune* (Paris: Société d'éditions littéraires et artistiques, Libraire Paul Ollendorff, 1971), 305.

68. "Graveurs cabaret du Père Lunette," *L'Illustration*, 25 May 1889, 452; "Paris," *Lanterne*, 31 March 1880, 3, and 11 March 1879, 2.

69. On Italians, see ADS and "Paris," *Lanterne*, 24 April 1880, 3. On the Auvergnats, see Françoise Raison-Jourde, *La Colonie auvergnate de Paris au XIXe siècle* (Paris: Imprimerie municipale, 1977), 301–3.

70. Peter Amann, *Revolution and Mass Democracy: The Paris Club Movement in 1848* (Princeton: Princeton University Press, 1975), 30.

71. Chevalier, *Formation de la population parisienne*, 239.

72. Raison-Jourde, *Colonie auvergnate*, 301–3.

73. Nancy L. Green, *The Pletzl of Paris: Jewish Immigrant Workers in the Belle Epoque* (New York: Holmes & Meier, 1986), 123, 71–99.

74. "Paris," *Lanterne*, 9 October 1880, 3.

75. Saint John, *Purple Tints*, 183.

76. ADS D3U6, no. 29, affaire Dejour et al., and no. 31, affaire Duchatet; D2U6, no. 37, affaire Walker et al., and no. 72, affaire Knopf.

77. "S.F.T.," "Le Pari mutuel," *L'Illustration*, 22 March 1890, 244–46, and 10 May 1890, 411; "Tom," "La Société parisienne: Le Monde et les courses," *L'Illustration*, 10 May 1890, 411.

78. Brennan, *Public Drinking and Popular Culture*, 282–85.

79. See, respectively, ADS D2U6, no. 32, affaire Patou et al., and no. 53, affaire Penot et al.

80. "Youth and Drink in Late Nineteenth-Century Paris: Rhetoric and Reality," *Contemporary French Civilization* 12, no. 1 (Winter–Spring 1988): 87–101.

81. Brennan, "Cabarets and Laboring Class Communities," 167.

82. See ADS D4U9, no. 9, affaire Costa et al., for the phrase "café friend," and Victor Henri Rocheforts-Lucary, *The Adventures of My Life*, trans. Ernest W. Smith (London: E. Arnold, 1896), 1: 28, for the phrase "café talk." See also "Chronique," *Gdt*, 5 August 1871, 405.

83. Honoré de Balzac, *César Birotteau*, trans. Ellen Marriage (New York: Dutton, 1912), 312.

84. *The Masterpieces of Charles-Paul de Kock*, vol. 2: *Monsieur Cherami* (Philadelphia: George Barrie & Sons, 1903), 177–182.

85. P[atrice] B[ousel], "Cafés," in *Dictionnaire de Paris* (Paris: Larousse, 1964), 77.

86. Benjamin F. Martin, *Crime and Criminal Justice under the Third Republic: The Shame of Marianne* (Baton Rouge: Louisiana State University Press, 1990), 66.

87. ADS D2U8, no. 56, affaire Billoir.

88. ADS D4U9, no. 9, affaire Costa et al.

89. PV, 333.

90. Respectively, AP D2U6, no. 41, affaire Ferrant; no. 40, affaire Rainot; no. 73, affaire Houdremont.

91. Respectively, D3U6, no. 40, affaire Fuchs; no. 37, affaire Chevalier.

92. "Chronique," *Gdt*, 17 January 1868, 2.

93. Erving Goffman, *Relations in Public: Microstudies of the Public Order* (1971; New York: Harper Colophon Books, 1972), 330–31, 260.

94. Léon and Maurice Bonneff, *Marchands de folie*, 2d ed. (Paris: Rivière, 1913), 76.

95. ADS D2U6, no. 58, affaire Gabot et al.

96. Tristan Bernard, *Le Petit Café*, in *L'Illustration théâtrale*, 18 May 1912, 4–5.

97. Brennan, "Cabarets and Laboring Class Communities," 171.

98. For the nicknames "Bretonne," "Jardinier," and "Décoré," see ADS D2U8, no. 56, affaire Billoir; for "la Patte," see D2U6, no. 53, affaire Huot et al.; for "Turio" (which seems to have meant "Fury"), see D3U6, no. 24; for "Pinsonneau," see D2U6, no. 162; for "Charlot," see D2U6, no. 105; for "Aglaré," see D3U6, no. 37; "Vierge de la Commune," "Chronique," *Gdt*, 23 December 1871, 883.

99. René Michaud, *J'avais vingt ans: Une Jeune Ouvrier au début du siècle* (Paris: Editions syndicalistes, 1967), 86.

100. Marcel Edant, "La Misère à Paris," *L'Illustration*, 9 October 1886, 248.

101. Charles Bonnet, *L'Alcoolisation dans differents professions de la region parisienne* (Paris: Jouvet, 1914), 47, and APP BA 497, "Réunions . . . au café Frontin."

102. "Chronique," *Gdt*, 13 February 1868, 147.

103. AP D2U6, no. 46, affaire Tellier.

104. AP D2U8, no. 56, affaire Billoir.

105. For example, see AP D2U6, no. 53, affaire Baudin et al.

106. Stewart Edwards, *The Paris Commune of 1871* (New York: Quadrangle, 1971), 312–50; Robert Toombs, *The War against Paris, 1871* (Cambridge: Cambridge University Press, 1981), 162–93.

107. See, respectively, ADS D2U6, no. 12, affaire Jardinot, and no. 7, affaire Wallard.

108. See Chapter 4.

109. Bernard, *Petit Café*, 11.

110. AN F7 3874, report of 19 April 1819.

111. "Les Planches," *Lune rousse*, 27 May 1877, 4; 15 April 1877, 4.

112. AN F7 3877, report of 17 March 1823.

113. "Chronique," *Gdt*, 30 January 1868, 98.

114. ADS D2U6, no. 105, affaire Calvet.

115. On police work in London, see Nancy Tomes, "A 'Torrent Of Abuse': Crimes of Violence between Working-Class Men and Women in London, 1840–1875," *Journal of Social History* 11, no. 3 (Spring 1978): 336.

116. For notion of time out in relation to bars, see Sherri Cavan, *Liquor License: An Ethnography of Bar Behavior* (Chicago: Aldine, 1966); on the aristocratic code of honor, see Robert Nye, "Honor Codes and Medical Ethics in Modern France" (paper delivered at the 20th annual meeting of the Western Society for French History, 22–24 October 1992).

117. AN F7 3880, report of 4 January 1826.

118. "Chronique," *Gdt*, 10 January 1829, 240; ibid., 4 February 1831, 324, and 19 March 1831, 484.

119. "Tribunal correctionnel," *Gdt*, 4 June 1848, 761.

120. ADS D3U6, no. 40, affaire Barrière.

121. See AP D2U6, no. 13, affaire Higler et al., and no. 73, affaire Marin et al.

122. "Paris," *Lanterne*, 15 September 1880, 3.

123. ADS D2U6, no. 65, affaire Bordet.

124. ADS D2U6, no. 51, affaire Palat.

125. Urbain Guérin, "Ouvrier cordonnier de Malakoff," *Ouvriers des deux mondes*, 1st ser., 5, no. 41 (1878): 193–94, 180.

126. Theodore Reff, "Manet and the Paris of Haussmann and Baudelaire," in *Visions of the Modern City*, ed. William Sharpe and Leonard Wallock (New York: Proceedings of the Heyman Center for the Humanities, 1983), 153, 158.

127. Brennan, "Cabarets and Laboring Class Communities," 147–48.

128. ADS D2U8, no. 56, affaire Billoir.

129. Joseph Reinach, *Contre l'alcoolisme* (Paris: Charpentier, 1911), 97–118.

130. ADS D2U6, no. 55, affaire Protche et al.

131. Jean-Claude Chesnais, *Histoire de la violence* (Paris: Robert Laffont, 1981), 22, 57.

132. Armand Audigane, *Les Populations ouvrières et les industries de la France* (1854; repr., New York: Burt Franklin, 1970), 283.

133. Saint John, *Purple Tints*, 407

134. See, e.g., Matilda Bentham-Edwards, *Home Life in France*, 6th ed. (London: Methuen, 1913), 87.

135. Saint John, *Purple Tints*, 406.

136. Nye, "Honor Codes and Medical Ethics in Modern France," 8.

137. B[oussel], "Cafés," in *Dictionnaire de Paris*, 84; François Fosca, *Histoire des cafés de Paris* (Paris: Firmin-Didot, 1934), 213.

Chapter 7.
Women and Gender Politics

1. David Garrioch, *Neighborhood and Community in Paris, 1740–1790* (Cambridge: Cambridge University Press, 1986), 24; Thomas Brennan, *Public Drinking and Popular Culture in Eighteenth-Century Paris* (Princeton: Princeton University Press, 1988), 148.

2. Dominique Godineau, *Citoyennes tricoteuses: Les Femmes du peuple à Paris pendant la Révolution française* (Aix-en-Provence: Alinea, 1988), 216.

3. Ouzi Elyada, pref., *Lettres bougrement patriotiques de la Mère Duchesne; suivi du Journal des femmes* (1791; Paris: Editions de Paris / EDHIS, 1989), 9–11, 158, 163–70.

4. *Paris pendant la terreur: Rapports des agents secrets du ministre de l'intérieur*, ed. Pierre Caron, in 6 vols. (Paris: Société de l'histoire contemporaine et Société de l'histoire de France, 1919–58), 2: 64, 165, 296.

5. Ibid., 3: 67.

6. For this view, see *Women in Revolutionary Paris, 1789–1795*, ed. Darline G. Levy, Harriet B. Applewhite, and Mary D. Johnson (Urbana: University of Illinois Press, 1979), 4–5; Olwen Hufton, "Women in Revolution, 1789–1796," in *French Society and the Revolution*, ed. Douglas Johnson (Cambridge: Cambridge University Press, 1976), 148, 159.

7. *Paris pendant la terreur*, 1: 164, 3: 279, 280.

8. Olwen Hufton, "Women in Revolution," *French Politics and Society* 7, no. 3 (Summer 1989): 65–81.

9. See *Women in Revolutionary Paris*, 213–20.

10. Political repression frequently drove political discussion underground and into cafés. A good example is nineteenth-century Toulouse. See Ronald Aminzade, *Class, Politics, and Early Industrial Capitalism: A Study of Mid-Nineteenth-Century Toulouse, France* (Albany: State University of New York Press, 1981), 194.

11. *Paris pendant la terreur*, 1: 184; 2: 85, 102, 279, 370; 5: 171.

12. Alphonse Aulard, *Paris pendant la réaction thermidorienne et sous le Directoire* (Paris, 1898; New York: AMS, 1974), 1: 452; 2: 7.

13. On the paucity of women who were publicly drunk, see Henri Wallon, *Histoire du tribunal révolutionnaire de Paris avec le journal de ses actes* (Paris, 1880), 1: 130–40; 324–27; 2: 190–99; 204, 266; 427–29; 455; 445.

14. Aulard, *Paris pendant la réaction thermidorienne et sous le Directoire*, 3: 359.

15. Dominique Godineau, "Masculine and Feminine Political Practice during the French Revolution, 1793–Year III," in *Women and Politics in the Age of Democratic Revolution*, ed. Harriet B. Applewhite and Darline G. Levy (Ann Arbor: University of Michigan Press, 1990), 61.

16. Susan P. Conner, "Politics, Prostitution, and the Pox in Revolutionary Paris, 1789–1799," *Journal of Social History* 22, no. 4 (Summer 1989): 718; Aulard, *Paris pendant la réaction thermidorienne et sous le Directoire*, 1: 230, 351, 380, 398, 408, 411, 420, 430, 535, 606; 2: 7, 398, 495, 529, 574, 754; 3: 90, 126, 140, 209, 216–17, 292, 313.

17. C. J. Lecour, *La Prostitution à Paris et à Londres* (Paris: P. Asselin, 1877), 213, 219, 223.

18. Richard Le Gallienne, *From a Paris Scrapbook* (New York: Ives Washburn, 1938), 116–17.

19. Doctor Véron, *Memoires d'un bourgeois de Paris*, ed. Gabriel de Gonet (Paris: Gabriel de Gonet, 1853), 1: 12–13; E. F. Bazot, *Les Cafés de Paris, ou revue politique, critique et littéraire des moeurs du siècle par un flâneur patente* (Paris: Lecrivain, 1819), 12.

20. "Fieschi and the Infernal Machine," *Every Saturday*, April 20, 1867, 504.

21. "Chronique," *Gazette des tribunaux* (hereafter cited as *Gdt*), 11 January 1872, 35; Léon and Maurice Bonneff, *Marchands de folie*, 2d ed. (Paris: Rivière, 1913), 13.

22. James Rousseau, "Les Cafés et les estaminets," in *Nouveau tableau de Paris au XIXe siècle* (Paris: Librairie de Madame Charles Béchet, 1834), 4: 68–69.

23. René Michaud, *J'avais vingt ans: Une Jeune Ouvrier au début du siècle* (Paris: Editions syndicalistes, 1967), 42.

24. James Rousseau, "Les Barrières et les guinguettes," in *Nouveau tableau de Paris aux XIXe siècle* (Paris: Librairie de Madame Charles Béchet, 1834), 5: 286.

25. Sîan Reynolds, "Allemane avant l'allemanisme: Jeunesse d'un militant," *Mouvement sociale*, no. 126 (January–March 1984): 7.

26. Joseph Barberet, *Le Travail en France: Monographies professionnelles* (Paris: Berger-Levrault, 1890), 23–24.

27. "La Vie à Paris depeinté par un Allemand," *L'Illustration*, 15 October 1881, 247.

28. See ADS series D10U3 for registers, and series D11U3 for dossiers.

29. See esp. ADS D2U6, no. 11, affaire Protery, D2U6, no. 27, affaire Marié de Lisle.

30. Raymond Rudorff, *The Belle Epoque: Paris in the Nineties* (New York: Saturday Review Press, 1972), 74.

31. See, respectively, ADS D2U6, no. 73, affaire Houdremont, and no. 53,

affaire Penot et Legrand. The latter case shows the female networks in the café.

32. ADS D2U6, no. 165, affaire Guinet.

33. Marilyn Boxer, "Marriage and Mobility: Parisian Flowermakers and Seamstresses, 1860–1910" (MS), 12.

34. Rousseau, "Barrières," 297.

35. AN, report of 6 May 1823.

36. "Chronique," *Gdt*, 28 November 1828, 95.

37. *Un Ouvrier en 1820: Manuscrit inédit de Jacques-Etienne Bédé*, ed. Rémi Gossez (Paris: Presses universitaires de France, 1984), 211.

38. "Chronique," *Gdt*, 3 November 1830, 8.

39. "Justice criminelle . . . Cour d'assise," *Gdt*, 15 July 1848, 894.

40. "Chronique," *Gdt*, 9 December 1848, 877.

41. Eugene Schulkind, "Socialist Women during the 1871 Paris Commune," *Past and Present*, no. 106 (February 1985): 153.

42. Victoria Thompson, "The Rise and Fall of the 'Grisette': Images of Working-Class Women in Bourgeois Writings of the July Monarchy" (paper presented at the 20th annual conference of the Western Society for French History, October 1992); *Enquête parlementaire sur l'insurrection du 18 mars*, vol. 2 (Versailles: Cerf, 1872), 221 (Mace), 237 (Garcin), 127 (Cresson).

43. "B" [Victorine Brocher], *Souvenirs d'une morte vivante, 1848–1871* (1909; Paris: Maspero, 1976), 6, 168, 193, 210.

44. ADS D3U6, no. 1895; and see APP, report of 29 May 1898.

45. ADS D2U6, no. 8, affaire Paquet.

46. APP BA884, dossier 1, " . . . des surveillances exercées dans les brasseries ci-après desservies par des filles travesties."

47. See *Femme au café*, a painting by Jean Beraut, ca. 1890, at the Musée des Arts décoratifs, and Jean Claude Bologne, *Histoire des cafés et des cafetiers* (Paris: Larousse, 1993), 306–7.

48. A. J. B. Parent-Duchâtelet, *De la prostitution dans la ville de Paris, de l'hygiène publique, de la morale, et de l'administration* (Brussels: Haumann & Cattoir, 1836); Alain Corbin, *Les Filles de noce: Misère sexuelle et prostitution (19ᵉ siècle)* (1978; Paris: Flammarion, 1982); Jill Harsin, *Policing Prostitution in Nineteenth-Century Paris* (Princeton: Princeton University Press, 1985). For an especially good analysis of prostitution and café life, see Theresa Ann Grondberg's "Femmes de Brasserie," *Art History* 7, no. 3 (September 1984): 330.

49. Harsin, *Policing Prostitution*, 42–3.

50. O. Commenge, *Hygiène sociale: La Prostitution clandestine à Paris* (Paris: Schleicher, 1897), 53.

51. Paris, Conseil municipal, *Rapports et documents* (Paris: Imprimerie municipal, 1883), no. 26, 12, and Harsin, *Policing Prostitution*, 309–11.

52. Harsin, *Policing Prostitution*, 319.

53. J. V. Daubie, *La Femme pauvre au XIXe siècle* (Paris: Guillaumin, 1866), 257.

54. Harsin, *Policing Prostitution*, 317–318.

55. Edouard Ducret, *Paris canaille: Moeurs contemporaines* (Paris: E. Dentu, 1888), 23–26.

56. Fernand Vandèrem, "Un Garçon chez Véry," *L'Illustration*, 9 April 1892, 300–301.

57. "Chronique," *Gdt*, 20–21 November 1871, 769.

58. "Le Case de M. Bouchez," *XIXe siècle*, 31 January 1888.

59. ADS, D22U1, no. 88, appeal of Denis, 20 March 1901.

60. Lecour, *La Prostitution à Paris et à Londres*, 144–45; Commenge, *Hygiène sociale*, 327–28.

61. "Chronique," *Gdt*, 21 January 1868, 71.

62. Bonneffs, *Marchands de folie*, 78–87.

63. Peter de Polnay, *Aspects of Paris* (London: W. H. Allen, 1968), 58–59.

64. See police ordinance of 19 September 1861 in Gabriel Delessert, *Collection officielle des ordonnances de police* (Paris: Dupont, 1844), 7: 796–97.

65. ADS D2U6, no. 35, affaire Pernot et Hebrand, and "Chronique," *Gdt*, 21 February 1872, 175.

66. ADS D2U6, no. 31, affaire Séguin.

67. "Chronique," *Gdt*, 4 January 1868, 15; 7 February 1868, 127; and 11 February 1868, 143.

68. Corbin, *Filles de noce*, 296–98, 253.

69. J.-K. Huysmans, *Against Nature* (1884), trans. Robert Baldick (New York: Penguin Books, 1959), 175–76.

70. Emile Zola, *The Ladies' Delight*, trans. April Fitzlyon (New York: Abelard-Schuman, 1958), 131.

71. Bonneffs, *Marchands de folie*, 14.

72. Lecour, *Prostitution à Paris et à Londres*, 180.

73. For example, *Paris pendant la terreur*, 1: 337, 339; 2: 128, 270; 3: 314.

74. Lucien Descaves, preface to "B," *Souvenirs*, 6.

75. Data from the registers of the correctional tribunal, series D1U6, for 1871 to 1873 and 1880. Cases of insult were collected on the basis of whether or not they included a café owner, because in most cases of civil insult, the location is not listed.

76. H. A. Frégier, *Des classes dangereuses de la population dans les grandes villes et des moyens de les rendre meilleurs* (Brussels: Meline, Cans, 1840), 1: 73.

77. Commenge, *Hygiène sociale*, 335–37.

78. Theresa M. McBride, "A Woman's World: Department Stores and the

Evolution of Women's Employment, 1870–1920," *French Historical Studies* 10, no. 4 (Fall 1978): 680; Charles Rearick, *Pleasures of the Belle Epoque: Entertainment and Festivity in Turn-of-the-Century France* (New Haven: Yale University Press, 1985), 161.

79. McBride, "Woman's World," 680.

80. Theresa M. McBride, *The Domestic Revolution: The Modernisation of Household Service in England and France, 1820–1920* (London: Croom Helm, 1976).

81. See John W. Schaffer, "Family, Class, and Young Women: Occupational Expectations in Nineteenth-Century Paris," in *Family and Sexuality in French History*, ed. Robert Wheaton and Tamara K. Hareven (Philadelphia: University of Pennsylvania Press, 1980); Préfecture de la Seine, *Résultats statistiques: Denombrement de 1886 pour la ville de Paris et le département de la Seine* (Paris: G. Masson, 1887), 78–79, 90–91.

82. Barberet, *Travail en France*, 5: 265, 281, 345.

83. ADS D2U8, no. 59, affaire Georgel; ADS D2U6, no. 31, affaire Seguin et al.; "After the Insurrection," *The Times* (London), 3 June 1871, 5; Othenin d'Haussonville, "La Misère à Paris," *Revue des deux mondes* 45 (1881): 834; ADS D3U6, no. 105, affaire Calvet.

84. Paul Leroy-Beaulieu, *Le Travail des femmes au XIXᵉ siècle* (Paris: Charpentier, 1873), 114; Alain Faure, *Paris carême-prenant: Du carnaval à Paris au XIXᵉ siècle* (Paris: Hachette, 1978), 134–35; Emile Gaboriau, *Other People's Money* (New York: Charles Scribner's Sons, 1900), 258.

85. This conclusion is based on a frequency run on the SPSS (Statistical Package for the Social Sciences) batch system, which found that out of 138 prostitutes appearing before the correctional tribunal, 118 (85.5%) had insulted a policeman, whereas only 570 out of 772 (73.8%) of women who were not prostitutes had done so. The corrected chi-square significance of these frequencies is .0046 and the raw chi square is .0033.

86. Commenge, *Hygiène sociale*, 125, 110–15, 116–17, 122.

87. See ADS D22U1, nos. 70–80, for repeated infractions by street vendors.

88. ADS D2U6, no. 22, affaire Perreau.

89. ADS D2U8, no. 56, affaire Billoir.

90. ADS D2U6, no. 34, affaire Delest et Sabre.

91. ADS D2U6, no. 16, affaire Blanchert.

92. ADS D2U6, no. 80, affaire Morel.

93. Gaboriau, *Other People's Money*, 237.

94. Alvan Sanborn, "Paris Workingmen's Cafés," *North American Review* 158 (1894): 252.

95. ADS D2U6, no. 22, affaire Perreau, and no. 103, affaire Porte.

96. Emile Zola, *Savage Paris*, trans. David Hughes and Marie J. Mason (London: Elek Books, 1955), 153, 154.

97. ADS D2U8, no. 56, affaire Billoir.

98. Zola, *Savage Paris*, 153, 155.

99. "Chronique," *Gdt*, 3–4 January 1848.

100. ADS D2U6, no. 5, affaire Lars.

101. ADS D2U6, no. 65, affaire Bourdet.

102. P. du Maroussem, "Ouvrière mouleuse en cartonnage d'une fabrique collective de jouets parisiens," *Ouvriers de deux mondes*, 2d ser., 4, no. 76 (1892): 177.

103. "B," *Souvenirs*, 149; "L'Alcoolisme dans la famille," *Tempérance* 2d ser., 2, no. 4 (1881): 323–25.

104. ADS D2U6, no. 73, affaire Houdremont.

105. ADS D2U6, no. 27, affaire Marié de Lisle.

106. ADS D2U6, no. 55, affaire Proteche et al.

107. Paul Leroy-Beaulieu, *Le Travail des femmes au XIXᵉ siècle* (Paris: Charpentier, 1873), 233. See also Joan W. Scott, "Men and Women in the Parisian Garment Trades: Discussions of Family and Work in the 1830's and 1840's" (paper delivered at conference on Representations of Work in France, Cornell University, 28–30 April 1983), 24.

108. ADS D2U6, no. 55, affaire Proteche et al.

109. Tristan Bernard's play, *Le Petit Café*, in *L'Illustration théâtrale*, 18 May 1912, 4; "Flirt," "Restaurants et brasseries," *L'Illustration*, 9 February 1895, 111.

110. AN F7 3877, report of 29 July 1823; Flora Tristan, *The Worker's Union*, trans. Beverly Livingston (Urbana: University of Illinois Press, 1983), 95.

111. *Enquête sur le travail à domicile dans l'industrie de la lingerie* (Paris: Imprimerie nationale, 1907), 1: 64, 652, 662, 642, 655, 671.

112. A frequency run on the SPSS batch system for defendants appearing before the Correctional Tribunal showed that 688 of 910 women (75.6%) had insulted the police, whereas 4,951 of 6,688 men (74.0%) had done so. The corrected chi-square significance was .3274 and the raw chi-square significance was .3078.

113. Jacques Donzelot, *The Policing of Families*, trans. Robert Hurley (New York: Pantheon Books, 1979), 38–42.

Chapter 8.
Behavioral Politics

1. William Reddy, "The *Batteurs* and the Informer's Eye: A Labour Dispute under the French Second Empire," *History Workshop Journal*, no. 7 (Spring 1979): 36.

2. On the destruction or loss of cartons on cafés at the Archives nationales, see Susanna Barrows " 'Parliaments of the People': The Political Cul-

ture of Cafés in the Early Third Republic," in *Drinking: Behavior and Belief in Modern History*, ed. id. and Robin Room (Berkeley and Los Angeles: University of California Press, 1991), 87.

3. Alfred Franklin, *La Vie privée d'autrefois: Le Café, le thé, et le chocolat* (Paris: Plon, 1893), 100; Jean Leclant, "Le Café et les cafés à Paris, 1644–1693," *Annales: Economies, sociétés, civilisations* 6, no. 1 (January–March 1951): 4–5.

4. Theodore Child, "Characteristic Parisian Cafés," *Harper's New Monthly Magazine* 78, no. 467 (April 1889): 688.

5. Thomas E. Brennan, *Public Drinking and Popular Culture in Eighteenth-Century Paris* (Princeton: Princeton University Press, 1988); P[atrice] B[oussel], "Cafés," in *Dictionnaire de Paris* (Paris: Larousse, 1964), 76; Frantz Funck-Brentano, *Les Nouvellistes*, with the collaboration of Paul d'Estree, 3d ed. (Paris: Hachette, 1923), 234.

6. B[oussel], "Cafés," 76.

7. Louis-Sébastien Mercier, *Tableau de Paris* (Amsterdam, 1782–88), 7: 227–30.

8. Quoted by Robert Darnton, "The High Enlightenment and the Low-Life of Literature," in *The Literary Underground of the Old Regime* (Cambridge, Mass.: Harvard University Press, 1982), 1.

9. B[oussel], "Cafés," 77; James Billington, *Fire in the Minds of Men: Origins of the Revolutionary Faith* (New York: Basic Books, 1980); Robert Isherwood, "The Convergence of Popular and Elite Culture: The Palais-Royal," in id., *Farce and Fantasy: Popular Entertainment in Eighteenth-Century Paris* (New York: Oxford University Press, 1986), 217–49.

10. Elisabeth Roudinesco, *Madness and Revolution: The Lives and Legends of Théroigne de Méricourt*, trans. Martin Thom (London: Verso, 1991), 5.

11. Billington, *Fire in the Minds of Men*, 30.

12. Jean Robiquet, *Daily Life in the French Revolution*, trans. James Kirkup (New York: Macmillan, 1964), 4.

13. Alexandre Tuetey, *Répertoire général des sources manuscrites de l'histoire de Paris pendant la Révolution française* (Paris: Imprimerie Nouvelle association ouvrière, 1890), 1: 197, no. 1721 (22 May 1790); 156, no. 1375 (12 June 1790).

14. Camille Desmoulins and F. L. C. Montjoie quoted in Hippolyte Taine, *The Origins of Contemporary France* (1875–94), trans. John Durand, ed. Edward T. Gargan (Chicago: University of Chicago Press, 1974), 106.

15. Tuetey, *Répertoire général*, 2: 122, no. 1169 (9 July 1790); 316, no. 2910 (9 October 1789); 316–17, no. 2911.

16. Simon Schama, *Citizens: A Chronicle of the French Revolution* (New York: Knopf, 1989), 526.

17. It would take pages to enumerate all the references to drink, toasts, and epithets contained in the papers of Marat and Hébert. See, however, Jacques-René Hébert, *Le Père Duchesne* (September 1790–February 1794; Paris: Editions d'histoire sociale, 1969), vol. 2, no. 13: 4–7, no. 17: 4–7; vol. 3, no. 41: 5, no. 51: 4–5, no. 78: 8. And see Jean-Paul Marat, *L'Ami du peuple* (Tokyo: Society for the Reproduction of Rare Books, 1967), 16 February 1793, no. 124, vol. 17: 6543–49; 28 December 1789, no. 80, vol. 2: 141–43; 21 July 1790, no. 168, vol. 4: 147–49; 11 September 1790, no. 218, vol. 5: 1674–80.

18. Darnton, *Literary Underground*, 1; George Rudé, *The Crowd in the French Revolution* (Oxford: Oxford University Press, 1959), 217; Albert Soboul, *The French Revolution, 1787–1799*, trans. Alan Forrest and Colin Jones (New York: Random House, Vintage Books, 1975), 143.

19. W. C. Morrow, from notes by Edouard Cucuel, *Bohemian Paris of Today* (London: Chatto & Windus, 1899), 218.

20. Taine, *Origins of Contemporary France*, ed. Gargan, 106.

21. For example, *L'Ami du peuple*, 1 October 1791, no. 563, vol. 12: 4534; 1 August 1791, no. 526, vol. 11: 4226; 19 November 1791, no. 603, vol. 13: 4877; 3 December 1791, no. 616, vol. 13: 4980; 11 September 1790, no. 218, vol. 15: 1674; 12 September 1790, no. 219, vol. 5: 1680; 12 October 1790, no. 248, vol. 15: 1935.

22. Alphonse Aulard, *Paris pendant la réaction thermidorienne et sous le Directoire* (Paris, 1898; New York: AMS, 1974), 1: 452, for example.

23. Richard Cobb, *The People's Armies*, trans. Marianne Elliot (New Haven: Yale University Press, 1987), 619.

24. Jürgen Habermas, *The Structural Transformation of the Public Sphere: An Inquiry into a Category of Bourgeois Society*, trans. Thomas Burger (Cambridge, Mass.: MIT Press, 1989), xviii; Richard Cobb, *Reactions to the French Revolution* (London: Oxford University Press, 1972), 171.

25. Jacques Hillairet, *Dictionnaire historique des rues de Paris* (Paris: Editions de Minuet, 1963), 1: 663.

26. Billington, *Fire in the Minds of Men*, 31.

27. Aulard, *Paris pendant la réaction thermidorienne et sous le Directoire*, reports of 11 June, 18 July, and 17 and 18 September 1803.

28. AN F7 3874, report of 17 December 1819.

29. Maurice Agulhon, *Le Cercle dans la France bourgeoise, 1810–1848* (Paris: Armand Colin, 1977).

30. Maurice Agulhon, "Working-Class Sociability," in *The Power of the Past: Essays for Eric Hobsbawm*, ed. Pat Thane, Geoffrey Crossick, and Roderick Floud (Cambridge: Cambridge University Press; Paris: Editions de la Maison des sciences de l'homme, 1984), 49.

31. APP, ordinances of 5 January, 2 September, and 5 January 1822.

32. See, respectively, AN F7 3877, reports of 6 April, 3 January, 26 March, 6 May, 28 April 1823.

33. Alfred Cobban, *A History of Modern France*, vol 2: *1799–1871* (Baltimore: Penguin Books, 1965), 87; APP, ordinance of 11 May 1829.

34. Claude Liprandi, "Gavroche et Béranger," *Revue des sciences humaines*, n.s., fasc. 79, "Mélanges" (July–September 1955): 423–24.

35. Alain Faure, "Mouvements populaires et mouvement ouvrier à Paris (1830–1834)," *Mouvement social*, no. 88 (July–September 1974): 68.

36. Maurice Choury, *Les Poètes de la Commune* (Paris: Seghers, 1970), 10.

37. Louis Blanc, *1848: Historical Revelations* (New York: Howard Fertig, 1971), 177.

38. B[oussel], "Cafés," 82.

39. Blanc, *1848*, 39, 222.

40. Karl Marx, *The 18th Brumaire of Louis Bonaparte* (New York: International Publishers 1963), 66.

41. Alexis de Tocqueville, *Recollections*, trans. George Lawrence (Garden City, N.Y.: Doubleday, Anchor Books, 1971), 128–29.

42. "Chronique," *Gazette des tribunaux* (hereafter cited as *Gdt*), 22 June 1848, 821, and article opening with "Matin des cinq heures," *Gdt*, 23 June 1848, 825.

43. Louis Girard, *La Deuxième République et le Second Empire, 1848–1870* (Paris: Association pour la publication d'une histoire de Paris, distrib. Hachette, 1981), 40.

44. "Paris, 23 juin," *Gdt*, 24 June 1848, 827.

45. "Chronique," *Gdt*, 8 July 1848, 868; 5 July 1848, 861; 25 July 1848, 922; 2 July 1848, 853.

46. Girard, *La Deuxième République et le Second Empire*, 50.

47. Victor Hugo, *History of a Crime* (New York: Peter Fenelon Collier, n.d.), 1, pt. 2: 92, 6.

48. Charles da Costa, *Les Blanquistes* (Paris: M. Riviere, 1912), 29.

49. Hugo, *History of a Crime*, 1, pt. 2: 150.

50. Ibid., 2: 252, 254.

51. Blanc, *1848*, 36; "The French Police," *Every Saturday*, 2 February 1897, 150.

52. Bayle Saint John, *Purple Tints of Paris: Character and Manners in the New Empire* (New York: Riker, Thorne, 1854), 184–85.

53. Da Costa, *Les Blanquistes*, 4.

54. "French Police," 150.

55. Henri d'Aleméras, *La Vie parisienne sous le Second Empire* (Paris: Albin Michel, 1933), 348–49.

56. Saint John, *Purple Tints*, 185.

57. Alvan F. Sanborn, *Paris and the Social Revolution* (Boston: Small, Maynard, 1895), 185.

58. Philibert Audebrand, *Un Café sous Napoléon III* (Paris: E. Dentu, 1888), 8.

59. Maxime Vuillaume, *Mes Cahiers rouges au temps de la Commune* (Paris: Société d'éditions littéraires et artistiques, Libraire Paul Ollendorff, 1971), 219–22.

60. Emile Zola, *Savage Paris*, trans. David Hughes and Marie J. Mason (London: Elek Books, 1955), 151–54; d'Aleméras, *Vie parisienne sous le Second Empire*, 353.

61. Audebrand, *Café*, 8.

62. Armand Audiganne, *Mémoires d'un ouvrier de Paris depuis la Commune* (Paris: Charpentier, 1873), 13–14; Saint James, *Purple Tints*, 180; Anthime Corbon, *Le Secret du peuple de Paris* (Paris: Pagnerre, 1863), 92.

63. *The English Defense of the Commune*, ed. Royden Harrison (London: Merlin Press, 1971), 105; Eugene Schulkind, "Socialist Women during the 1871 Paris Commune," *Past and Present*, no. 106 (February 1985): 135.

64. Jeanne Gaillard, *Paris, la ville, 1852–1870* (Paris: Champion, 1977), 564.

65. Sanborn, *Paris and the Social Revolution*, 176.

66. For the 1830s, see, e.g., "Troubles de décembre," *Gdt*, 30 March 1831.

67. Girard, *La Deuxième République et le Second Empire*, 371, quoting Ludovic Halévy, *Carnets* (Paris: Calmann-Lévy, 1934–35), 33–67.

68. Gérard Jacquemet, *Belleville au XIXᵉ siècle: Du faubourg à la ville*, ed. Jean Touzot (Paris: Editions de l'Ecole des hautes études en sciences sociales, 1984), 168.

69. Alphonse Daudet, *Quarante ans de Paris, 1857–1897* (Geneva: La Palatine, 1945), 126–32.

70. B[oussel], "Cafés," 82.

71. Vuillaume, *Mes Cahiers rouges*, 305, 314; d'Aleméras, *Vie parisienne sous le Second Empire*, 345.

72. *Enquête parlementaire sur l'insurrection du 18 mars*, vol. 2: *Dépositions des témoins*, app. no. 740 (Versailles: Cerf, 1872), 115.

73. Vuillaume, *Mes Cahiers rouges*, 229, 234.

74. Melvin Kranzberg, *The Siege of Paris, 1870–1871* (Ithaca, N.Y.: Cornell University Press, 1950), 78; *Enquête parlementaire*, 24, 41, 53, 79, 170; Saint John, *Purple Tints*, 177; Ludovic Halévy, *Notes et souvenirs, 1871–1872*, 2d ed. (Paris: Calmann-Lévy, 1889), 134.

75. Schulkind, "Socialist Women," 135.

76. Ted W. Margadant, "The Paris Commune: A Revolution That Failed," review of *The Paris Commune, 1871*, by Steward Edwards (Chicago: Quadrangle Books, 1973), *Journal of Interdisciplinary History* 7, no. 1 (Summer 1976): 94.

77. *Enquête parlementaire*, 158.

78. Henri d'Aleméras, *La Vie parisienne pendant le siège et sous la Commune* (Paris: Albin Michel, 1927), 466–67.

79. Maxime du Camp, *Les Convulsions de Paris* (1881; repr., New York: AMS Press, n.d.), 4: 79; 1: 10; 2: 309; 1: 22, 48, 55, 84, 126, 217, 262, 278, 43, 214; 3: 11; 4: 291.

80. Lucien Descaves, preface to "B" [Victorine Brocher], *Souvenirs d'une morte vivante, 1848–1871* (1909; Paris: Maspero, 1976), 6.

81. "The Commune is first of all the city in festival [and] the cafés evidently played a big role," Bernard Noël, asserts in his *Dictionnaire de la Commune* (Paris: F. Hazen, 1971), 58, however; Noël believed that the cafés embodied the Commune's principles of perpetual discussion and camaraderie.

82. Kristen Ross, *The Emergence of Social Space: Rimbaud and the Paris Commune* (Minneapolis: University of Minnesota Press, 1988), 147.

83. Edgar Rodrigues, *Carnaval rouge* (Paris: E. Dentu, 1872), 39.

84. D'Aleméras, *La Vie parisienne pendant le siège et sous la Commune*, 466–67.

85. *Enquête parlementaire*, 206–7; Sanborn, *Paris and the Social Revolution*, 184; Auguste Lepage, *Les Cafés artistiques et littéraires de Paris* (Paris: Martin Boursin, 1882), 239.

86. Du Camp, *Convulsions*, 1: 46, 51–52, 126, 155; d'Aleméras, *Vie parisienne pendant le siege et sous la Commune*, 461; du Camp, *Convulsions*, 1: 84, 217; 3: 7; 4: 21.

87. Du Camp, *Convulsions*, 1: 84, 217; 2: 43; 1: 226, 280; 3: 317; 1: 235; 4: 1, 14.

88. *Enquête parlementaire*, 305, 343, 107.

89. Vuillaume, *Mes Cahiers rouges*, 171, 208, 11, 40, 161, 152–54, 186, 152.

90. Du Camp, *Convulsions*, 1: 300; Price, "Ideology and Motivation in the Paris Commune," 273.

91. D'Aleméras, *Vie parisienne pendant le siege et sous la Commune*, 466–67.

92. Gordon Wright, "The Anti-Commune: Paris 1871," *French Historical Studies* 10, no. 1 (Spring 1977): 166; Jacques Rougerie, *Paris Libre* (Paris: Seuil, 1971), 109–65; *Reimpression du journal officiel de la République française sous le Commune du 19 Mars au 24 mai 1871*, 1st ed. (Paris: Victor Brunel, 1871), 14; Ross, *Emergence of Social Space*, 138.

93. Paul Martine, *Souvenirs d'un insurgé: La Commune, 1871* (Paris: Libraire académique Perrin, 1971), 280–81, 295, 307.

94. Halévy, *Notes et souvenirs*, 82.

95. Jacquemet, *Belleville au XIXe siècle*, 188; Edmond and Jules de

Goncourt, *Paris under Siege, 1870–1871: From the Goncourt Journal*, ed. and trans. George J. Becker (Ithaca, N.Y.: Cornell University Press, 1969), 313.

96. Benjamin F. Martin, *Crime and Criminal Justice under the Third Republic: The Shame of Marianne* (Baton Rouge: Louisiana State University Press, 1990), 81, 44, 50.

97. ADS D2U6, no. 15, affaire Grosjean.

98. ADS D3U6 no. 1, affaire Brunat.

99. Wright, "Anti-Commune," 162.

100. Jacques Rougerie, *Procès des Communards* (Paris: Gallimard Archives, 1978), 106.

101. Jacquemet, *Belleville au XIXᵉ siècle*, 364.

102. APP, BA87, report of 1 June 1876, 4.

103. ADS D3U6, no. 24, affaire Girault et al.

104. ADS D3U6, no. 30, affaire Rouillon et al.

105. ADS D3U6, no. 30, affaire Rouillon et al.

106. Jean T. Joughin, *The Paris Commune in French Politics, 1871–1880* (Baltimore: Johns Hopkins Press, 1955), 155–81.

107. Guesde in the newspaper *Le Citoyen*, 19 June 1882, in Ann Louise Shapiro, *Housing the Poor of Paris, 1850–1902* (Madison: University of Wisconsin Press, 1985), 116.

108. Henri Lefebvre, *Le Droit à la ville suivi de espace et politique* (Paris: Editions anthropos, 1972).

109. APP, BA86, report of 18 March 1872, 1.

110. APP, BA 1545, semaine sanglante; Jacquemet, *Belleville au XIXᵉ siècle*, 374–5.

111. Shapiro, *Housing the Poor*, 196.

112. Jacquemet, *Belleville au XIXᵉ siècle*, 351; Raymond Rudorff, *The Belle Epoque: Paris in the Nineties* (New York: Saturday Review Press, 1972), 148.

113. Alain Cottereau, "The Distinctiveness of Working-Class Cultures in France, 1848–1900," in *Working-Class Formation: Nineteenth-Century Patterns in Western Europe and the United States*, ed. Ira Katznelson and Aristide R. Zolberg (Princeton: Princeton University Press, 1986), 143–44.

114. Eliot Gregory, "The Poetic Cabarets of Paris," *Scribner's Magazine* 27, no. 10 (1900): 93.

115. "Procès-verbaux de la commission chargée de faire une enquête sur la situation des ouvriers de l'industrie et de l'agriculture en France et de présenter un premier rapport sur la crise industrielle à Paris," *Annales de la Chambre des députés*, n.s., *Documents parlementaire*, 12 (March–April 1884), app., 333.

116. Gustave Le Bon, *The Crowd: A Study of the Popular Mind* (trans. 1897; New York: Viking, 1960), 128.

117. Claude-Albert Colliard, *Libertés publiques* (Paris: Dalloz, 1959), 580–609, and Henri Nuce de Lamothe, *La Liberté de réunion en France* (Toulouse: Sebille, 1911), 70–90.

118. APP, BA 115, 10 January 1906.

119. Henry Steele, *The Working Classes of France* (London: Twentieth-Century Press, 1904), 101.

120. Jacques Bonzon, *Le Crime et l'école* (Paris: Guillaumin, 1896), 33.

121. "P.A.," "Courrier de Paris," *L'Illustration*, 13 October 1877, 227.

122. ADSD2U6, no. 90, affaire Rousset.

123. "Perdican," "Courier de Paris," *L'Illustration*, 24 March 1883, 179.

124. "Nos graveurs . . . une soupe conférence," *L'Illustration*, 24 December 1892, 528, 532.

125. "P.A.," "Courrier de Paris," *L'Illustration*, 28 April 1877, 266–67.

126. Jacquemet, *Belleville au XIXe siècle*, 347–48.

127. Harold B. Segel, *Turn-of-the-Century Cabaret: Paris, Barcelona, Berlin, Munich, Vienna, Cracow, Moscow, St. Petersburg, Zurich* (New York: Columbia University Press, 1987), 48–50; Jerrold E. Seigel, *Bohemian Paris: Culture, Politics, and the Boundaries of Bourgeois Life, 1830–1930* (New York: Viking, 1986), 288–95.

128. Carter Jefferson, "Worker Education in France," *Comparative Studies in Society and History*, no. 6 (1964), 358; APP BA 115.

129. D. R. Watson, "The Politics of Educational Reform in France during the Third Republic, 1900–1940," *Past and Present*, no. 34 (July 1966), 86; Charles Gide, "Le Restaurant coopératif du quartier Latin," *Revue internationale de l'enseignement* 1, no. 10 (15 October 1905): 290–300, 311.

130. Jacqueline LaLouette, "Les Débits de boissons en France, 1871–1919," in 2 vols. (thesis, University of Paris, 1979), 82.

131. Jacquemet, *Belleville au XIXe siècle*, 373, 385, 374–75.

132. Maxwell Kelso, "The Inception of the Modern French Labor Movement (1871–1879)," *Journal of Modern History*, no. 8 (1936): 181; Samuel Bernstein, *The Beginnings of Marxian Socialism in France* (New York: Social Science Studies, 1933), 115.

133. Mermeix [Gabriel Terrail], *Le Socialisme* (Paris: Ollendorff, 1906), 118–19.

134. Bernstein, *Beginnings of Marxian Socialism in France*, 128–30; Joughin, *Paris Commune in French Politics*, 172.

135. ADS D2U6, no. 51, affaire Finance; APP BA 28, "Congrèses divers ouvrier socialiste, 1878," nos. 203, 206, 237, 239.

136. Paris, Conseil municipal, *Procès verbaux/débats* (Paris: Imprimerie municipale), 1881, pt. 1, 764–66, 424–28; 1887, pt. 1, 702–705, for Joffrin; 1885, pt. 1, 470–81; 1886, pt. 1, 632–42, 1093, for Vaillant.

137. Vincent Wright, "La Préfecture de police pendant le XIXe siècle," in

L'Administration de Paris, 1789–1977, Centre de recherches d'histoire et de philologie de la IVe section de l'Ecole pratique des hautes études (Paris: Champion, 1979), 117.

138. ADS D3U6, no. 40, affaire Odin; no. 34 has twenty-two cases; no. 48, affaire Nivet.

139. ADS D2U6, no. 53, affaire Baudin.

140. ADS D1U6, register, February 1885, affaire Andrieux.

141. See Philip Nord, *Paris Shopkeepers and the Politics of Resentment* (Princeton: Princeton University Press, 1986), 171–74.

142. ADS D3U6, no. 37, affaire Brousse et al., and no. 50, affaires Terrier et al., Bouvret et al., Le Boucher et al., Pellaz et al., Borderie, and Jorday.

143. ADS D3U6, no. 24, affaire Louiche; D3U6, no. 50, cases cited in n. 142 above.

144. ADS D3U6, no. 40, affaire Odin et Prades.

145. Ernest Barron Gordon, *The Anti-Alcohol Movement in Europe* (New York: Fleming H. Revell, [ca. 1913]), 167.

146. Pyotr Kropotkin, *Memoirs of a Revolutionist* (Boston: Houghton Mifflin, 1899), 406.

147. ADS D3U6, no. 50, affaire Pellez et al.

148. See, e.g., ADSD3U6, no. 50, affaire Mayence; APP BA 1503, surveillance of anarchists.

149. Rudorff, *Belle Epoque*, 157.

150. D3U6, no. 31, affaire Rousseau et al.

151. Rudorff, *Belle Epoque*, 158; Sanborn, *Paris and the Social Revolution*, 42.

152. Bernard Moss, *The Origins of the French Labor Movement: The Socialism of Skilled Workers, 1830–1914* (Berkeley and Los Angeles: University of California Press, 1976), 144.

153. Aaron Noland, *The Founding of the French Socialist Party, 1893–1905* (1956; New York: Howard Fertig, 1970), 189.

154. ADS D2U6, no. 169, affaire R.

155. ADS D2U6, no. 165, affaire G.

156. *L'Illustration*, 26 January 1907, 51.

157. ADS D2U6, no. 160, affaire B.

158. ADS D2U6, no. 160, affaire H.

159. Rudorff, *Belle Epoque*, 30.

160. This study has given a new twist to Eugen Weber's assertion that "in the enchantment of the Third Republic, words were equated with acts." See "The Politics of Maurice Barrès," in *My France: Politics, Culture, Myth* (Cambridge, Mass.: Harvard University Press, Belknap Press, 1991), 242.

161. A. Daude-Bancel, "L'Antialcoolisme ouvrier en France," *Annales antialcooliques* 7, no. 10 (October 1909): 162–63.

162. Stuart Hall, "Notes on Deconstructing the 'Popular,'" in *People's History and Socialist Theory*, ed. Ralph Samuel (London: Routledge & Kegan Paul, 1981), 235–36.

163. Arthur Hirsch, *The French New Left: An Intellectual History From Sartre to Gorz* (Boston: South End Press, 1981), 145.

Conclusion

1. Raymond Williams, *The City and the Country* (New York: Oxford University Press, 1973), 249.

2. See esp. Vernon Lidke, *The Alternative Culture: Socialist Labor in Imperial Germany* (Oxford: Oxford University Press, 1985).

3. Michel Foucault, *Power/Knowledge: Selected Interviews and Other Writings, 1972–1977*, ed. Colin Gordon, trans. id. et al. (New York: Pantheon Books, 1980), 41–42.

4. See Tyler Stovall, *The Rise of the Paris Red Belt* (Berkeley and Los Angeles: University of California Press, 1990), esp. 75–76, 150–65.

5. Victor Turner, *Dramas, Fields, and Metaphors* (Ithaca, N.Y.: Cornell University Press, 1974), 41.

6. Temma Kaplan, "Civic Rituals and Patterns of Resistance in Barcelona, 1890–1930," in *The Power of the Past: Essays for Eric Hobsbawm*, ed. Pat Thane et al. (Cambridge: Cambridge University Press; Paris: Editions de la Maison des sciences de l'homme, 1984), 178.

7. See, e.g., Louis Chevalier, *Laboring Classes and Dangerous Classes in Paris during the First Half of the Nineteenth Century*, trans. Frank Jellinek (Princeton: Princeton University Press, 1981), and id., *La Formation de la population parisienne au XIXe siècle*, Institut national d'études démographiques, Travaux et documents, cahier no. 10 (Paris, 1950). Another statement of the "culture of poverty" paradigm is to be found in Jeffrey Kaplow, *The Names of Kings: The Parisian Laboring Poor in the Eighteenth Century* (New York: Basic Books, 1972). In contrast, see Barrie M. Ratcliffe, "Classes laborieuses et classes dangereuses à Paris pendant la première moitié du XIXe siècle? The Chevalier Thesis Reexamined," *French Historical Studies* 17, no. 2 (Fall 1991), 542–74, and *Un Ouvrier en 1820: Manuscrit inédit de Jacques-Etienne Bédé*, ed. Rémi Gossez (Paris: Presses universitaires de France, 1984), introduction.

8. Peter Stearns, "The Effort at Continuity in Working-Class Culture," *Journal of Modern History* 52 (December 1980): 628–46; quotation from p. 639.

9. See Christopher Lasch, *The True and Only Heaven: Progress and Its Critics* (New York: Norton, 1991), esp. 49–72 and his discussion of civic humanism and the consumer ethic.

Appendix:
Historiography and Methodology

1. The paucity of studies of informal sociability is noted by François Bedarida and Anthony Sutcliff, "The Street in the Structure and Life of the City: Reflections on Nineteenth-Century London and Paris," *Journal of Urban History*, no. 4 (1980): 378, 383.

2. Peter Clark, *The English Alehouse: A Social History, 1200–1830* (London: Longman, 1983); Perry R. Duis, *The Saloon: Public Drinking in Chicago and Boston, 1880–1920* (Urbana: University of Illinois Press, 1983); Roy Rosenzweig, *Eight Hours for What We Will: Workers & Leisure in an Industrial City, 1870–1920* (Cambridge: Cambridge University Press, 1986).

3. Thomas E. Brennan, *Public Drinking and Popular Culture in Eighteenth-Century Paris* (Princeton: Princeton University Press, 1988); Henri-Melchior de Langle, *Le Petit Monde des cafés et débits parisiens au XIXᵉ siècle* (Paris: Presses universitaires de France, 1990). Other writings on Parisian cafés have appeared recently, but they are in the long tradition of histories based more on anecdotal than on archival evidence. See Beatrice Malki-Thouvenel, *Cabarets, cafés et bistrots de Paris* (Paris: Editions Horvath, 1987), and Jean-Claude Bologne, *Histoire des cafés et des cafetiers* (Paris: Larousse, 1993).

4. See Peter Clark, "The Alehouse and Social Integration in English Towns (1500–1700)," in *Habiter la ville, XVᵉ–XXᵉ siècles*, ed. Maurice Garden and Yves Lequin (Lyon: Presses universitaires de Lyon, 1984), 225–31, and id., *English Alehouse*.

5. Hayden White, *Metahistory: The Historical Imagination in Nineteenth-Century Europe* (Baltimore: Johns Hopkins University Press, 1973), 5–11, 93–97, and id., *The Content of the Form: Narrative Discourse and Historical Representation* (Baltimore: Johns Hopkins University Press, 1987), 44–67.

6. Peter Burke, *Popular Culture in Early Modern Europe* (New York: Harper Torchbooks, 1978); Beverly Ann Tlusty, "Gender and Alcohol Abuse in Early Modern Augsburg" (paper presented at the International Congress on the Social History of Alcohol, 1993).

7. Lawrence Klein, "Coffee Clashes: The Politics of Discourse in the English Coffeehouse" (paper given at the annual meeting of the American Historical Association, 1991).

8. Lillian Faderman, *Odd Girls and Twilight Lovers: A History of Lesbian Life in Twentieth-Century America* (New York: Columbia University Press, 1991), 79–80, 306; Martin B. Duberman, *Stonewall* (New York: Dutton, 1993).

9. Maurice Agulhon, *The Republican Experiment, 1848–1852*, Cambridge History of Modern France (Cambridge: Cambridge University Press; Paris: Editions de la Maison des sciences de l'homme, 1983).

10. Peter Burke, review of *Sociabilité, pouvoirs et société: Actes du Colloque de Rouen, Novembre 1983*, ed. F. Thelamon (Rouen: Publications du l'Université de Rouen, 1987), *French History* 2, no. 4 (December 1988): 490–91.

11. Susanna Barrows, "'Parliaments of the People': The Political Culture of Cafés in the Early Third Republic," in *Drinking: Behavior and Belief in Modern History*, ed. id. and Robin Room (Berkeley and Los Angeles: University of California Press, 1991), 87–97.

12. Iain McCalman, *Radical Underworld: Prophets, Revolutionaries and Pornographers in London, 1795–1840* (Cambridge: Cambridge University Press, 1988).

13. David W. Gutzke, *Protecting the Pub: Brewers and Publicans against Temperance* (Suffolk: Royal Historical Society / Boydell & Brewer, 1989), and id., "Trust Your Pub: Sociability as Social Control, 1895–1914" (paper presented at the International Congress on the Social History of Alcohol, 1993).

14. See esp. Madelon Powers, "'The Poorman's Friend': Saloonkeepers, Workers, and the Code of Reciprocity in U.S. Barrooms, 1870–1920," *Internal Labor and Working-Class History*, no. 45 (Spring 1994): 1–15.

15. On Banlieues '89 (Suburbs '89), the French program to reanimate suburban life headed by Roland Castro, see several articles in *Libération*, 17 May 1985; "Hep! architecte, un café, un," in ibid., 26–27 December 1987, 12; and an article in ibid., 30 January 1990, 8.

16. James C. Scott, *Domination and the Arts of Resistance: Hidden Transcripts* (New Haven: Yale University Press, 1990).

17. See, e.g., Erving Goffman, *Relations in Public* (New York: Harper & Row, 1971); Carlo Ginzburg, *The Cheese and the Worms: The Cosmos of a Sixteenth-Century Miller* (Baltimore: Johns Hopkins University Press, 1980); Natalie Z. Davis, *The Return of Martin Guerre* (Cambridge, Mass.: Harvard University Press, 1983). *Microhistory and the Lost Peoples of Europe*, a selection from the Italian historical journal *Quaderni storici*, trans. Eren Branch, ed. Edward Muir and Guido Ruggiero (Baltimore: Johns Hopkins University Press, 1991), offers an excellent overview of the work of Ginzburg and other Italian scholars.

18. Steven G. Reinhardt, "The Selective Prosecution of Crime in Ancien Régime France: Theft in the Sénéchaussée of Sarlat," *European History Quarterly* 16, no. 1 (January 1986): 3.

19. ADS D2U6, no. 18, affaire Pipon contre Dompte.

20. *Un Ouvrier en 1820: Manuscrit inédit de Jacques-Etienne Bédé*, ed. Rémi Gossez (Paris: Presses universitaires de France, 1984); see Gossez's perceptive introduction, 6–9.

21. ADS D3U6, no. 20, affaire Rouyer et al.

22. Alain Cottereau, "Denis Poulot's *Le Sublime*—A Preliminary Study," in *Voices of the People: The Social Life of "La Sociale" at the End of the Second*

Empire, trans. John Moore, ed. Adrian Rifkin and Roger Thomas (London: Routledge & Kegan Paul, 1988), 97–177.

23. Louis Chevalier, *Laboring Classes and Dangerous Classes in Paris during the First Half of the Nineteenth Century*, trans. Frank Jellinek (Princeton: Princeton University Press, 1981), 76–77.

24. Henri Imbert, *L'Alcoolisme chronique dans ses rapports avec les professions* (Paris: Société d'éditions scientifiques, 1897); Charles Bonnet, *L'Alcoolisation dans différents professions de la région Parisienne* (Paris: Thèse medecine, 1914).

25. Arlette Farge, *Vivre dans la rue à Paris au XVIIIe siècle* (Paris: Gallimard-Archives, 1979), 241–44.

26. For an overview of the emergence of the modern shop, see Fernand Braudel, *Civilization and Capitalism, Fifteenth–Eighteenth Century*, vol. 2: *The Wheels of Commerce*, trans. Sîan Reynolds (New York: Harper & Row, 1982, 25–80.

27. Quoting a penal reformer named Rossi, Foucault notes these points about crowds and, obliquely, also about taverns (Michel Foucault, *Discipline and Punish: The Birth of the Prison*, trans. Alan Sheridan [New York: Pantheon Books, 1977]), 201, 276.

28. Michel Foucault, *The History of Sexuality*, vol. 1, trans. Robert Hurley (New York: Random House, Vintage Books, 1980), 225.

29. Charles Tilly regretted that he could not deal with these questions. See his *From Mobilization to Revolution* (Reading, Mass.: Addison-Wesley, 1978), 8.

30. Jürgen Habermas, *The Structural Transformation of the Public Sphere: An Inquiry into a Category of Bourgeois Society*, trans. Thomas Burger (Cambridge, Mass.: MIT Press, 1989), xviii.

31. A classic representation of the carnivalesque and its relation to popular culture is Mikhail Bakhtin's *Rabelais and His World*, trans. Hélène Iswolsky (Bloomington: Indiana University Press, 1984). By the nineteenth century, much of the ribald and contestatory culture that Bakhtin locates in the medieval marketplace had been transferred to the café.

Index

319

Class consciousness, 2, 152, 156–58, 233, 262n. 108
Clémenceau, Prime Minister Georges, 84
Cobb, Richard, 31, 155
Coffeehouses, advent of, 7
Commenge, O., 195–96
Commune, 11–12, 219–25; alcohol consumption, 112, 116; and café owners, 144–46
Confédération general du travail (CGT), 84, 228
Conference of the French Socialists (CFIO), 13
Conner, Susan, 183
Conseil d'état, 21
Constituent Assembly, 14, 15
Construction trades, 46, 71–72, 80
Contat, Nicolas, 66
Cooperatives, 65, 129, 148, 214
Corbin, Alain, 189, 191–92
Corbon, Anthime, 37, 217
Corps législatif, 11
Cottereau, Alain, 60, 67, 74, 226
Courts: decisions, 258n. 40; records, 100, 251; system, xi; testimony in, 91, 105–16, 166–75, 200–202, 215, 234
Courts, types of: Appeals (*cour d'appel*), xi; Assize (*cour d'assises*), xi; correctional tribunal (*tribunal de police correctionnelle*), xi, 18, 112; police (*tribunal de simple police*), xi, 18; Supreme court of appeals (*cour de cassation*), 16, 20
Crime, 136, 165. *See also* Offenses, criminal
Cross, Gary, 86

Dairies (*crémeries*), 122
d'Aleméras, Henri, 220
Dance halls, 28
Darnton, Robert, 7
Daudet, Alphonse, 50, 78, 95, 103, 157, 159, 218
Daudet, Léon, 35
Davis, Natalie Z., ix, 74
Day laborers, 45–47, 72–73, 223, 271n. 42
Decoration, of cafés, 3, 4, 124–25, 131, 146
Degas, 176
Delamare, Nicolas, 7
Delveau, Alfred, 100
Demonstrations. *See* Labor: organization of; Strikes

Department store, 156
Desmoulins, Camille, 2, 7, 210
Diderot, Denis, 209
Diet. *See* Workers
Dietz-Monnin, M., 85
Dion, Roger, 89
Divorce, 130
Domesticity, in cafés, 53, 57. *See also* Privacy
Domestic laborers, 72–73, 197
Drinking establishments, 3–4, 28–29
Drinking rituals. *See* Workers
Drunkenness, public, 25, 195; arrests for, 30–31, 41–44; Holy Monday and, 77–78; law repressing, 11–13, 18–20, 111–15; occupation and, 46, 68–73, 223, 272n. 50; terms for, 103–7
Dumas, Alexandre, 142, 187, 193
Dupont, Pierre, 231
Duprat, G. L., 67
Duveau, Georges, 12, 60, 67, 161

Economic crisis, 93–95, 126, 147
Emerson, Ralph Waldo, 1
Employers, and workplace sociability, 64, 85
Employment agencies, 65
Engels, Friedrich, 152, 232

Factory workers, 78, 80, 87
Family: fights, in public, 53–54; parent-child relations, 49–51; and social order, 8. *See also* Domesticity, in cafés
Farge, Arlette, 34, 52, 154, 177
Faure, Alain, 213
Fauré, Sébastien, 188
Femme publique. See Prostitution
Feuillet, Octave, 36
Fillassier, Dr. A., 110–11
Filouterie, 42
Food trade, 119–20
Fosca, François, 178
Foucault, Michel, 10, 236
Frégier, H. A., 9, 73, 101, 195
French Revolution, 7–8, 15–16, 24, 61, 91; café perceptions of, 8; regulations during, 21
Fuchs, Rachel, 50

Gaboriau, Emile, 11, 23–24, 28, 103, 111, 122, 134, 200

Lefort, Dr. Joseph, 67, 99
Leisure: activities, 63, 79, 87, 276n. 133; growth of, 177; and the workplace, 59
Le Mel, Nathalie, 187
Lepelletier, Edmond, 218
Le Petit Parisien, 106, 149
Le Play school, 39, 67
Le Père Duchêne, 220
Le Père Duchesne, 119, 180, 210
Le Rappel, 149
Le Sage, Alain-René, 166
Le Siècle, 141, 143
Le Sublime, ou le travailleur comme il est en 1870, 66
Levasseur, Emile, 67–68
Leyret, Henri, 2, 13, 51, 100, 130, 151, 158
Licenses, business (*patentes*), 16, 124, 148, 156
L'Illustration, 36, 190
Ligue syndicale du travail de l'industrie et du commerce, 148–49
Lodging houses (*garni*), 40
London, 4, 35
Louis XIV, 14, 208
Lumière brothers, 2

Magnan, Dr., 110–11
Manet, 176
Marat, Jean-Paul, 7, 210–11
Mardi Gras, 135
Margadant, Ted, 219
Marie-Berce, Yves, 63
Marx, Karl, 1, 10, 142, 214
Maurras, Michael, 89
McBride, Theresa, 197
Meeting halls, 227–28
Ménétra, Jacques-Louis, 52, 66
Mercier, Louis-Sébastien, 45, 66, 154, 209
Méricourt, Théroigne de, 209
Merriman, John, 130
Michelet, Jules, 122
Mirbeau, Octave, 95
Modernization. *See* Urban renewal
Monin, Dr. Ernest, 104
Montjoie, F. L. C., 210
Montorgeuil, Georges, 124–25
Morality, 6–8
Moreau, Edouard, 19

Nadaud, Martin, 11, 139
National Assembly, 11, 19

National Workshops, 214–15
Neighborhood ties, and café life, 162–63
Newspapers, 119, 210–12. *See also names of individual papers*
Nicknames, for café customers, 134, 169
Niethammer, Lutz, 150
Nourrisson, Didier, 116
Nouveau tableau de Paris, 122, 134
Nye, Robert, 173, 177

Occupation: of cafégoers, 45–47, 65–67, 193–99; and public drunkenness, 46, 68–73, 223, 272n. 50
Offenses, criminal: felonies (*crimes*), xi; misdemeanors (*délits*), xi; petty (*contraventions*), xi
Old Regime, 108–9
Opéra-Comique, 27

Palais-Royal cafés, 2, 25, 53, 158
Parent-Duchâtelet, Alexandre, 189
Pawnbrokers, 136
Pelloutier, Fernand and Maurice, 65, 94–96, 162
Père Lachaise cemetery, 225
Perrot, Michelle, 77, 85
Picot, Georges, 40
Police, 22–32, 195; class consciousness of, 2, 262n. 108; detectives (Sûreté), 28; innovations, 14–15, 154–55; laxity, 5, 114; restrictions, 227; strategies, 55, 62, 216–17. *See also* Regulations
Police, insults against (*outrage-aux-agents*), 20; age of attackers, 42; arrests for, 112–13; language of, 79, 223, 233; occupation of attackers, 68, 271n. 39; women and, 198, 205, 304n. 85, 305n. 112
Police prefects: Andrieux, Louis, 21, 24, 199; Camescasse, Jean, 125, 167, 199, 227; Caussidière, Marc, 17, 142; Cresson, Ernest, 187, 221; Gigot, Albert, 198; Haussmann, Georges Eugène, 17; Lenoir, Jean, 154; Mangin, Jean, 189; Sartine, Gabriel de, 24; Voisin, Felix, 19; Volvic, G. J. C. Chabrol de, 8
Politics: and alcohol, 116; and the café, 7, 25, 27, 228–30, 234; of café owners, 135, 141–49; fragmentation of, 226; in the Palais-Royal cafés, 209–11; and police insults, 223, 233; repression of,

Union des syndicats, 84
Unions. *See* Labor
Urban renewal, 27–29, 35, 62; and alcohol, 89–93; and new cafés, 124; police surveillance, 26–27

Vaillant, Edouard, 56
Vallès, Jules, 50
Verrière, Emile, 122
Vigilance Committees, 19
Villeneuve-Bargemont, Count Alban de, 8
Villermé, Louis René, 9, 66
Vinçard, Jules, 9
Violence, in cafés, 25–26, 108, 170–77
Vuillaume, Maxime, 139, 143, 217, 221

Warnod, André, 135
Weddings, 47–49, 57, 134–35, 266n. 69, 289n. 91
White-collar clerks, 45
Wine: adulteration of, 95, 99; consumption, 91–92; cost, 95, 97
Women: alcohol consumption by, 71, 204–5; as café customers, 21, 137, 200; as café owners, 183, 185, 188; "furies," 182, 187, 193; *grisette,* 187; insults against police, 304n. 84; *lorette,* 187; mediators, 172; occupations, 47, 196; political club, 181; reformers, 19; working conditions, 197; in Zola's novels, 201
Workers, 9; accidents of, 78–79; and café breaks, 75–76; diet, 90–94, 100; discipline, 64, 71–72; drinking rituals, 73–74, 76, 101–2, 169; wage reduction, 91
Worker's associations, 61, 215, 228
Working-class movements, 167, 212–15. *See also* Labor; Socialism

Youths, 267n. 90; alcohol consumption by, 18, 51; arrest of, 42–43, 50, 54, 265n. 53; delinquency of, 165

Zinc. See Café counter
Zola, Emile, 12, 36, 53, 67, 75, 131, 201, 217

Library of Congress Cataloging-in-Publication Data

Haine, W. Scott.
   The world of the Paris café : sociability among the French working class, 1789–1914 /
W. Scott Haine.
        p.   cm. — (The Johns Hopkins University studies in historical and political
science : 114th ser., 2)
   Includes bibliographical references and index.
   ISBN 0-8018-5104-1 (hc : alk. paper)
   1. Paris (France)—Social life and customs—19th century. 2. Social interaction—
France—Paris—History—19th century.   3. Bars (Drinking establishments)—
France—Paris—Social aspects.   I. Title. II. Series.
DC715.H275   1996
306'.0944—dc20   95-30624
                                                                                              CIP

ISBN 0-8018-6070-9 (pbk.)